# CASE CLOSED™

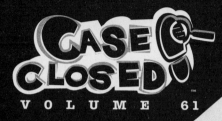

VOLUME 61

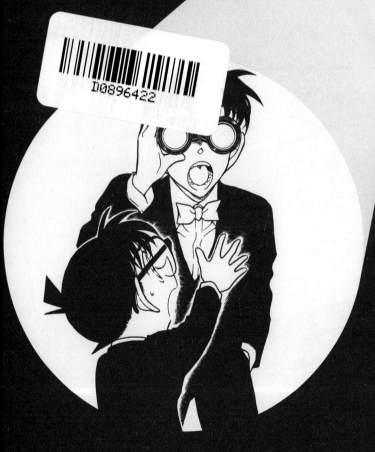

Gosho Aoyama

# Case Briefing:

Subject:
Occupation:
Special Skills:
Equipment:

Jimmy Kudo, a.k.a. Conan Edogawa
High School Student/Detective
Analytical thinking and deductive reasoning, Soccer
Bow Tie Voice Transmitter, Super Sneakers,
Homing Glasses, Stretchy Suspenders

The subject is hot on the trail of a pair of suspicious men in black when he is attacked from behind and administered a strange substance which physically transforms him into a first grader. When the subject confides in the eccentric inventor Dr. Agasa, they decide to keep the subject's true identity a secret for the safety of everyone around him. Assuming the new identity of first-grader Conan Edogawa, the subject continues to assist the police force on their most baffling cases. The only problem is that most crime-solving professionals won't take a little kid's advice!

# Table of Contents

CONFIDEN

# CASE CLOSED

## Volume 61
### Shonen Sunday Edition

### Story and Art by GOSHO AOYAMA

MEITANTEI CONAN Vol. 61
by Gosho AOYAMA
© 1994 Gosho AOYAMA
All rights reserved.
Original Japanese edition published by SHOGAKUKAN.
English translation rights in the United States of America, Canada,
the United Kingdom and Ireland arranged with SHOGAKUKAN.

**Translation**
**Tetsuichiro Miyaki**

**Touch-up & Lettering**
**Freeman Wong**

**Cover & Graphic Design**
**Andrea Rice**

**Editor**
**Shaenon K. Garrity**

Printed in the U.S.A.

Published by VIZ Media, LLC
P.O. Box 77010
San Francisco, CA 94107

10 9 8 7 6 5 4 3 2 1
First printing, January 2017

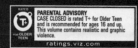

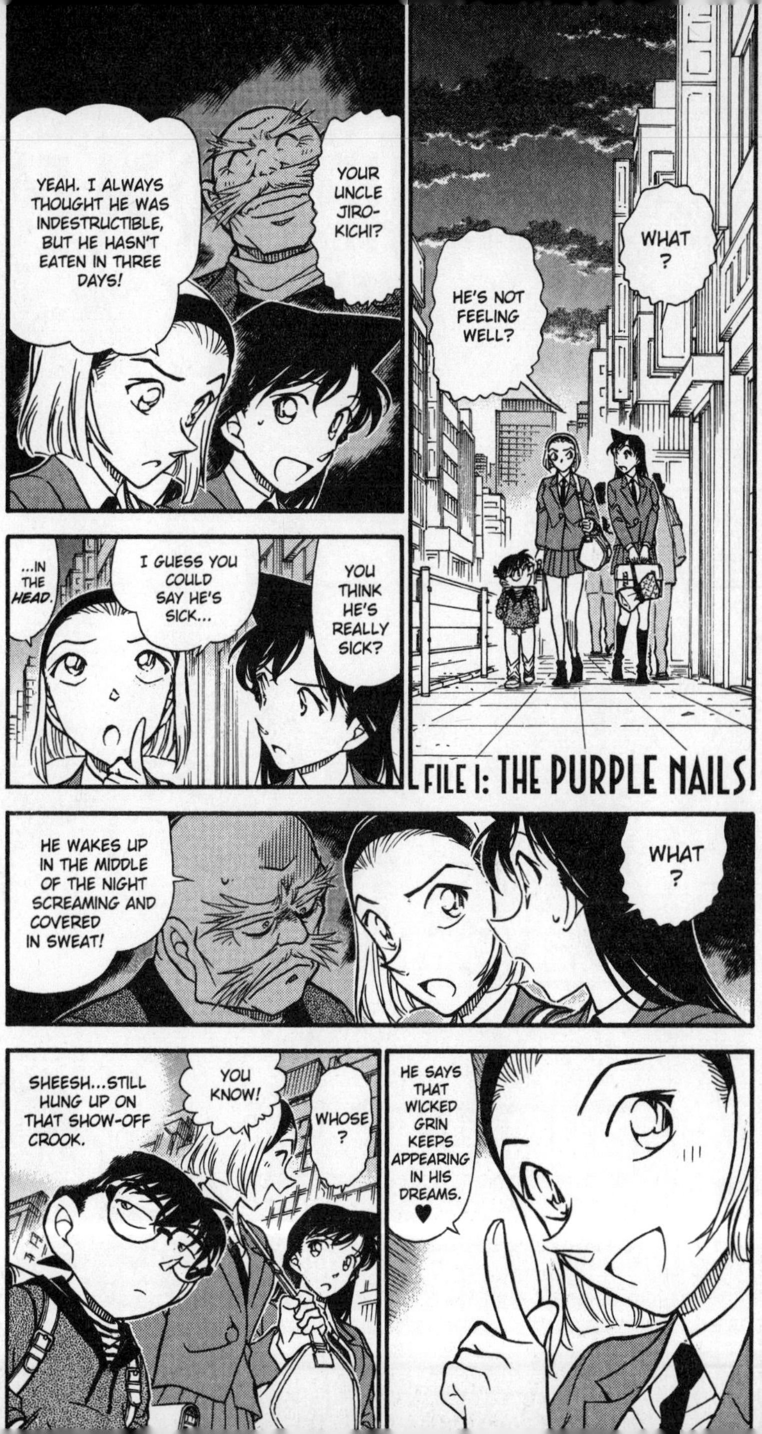
WHAT ?
HE'S NOT FEELING WELL?
FILE 1: THE PURPLE NAILS
YOUR UNCLE JIRO-KICHI?
YEAH. I ALWAYS THOUGHT HE WAS INDESTRUCTIBLE, BUT HE HASN'T EATEN IN THREE DAYS!
YOU THINK HE'S REALLY SICK?
I GUESS YOU COULD SAY HE'S SICK...
...IN THE HEAD.
WHAT ?
HE WAKES UP IN THE MIDDLE OF THE NIGHT SCREAMING AND COVERED IN SWEAT!
HE SAYS THAT WICKED GRIN KEEPS APPEARING IN HIS DREAMS. ♥
WHOSE ?
YOU KNOW!
SHEESH...STILL HUNG UP ON THAT SHOW-OFF CROOK.

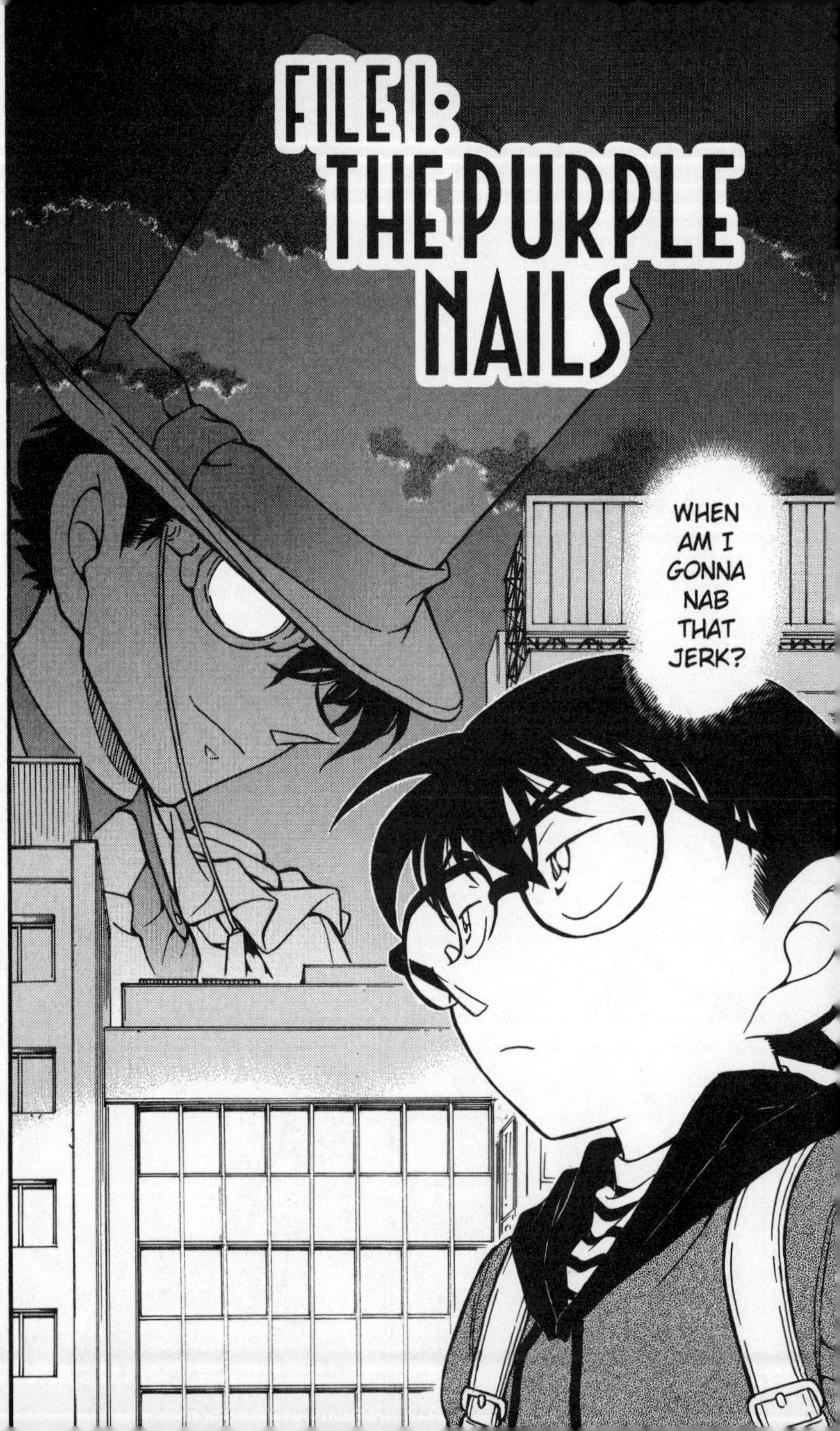
FILE 1:
THE PURPLE NAILS
WHEN AM I GONNA NAB THAT JERK?

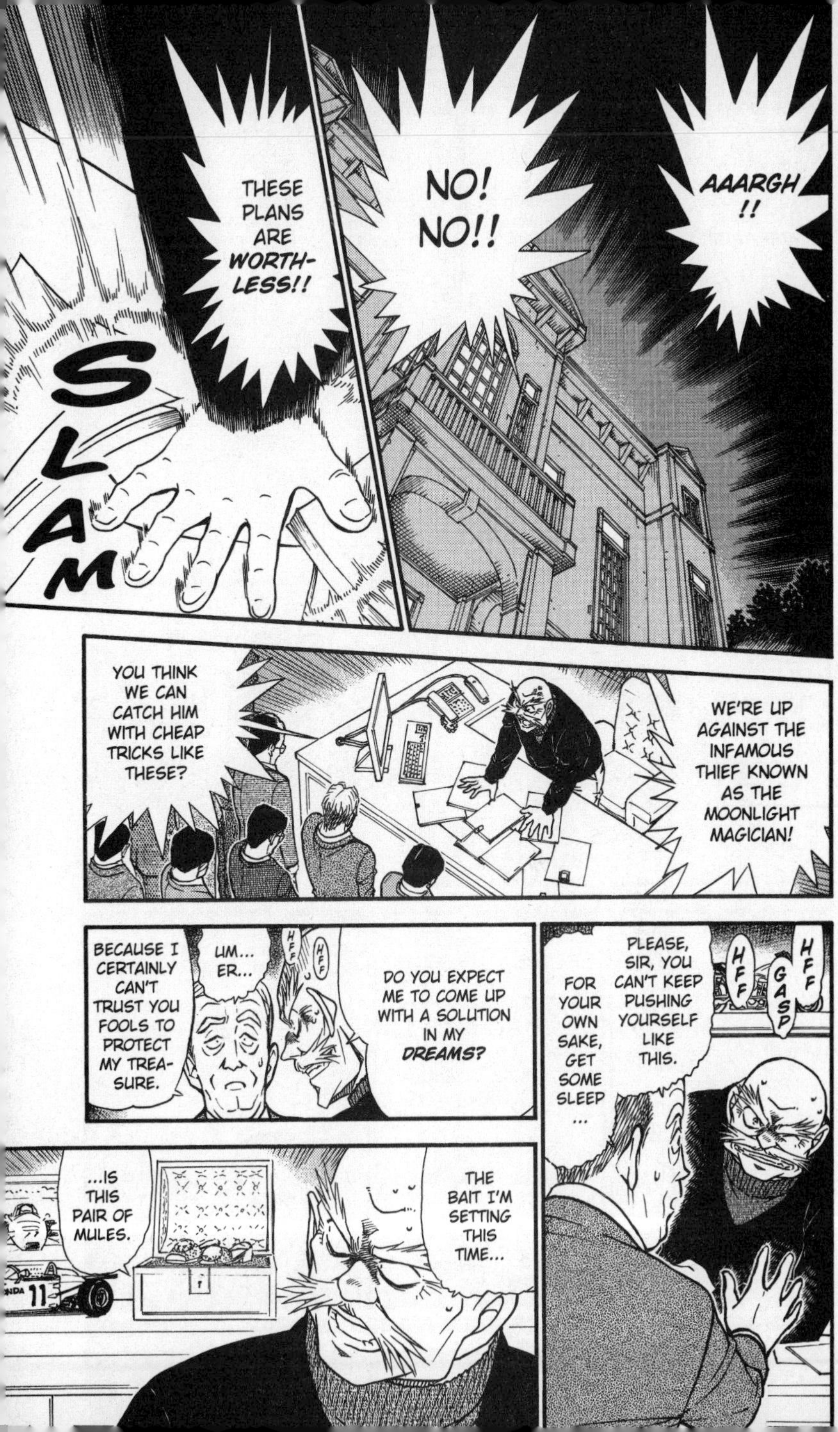
AAARGH!!
NO! NO!!
THESE PLANS ARE WORTHLESS!!
SLAM
WE'RE UP AGAINST THE INFAMOUS THIEF KNOWN AS THE MOONLIGHT MAGICIAN!
YOU THINK WE CAN CATCH HIM WITH CHEAP TRICKS LIKE THESE?
HFF
GASP
HFF
PLEASE, SIR, YOU CAN'T KEEP PUSHING YOURSELF LIKE THIS.
FOR YOUR OWN SAKE, GET SOME SLEEP...
DO YOU EXPECT ME TO COME UP WITH A SOLUTION IN MY DREAMS?
HFF
HFF
UM... ER...
BECAUSE I CERTAINLY CAN'T TRUST YOU FOOLS TO PROTECT MY TREASURE.
THE BAIT I'M SETTING THIS TIME...
...IS THIS PAIR OF MULES.

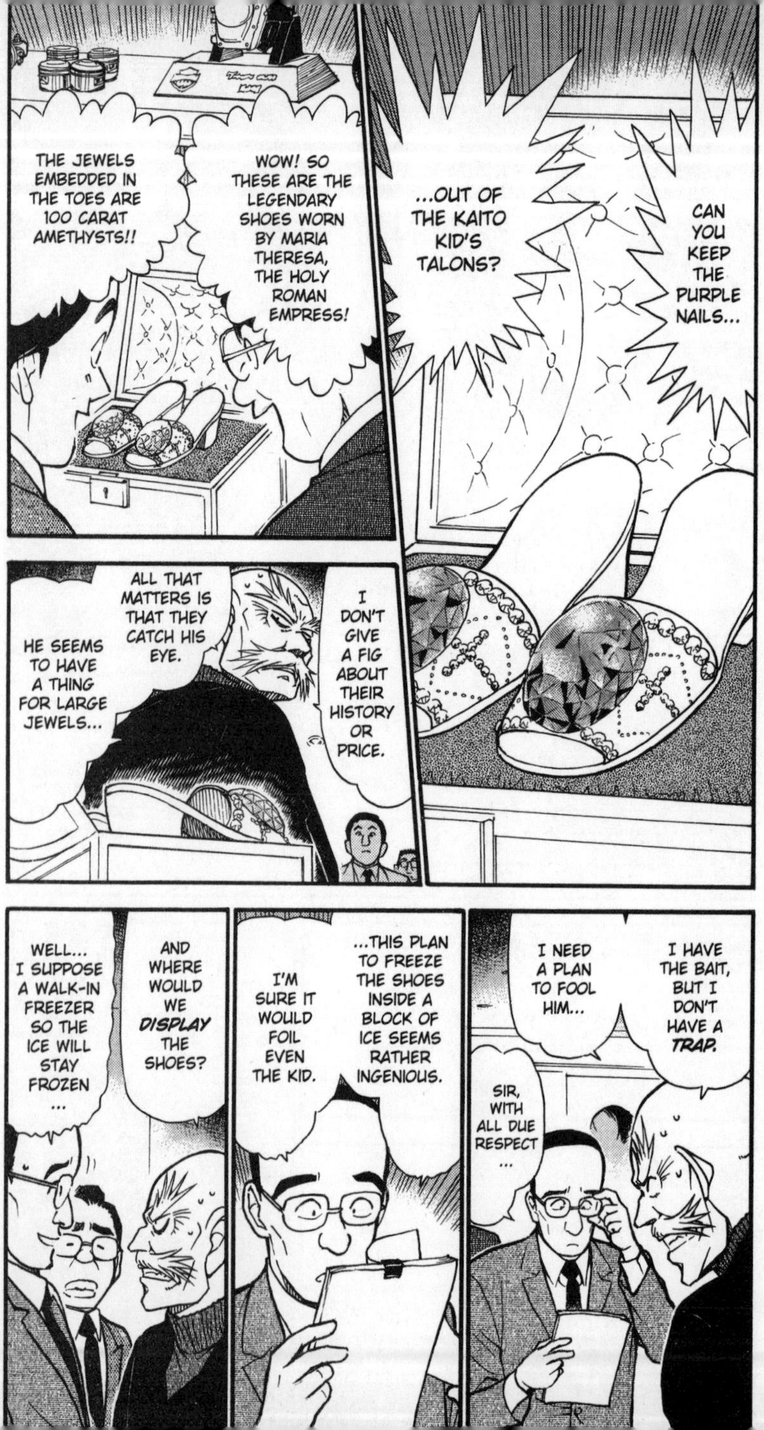
CAN YOU KEEP THE PURPLE NAILS...
...OUT OF THE KAITO KID'S TALONS?
WOW! SO THESE ARE THE LEGENDARY SHOES WORN BY MARIA THERESA, THE HOLY ROMAN EMPRESS!
THE JEWELS EMBEDDED IN THE TOES ARE 100 CARAT AMETHYSTS!!
I DON'T GIVE A FIG ABOUT THEIR HISTORY OR PRICE.
ALL THAT MATTERS IS THAT THEY CATCH HIS EYE.
HE SEEMS TO HAVE A THING FOR LARGE JEWELS...
I HAVE THE BAIT, BUT I DON'T HAVE A *TRAP.*
I NEED A PLAN TO FOOL HIM...
SIR, WITH ALL DUE RESPECT...
...THIS PLAN TO FREEZE THE SHOES INSIDE A BLOCK OF ICE SEEMS RATHER INGENIOUS.
I'M SURE IT WOULD FOIL EVEN THE KID.
AND WHERE WOULD WE *DISPLAY* THE SHOES?
WELL... I SUPPOSE A WALK-IN FREEZER SO THE ICE WILL STAY FROZEN...

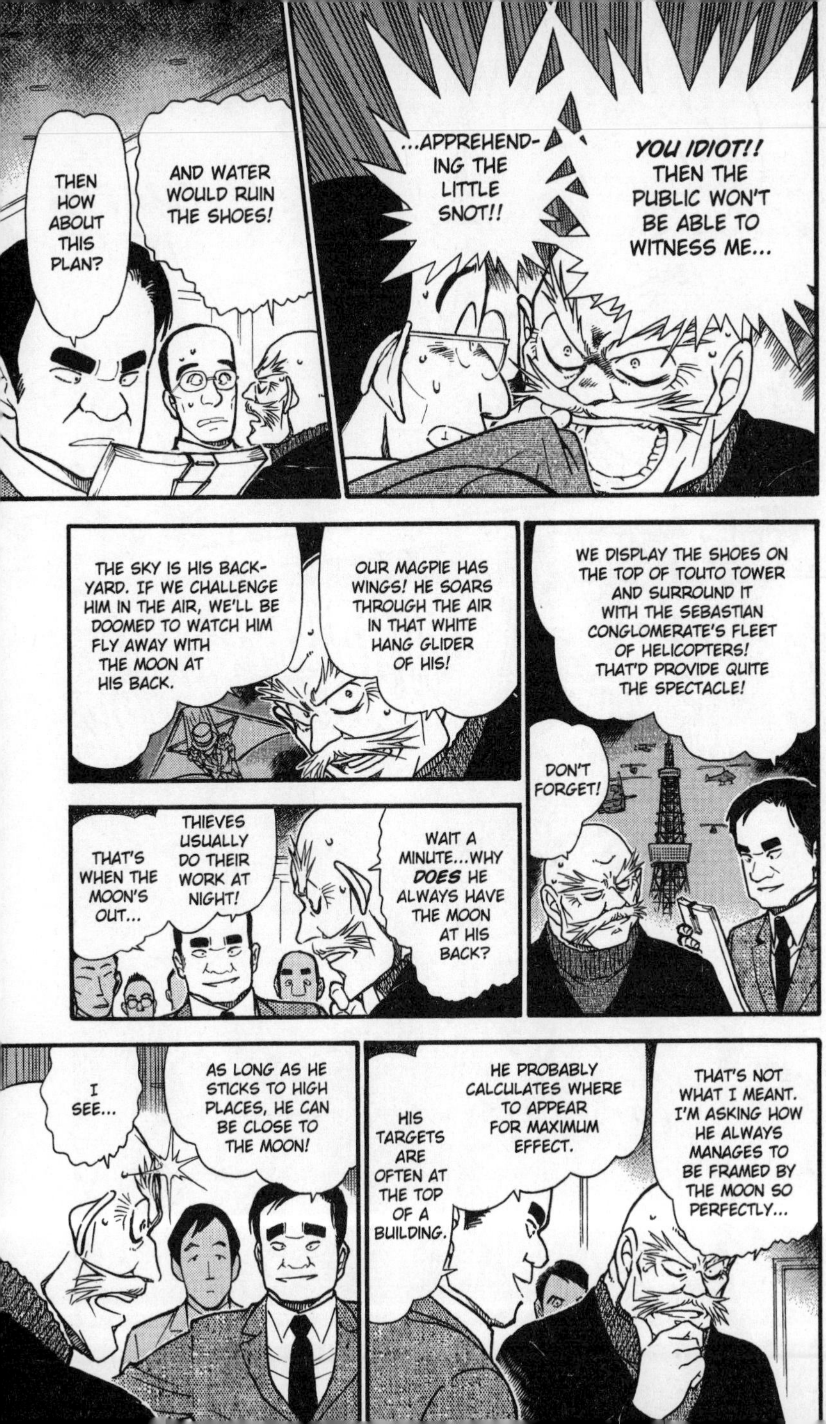
...APPREHENDING THE LITTLE SNOT!!
*YOU IDIOT!!* THEN THE PUBLIC WON'T BE ABLE TO WITNESS ME...
AND WATER WOULD RUIN THE SHOES!
THEN HOW ABOUT THIS PLAN?
WE DISPLAY THE SHOES ON THE TOP OF TOUTO TOWER AND SURROUND IT WITH THE SEBASTIAN CONGLOMERATE'S FLEET OF HELICOPTERS! THAT'D PROVIDE QUITE THE SPECTACLE!
DON'T FORGET!
OUR MAGPIE HAS WINGS! HE SOARS THROUGH THE AIR IN THAT WHITE HANG GLIDER OF HIS!
THE SKY IS HIS BACKYARD. IF WE CHALLENGE HIM IN THE AIR, WE'LL BE DOOMED TO WATCH HIM FLY AWAY WITH THE MOON AT HIS BACK.
WAIT A MINUTE...WHY *DOES* HE ALWAYS HAVE THE MOON AT HIS BACK?
THIEVES USUALLY DO THEIR WORK AT NIGHT!
THAT'S WHEN THE MOON'S OUT...
THAT'S NOT WHAT I MEANT. I'M ASKING HOW HE ALWAYS MANAGES TO BE FRAMED BY THE MOON SO PERFECTLY...
HE PROBABLY CALCULATES WHERE TO APPEAR FOR MAXIMUM EFFECT.
HIS TARGETS ARE OFTEN AT THE TOP OF A BUILDING.
AS LONG AS HE STICKS TO HIGH PLACES, HE CAN BE CLOSE TO THE MOON!
I SEE...

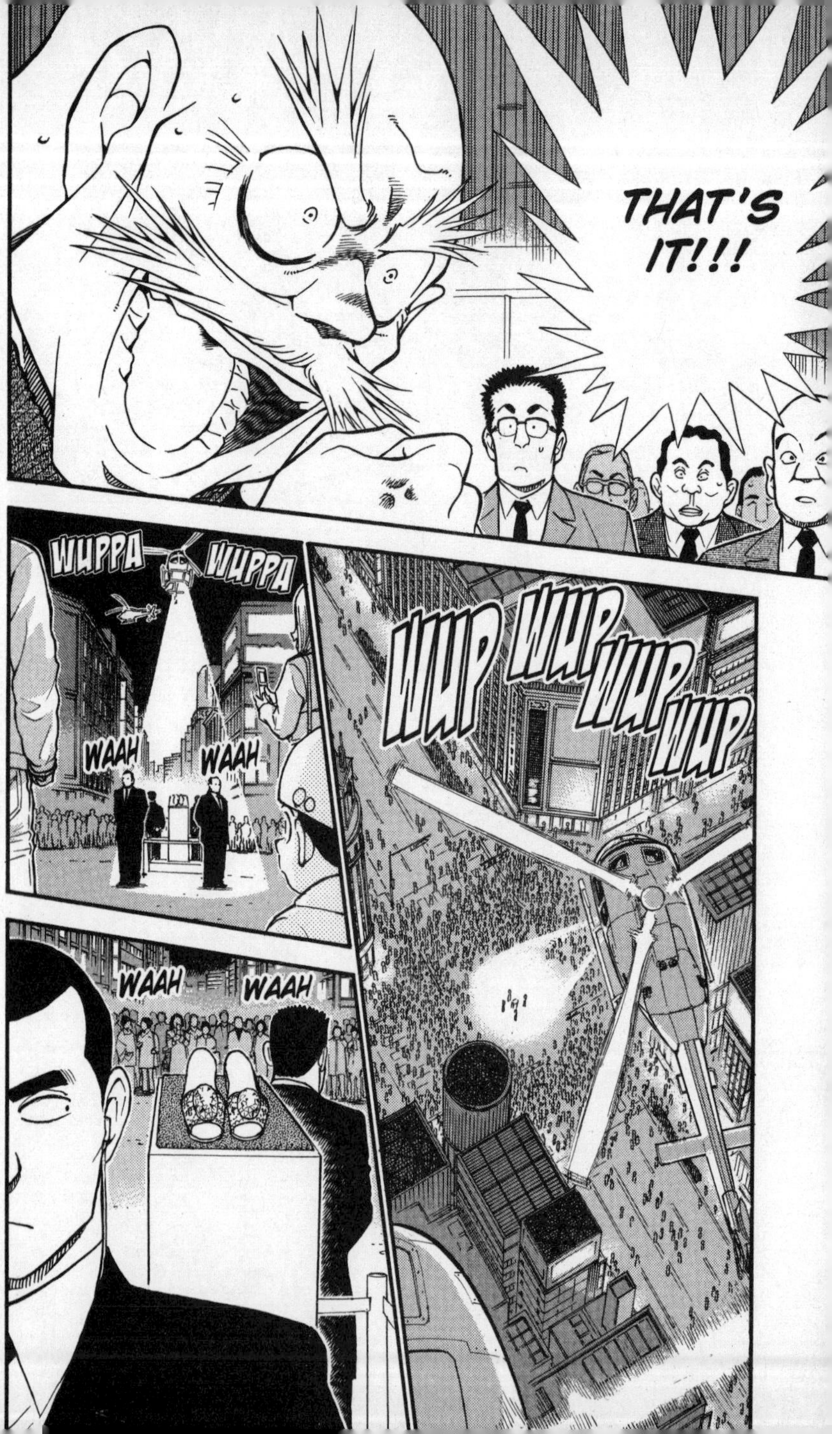
THAT'S IT!!!
WUP WUP WUP WUP
WUPPA
WUPPA
WAAH
WAAH
WAAH
WAAH

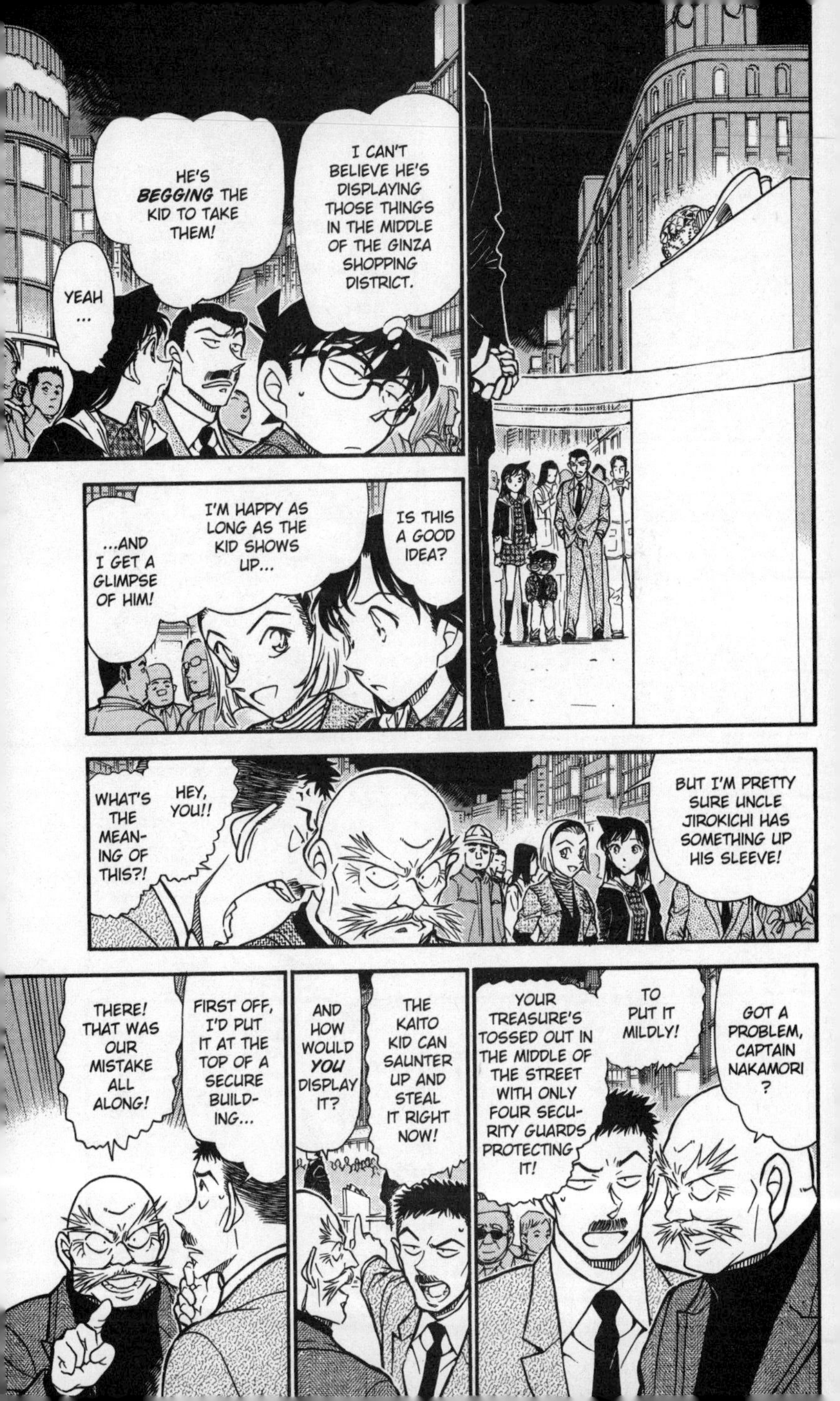

I CAN'T BELIEVE HE'S DISPLAYING THOSE THINGS IN THE MIDDLE OF THE GINZA SHOPPING DISTRICT.
HE'S *BEGGING* THE KID TO TAKE THEM!
YEAH ...
IS THIS A GOOD IDEA?
I'M HAPPY AS LONG AS THE KID SHOWS UP...
...AND I GET A GLIMPSE OF HIM!
BUT I'M PRETTY SURE UNCLE JIROKICHI HAS SOMETHING UP HIS SLEEVE!
HEY, YOU!!
WHAT'S THE MEAN-ING OF THIS?!
GOT A PROBLEM, CAPTAIN NAKAMORI ?
TO PUT IT MILDLY!
YOUR TREASURE'S TOSSED OUT IN THE MIDDLE OF THE STREET WITH ONLY FOUR SECU-RITY GUARDS PROTECTING IT!
THE KAITO KID CAN SAUNTER UP AND STEAL IT RIGHT NOW!
AND HOW WOULD *YOU* DISPLAY IT?
FIRST OFF, I'D PUT IT AT THE TOP OF A SECURE BUILD-ING...
THERE! THAT WAS OUR MISTAKE ALL ALONG!

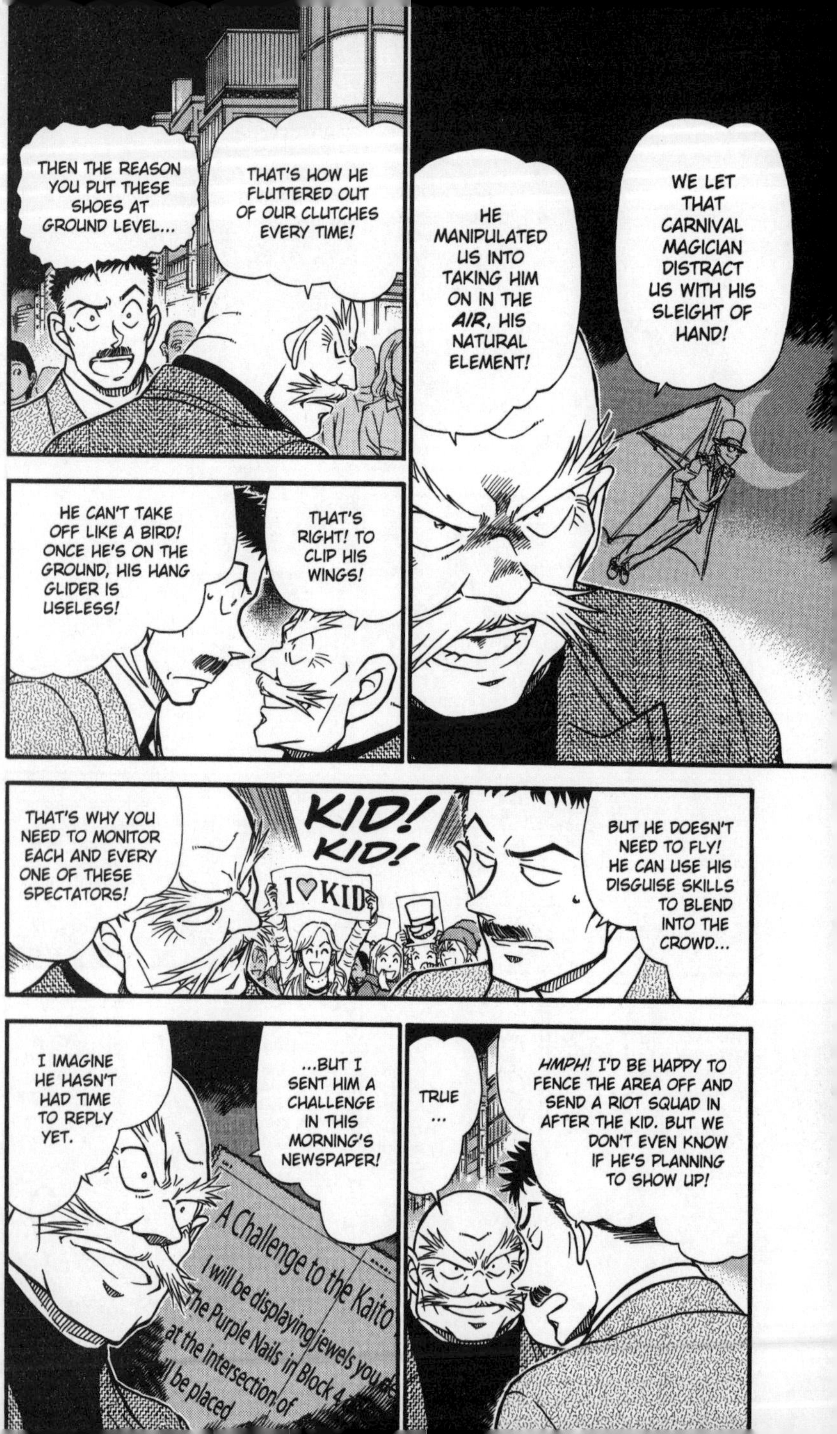
WE LET THAT CARNIVAL MAGICIAN DISTRACT US WITH HIS SLEIGHT OF HAND!
HE MANIPULATED US INTO TAKING HIM ON IN THE *AIR*, HIS NATURAL ELEMENT!
THAT'S HOW HE FLUTTERED OUT OF OUR CLUTCHES EVERY TIME!
THEN THE REASON YOU PUT THESE SHOES AT GROUND LEVEL...
THAT'S RIGHT! TO CLIP HIS WINGS!
HE CAN'T TAKE OFF LIKE A BIRD! ONCE HE'S ON THE GROUND, HIS HANG GLIDER IS USELESS!
BUT HE DOESN'T NEED TO FLY! HE CAN USE HIS DISGUISE SKILLS TO BLEND INTO THE CROWD...
KID! KID!
I♥KID
THAT'S WHY YOU NEED TO MONITOR EACH AND EVERY ONE OF THESE SPECTATORS!
*HMPH!* I'D BE HAPPY TO FENCE THE AREA OFF AND SEND A RIOT SQUAD IN AFTER THE KID. BUT WE DON'T EVEN KNOW IF HE'S PLANNING TO SHOW UP!
TRUE...
...BUT I SENT HIM A CHALLENGE IN THIS MORNING'S NEWSPAPER!
I IMAGINE HE HASN'T HAD TIME TO REPLY YET.
A Challenge to the Kaito
I will be displaying jewels you
The Purple Nails in Block 4
at the intersection of
be placed

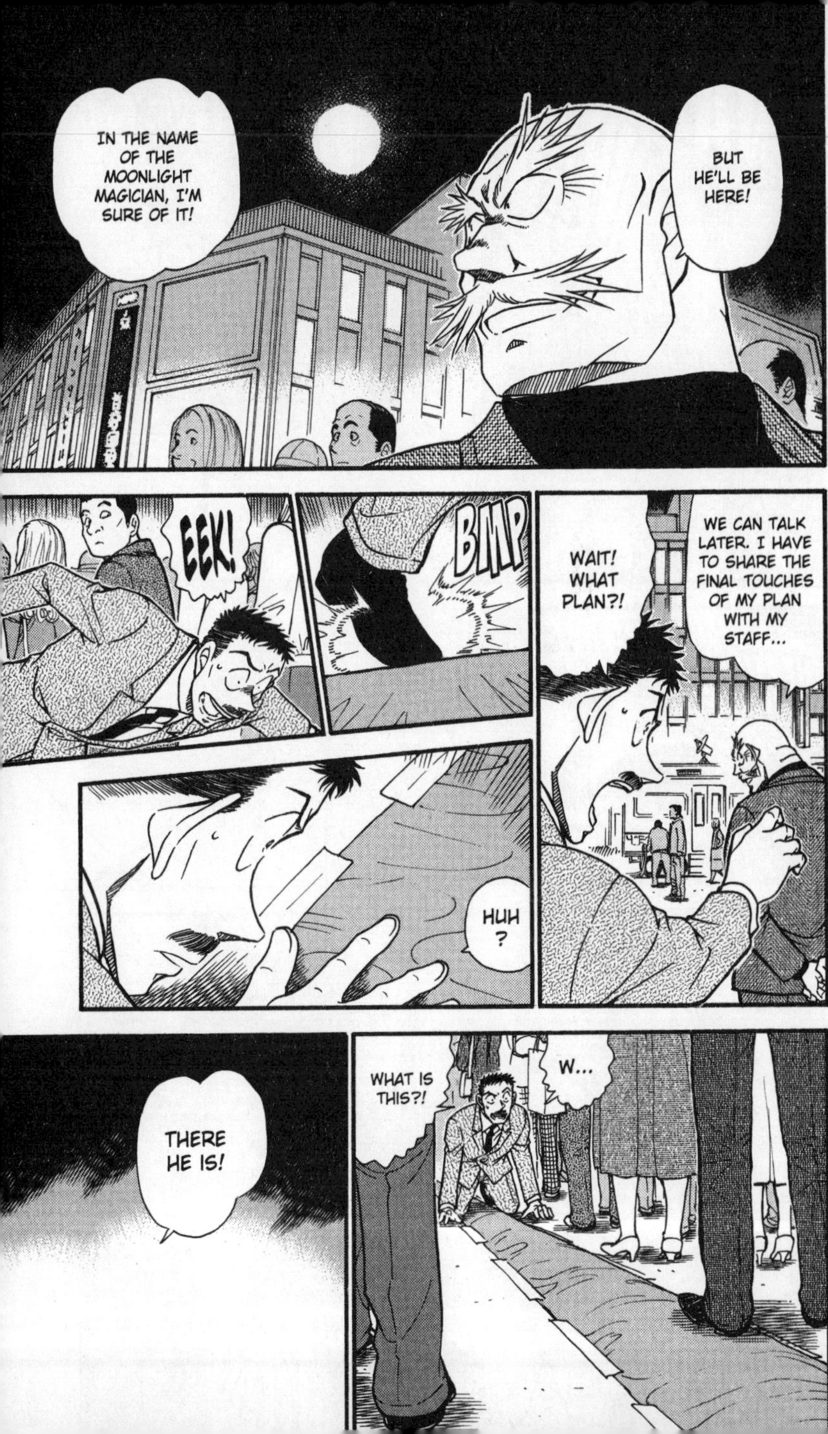
BUT HE'LL BE HERE!
IN THE NAME OF THE MOONLIGHT MAGICIAN, I'M SURE OF IT!
WE CAN TALK LATER. I HAVE TO SHARE THE FINAL TOUCHES OF MY PLAN WITH MY STAFF...
WAIT! WHAT PLAN?!
BMP
EEK!
HUH?
W...
WHAT IS THIS?!
THERE HE IS!

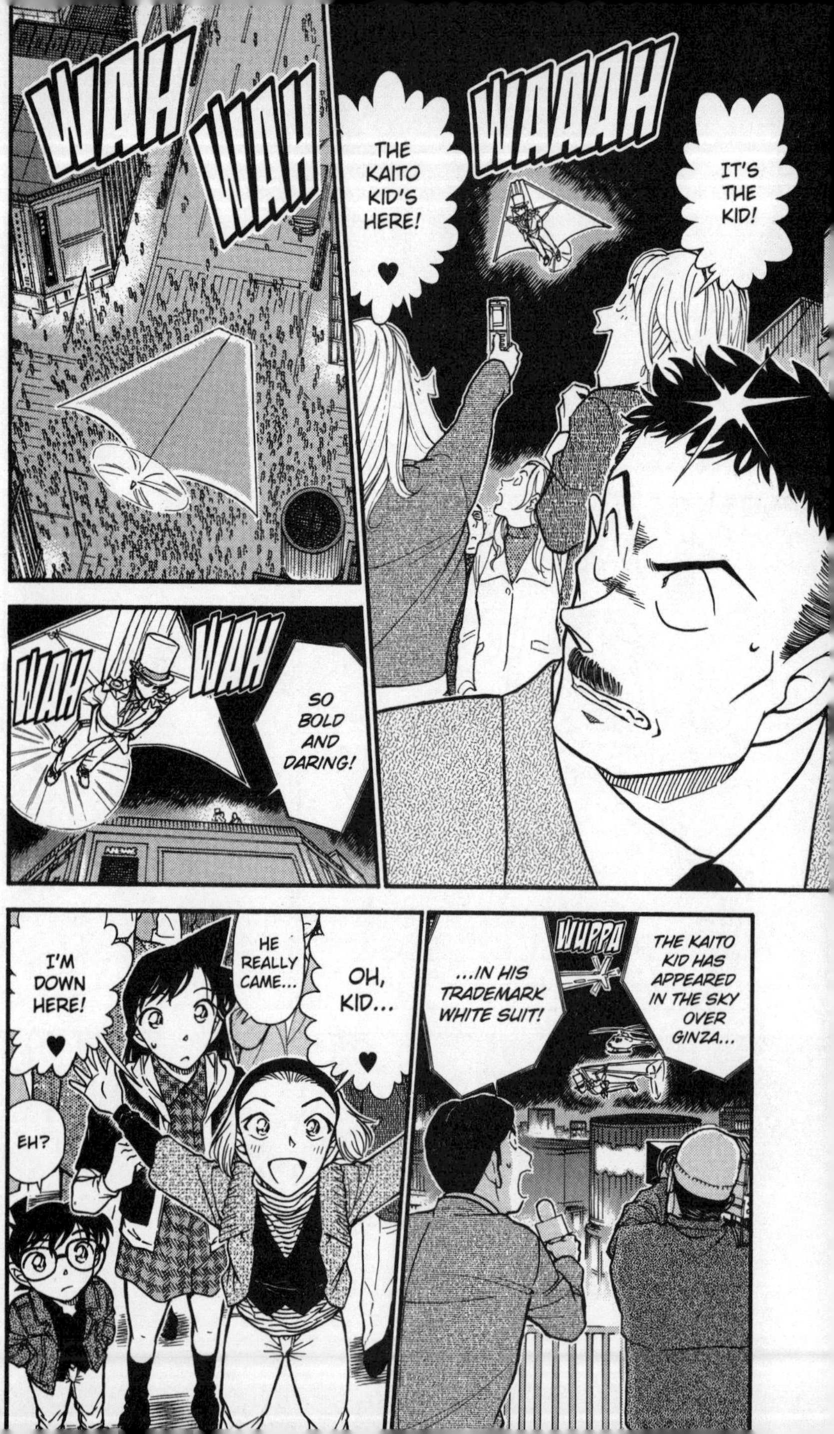
IT'S THE KID!
WAAAH
THE KAITO KID'S HERE! ♥
WAH WAH
WAH WAH
SO BOLD AND DARING!
THE KAITO KID HAS APPEARED IN THE SKY OVER GINZA...
WUPPA
...IN HIS TRADEMARK WHITE SUIT!
OH, KID... ♥
HE REALLY CAME...
I'M DOWN HERE! ♥
EH?

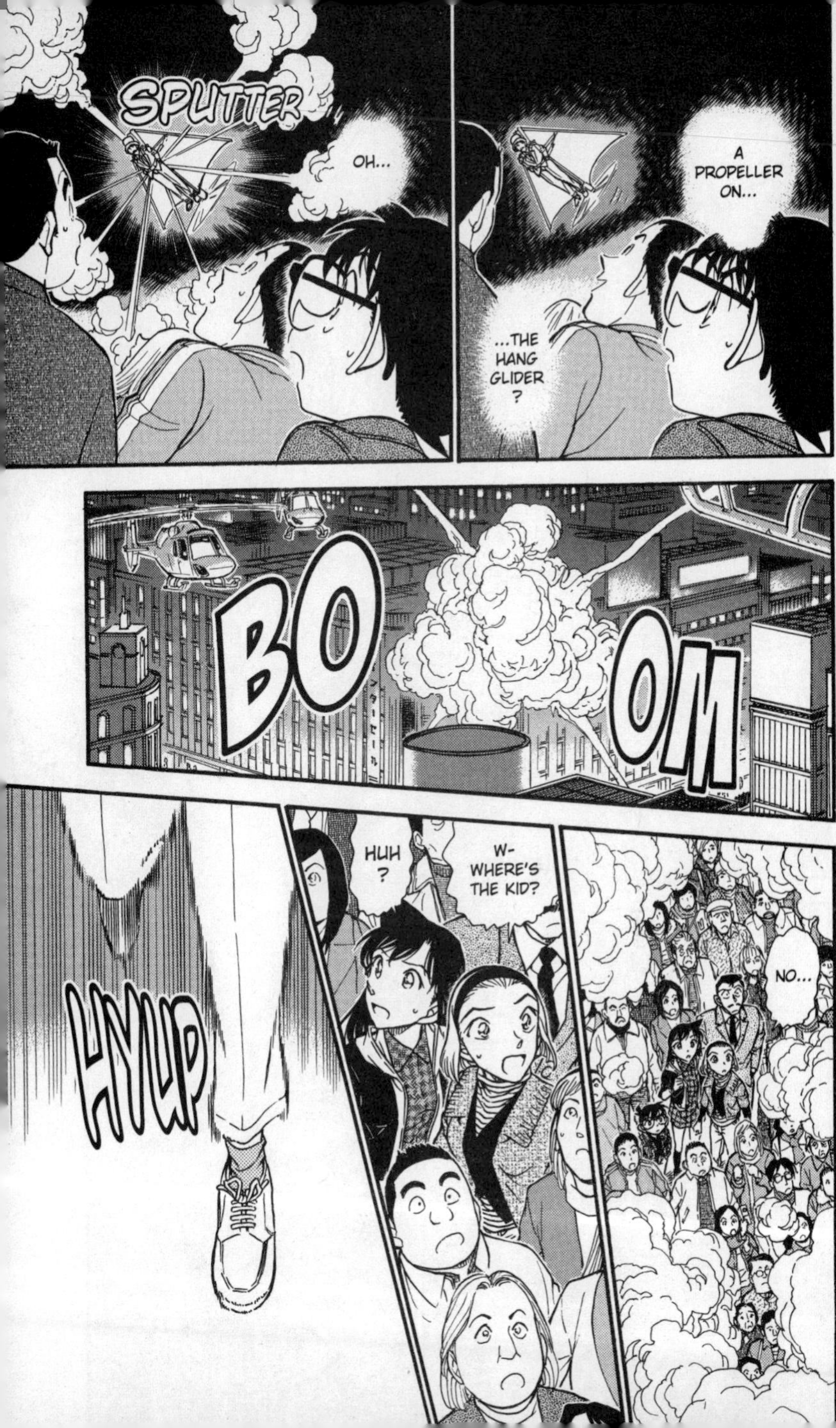
A PROPELLER ON...
...THE HANG GLIDER ?
SPUTTER
OH...
BOOM
NO...
W-WHERE'S THE KID?
HUH ?
HYUP

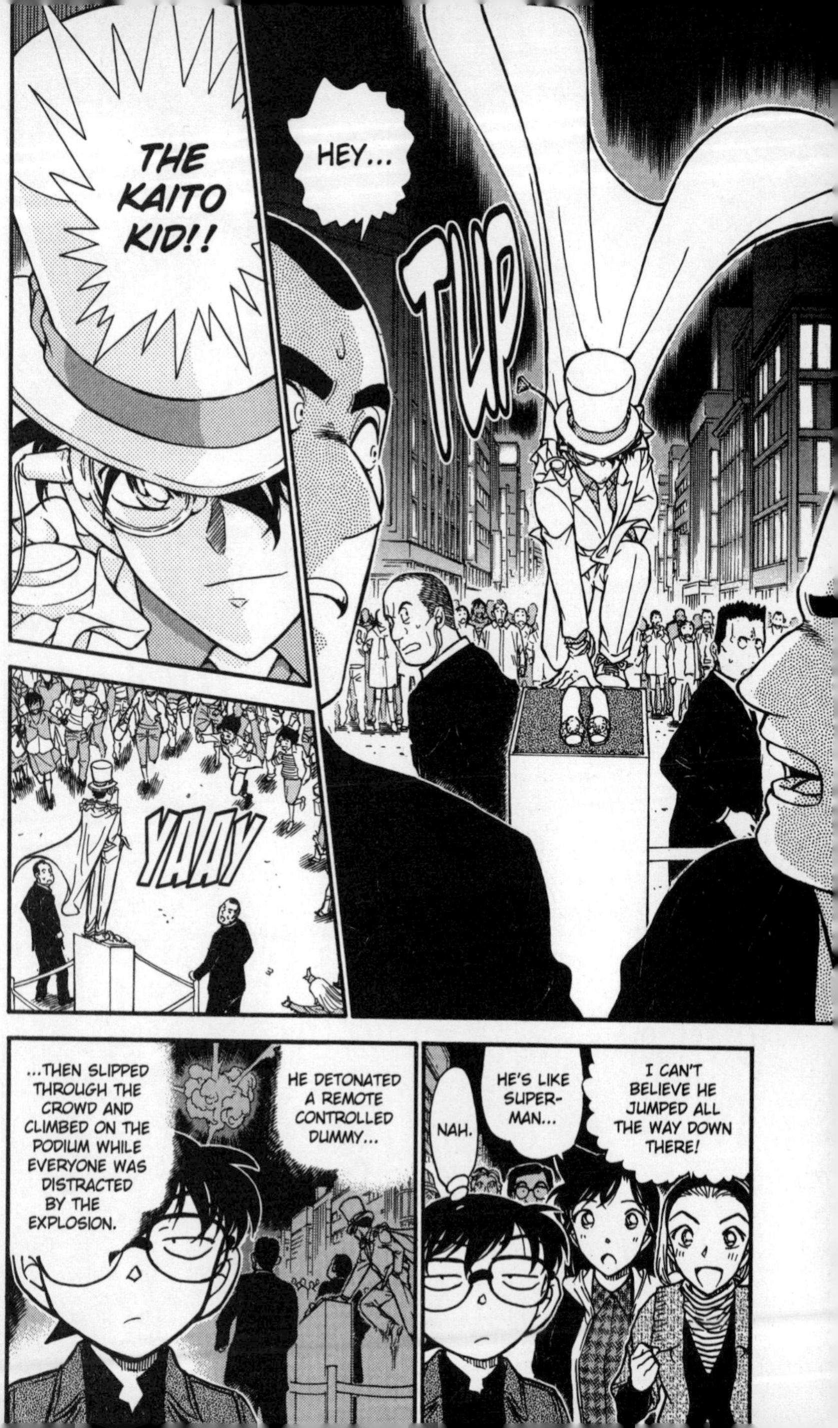
HEY...
TUP
THE KAITO KID!!
YAAY
I CAN'T BELIEVE HE JUMPED ALL THE WAY DOWN THERE!
HE'S LIKE SUPER-MAN...
NAH.
HE DETONATED A REMOTE CONTROLLED DUMMY...
...THEN SLIPPED THROUGH THE CROWD AND CLIMBED ON THE PODIUM WHILE EVERYONE WAS DISTRACTED BY THE EXPLOSION.

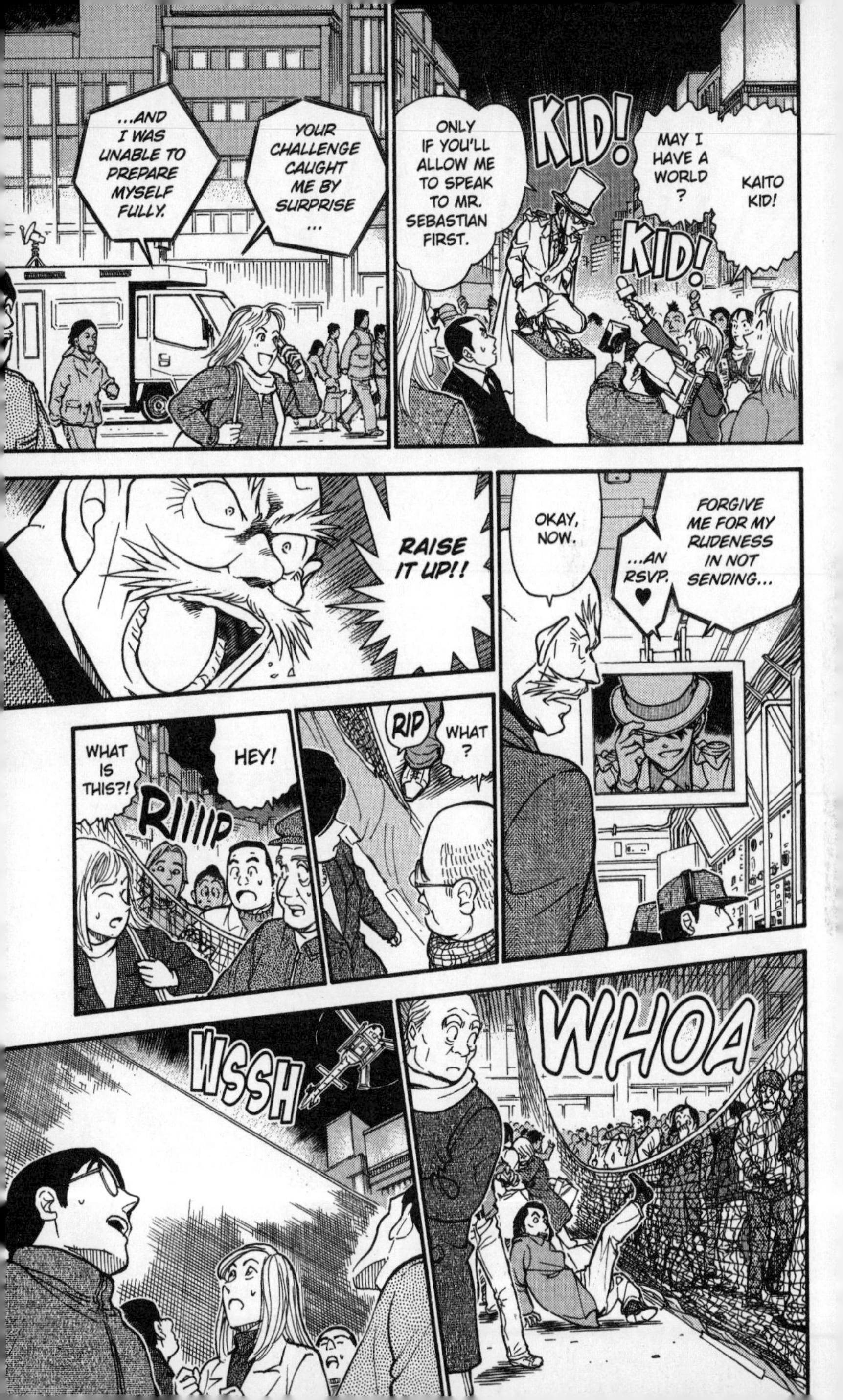

MAY I HAVE A WORLD ?
KAITO KID!
KID!
KID!
ONLY IF YOU'LL ALLOW ME TO SPEAK TO MR. SEBASTIAN FIRST.
YOUR CHALLENGE CAUGHT ME BY SURPRISE ...
...AND I WAS UNABLE TO PREPARE MYSELF FULLY.
FORGIVE ME FOR MY RUDENESS IN NOT SENDING...
...AN RSVP. ♥
OKAY, NOW.
RAISE IT UP!!
WHAT ?
RIP
HEY!
WHAT IS THIS?!
RIIIIP
WHOA
WSSH

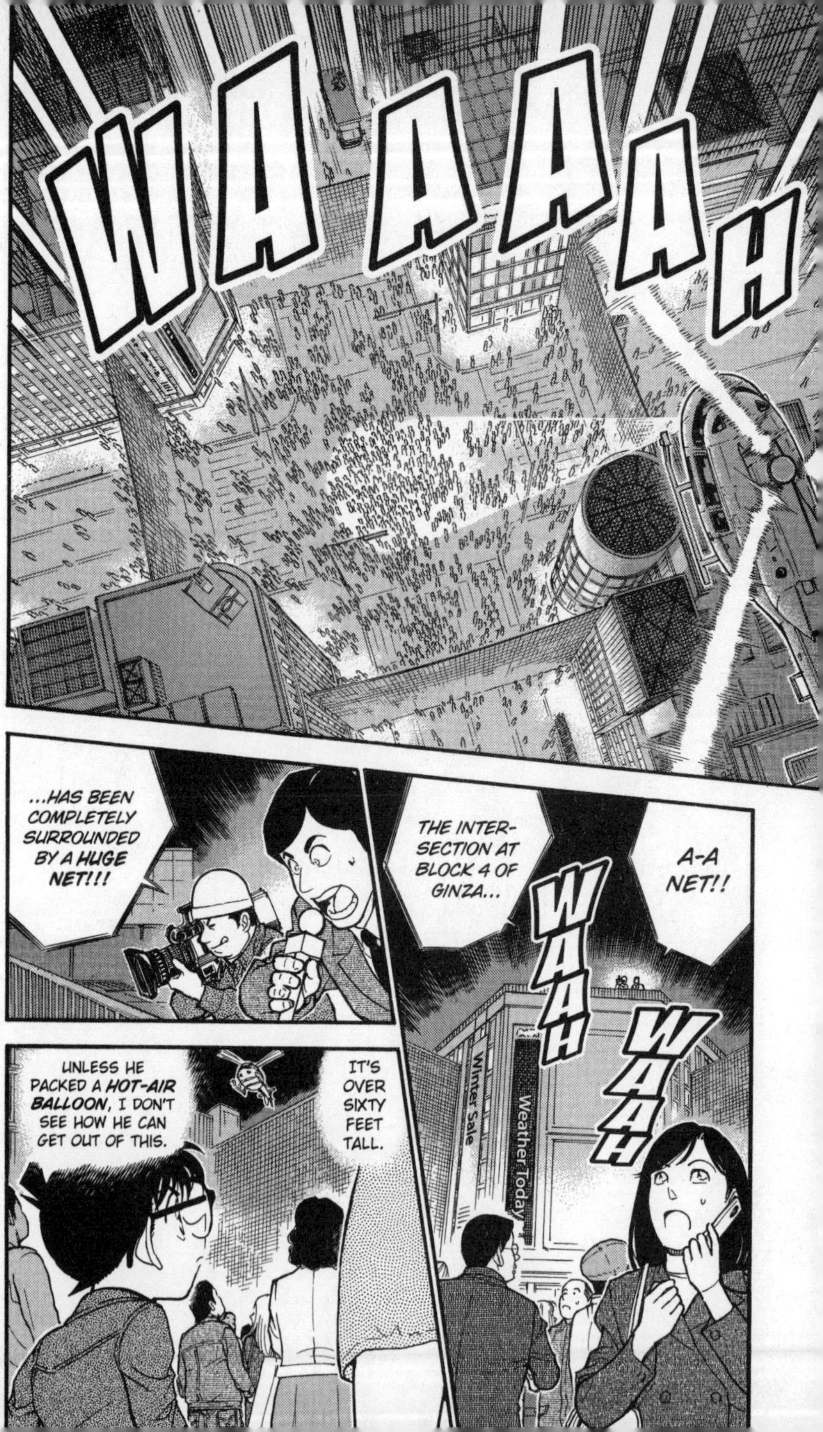

WAAAAH
A-A NET!!
THE INTER-SECTION AT BLOCK 4 OF GINZA...
WAAAH
WAAAH
Winter Sale
Weather Today
...HAS BEEN COMPLETELY SURROUNDED BY A HUGE NET!!!
IT'S OVER SIXTY FEET TALL.
UNLESS HE PACKED A HOT-AIR BALLOON, I DON'T SEE HOW HE CAN GET OUT OF THIS.

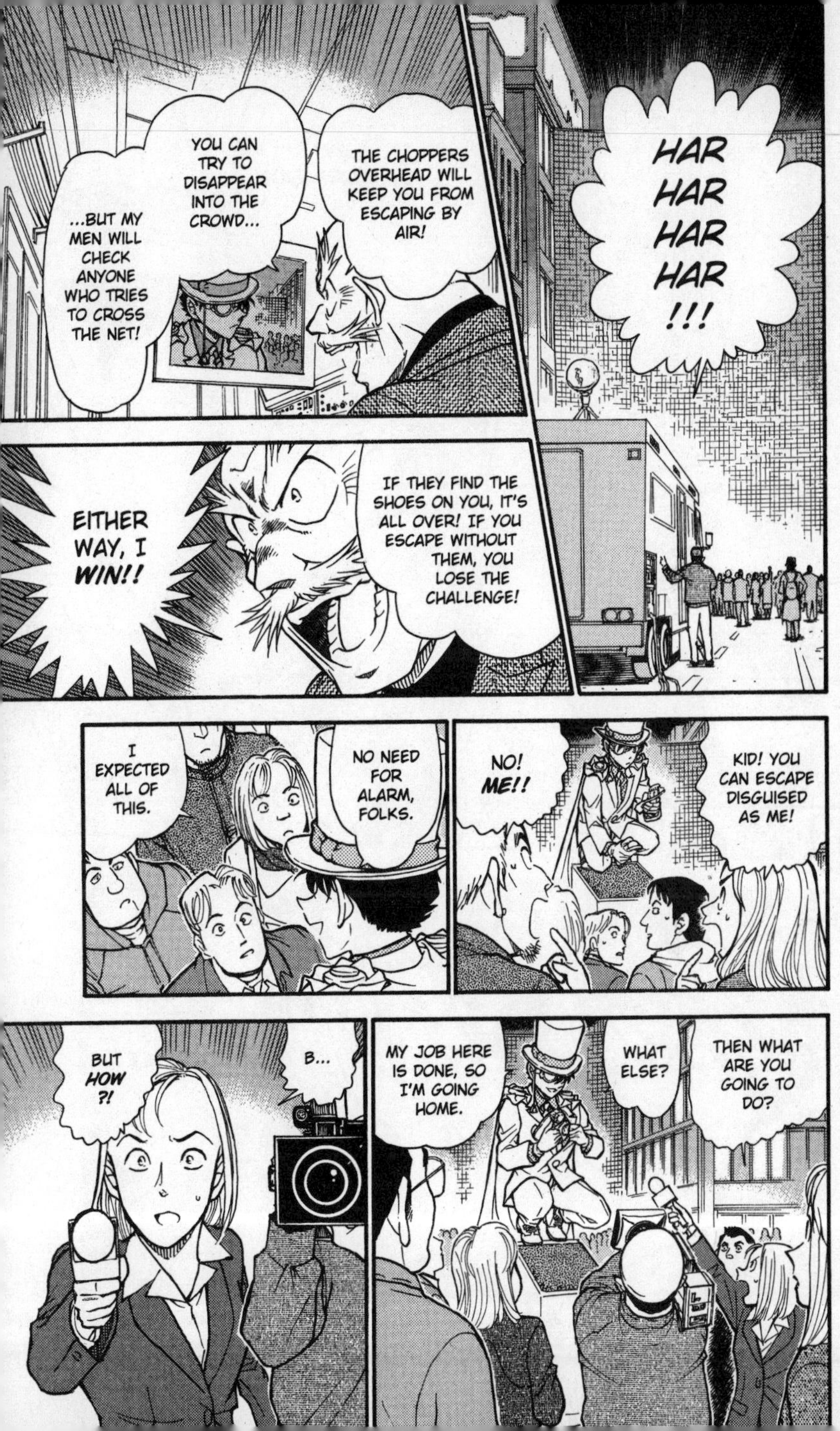
HAR HAR HAR HAR !!!
THE CHOPPERS OVERHEAD WILL KEEP YOU FROM ESCAPING BY AIR!
YOU CAN TRY TO DISAPPEAR INTO THE CROWD...
...BUT MY MEN WILL CHECK ANYONE WHO TRIES TO CROSS THE NET!
IF THEY FIND THE SHOES ON YOU, IT'S ALL OVER! IF YOU ESCAPE WITHOUT THEM, YOU LOSE THE CHALLENGE!
EITHER WAY, I *WIN!!*
KID! YOU CAN ESCAPE DISGUISED AS ME!
NO! *ME!!*
NO NEED FOR ALARM, FOLKS.
I EXPECTED ALL OF THIS.
THEN WHAT ARE YOU GOING TO DO?
WHAT ELSE?
MY JOB HERE IS DONE, SO I'M GOING HOME.
B...
BUT *HOW* ?!

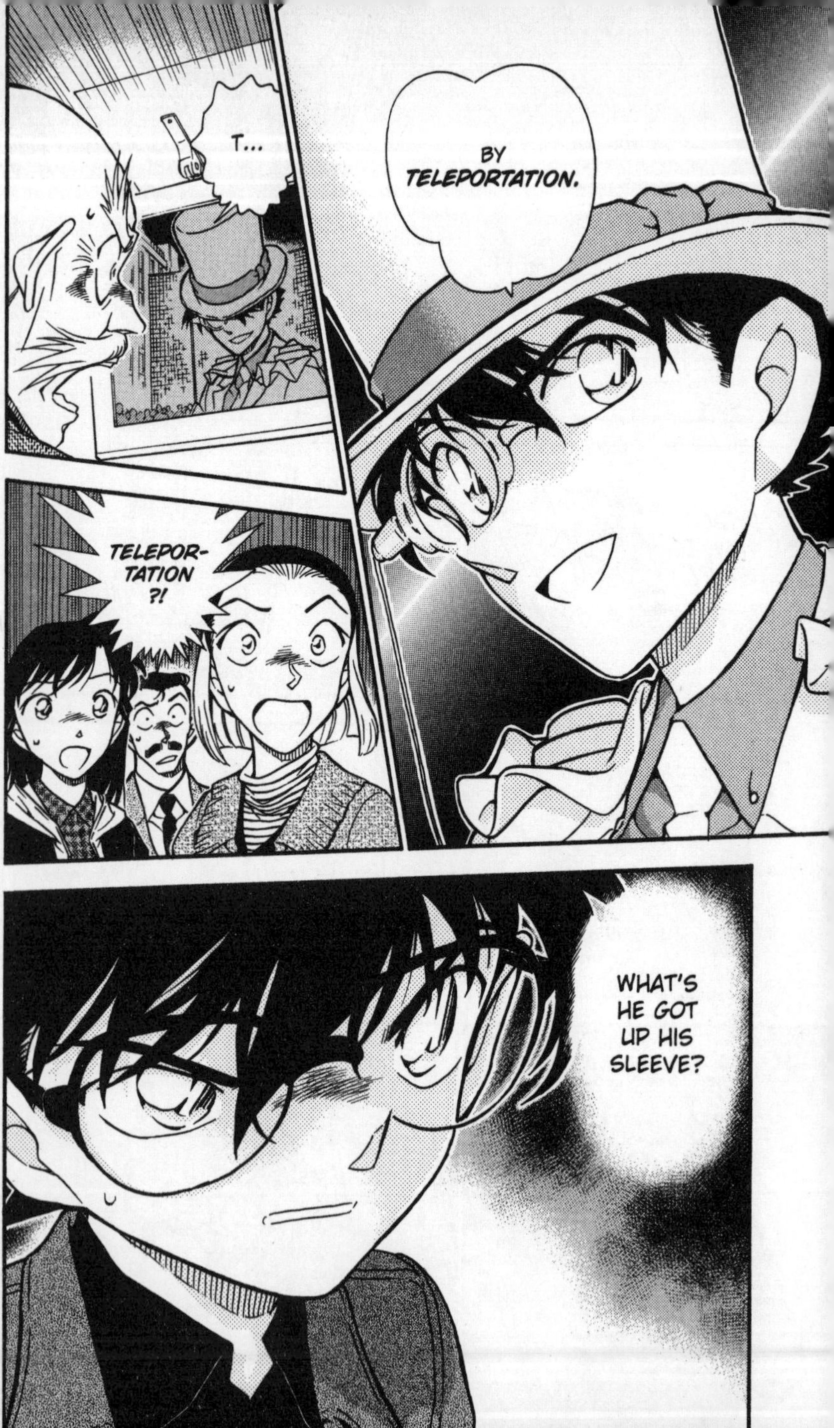
BY TELEPORTATION.
T...
TELEPOR-TATION ?!
WHAT'S HE GOT UP HIS SLEEVE?

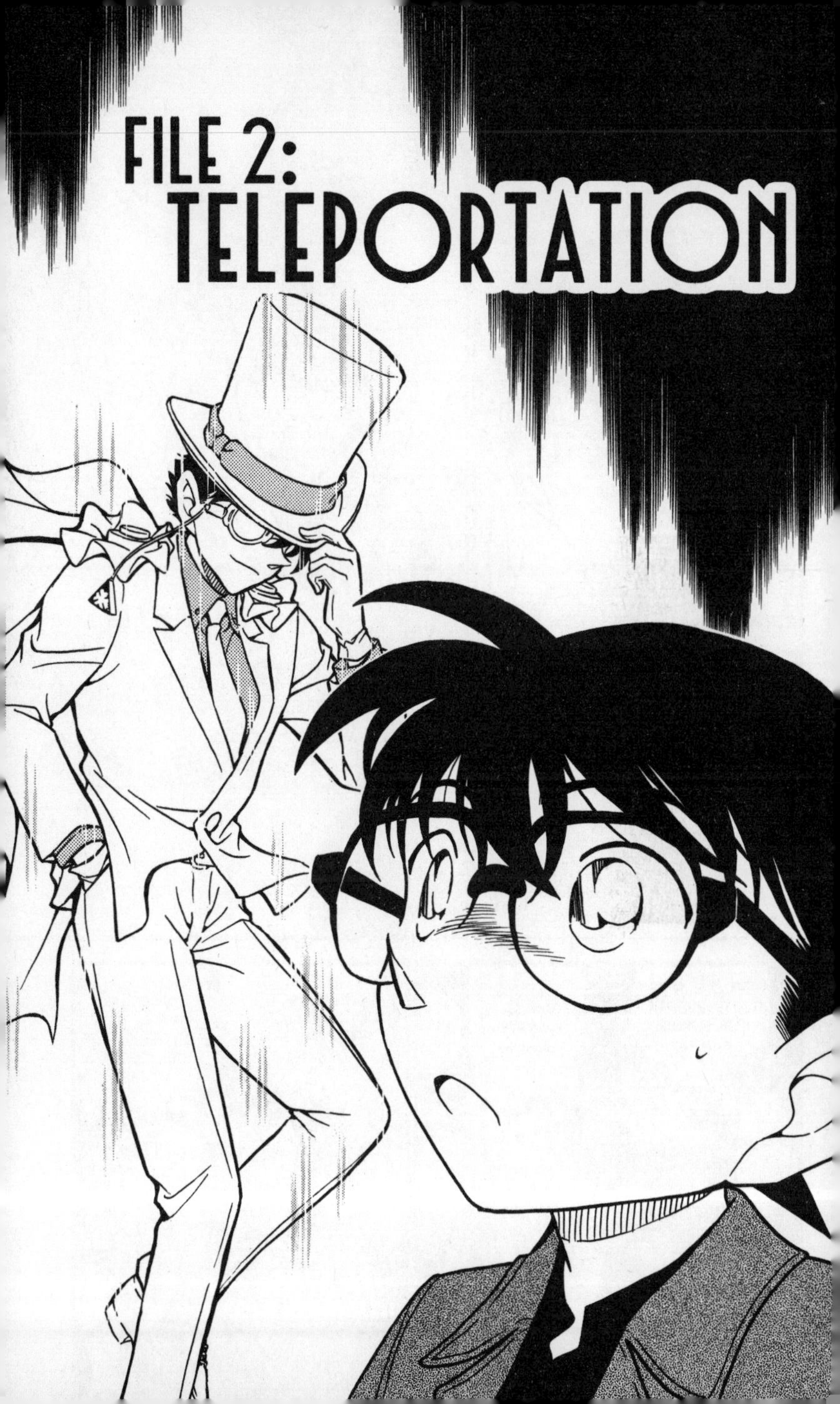
FILE 2:
TELEPORTATION

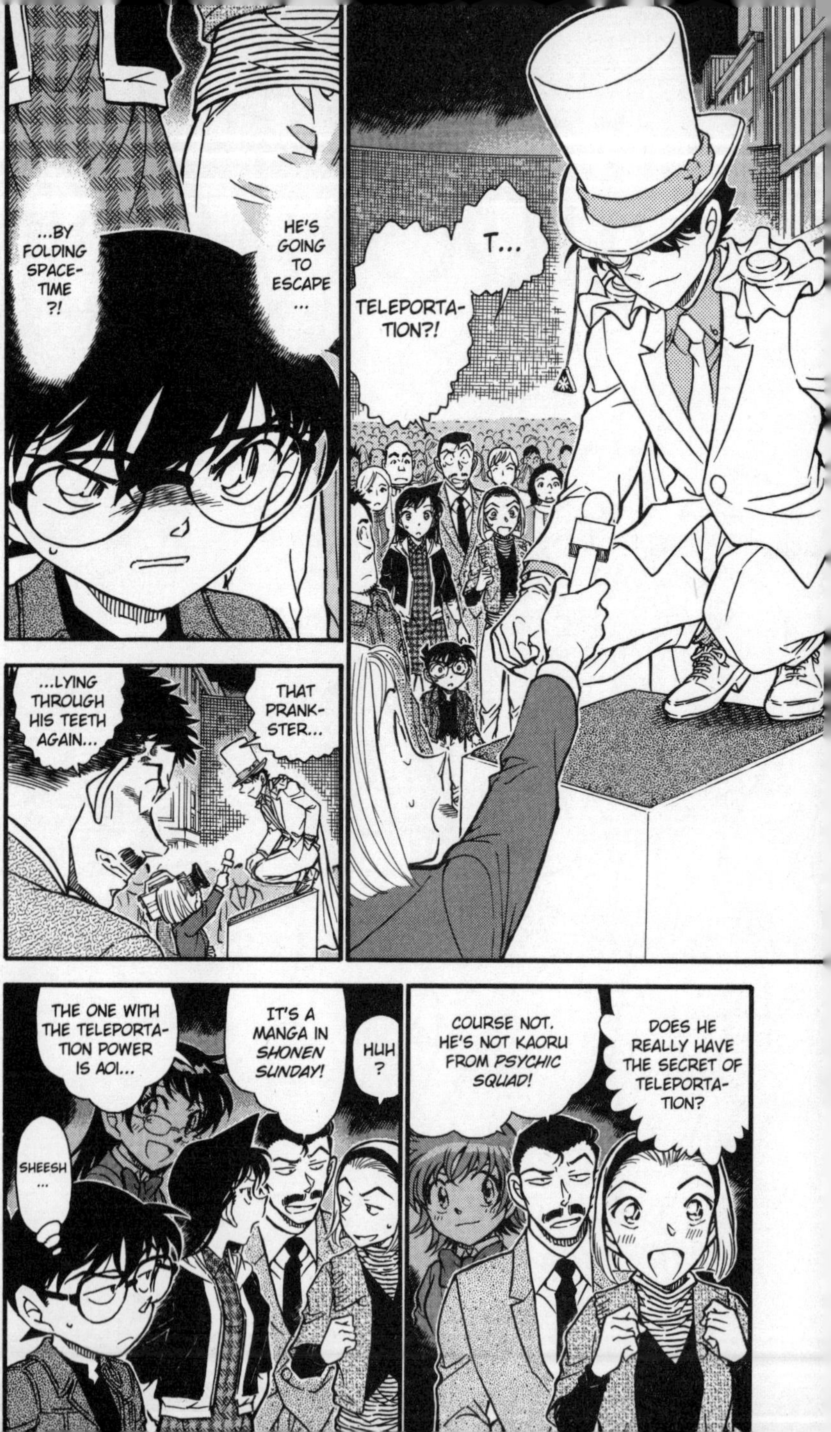
T...
TELEPORTATION?!
HE'S GOING TO ESCAPE...
...BY FOLDING SPACE-TIME?!
THAT PRANKSTER...
...LYING THROUGH HIS TEETH AGAIN...
DOES HE REALLY HAVE THE SECRET OF TELEPORTATION?
COURSE NOT. HE'S NOT KAORU FROM *PSYCHIC SQUAD*!
HUH?
IT'S A MANGA IN *SHONEN SUNDAY*!
THE ONE WITH THE TELEPORTATION POWER IS AOI...
SHEESH...

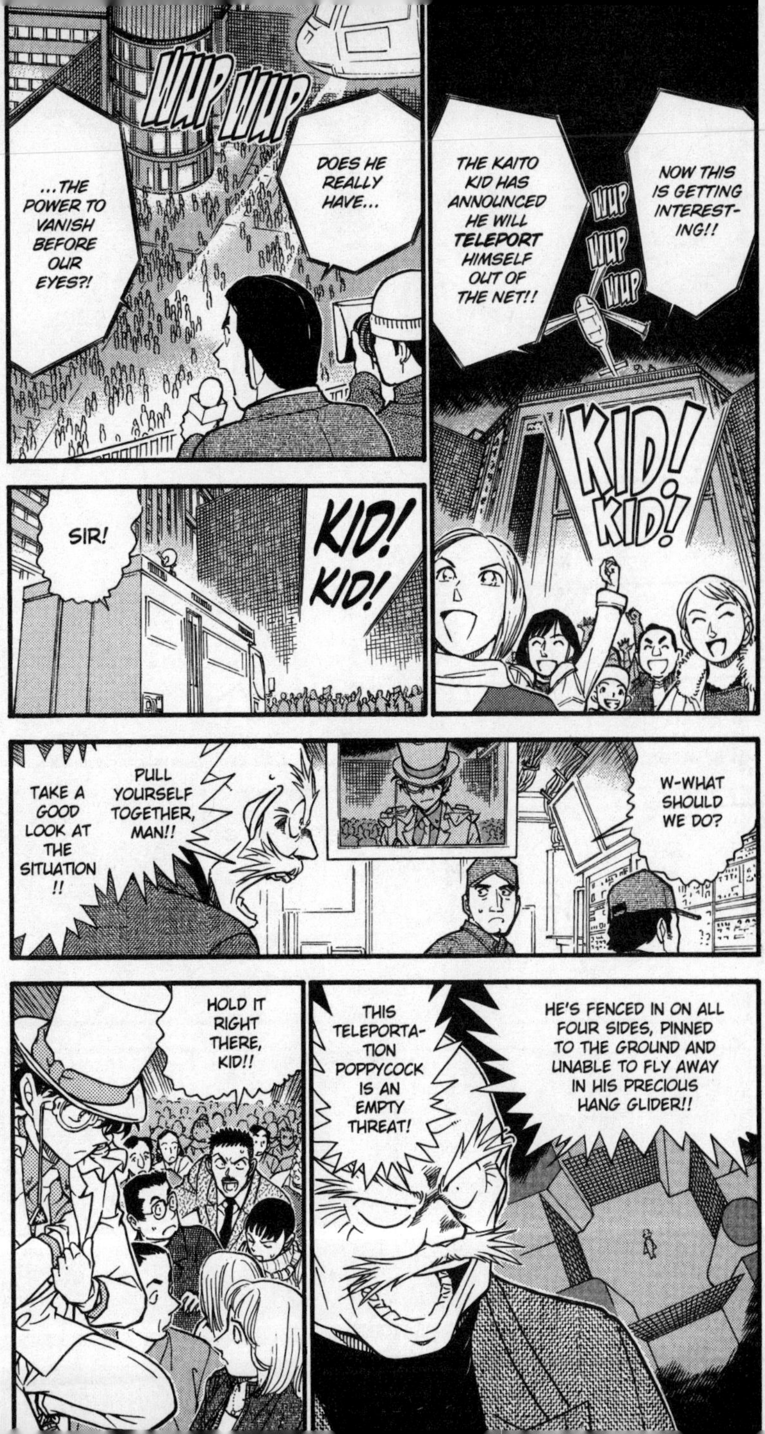
NOW THIS IS GETTING INTEREST-ING!!
THE KAITO KID HAS ANNOUNCED HE WILL TELEPORT HIMSELF OUT OF THE NET!!
WUP WUP WUP
KID! KID!
WUP WUP
DOES HE REALLY HAVE...
...THE POWER TO VANISH BEFORE OUR EYES?!
KID! KID!
SIR!
W-WHAT SHOULD WE DO?
PULL YOURSELF TOGETHER, MAN!!
TAKE A GOOD LOOK AT THE SITUATION!!
HE'S FENCED IN ON ALL FOUR SIDES, PINNED TO THE GROUND AND UNABLE TO FLY AWAY IN HIS PRECIOUS HANG GLIDER!!
THIS TELEPORTA-TION POPPYCOCK IS AN EMPTY THREAT!
HOLD IT RIGHT THERE, KID!!

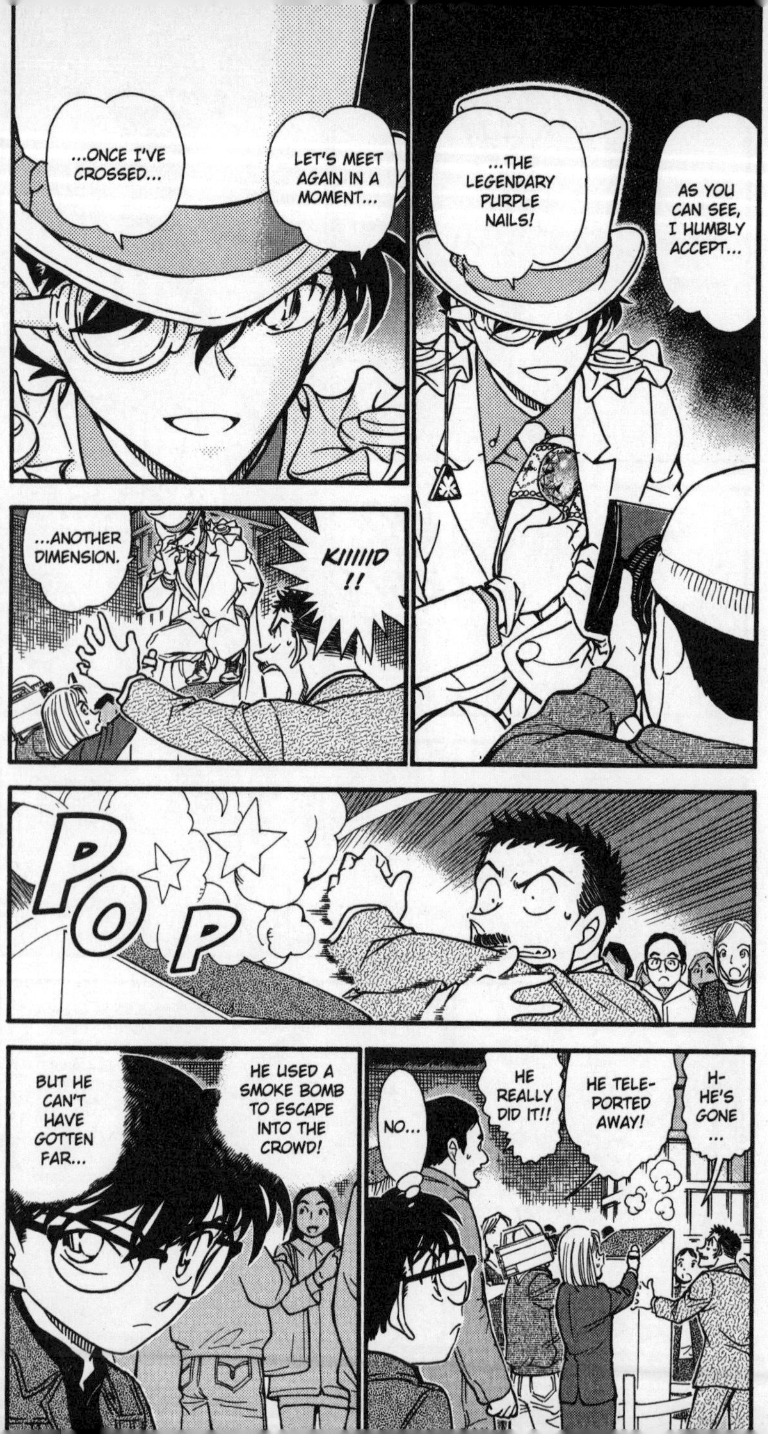
AS YOU CAN SEE, I HUMBLY ACCEPT...
...THE LEGENDARY PURPLE NAILS!
LET'S MEET AGAIN IN A MOMENT...
...ONCE I'VE CROSSED...
KIIIIID!!
...ANOTHER DIMENSION.
POP
H- HE'S GONE ...
HE TELE- PORTED AWAY!
HE REALLY DID IT!!
NO...
HE USED A SMOKE BOMB TO ESCAPE INTO THE CROWD!
BUT HE CAN'T HAVE GOTTEN FAR...

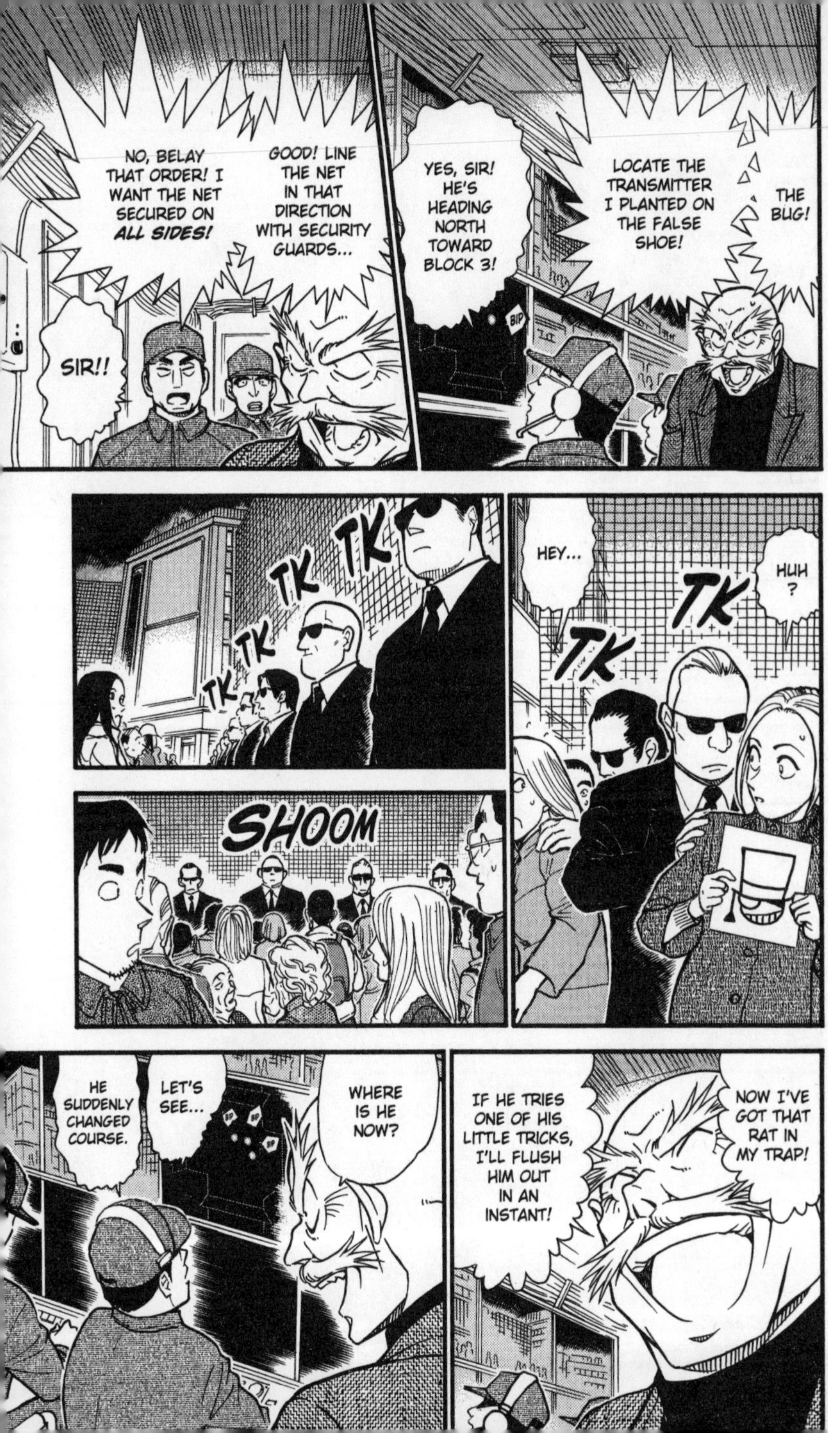
THE BUG!
LOCATE THE TRANSMITTER I PLANTED ON THE FALSE SHOE!
BIP
YES, SIR! HE'S HEADING NORTH TOWARD BLOCK 3!
GOOD! LINE THE NET IN THAT DIRECTION WITH SECURITY GUARDS...
NO, BELAY THAT ORDER! I WANT THE NET SECURED ON ALL SIDES!
SIR!!
HUH ?
HEY...
TK
TK
TK
TK
TK
TK
TK
SHOOM
NOW I'VE GOT THAT RAT IN MY TRAP!
IF HE TRIES ONE OF HIS LITTLE TRICKS, I'LL FLUSH HIM OUT IN AN INSTANT!
WHERE IS HE NOW?
LET'S SEE...
HE SUDDENLY CHANGED COURSE.

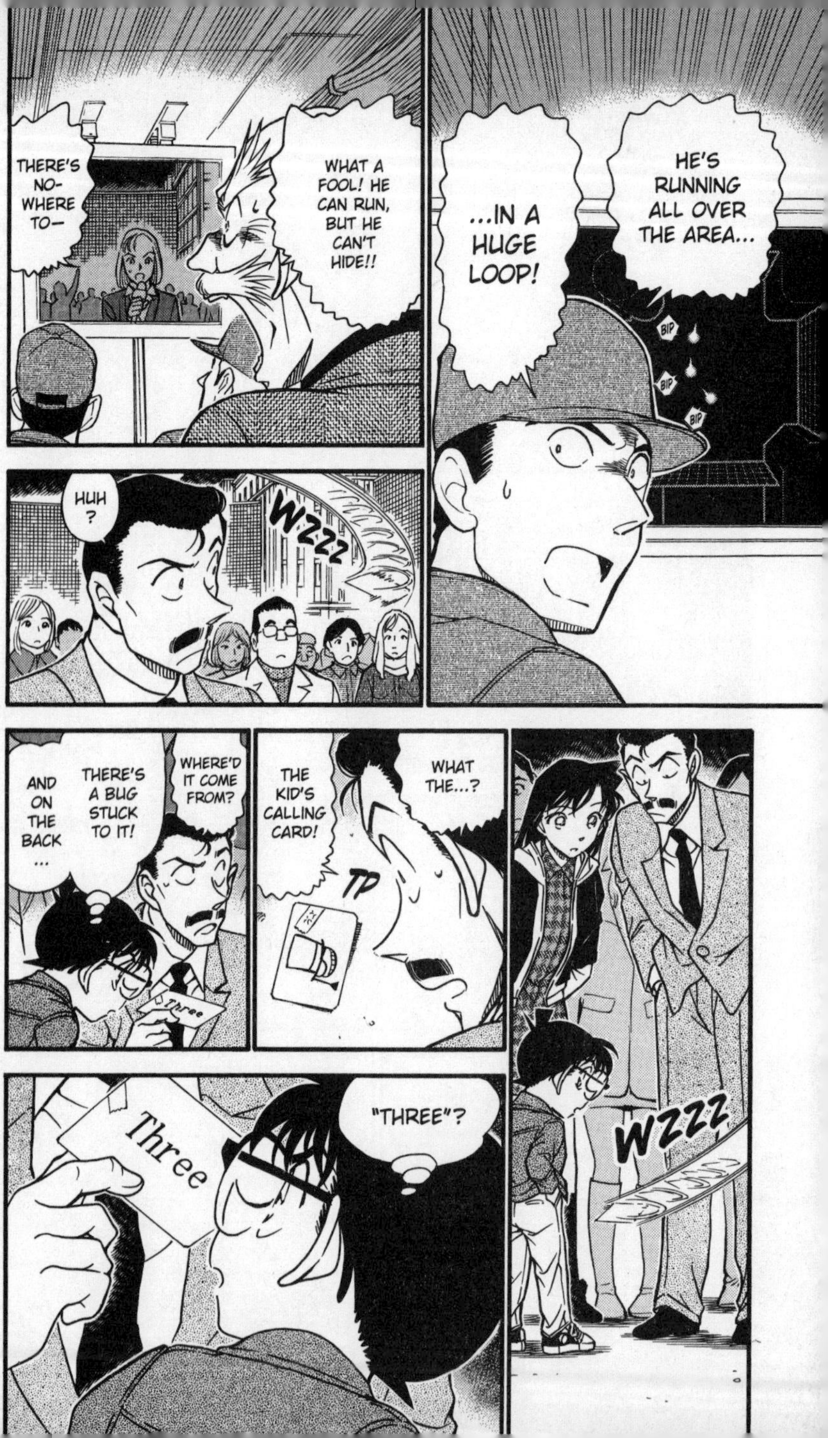
HE'S RUNNING ALL OVER THE AREA...
...IN A HUGE LOOP!
BIP
BIP
BIP
WHAT A FOOL! HE CAN RUN, BUT HE CAN'T HIDE!!
THERE'S NO-WHERE TO—
WZZZ
HUH?
WZZZ
WHAT THE...?
THE KID'S CALLING CARD!
TP
WHERE'D IT COME FROM?
THERE'S A BUG STUCK TO IT!
AND ON THE BACK...
Three
"THREE"?
Three

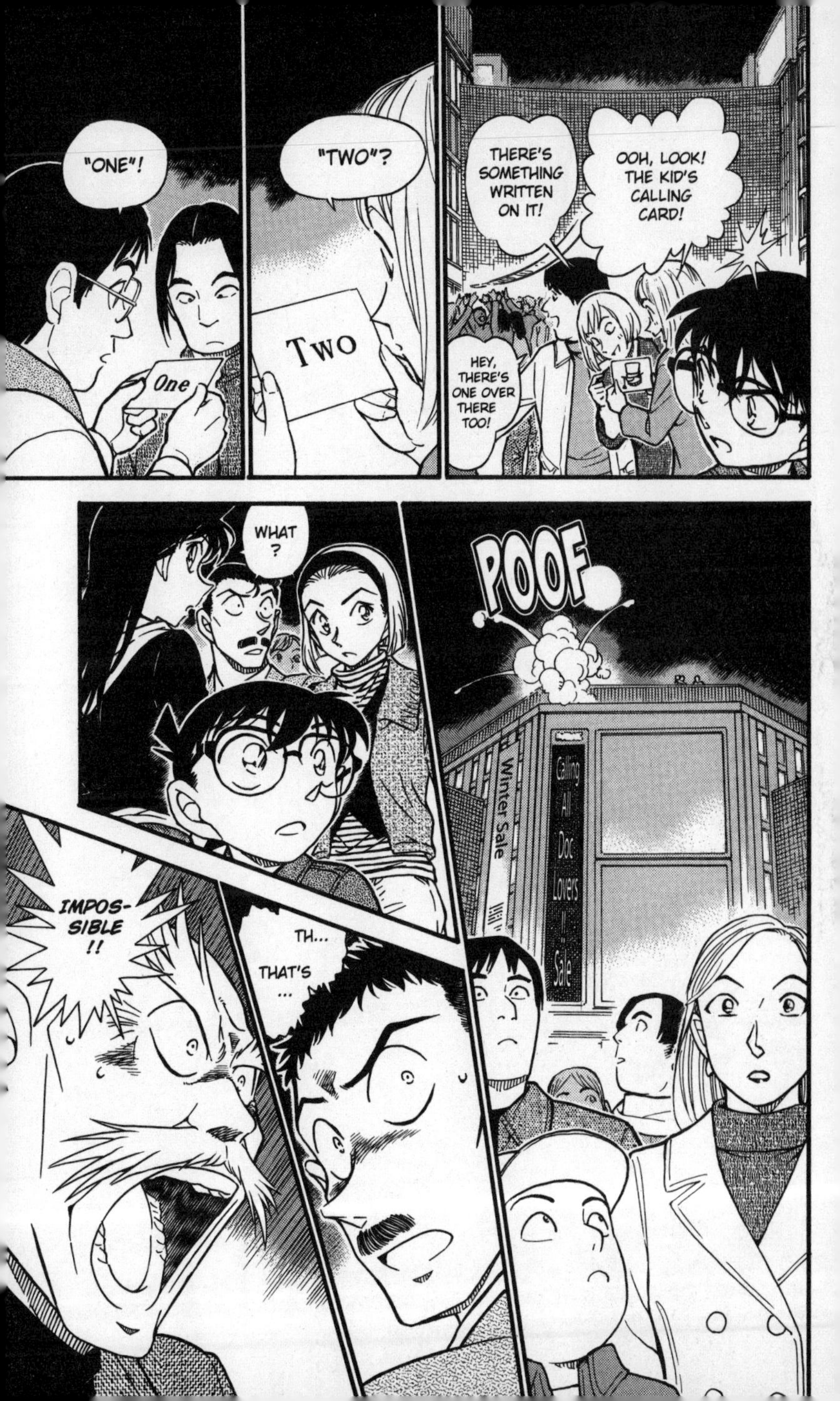
OOH, LOOK! THE KID'S CALLING CARD!
THERE'S SOMETHING WRITTEN ON IT!
HEY, THERE'S ONE OVER THERE TOO!
"TWO"?
Two
"ONE"!
One
POOF
Winter Sale
Calling All Doc Lovers!! Sale
WHAT?
TH... THAT'S ...
IMPOS-SIBLE!!

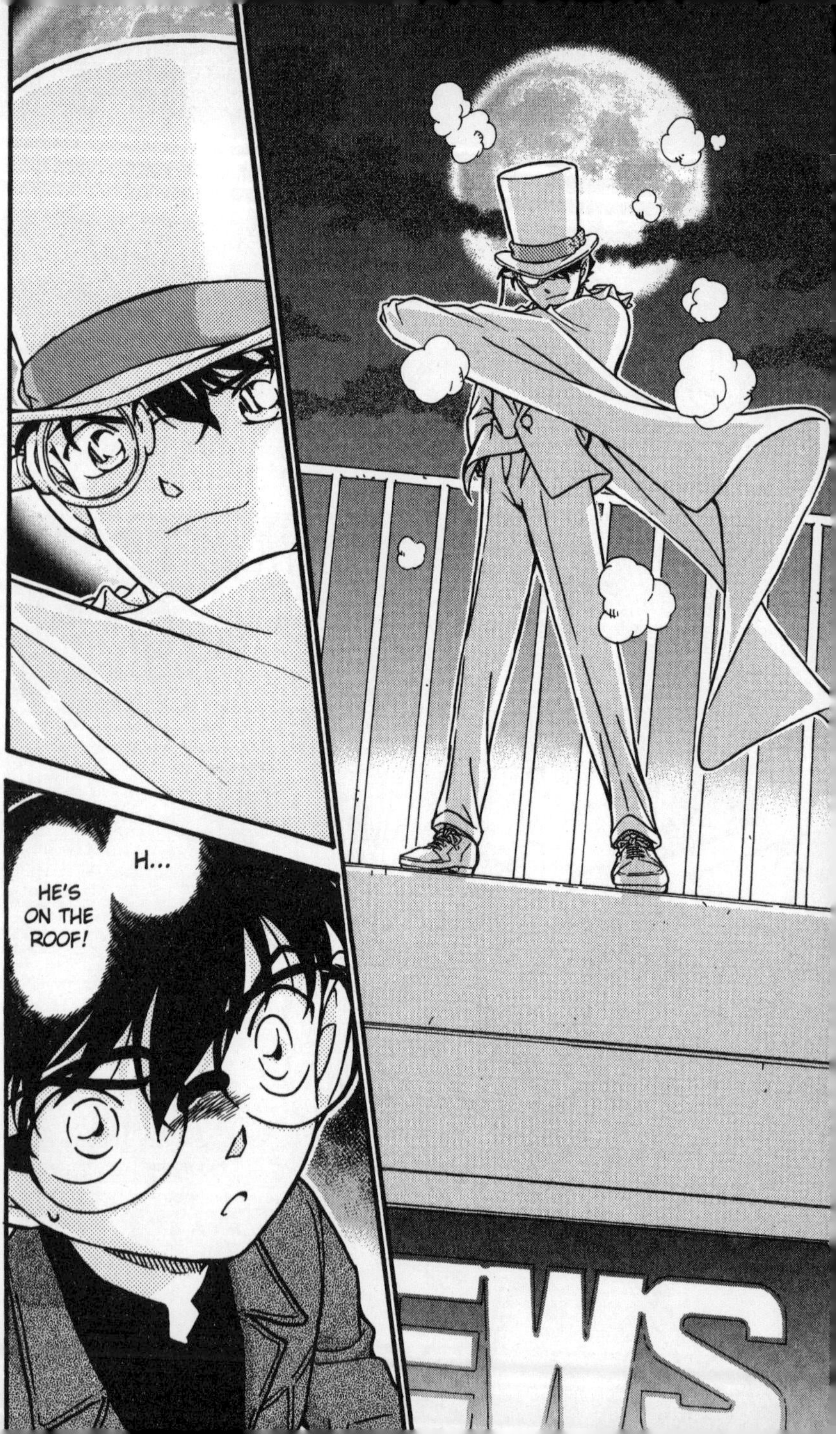
H...
HE'S ON THE ROOF!

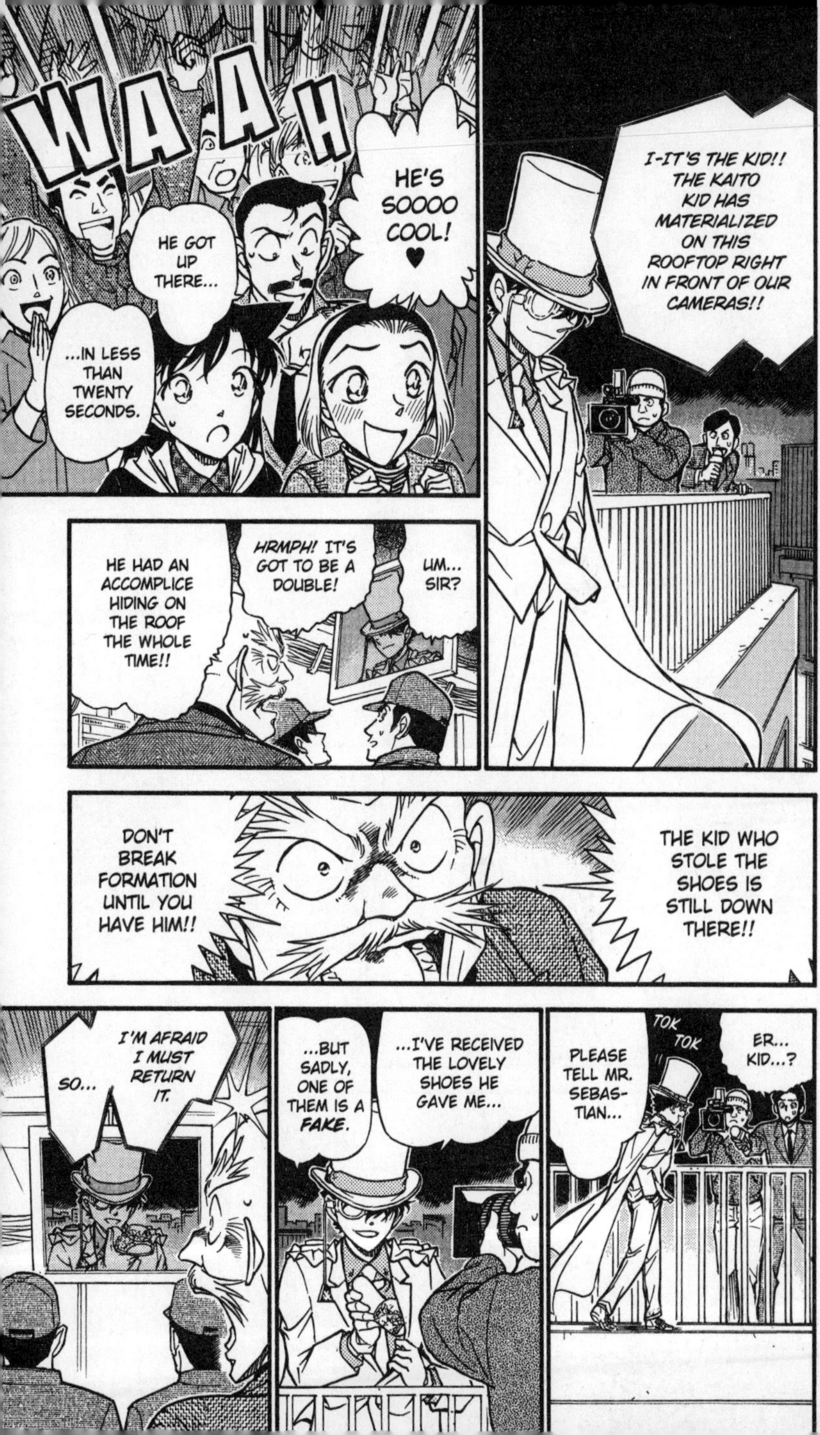
I-IT'S THE KID!! THE KAITO KID HAS MATERIALIZED ON THIS ROOFTOP RIGHT IN FRONT OF OUR CAMERAS!!
WAAH
HE'S SOOOO COOL! ♥
HE GOT UP THERE...
...IN LESS THAN TWENTY SECONDS.
UM... SIR?
HRMPH! IT'S GOT TO BE A DOUBLE!
HE HAD AN ACCOMPLICE HIDING ON THE ROOF THE WHOLE TIME!!
THE KID WHO STOLE THE SHOES IS STILL DOWN THERE!!
DON'T BREAK FORMATION UNTIL YOU HAVE HIM!!
ER... KID...?
TOK TOK
PLEASE TELL MR. SEBAS-TIAN...
...I'VE RECEIVED THE LOVELY SHOES HE GAVE ME...
...BUT SADLY, ONE OF THEM IS A FAKE.
I'M AFRAID I MUST RETURN IT.
SO...

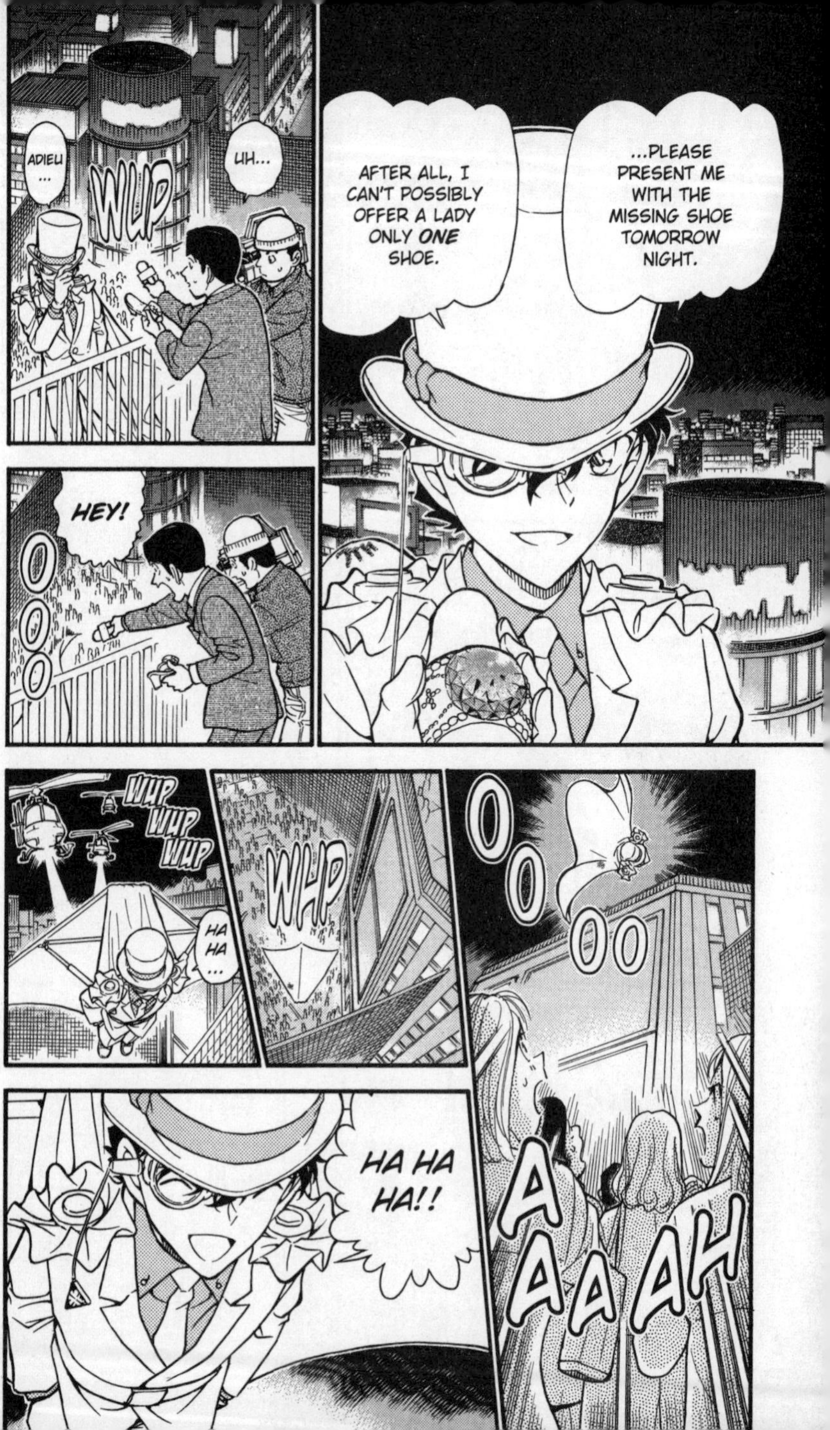
...PLEASE PRESENT ME WITH THE MISSING SHOE TOMORROW NIGHT.
AFTER ALL, I CAN'T POSSIBLY OFFER A LADY ONLY *ONE* SHOE.
UH...
WUP
ADIEU ...
HEY!
OOOO
OOOOO
AAAAAH
WHP
WUP WUP WUP
HA HA ...
HA HA HA!!

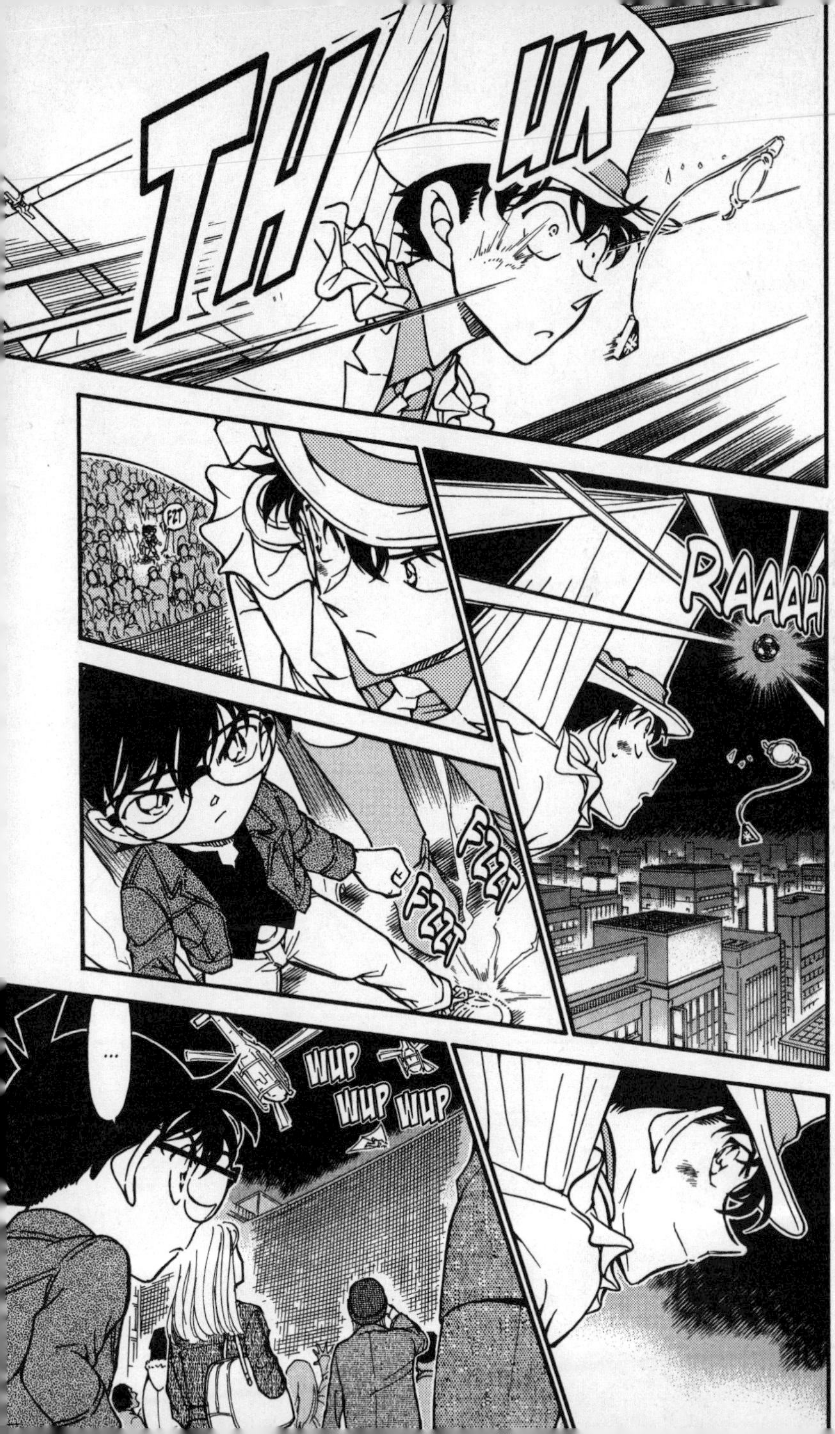

TH UK
RAAAH
FZT
FZZT
FZZT
...
WUP
WUP WUP

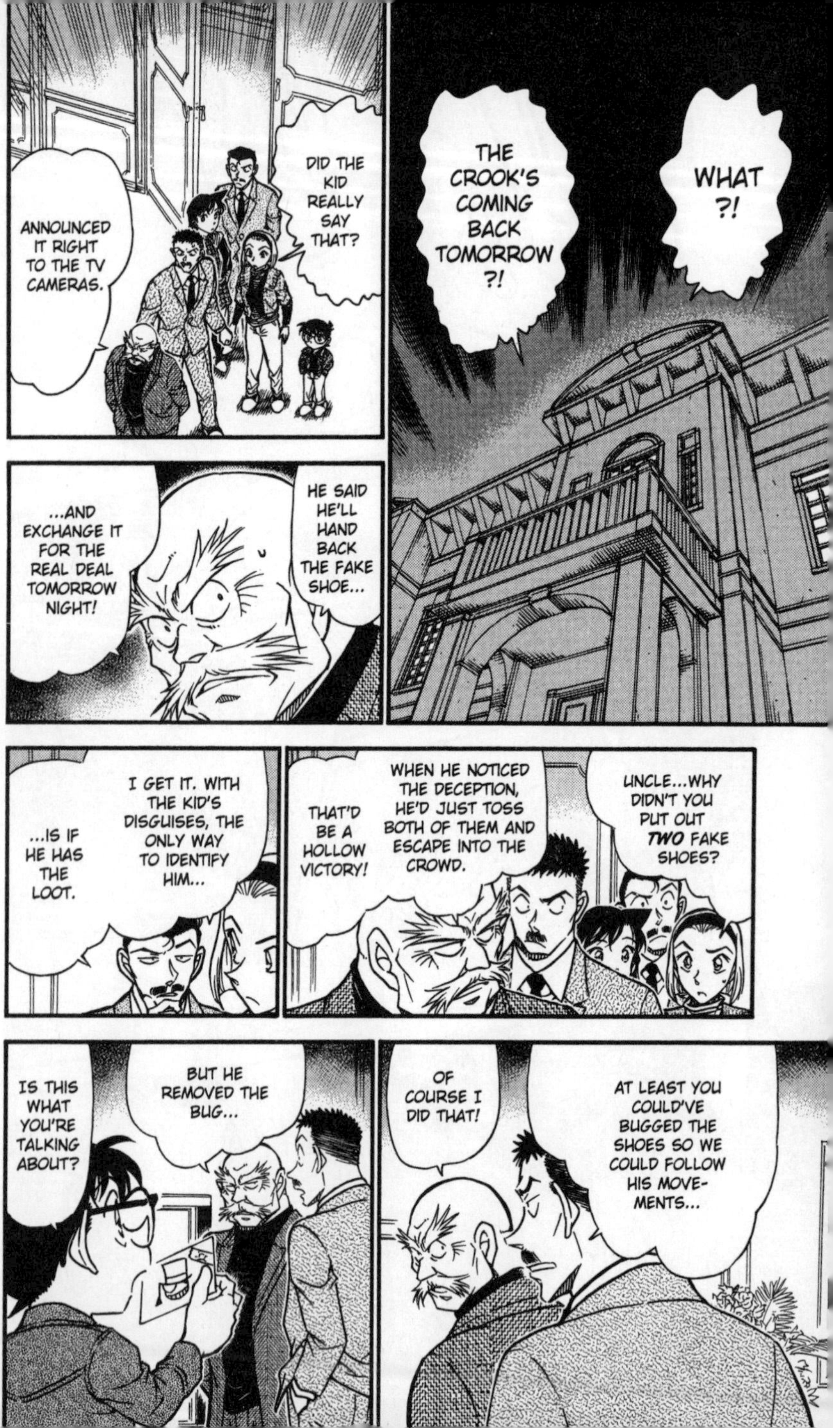
WHAT?!
THE CROOK'S COMING BACK TOMORROW?!
DID THE KID REALLY SAY THAT?
ANNOUNCED IT RIGHT TO THE TV CAMERAS.
HE SAID HE'LL HAND BACK THE FAKE SHOE...
...AND EXCHANGE IT FOR THE REAL DEAL TOMORROW NIGHT!
UNCLE...WHY DIDN'T YOU PUT OUT TWO FAKE SHOES?
WHEN HE NOTICED THE DECEPTION, HE'D JUST TOSS BOTH OF THEM AND ESCAPE INTO THE CROWD.
THAT'D BE A HOLLOW VICTORY!
I GET IT. WITH THE KID'S DISGUISES, THE ONLY WAY TO IDENTIFY HIM...
...IS IF HE HAS THE LOOT.
AT LEAST YOU COULD'VE BUGGED THE SHOES SO WE COULD FOLLOW HIS MOVE-MENTS...
OF COURSE I DID THAT!
BUT HE REMOVED THE BUG...
IS THIS WHAT YOU'RE TALKING ABOUT?

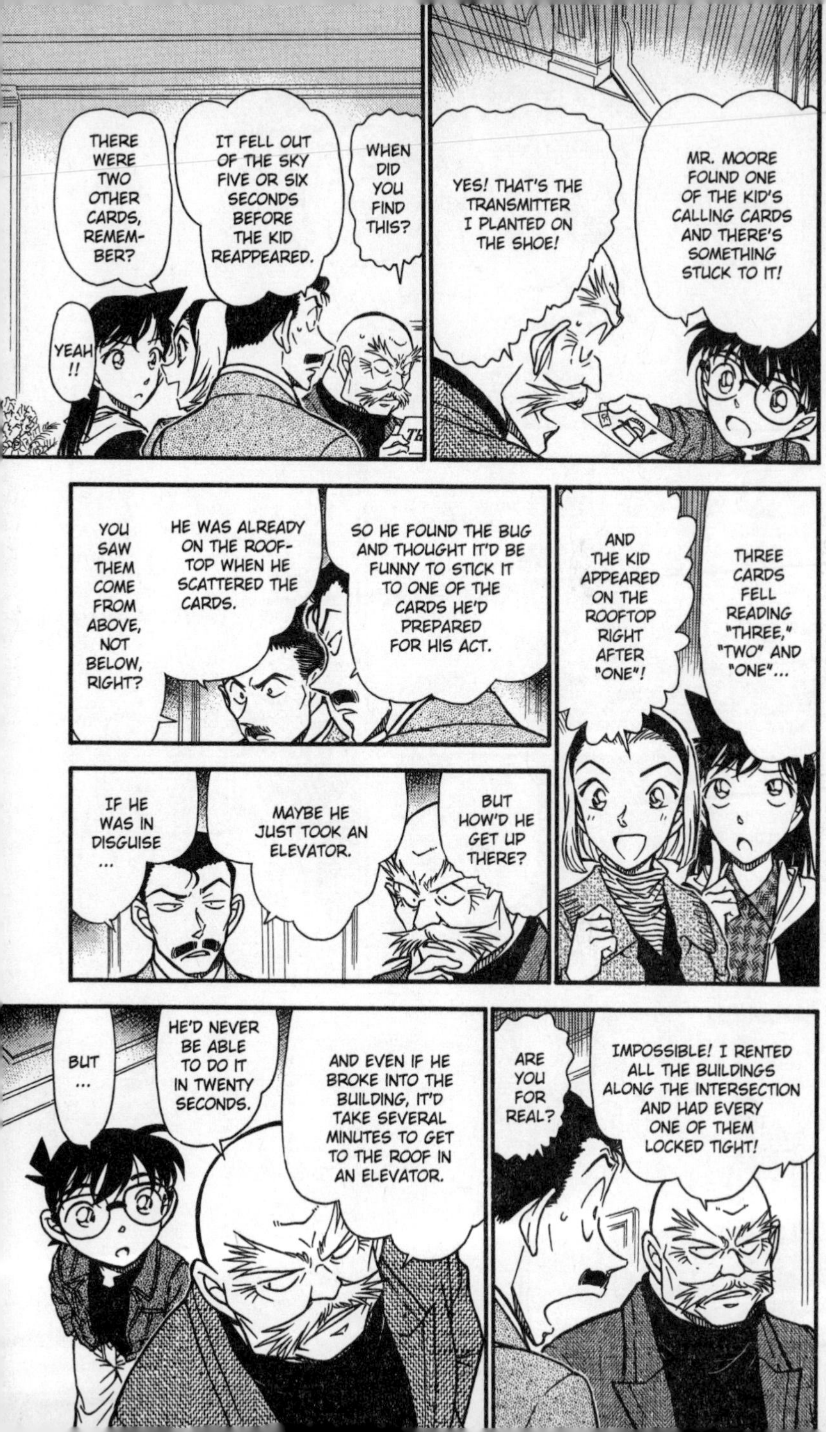
MR. MOORE FOUND ONE OF THE KID'S CALLING CARDS AND THERE'S SOMETHING STUCK TO IT!
YES! THAT'S THE TRANSMITTER I PLANTED ON THE SHOE!
WHEN DID YOU FIND THIS?
IT FELL OUT OF THE SKY FIVE OR SIX SECONDS BEFORE THE KID REAPPEARED.
THERE WERE TWO OTHER CARDS, REMEMBER?
YEAH!!
THREE CARDS FELL READING "THREE," "TWO" AND "ONE"...
AND THE KID APPEARED ON THE ROOFTOP RIGHT AFTER "ONE"!
SO HE FOUND THE BUG AND THOUGHT IT'D BE FUNNY TO STICK IT TO ONE OF THE CARDS HE'D PREPARED FOR HIS ACT.
HE WAS ALREADY ON THE ROOF-TOP WHEN HE SCATTERED THE CARDS.
YOU SAW THEM COME FROM ABOVE, NOT BELOW, RIGHT?
BUT HOW'D HE GET UP THERE?
MAYBE HE JUST TOOK AN ELEVATOR.
IF HE WAS IN DISGUISE ...
IMPOSSIBLE! I RENTED ALL THE BUILDINGS ALONG THE INTERSECTION AND HAD EVERY ONE OF THEM LOCKED TIGHT!
ARE YOU FOR REAL?
AND EVEN IF HE BROKE INTO THE BUILDING, IT'D TAKE SEVERAL MINUTES TO GET TO THE ROOF IN AN ELEVATOR.
HE'D NEVER BE ABLE TO DO IT IN TWENTY SECONDS.
BUT ...

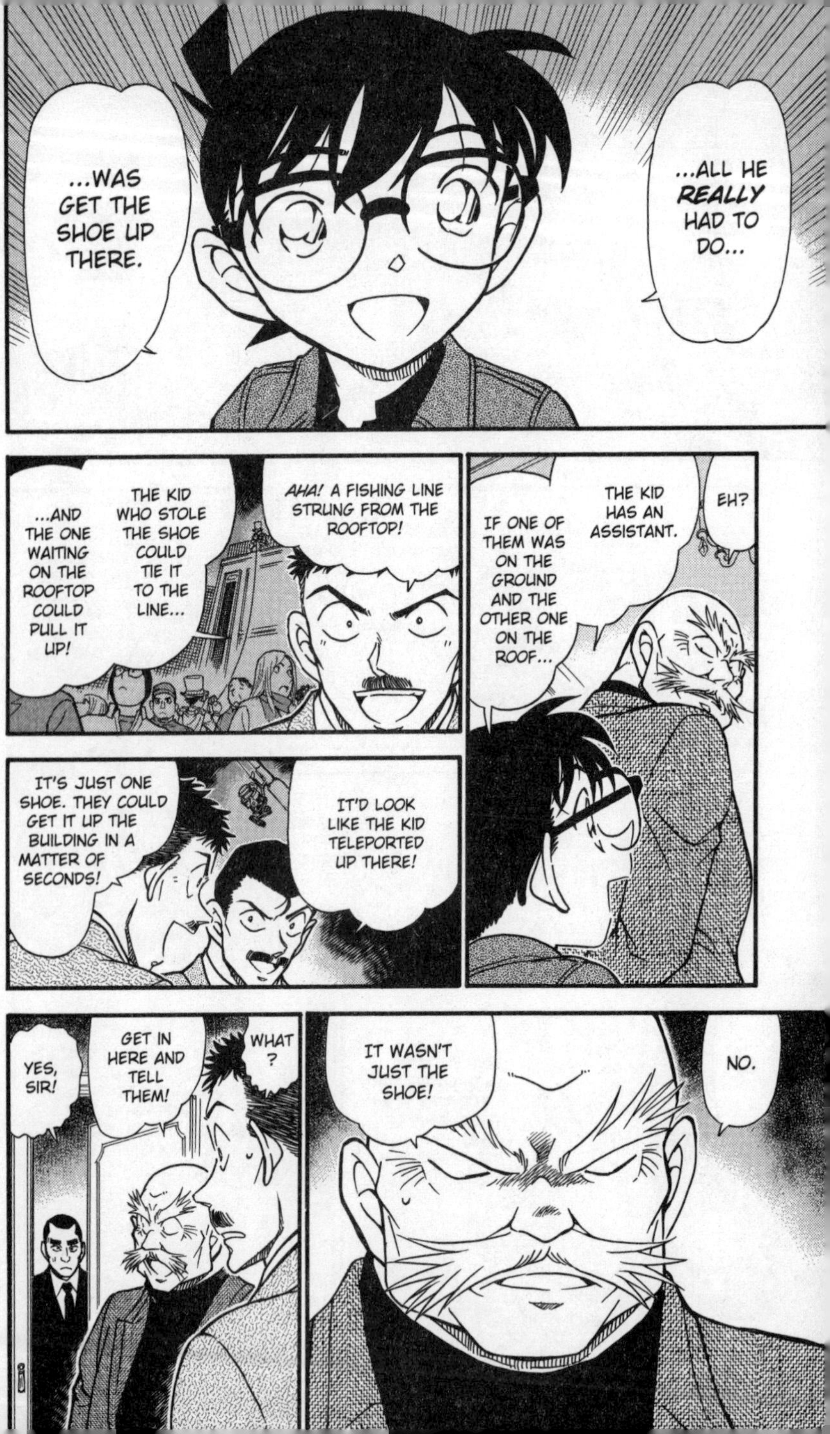

...ALL HE *REALLY* HAD TO DO...
...WAS GET THE SHOE UP THERE.
EH?
THE KID HAS AN ASSISTANT.
IF ONE OF THEM WAS ON THE GROUND AND THE OTHER ONE ON THE ROOF...
*AHA!* A FISHING LINE STRUNG FROM THE ROOFTOP!
THE KID WHO STOLE THE SHOE COULD TIE IT TO THE LINE...
...AND THE ONE WAITING ON THE ROOFTOP COULD PULL IT UP!
IT'D LOOK LIKE THE KID TELEPORTED UP THERE!
IT'S JUST ONE SHOE. THEY COULD GET IT UP THE BUILDING IN A MATTER OF SECONDS!
NO.
IT WASN'T JUST THE SHOE!
WHAT?
GET IN HERE AND TELL THEM!
YES, SIR!

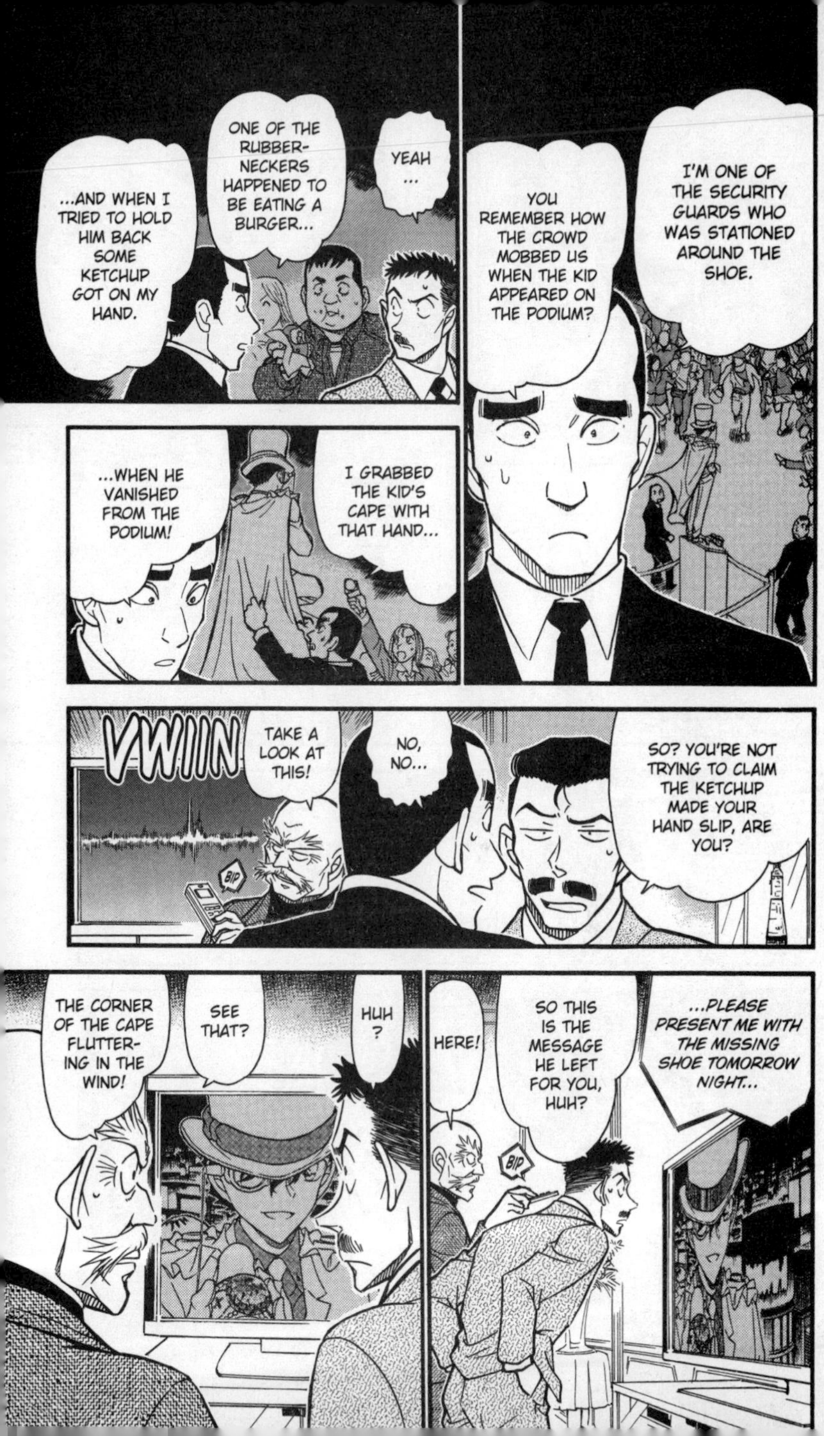
I'M ONE OF THE SECURITY GUARDS WHO WAS STATIONED AROUND THE SHOE.
YOU REMEMBER HOW THE CROWD MOBBED US WHEN THE KID APPEARED ON THE PODIUM?
YEAH...
ONE OF THE RUBBER-NECKERS HAPPENED TO BE EATING A BURGER...
...AND WHEN I TRIED TO HOLD HIM BACK SOME KETCHUP GOT ON MY HAND.
I GRABBED THE KID'S CAPE WITH THAT HAND...
...WHEN HE VANISHED FROM THE PODIUM!
SO? YOU'RE NOT TRYING TO CLAIM THE KETCHUP MADE YOUR HAND SLIP, ARE YOU?
NO, NO...
TAKE A LOOK AT THIS!
BIP
VWIIN
...PLEASE PRESENT ME WITH THE MISSING SHOE TOMORROW NIGHT...
SO THIS IS THE MESSAGE HE LEFT FOR YOU, HUH?
BIP
HERE!
HUH?
SEE THAT?
THE CORNER OF THE CAPE FLUTTERING IN THE WIND!

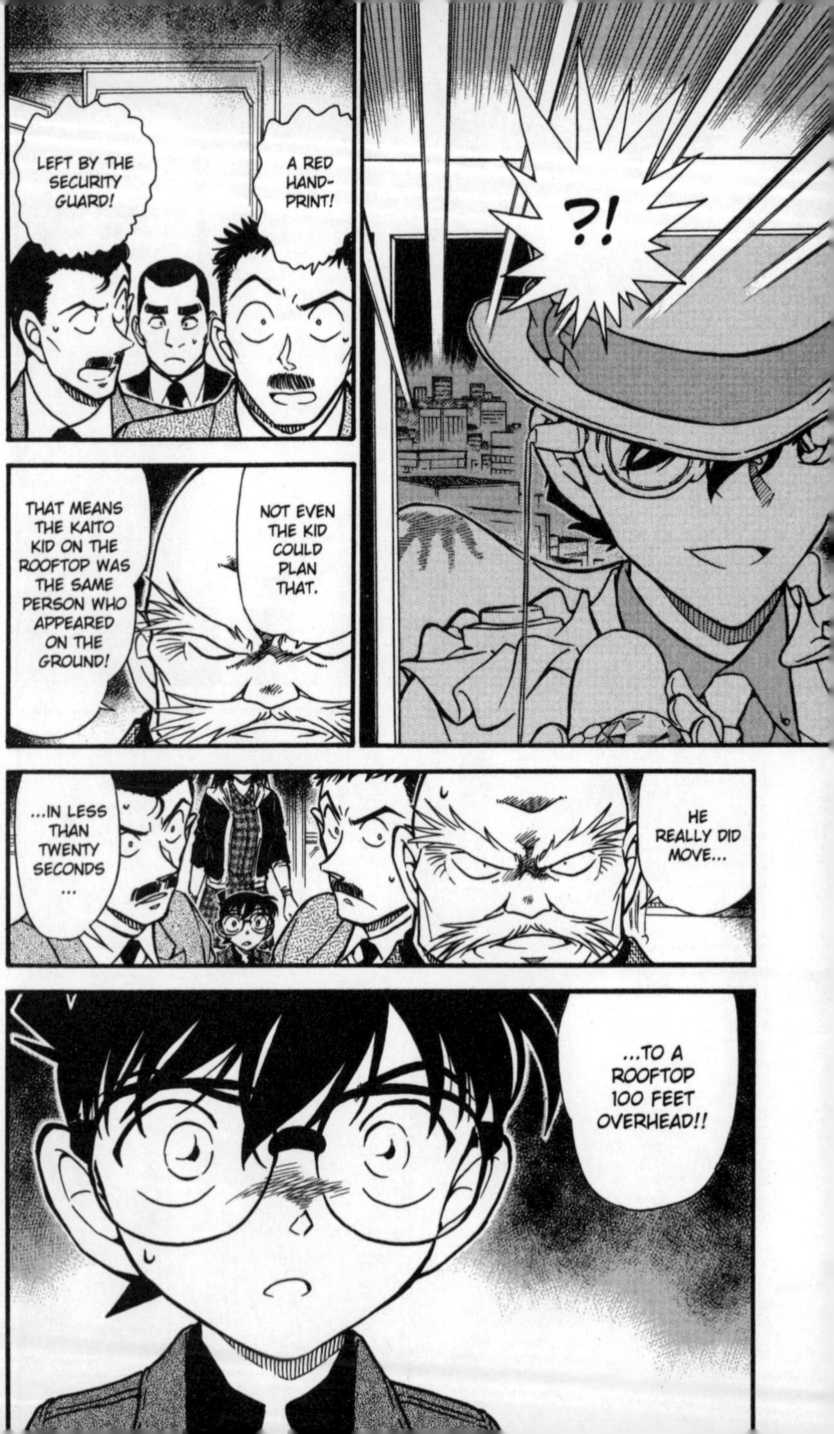
?!
A RED HAND-PRINT!
LEFT BY THE SECURITY GUARD!
NOT EVEN THE KID COULD PLAN THAT.
THAT MEANS THE KAITO KID ON THE ROOFTOP WAS THE SAME PERSON WHO APPEARED ON THE GROUND!
HE REALLY DID MOVE...
...IN LESS THAN TWENTY SECONDS ...
...TO A ROOFTOP 100 FEET OVERHEAD!!

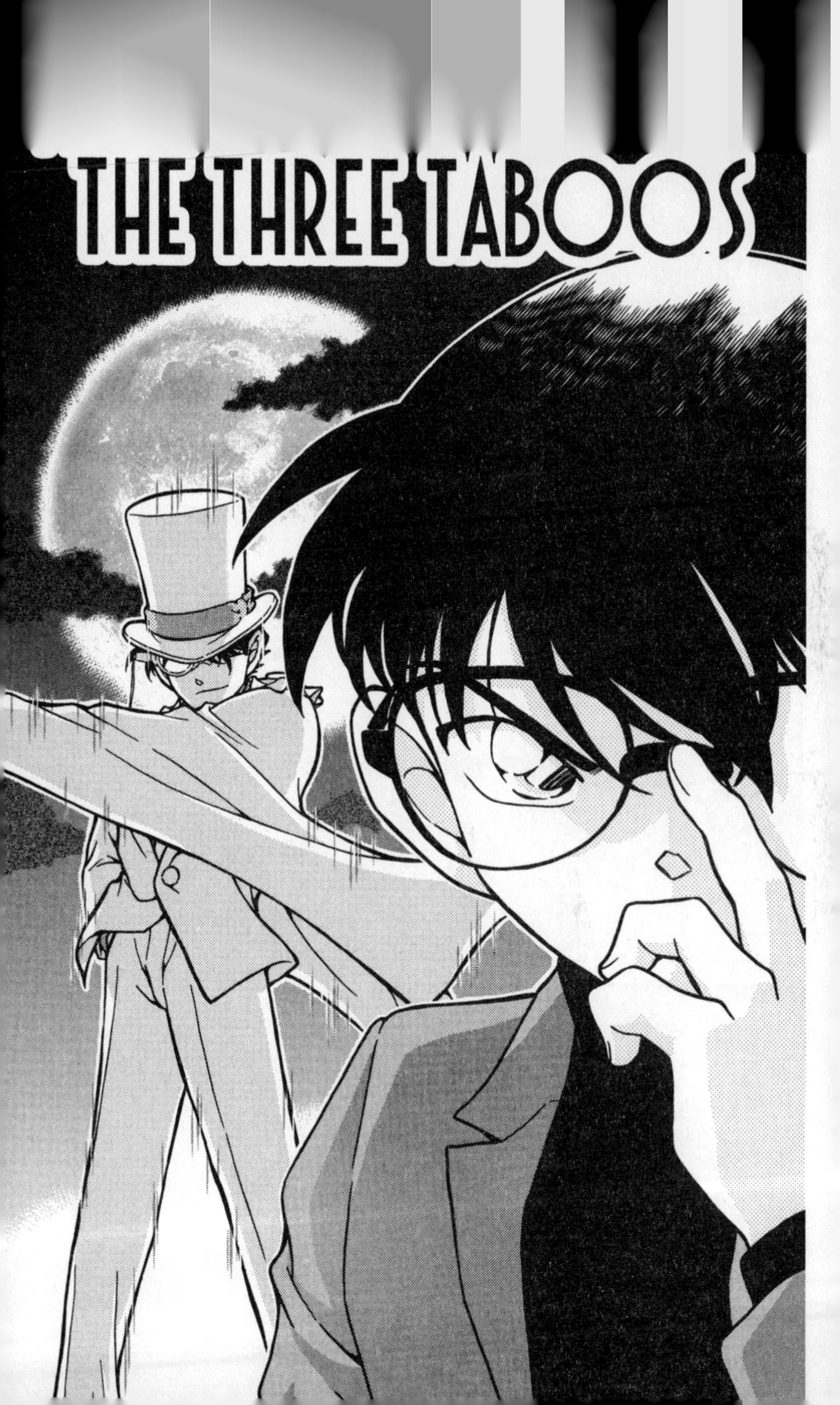
THE THREE TABOOS

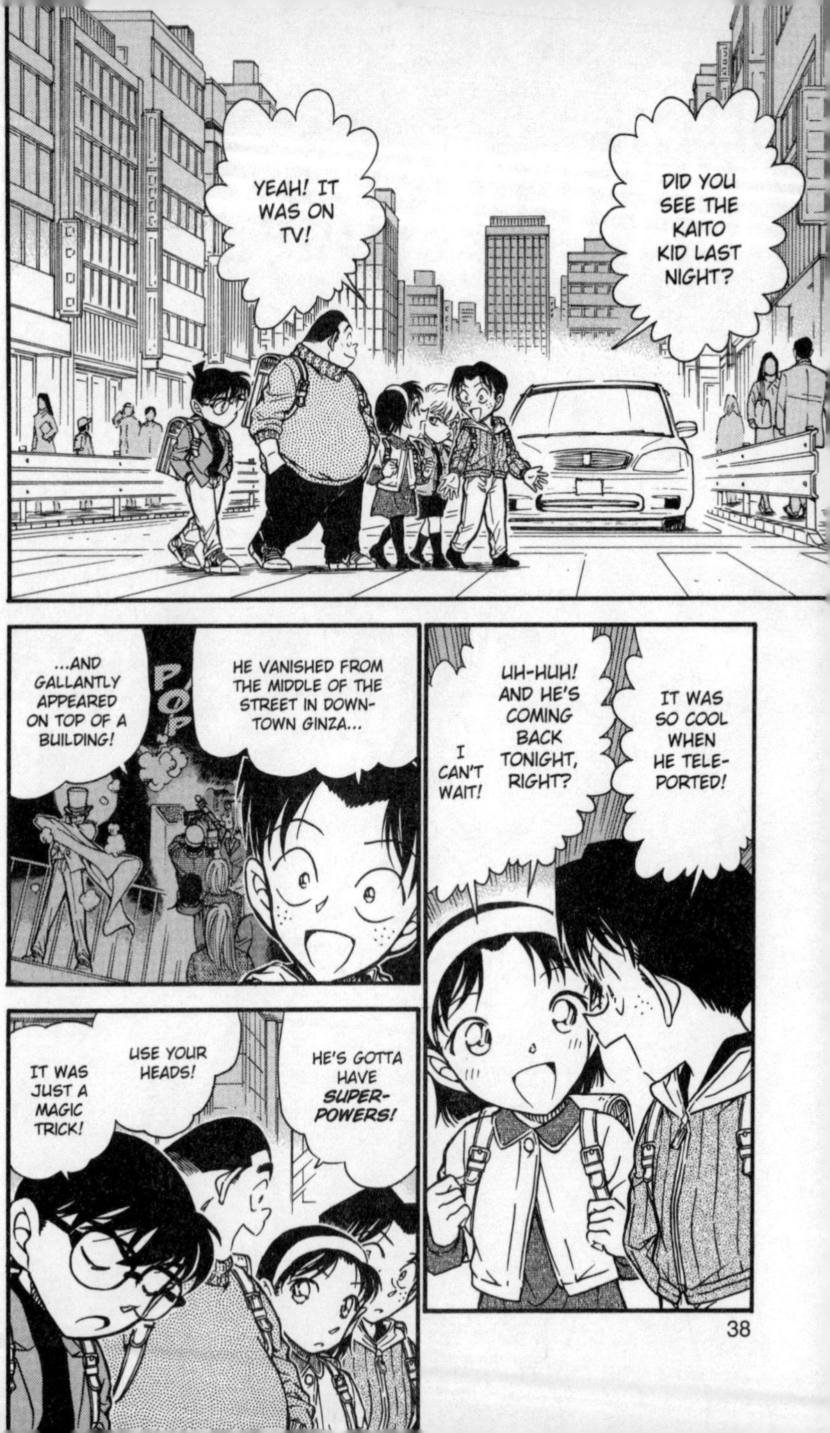
DID YOU SEE THE KAITO KID LAST NIGHT?
YEAH! IT WAS ON TV!
IT WAS SO COOL WHEN HE TELE-PORTED!
UH-HUH! AND HE'S COMING BACK TONIGHT, RIGHT?
I CAN'T WAIT!
HE VANISHED FROM THE MIDDLE OF THE STREET IN DOWN-TOWN GINZA...
POP
...AND GALLANTLY APPEARED ON TOP OF A BUILDING!
HE'S GOTTA HAVE *SUPER-POWERS!*
USE YOUR HEADS!
IT WAS JUST A MAGIC TRICK!

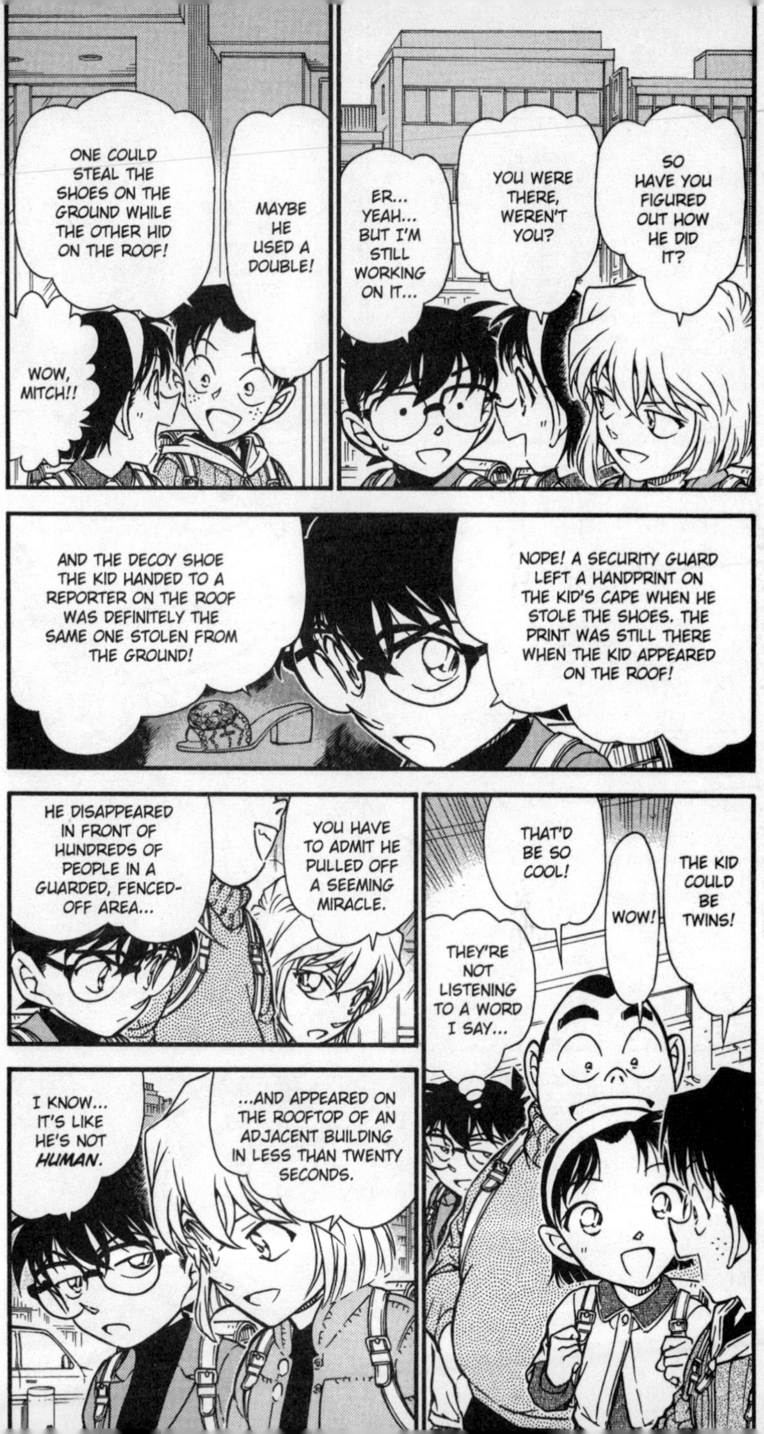
SO HAVE YOU FIGURED OUT HOW HE DID IT?
YOU WERE THERE, WEREN'T YOU?
ER... YEAH... BUT I'M STILL WORKING ON IT...
MAYBE HE USED A DOUBLE!
ONE COULD STEAL THE SHOES ON THE GROUND WHILE THE OTHER HID ON THE ROOF!
WOW, MITCH!!
NOPE! A SECURITY GUARD LEFT A HANDPRINT ON THE KID'S CAPE WHEN HE STOLE THE SHOES. THE PRINT WAS STILL THERE WHEN THE KID APPEARED ON THE ROOF!
AND THE DECOY SHOE THE KID HANDED TO A REPORTER ON THE ROOF WAS DEFINITELY THE SAME ONE STOLEN FROM THE GROUND!
THE KID COULD BE TWINS!
WOW!
THAT'D BE SO COOL!
THEY'RE NOT LISTENING TO A WORD I SAY...
YOU HAVE TO ADMIT HE PULLED OFF A SEEMING MIRACLE.
HE DISAPPEARED IN FRONT OF HUNDREDS OF PEOPLE IN A GUARDED, FENCED-OFF AREA...
...AND APPEARED ON THE ROOFTOP OF AN ADJACENT BUILDING IN LESS THAN TWENTY SECONDS.
I KNOW... IT'S LIKE HE'S NOT ***HUMAN***.

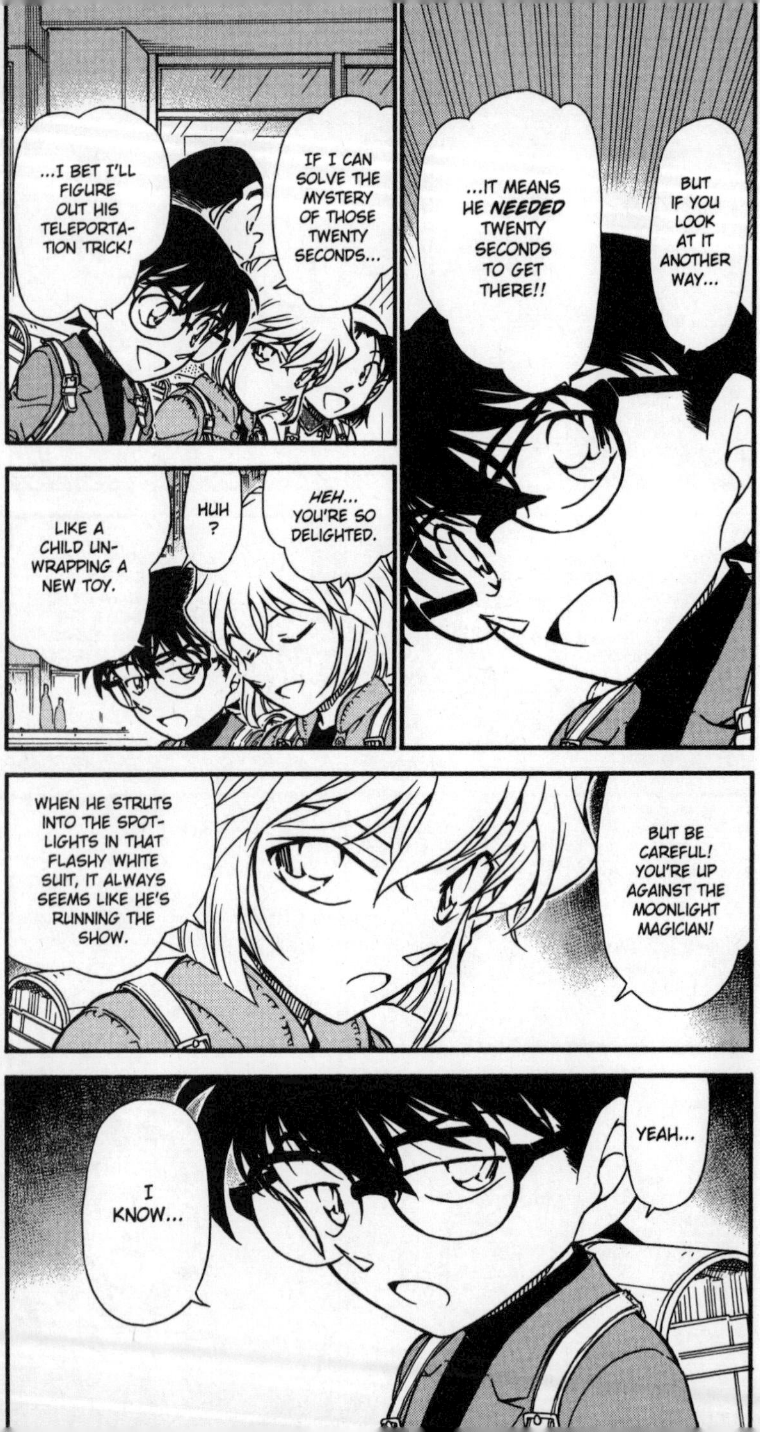
BUT IF YOU LOOK AT IT ANOTHER WAY...
...IT MEANS HE ***NEEDED*** TWENTY SECONDS TO GET THERE!!
IF I CAN SOLVE THE MYSTERY OF THOSE TWENTY SECONDS...
...I BET I'LL FIGURE OUT HIS TELEPORTATION TRICK!
*HEH...* YOU'RE SO DELIGHTED.
HUH?
LIKE A CHILD UNWRAPPING A NEW TOY.
BUT BE CAREFUL! YOU'RE UP AGAINST THE MOONLIGHT MAGICIAN!
WHEN HE STRUTS INTO THE SPOTLIGHTS IN THAT FLASHY WHITE SUIT, IT ALWAYS SEEMS LIKE HE'S RUNNING THE SHOW.
YEAH...
I KNOW...

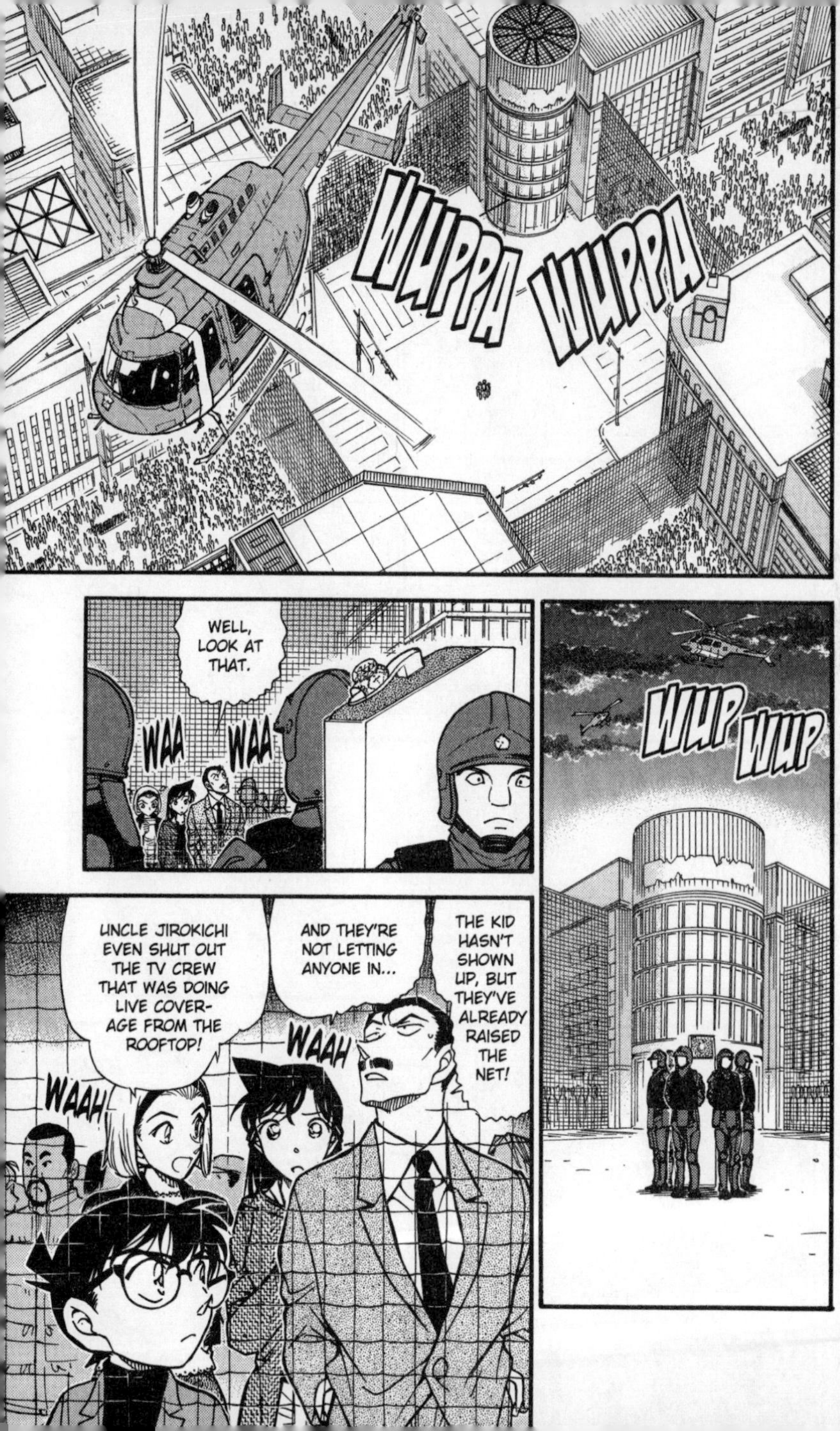
WUPPA WUPPA
WUP WUP
WELL, LOOK AT THAT.
WAA WAA
THE KID HASN'T SHOWN UP, BUT THEY'VE ALREADY RAISED THE NET!
WAAH
AND THEY'RE NOT LETTING ANYONE IN...
UNCLE JIROKICHI EVEN SHUT OUT THE TV CREW THAT WAS DOING LIVE COVER-AGE FROM THE ROOFTOP!
WAAH

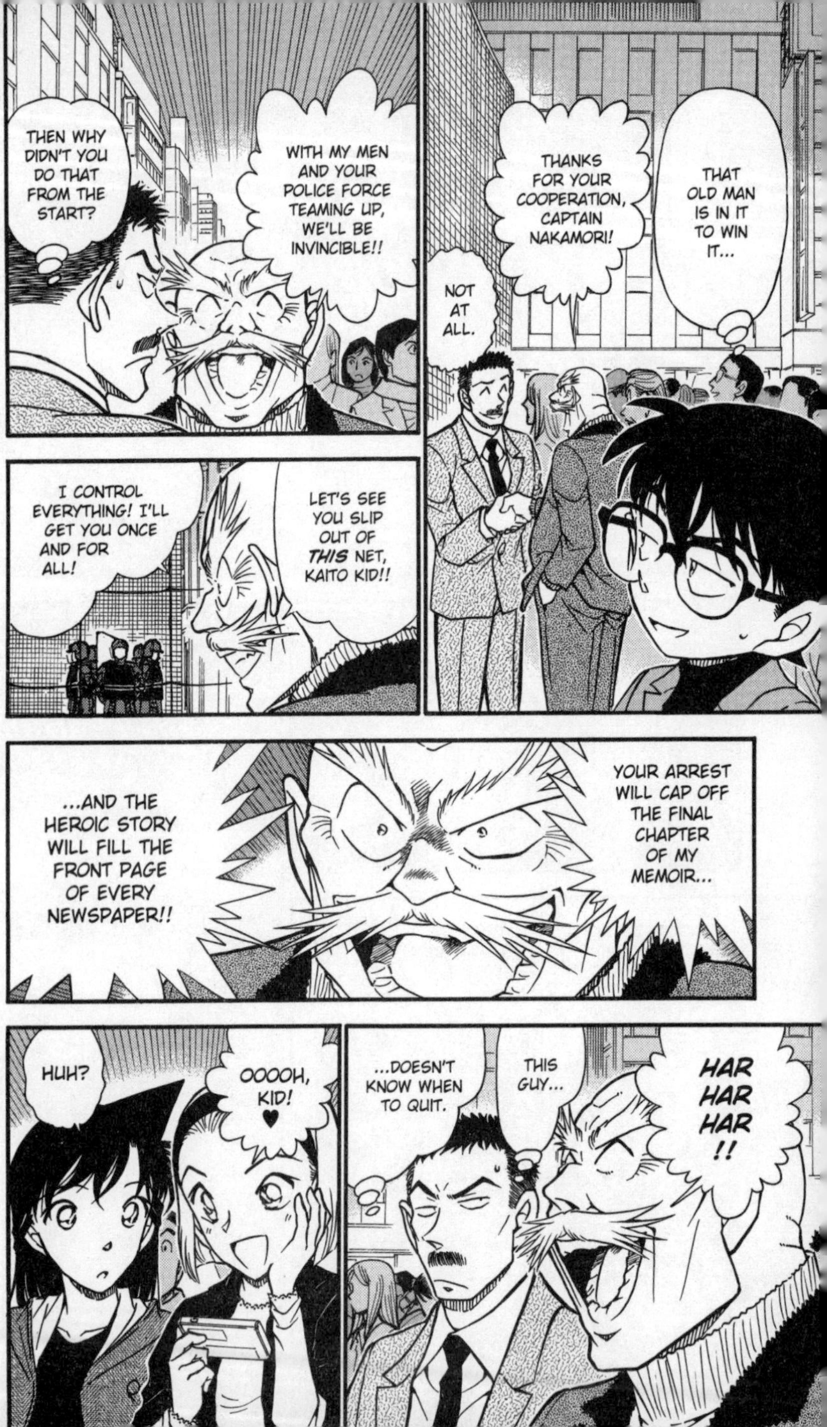
THAT OLD MAN IS IN IT TO WIN IT...
THANKS FOR YOUR COOPERATION, CAPTAIN NAKAMORI!
NOT AT ALL.
WITH MY MEN AND YOUR POLICE FORCE TEAMING UP, WE'LL BE INVINCIBLE!!
THEN WHY DIDN'T YOU DO THAT FROM THE START?
LET'S SEE YOU SLIP OUT OF *THIS* NET, KAITO KID!!
I CONTROL EVERYTHING! I'LL GET YOU ONCE AND FOR ALL!
YOUR ARREST WILL CAP OFF THE FINAL CHAPTER OF MY MEMOIR...
...AND THE HEROIC STORY WILL FILL THE FRONT PAGE OF EVERY NEWSPAPER!!
HAR HAR HAR !!
THIS GUY...
...DOESN'T KNOW WHEN TO QUIT.
OOOOH, KID! ♥
HUH?

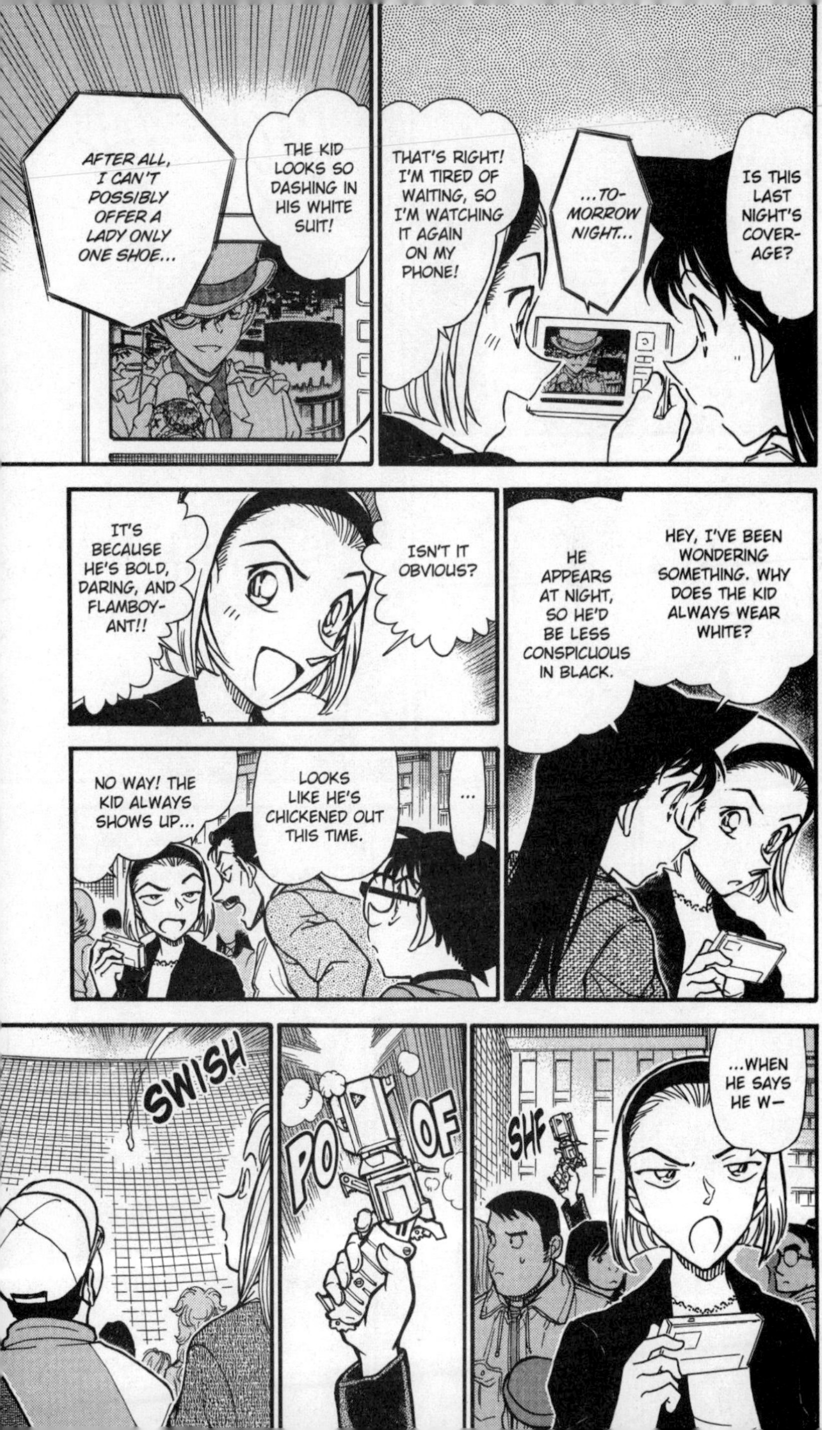
IS THIS LAST NIGHT'S COVER-AGE?
...TO-MORROW NIGHT...
THAT'S RIGHT! I'M TIRED OF WAITING, SO I'M WATCHING IT AGAIN ON MY PHONE!
THE KID LOOKS SO DASHING IN HIS WHITE SUIT!
AFTER ALL, I CAN'T POSSIBLY OFFER A LADY ONLY ONE SHOE...
HEY, I'VE BEEN WONDERING SOMETHING. WHY DOES THE KID ALWAYS WEAR WHITE?
HE APPEARS AT NIGHT, SO HE'D BE LESS CONSPICUOUS IN BLACK.
ISN'T IT OBVIOUS?
IT'S BECAUSE HE'S BOLD, DARING, AND FLAMBOY-ANT!!
...
LOOKS LIKE HE'S CHICKENED OUT THIS TIME.
NO WAY! THE KID ALWAYS SHOWS UP...
...WHEN HE SAYS HE W—
SHF
POOF
SWISH

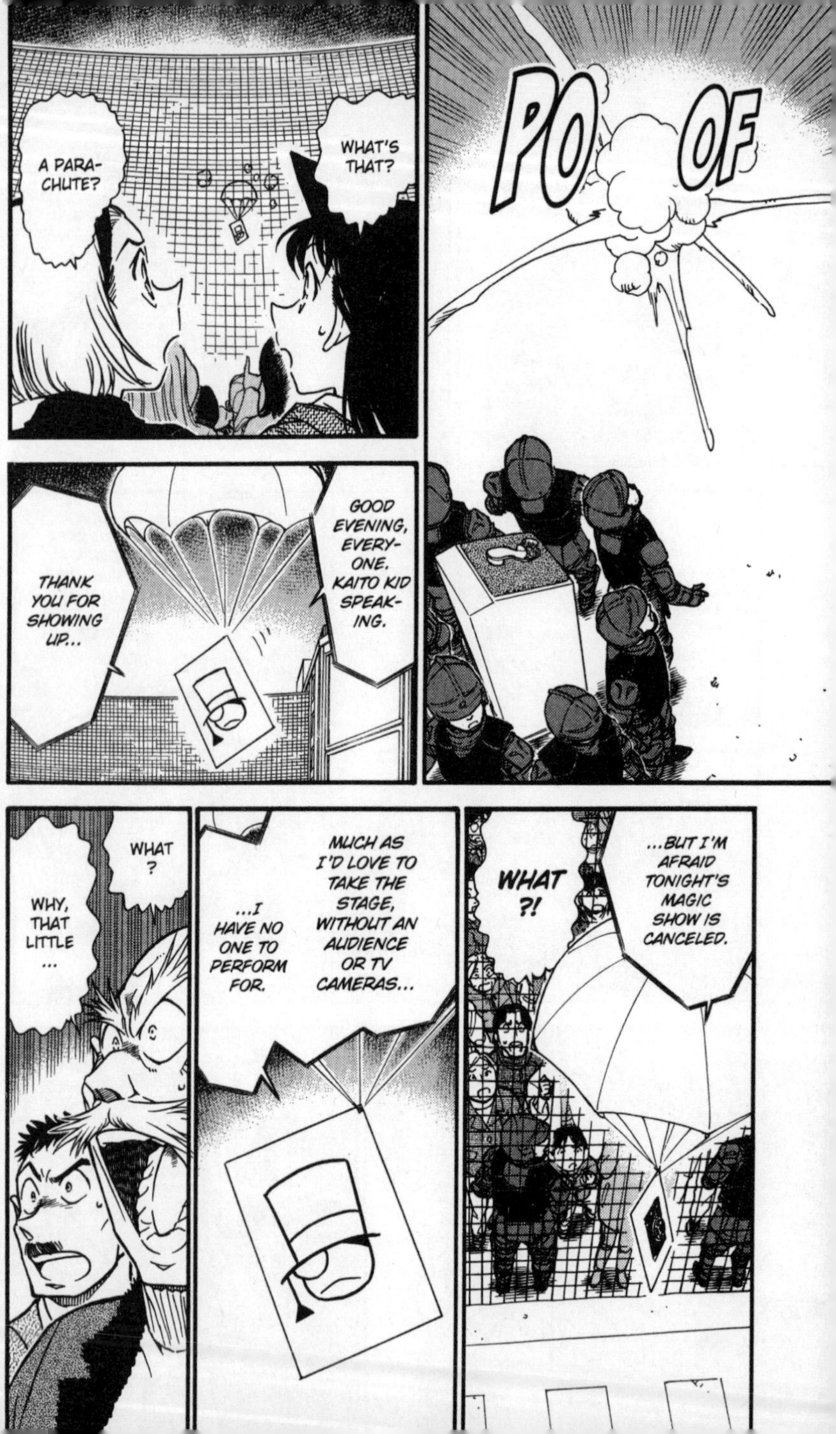
POOF
WHAT'S THAT?
A PARA-CHUTE?
GOOD EVENING, EVERY-ONE. KAITO KID SPEAK-ING.
THANK YOU FOR SHOWING UP...
...BUT I'M AFRAID TONIGHT'S MAGIC SHOW IS CANCELED.
WHAT ?!
MUCH AS I'D LOVE TO TAKE THE STAGE, WITHOUT AN AUDIENCE OR TV CAMERAS...
...I HAVE NO ONE TO PERFORM FOR.
WHAT ?
WHY, THAT LITTLE ...

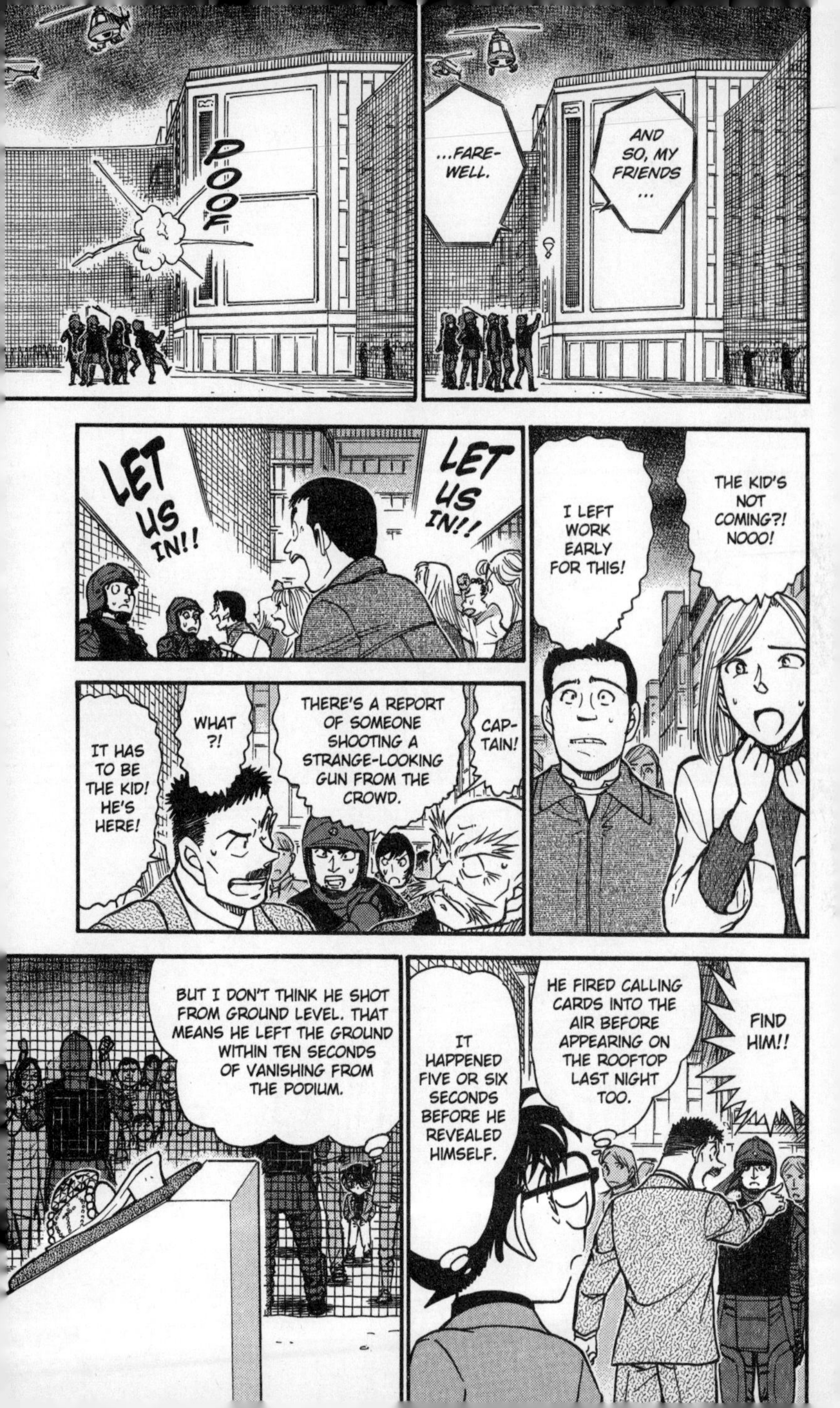
AND SO, MY FRIENDS ...
...FARE-WELL.
POOF
THE KID'S NOT COMING?! NOOO!
I LEFT WORK EARLY FOR THIS!
LET US IN!!
LET US IN!!
CAP-TAIN!
THERE'S A REPORT OF SOMEONE SHOOTING A STRANGE-LOOKING GUN FROM THE CROWD.
WHAT ?!
IT HAS TO BE THE KID! HE'S HERE!
FIND HIM!!
HE FIRED CALLING CARDS INTO THE AIR BEFORE APPEARING ON THE ROOFTOP LAST NIGHT TOO.
IT HAPPENED FIVE OR SIX SECONDS BEFORE HE REVEALED HIMSELF.
BUT I DON'T THINK HE SHOT FROM GROUND LEVEL. THAT MEANS HE LEFT THE GROUND WITHIN TEN SECONDS OF VANISHING FROM THE PODIUM.

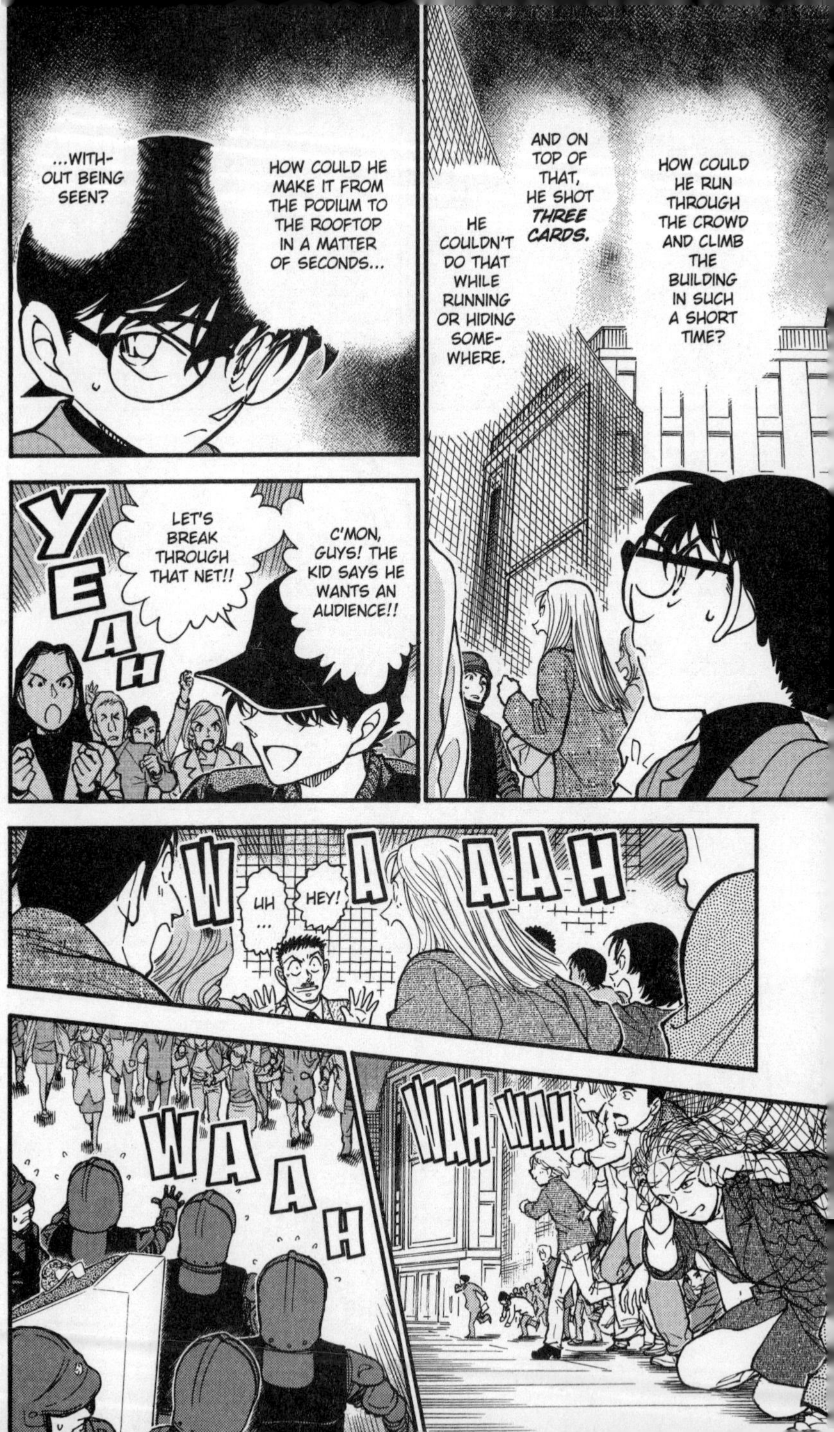
HOW COULD HE RUN THROUGH THE CROWD AND CLIMB THE BUILDING IN SUCH A SHORT TIME?
AND ON TOP OF THAT, HE SHOT *THREE CARDS.*
HE COULDN'T DO THAT WHILE RUNNING OR HIDING SOME-WHERE.
HOW COULD HE MAKE IT FROM THE PODIUM TO THE ROOFTOP IN A MATTER OF SECONDS...
...WITH-OUT BEING SEEN?
C'MON, GUYS! THE KID SAYS HE WANTS AN AUDIENCE!!
LET'S BREAK THROUGH THAT NET!!
YEAH
WAAAH
HEY!
UH...
WAH WAH
WAAAH

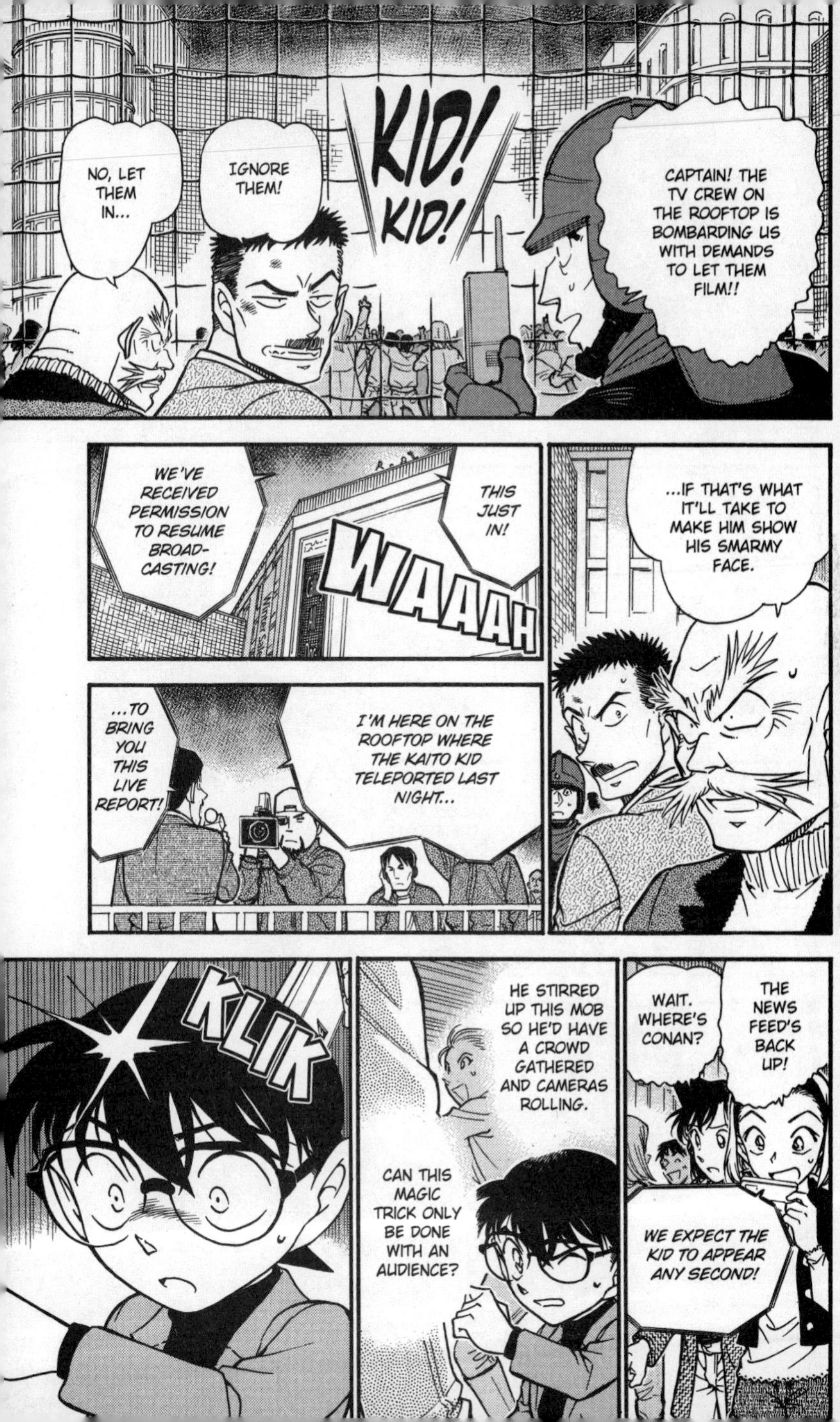
CAPTAIN! THE TV CREW ON THE ROOFTOP IS BOMBARDING US WITH DEMANDS TO LET THEM FILM!!
KID! KID!
IGNORE THEM!
NO, LET THEM IN...
...IF THAT'S WHAT IT'LL TAKE TO MAKE HIM SHOW HIS SMARMY FACE.
THIS JUST IN!
WAAAAH
WE'VE RECEIVED PERMISSION TO RESUME BROAD-CASTING!
I'M HERE ON THE ROOFTOP WHERE THE KAITO KID TELEPORTED LAST NIGHT...
...TO BRING YOU THIS LIVE REPORT!
THE NEWS FEED'S BACK UP!
WAIT. WHERE'S CONAN?
WE EXPECT THE KID TO APPEAR ANY SECOND!
HE STIRRED UP THIS MOB SO HE'D HAVE A CROWD GATHERED AND CAMERAS ROLLING.
CAN THIS MAGIC TRICK ONLY BE DONE WITH AN AUDIENCE?
KLIK

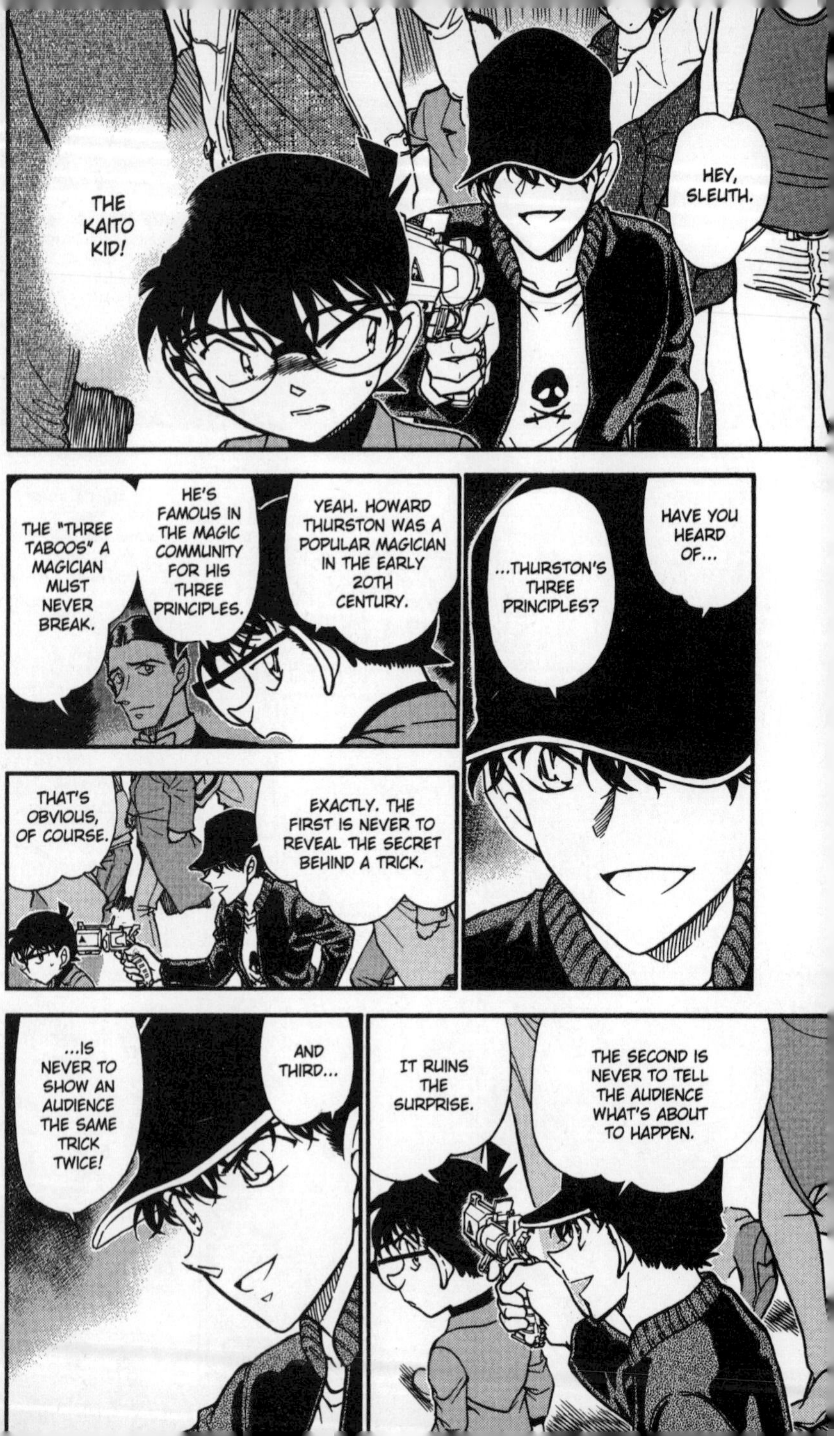
HEY, SLEUTH.
THE KAITO KID!
HAVE YOU HEARD OF...
...THURSTON'S THREE PRINCIPLES?
YEAH. HOWARD THURSTON WAS A POPULAR MAGICIAN IN THE EARLY 20TH CENTURY.
HE'S FAMOUS IN THE MAGIC COMMUNITY FOR HIS THREE PRINCIPLES.
THE "THREE TABOOS" A MAGICIAN MUST NEVER BREAK.
EXACTLY. THE FIRST IS NEVER TO REVEAL THE SECRET BEHIND A TRICK.
THAT'S OBVIOUS, OF COURSE.
THE SECOND IS NEVER TO TELL THE AUDIENCE WHAT'S ABOUT TO HAPPEN.
IT RUINS THE SURPRISE.
AND THIRD...
...IS NEVER TO SHOW AN AUDIENCE THE SAME TRICK TWICE!

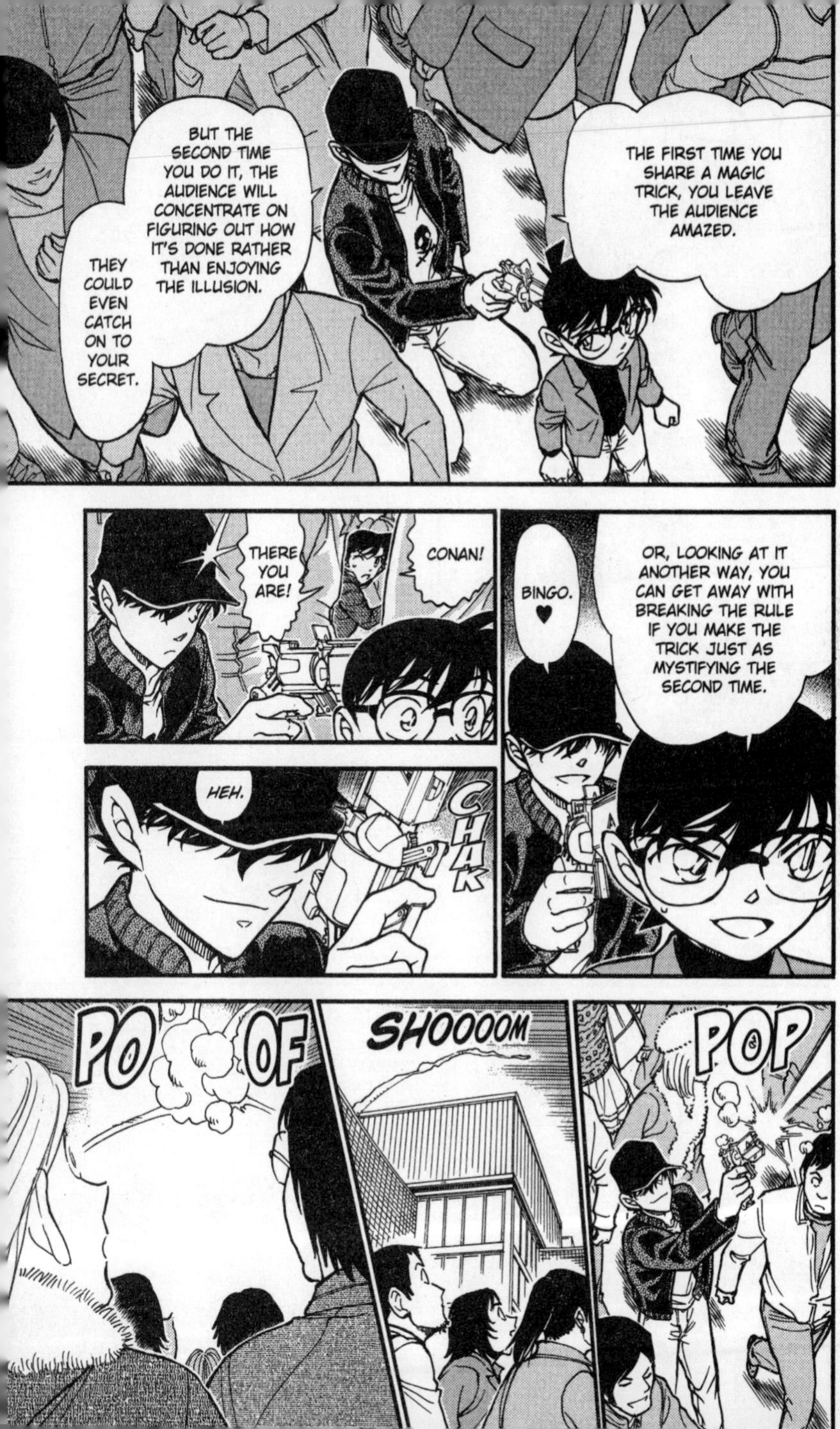
THE FIRST TIME YOU SHARE A MAGIC TRICK, YOU LEAVE THE AUDIENCE AMAZED.
BUT THE SECOND TIME YOU DO IT, THE AUDIENCE WILL CONCENTRATE ON FIGURING OUT HOW IT'S DONE RATHER THAN ENJOYING THE ILLUSION.
THEY COULD EVEN CATCH ON TO YOUR SECRET.
OR, LOOKING AT IT ANOTHER WAY, YOU CAN GET AWAY WITH BREAKING THE RULE IF YOU MAKE THE TRICK JUST AS MYSTIFYING THE SECOND TIME.
BINGO. ♥
CONAN!
THERE YOU ARE!
HEH.
CHAK
POP
SHOOOOM
PO OF

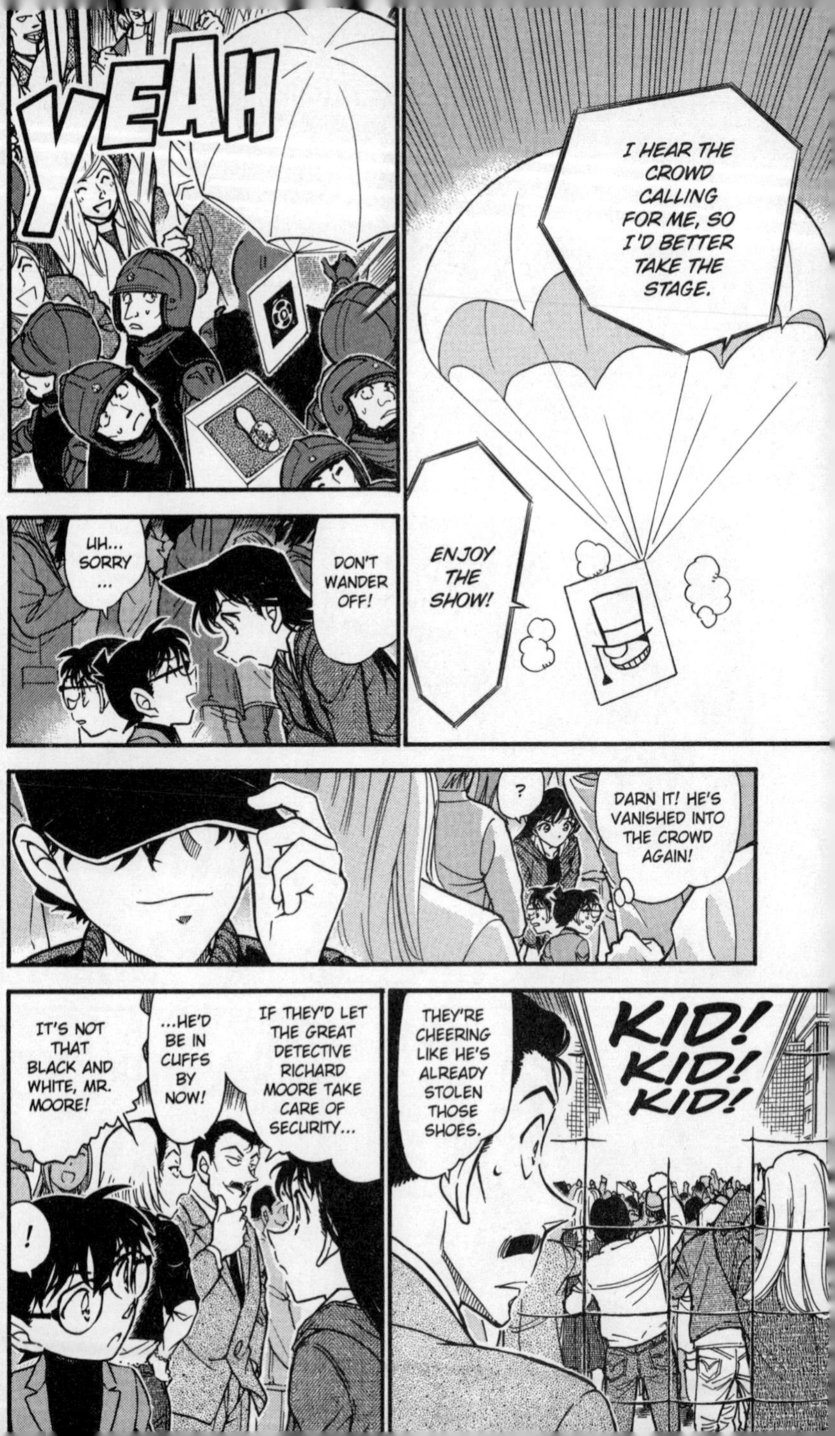

I HEAR THE CROWD CALLING FOR ME, SO I'D BETTER TAKE THE STAGE.
ENJOY THE SHOW!
YEAH
DON'T WANDER OFF!
UH... SORRY ...
DARN IT! HE'S VANISHED INTO THE CROWD AGAIN!
?
KID! KID! KID!
THEY'RE CHEERING LIKE HE'S ALREADY STOLEN THOSE SHOES.
IF THEY'D LET THE GREAT DETECTIVE RICHARD MOORE TAKE CARE OF SECURITY...
...HE'D BE IN CUFFS BY NOW!
IT'S NOT THAT BLACK AND WHITE, MR. MOORE!
!

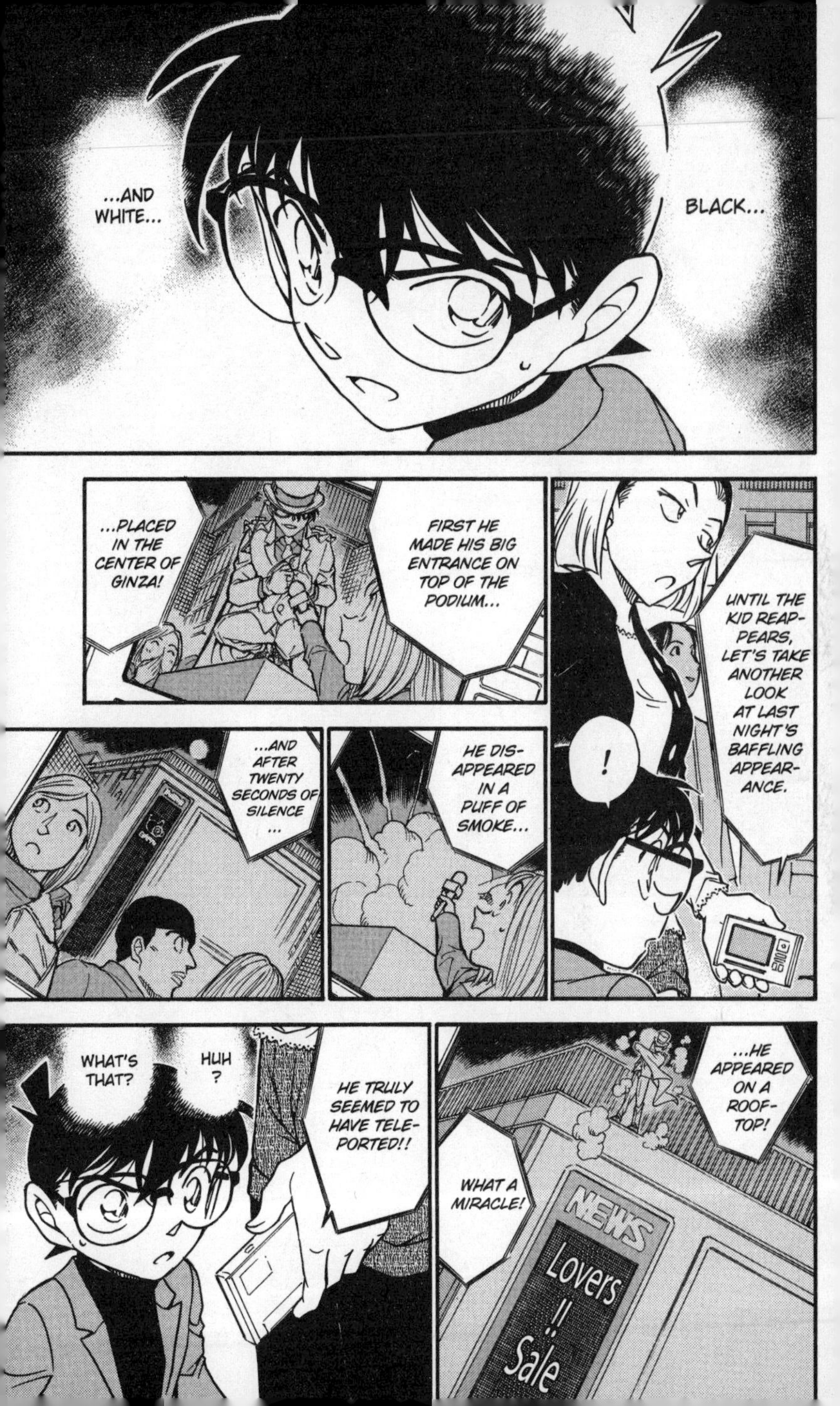
BLACK...
...AND WHITE...
UNTIL THE KID REAPPEARS, LET'S TAKE ANOTHER LOOK AT LAST NIGHT'S BAFFLING APPEARANCE.
!
FIRST HE MADE HIS BIG ENTRANCE ON TOP OF THE PODIUM...
...PLACED IN THE CENTER OF GINZA!
HE DISAPPEARED IN A PUFF OF SMOKE...
...AND AFTER TWENTY SECONDS OF SILENCE...
...HE APPEARED ON A ROOFTOP!
WHAT A MIRACLE!
NEWS
Lovers !! Sale
HE TRULY SEEMED TO HAVE TELEPORTED!!
HUH?
WHAT'S THAT?

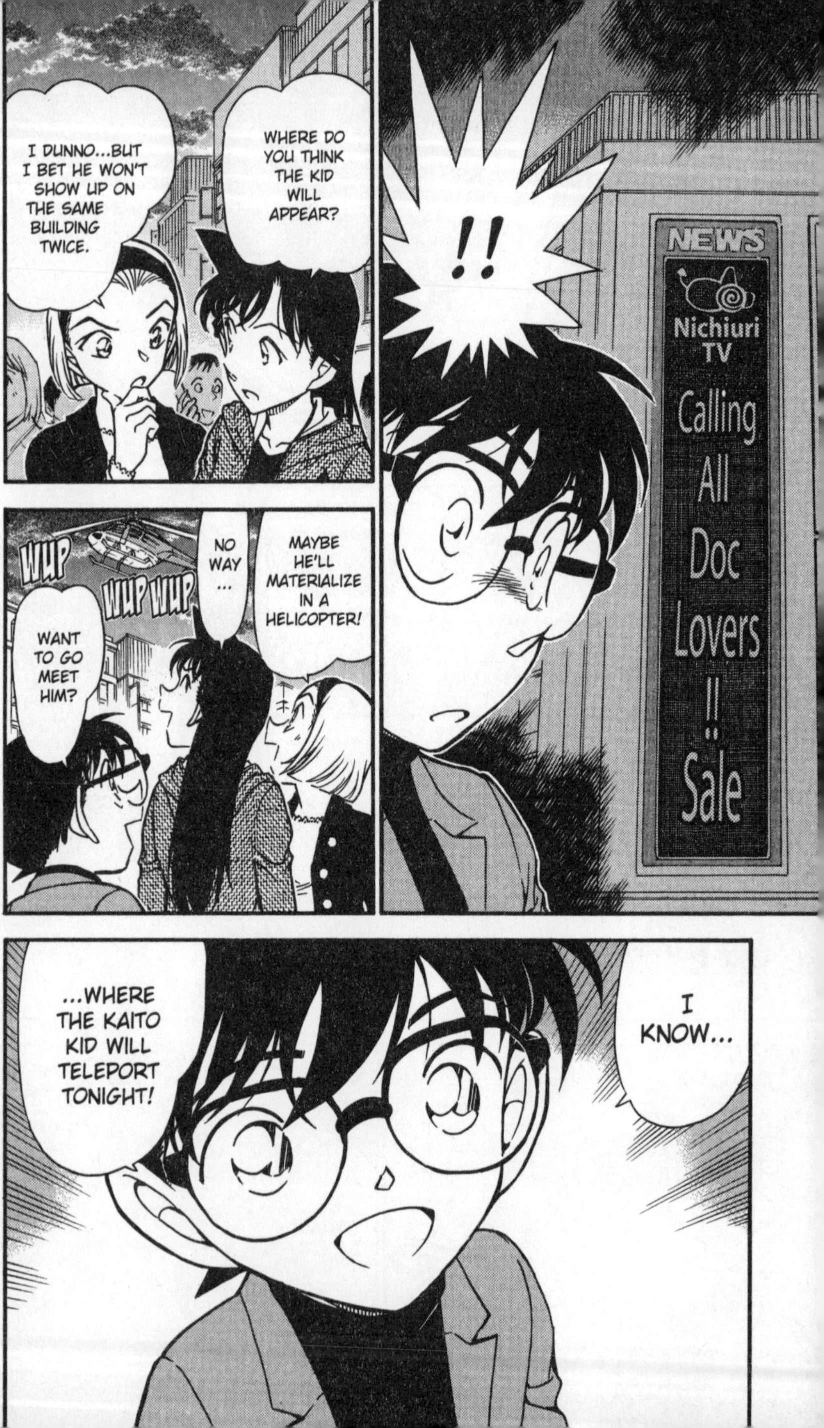
!!
NEWS
Nichiuri TV
Calling All Doc Lovers!! Sale
WHERE DO YOU THINK THE KID WILL APPEAR?
I DUNNO...BUT I BET HE WON'T SHOW UP ON THE SAME BUILDING TWICE.
WUP
WUP WUP
MAYBE HE'LL MATERIALIZE IN A HELICOPTER!
NO WAY...
WANT TO GO MEET HIM?
I KNOW...
...WHERE THE KAITO KID WILL TELEPORT TONIGHT!

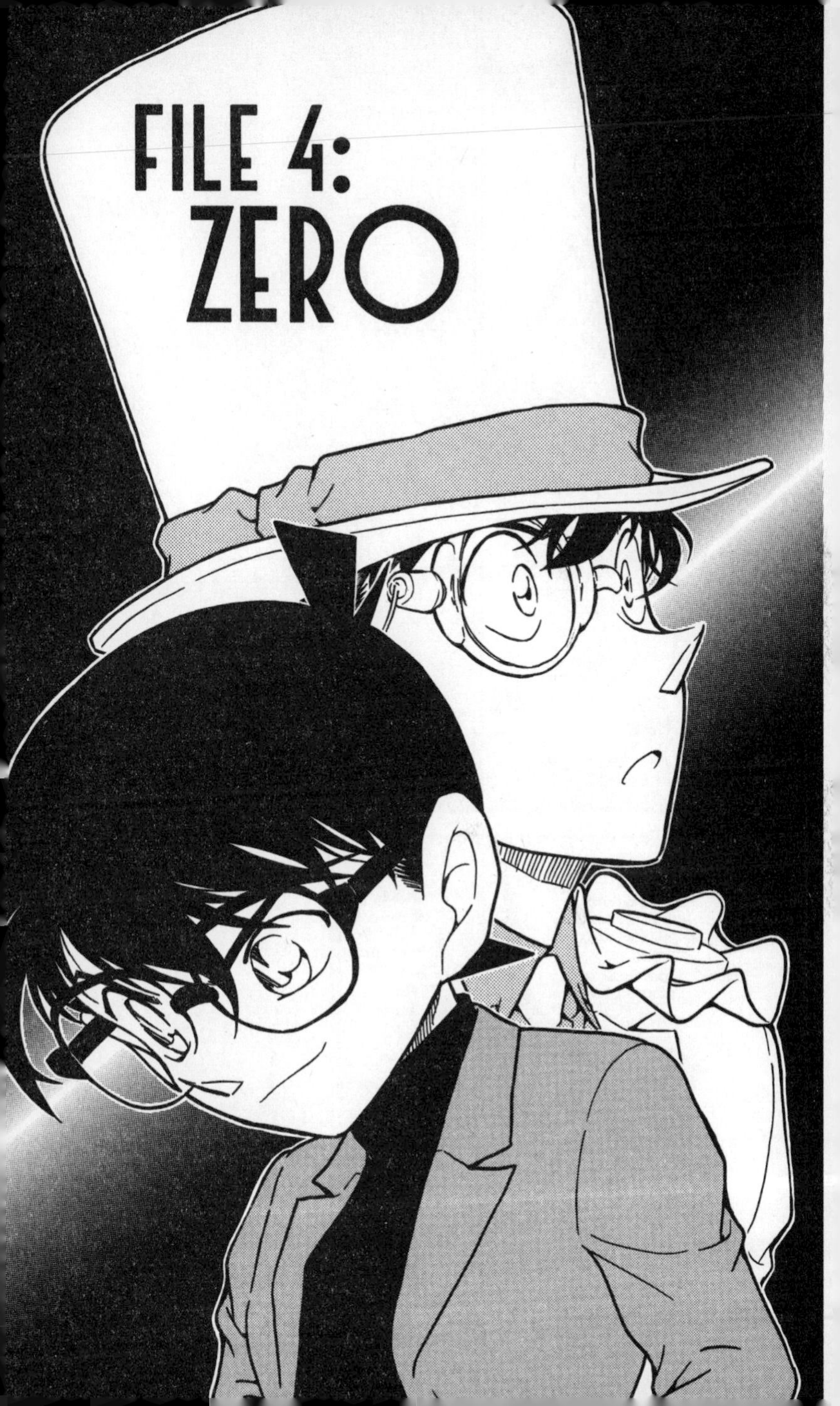
FILE 4:
ZERO

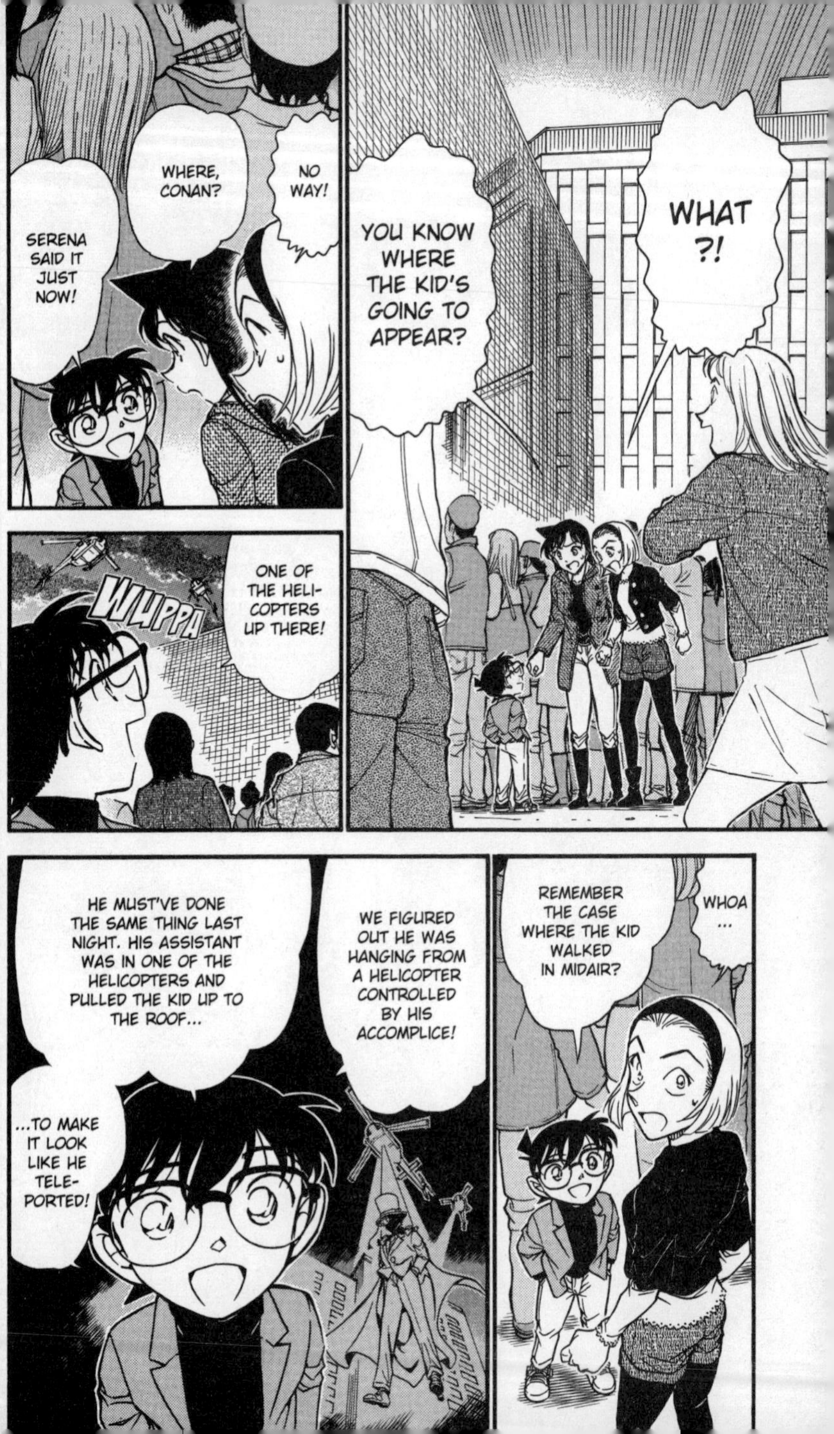
WHAT ?!
YOU KNOW WHERE THE KID'S GOING TO APPEAR?
NO WAY!
WHERE, CONAN?
SERENA SAID IT JUST NOW!
ONE OF THE HELICOPTERS UP THERE!
WUPPA
WHOA ...
REMEMBER THE CASE WHERE THE KID WALKED IN MIDAIR?
WE FIGURED OUT HE WAS HANGING FROM A HELICOPTER CONTROLLED BY HIS ACCOMPLICE!
HE MUST'VE DONE THE SAME THING LAST NIGHT. HIS ASSISTANT WAS IN ONE OF THE HELICOPTERS AND PULLED THE KID UP TO THE ROOF...
...TO MAKE IT LOOK LIKE HE TELEPORTED!

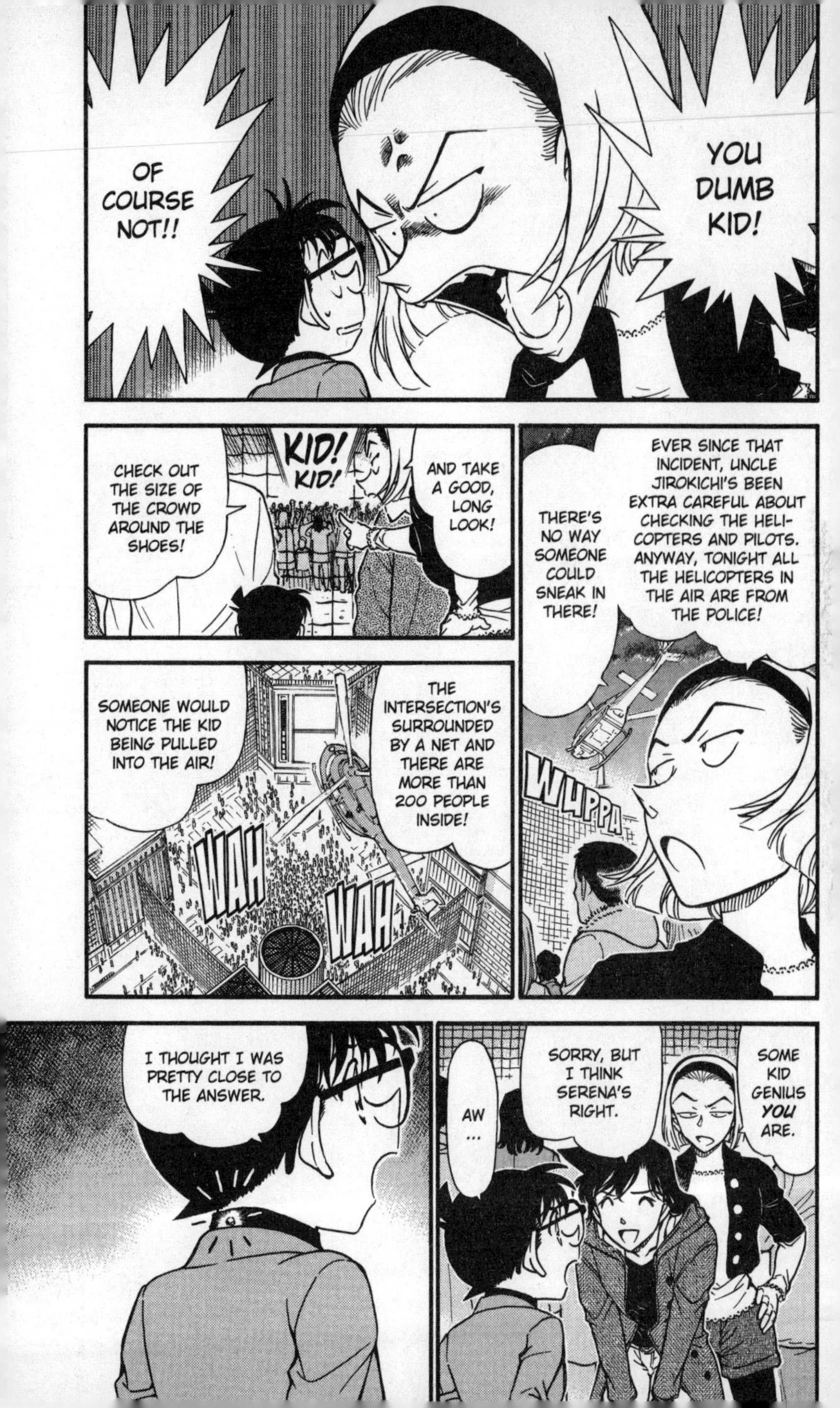
YOU DUMB KID!
OF COURSE NOT!!
EVER SINCE THAT INCIDENT, UNCLE JIROKICHI'S BEEN EXTRA CAREFUL ABOUT CHECKING THE HELI-COPTERS AND PILOTS. ANYWAY, TONIGHT ALL THE HELICOPTERS IN THE AIR ARE FROM THE POLICE!
THERE'S NO WAY SOMEONE COULD SNEAK IN THERE!
WUPPA
AND TAKE A GOOD, LONG LOOK!
KID! KID!
CHECK OUT THE SIZE OF THE CROWD AROUND THE SHOES!
THE INTERSECTION'S SURROUNDED BY A NET AND THERE ARE MORE THAN 200 PEOPLE INSIDE!
SOMEONE WOULD NOTICE THE KID BEING PULLED INTO THE AIR!
WAH
WAH
SOME KID GENIUS *YOU* ARE.
SORRY, BUT I THINK SERENA'S RIGHT.
AW ...
I THOUGHT I WAS PRETTY CLOSE TO THE ANSWER.

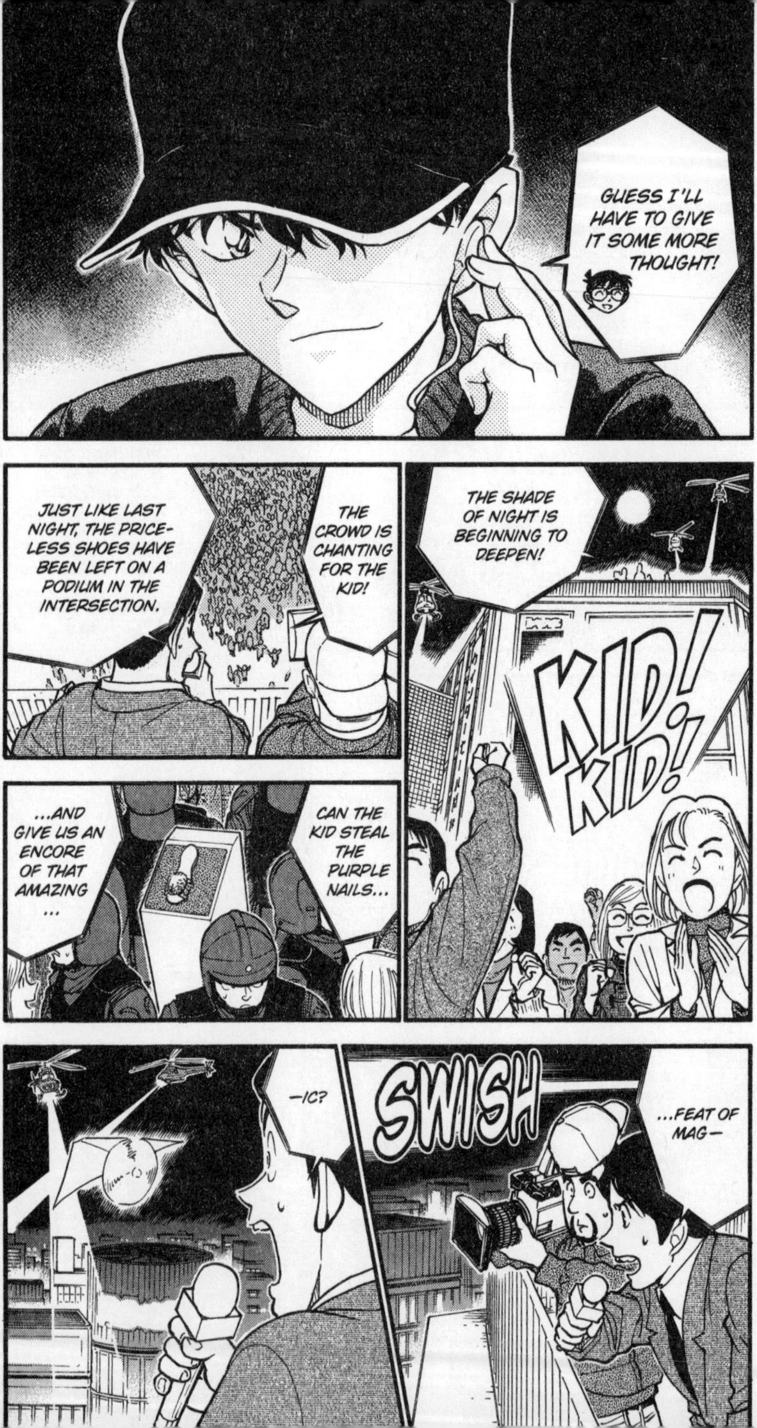
GUESS I'LL HAVE TO GIVE IT SOME MORE THOUGHT!
THE SHADE OF NIGHT IS BEGINNING TO DEEPEN!
KID! KID!
THE CROWD IS CHANTING FOR THE KID!
JUST LIKE LAST NIGHT, THE PRICELESS SHOES HAVE BEEN LEFT ON A PODIUM IN THE INTERSECTION.
CAN THE KID STEAL THE PURPLE NAILS...
...AND GIVE US AN ENCORE OF THAT AMAZING ...
...FEAT OF MAG—
SWISH
—IC?

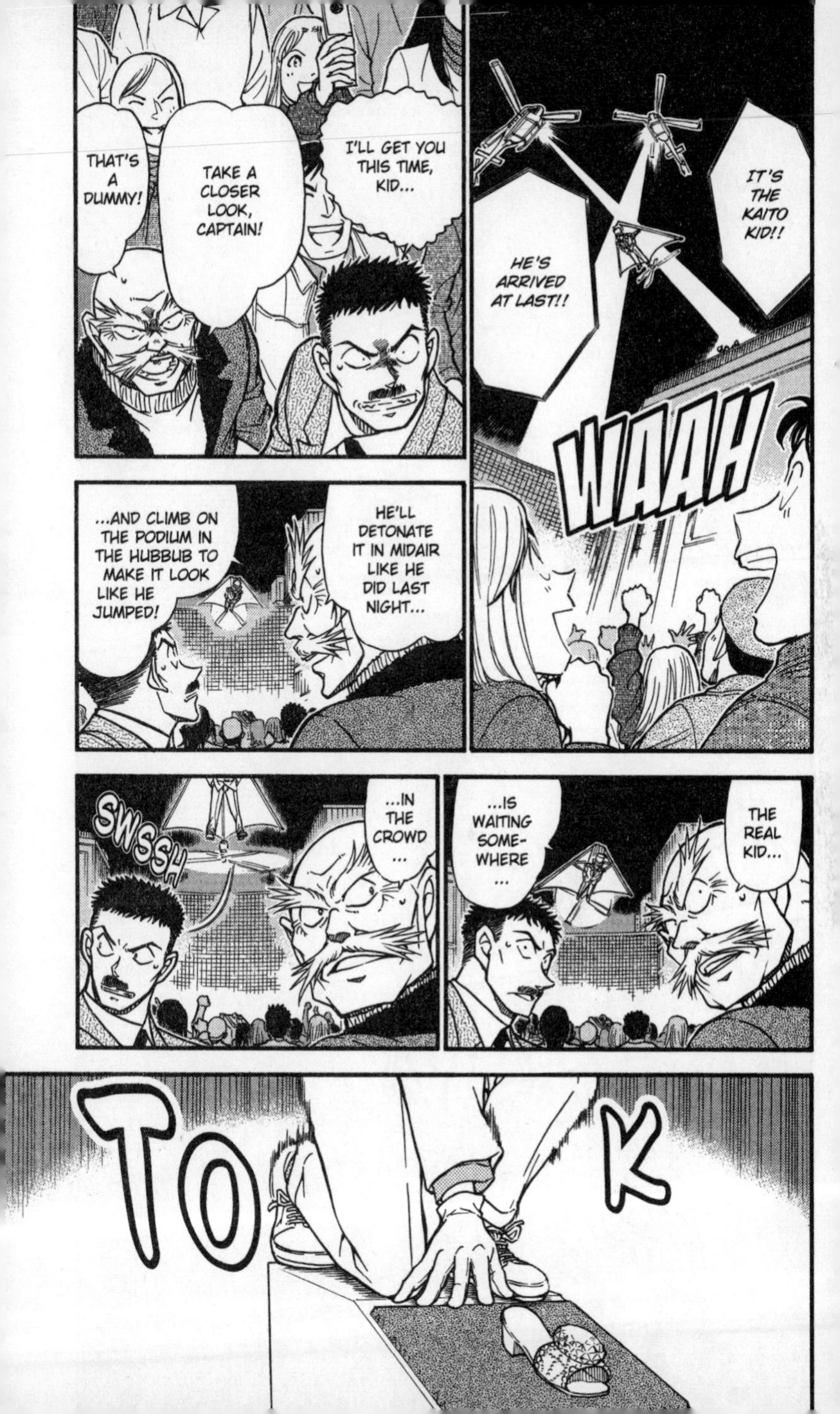
IT'S THE KAITO KID!!
HE'S ARRIVED AT LAST!!
WAAH
I'LL GET YOU THIS TIME, KID...
TAKE A CLOSER LOOK, CAPTAIN!
THAT'S A DUMMY!
HE'LL DETONATE IT IN MIDAIR LIKE HE DID LAST NIGHT...
...AND CLIMB ON THE PODIUM IN THE HUBBUB TO MAKE IT LOOK LIKE HE JUMPED!
THE REAL KID...
...IS WAITING SOME-WHERE...
...IN THE CROWD...
SWSSH
TOK

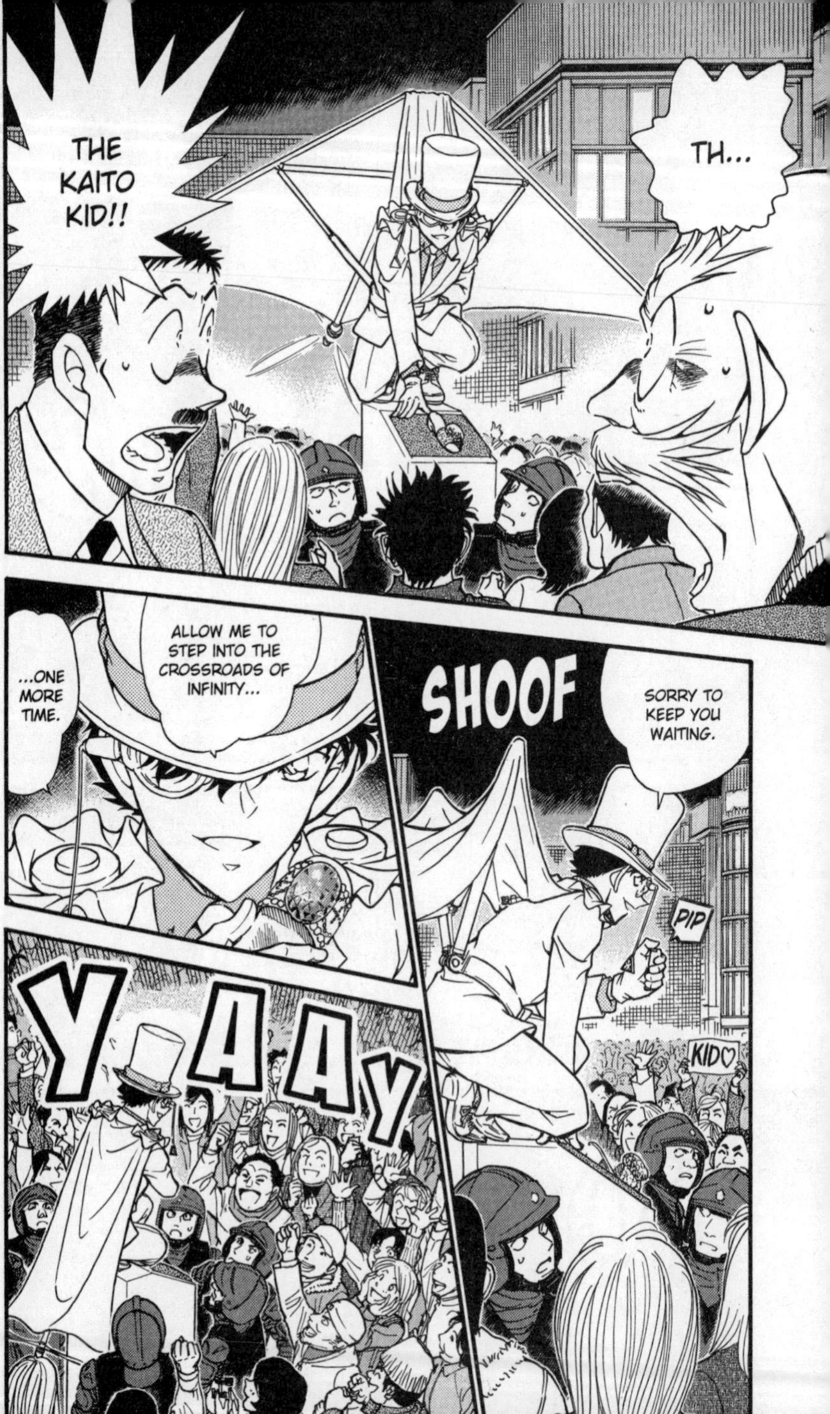
TH...
THE KAITO KID!!
SORRY TO KEEP YOU WAITING.
SHOOF
PIP
KID♡
ALLOW ME TO STEP INTO THE CROSSROADS OF INFINITY...
...ONE MORE TIME.
YAAAY

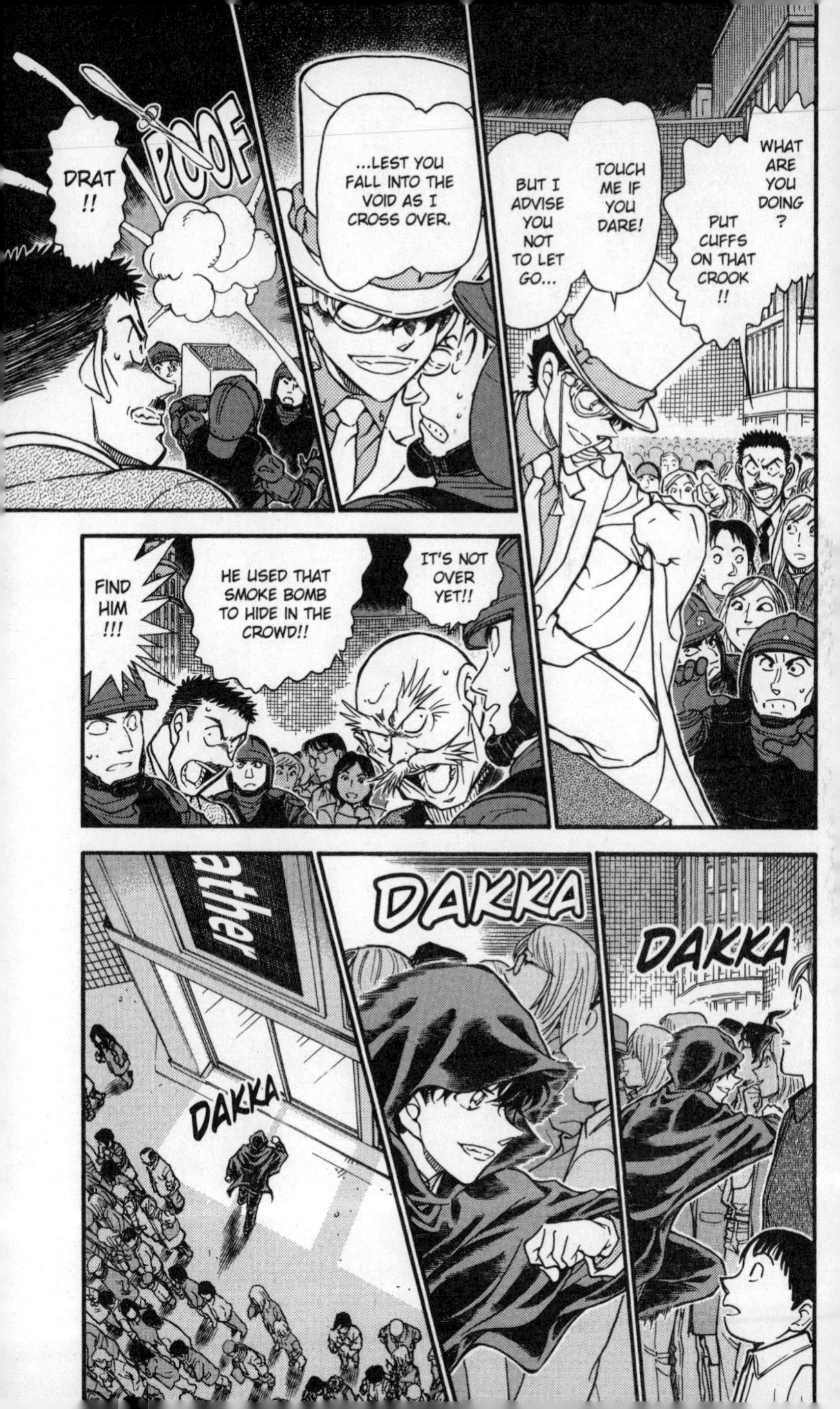
WHAT ARE YOU DOING?
PUT CUFFS ON THAT CROOK!!
TOUCH ME IF YOU DARE!
BUT I ADVISE YOU NOT TO LET GO...
...LEST YOU FALL INTO THE VOID AS I CROSS OVER.
POOF
DRAT!!
IT'S NOT OVER YET!!
HE USED THAT SMOKE BOMB TO HIDE IN THE CROWD!!
FIND HIM!!!
DAKKA
DAKKA
ather
DAKKA

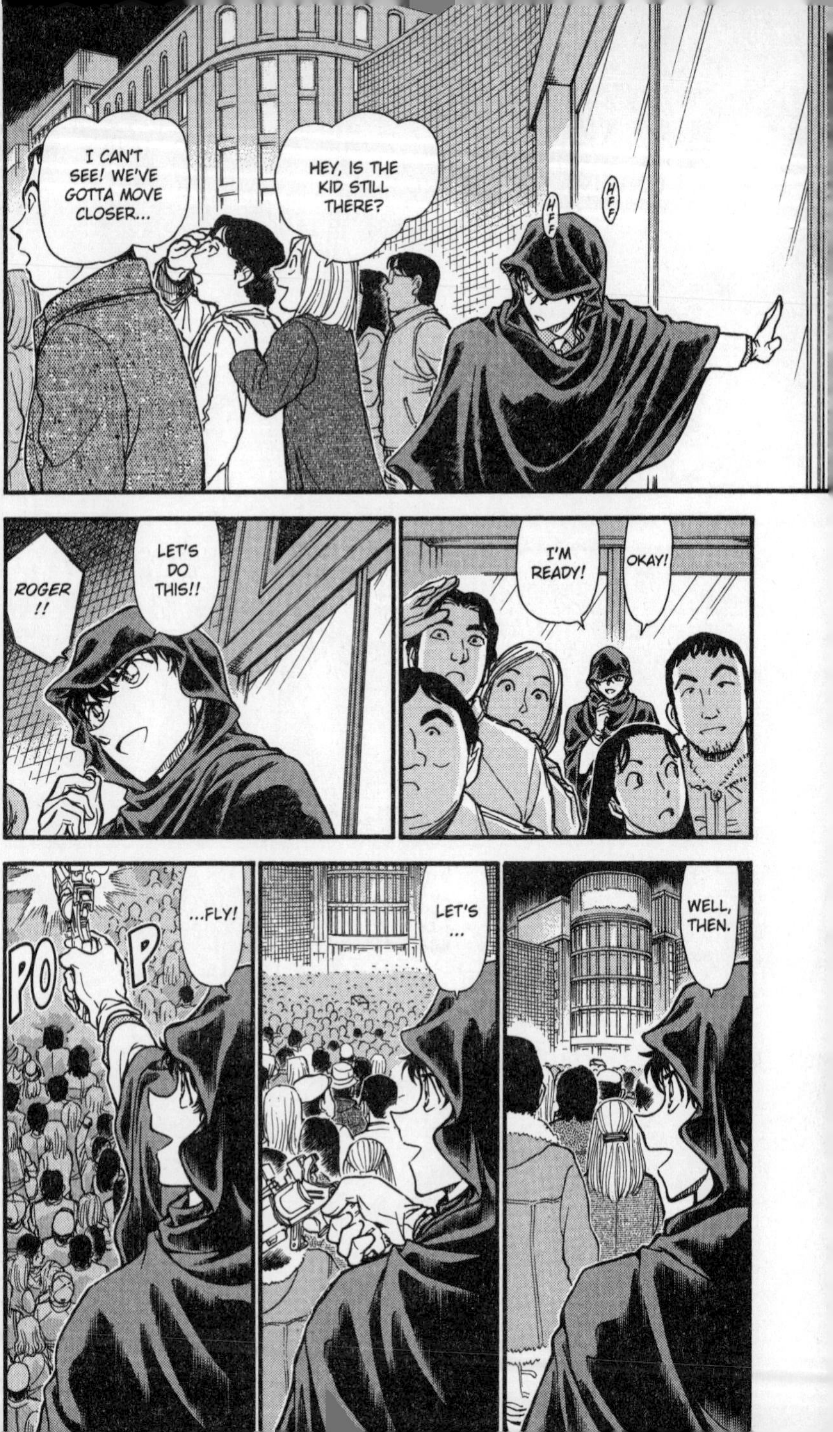
HFF HFF
HEY, IS THE KID STILL THERE?
I CAN'T SEE! WE'VE GOTTA MOVE CLOSER...
OKAY!
I'M READY!
LET'S DO THIS!!
ROGER!!
WELL, THEN.
LET'S ...
...FLY!
POP

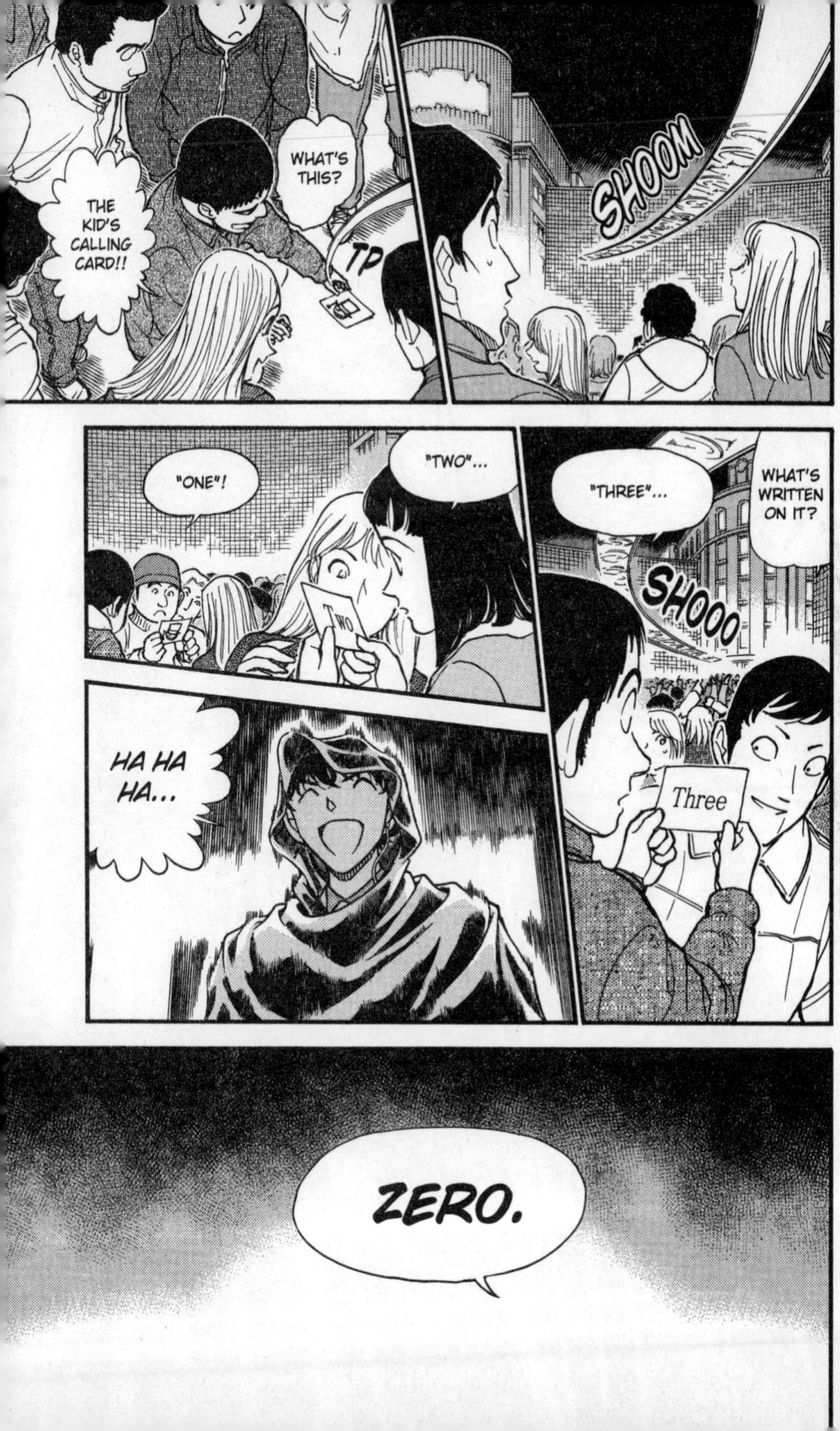
SHOOM
WHAT'S THIS?
TP
THE KID'S CALLING CARD!!
WHAT'S WRITTEN ON IT?
"THREE"...
SHOOO
Three
"TWO"...
"ONE"!
TWO
HA HA HA...
ZERO.

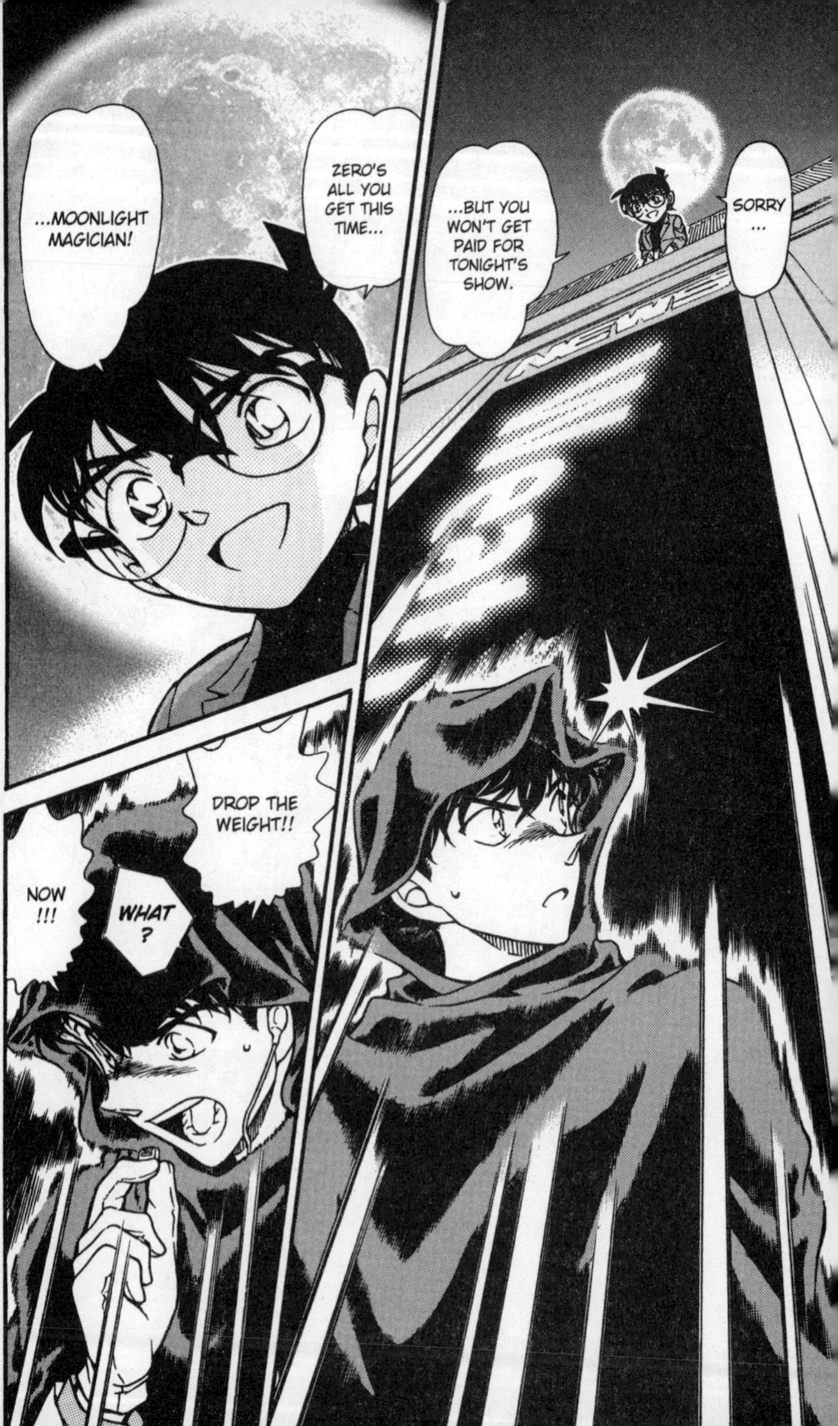
SORRY ...
...BUT YOU WON'T GET PAID FOR TONIGHT'S SHOW.
ZERO'S ALL YOU GET THIS TIME...
...MOONLIGHT MAGICIAN!
DROP THE WEIGHT!!
WHAT ?
NOW !!!

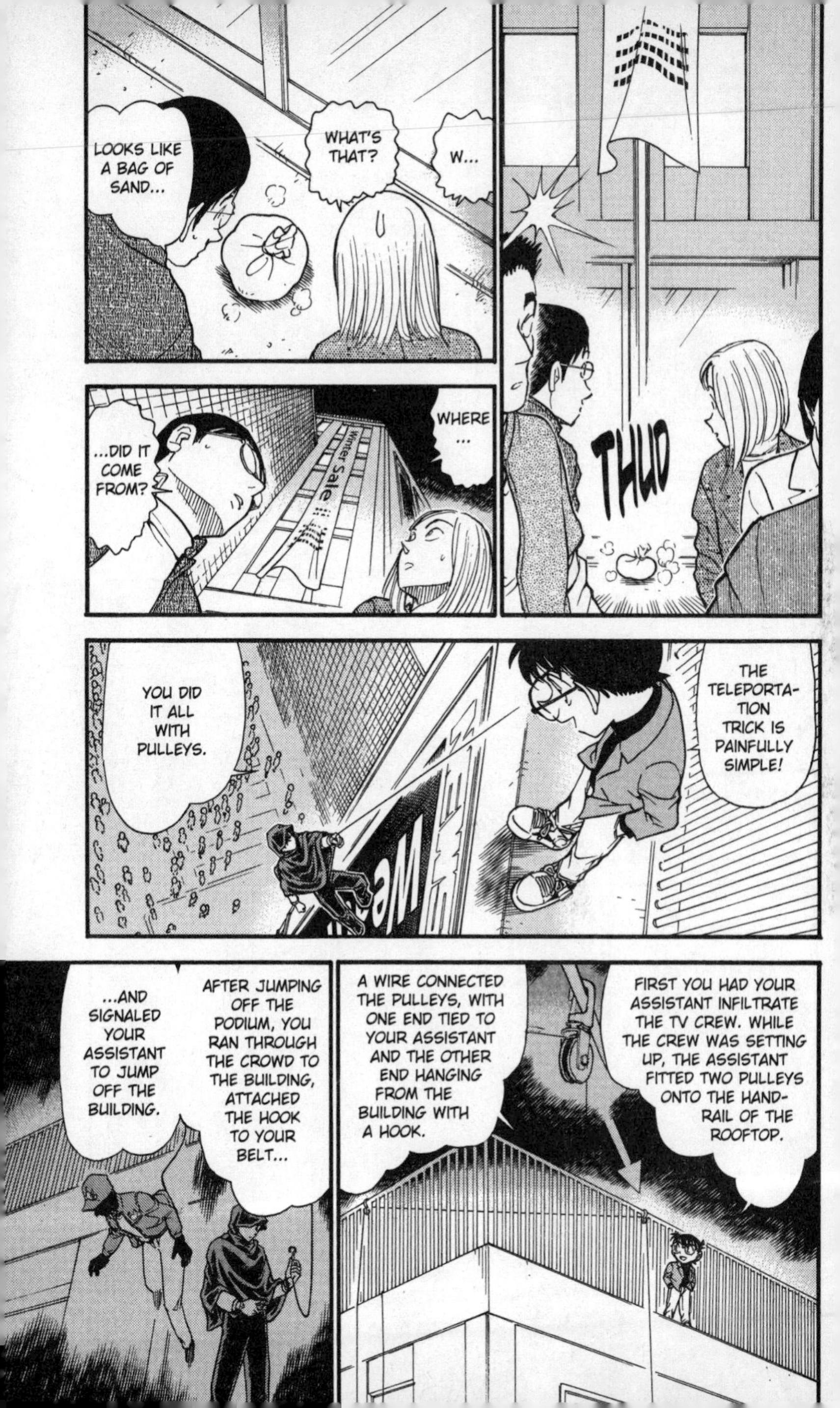
THUD
W...
WHAT'S THAT?
LOOKS LIKE A BAG OF SAND...
WHERE...
...DID IT COME FROM?
Winter Sale
THE TELEPORTATION TRICK IS PAINFULLY SIMPLE!
YOU DID IT ALL WITH PULLEYS.
FIRST YOU HAD YOUR ASSISTANT INFILTRATE THE TV CREW. WHILE THE CREW WAS SETTING UP, THE ASSISTANT FITTED TWO PULLEYS ONTO THE HANDRAIL OF THE ROOFTOP.
A WIRE CONNECTED THE PULLEYS, WITH ONE END TIED TO YOUR ASSISTANT AND THE OTHER END HANGING FROM THE BUILDING WITH A HOOK.
AFTER JUMPING OFF THE PODIUM, YOU RAN THROUGH THE CROWD TO THE BUILDING, ATTACHED THE HOOK TO YOUR BELT...
...AND SIGNALED YOUR ASSISTANT TO JUMP OFF THE BUILDING.

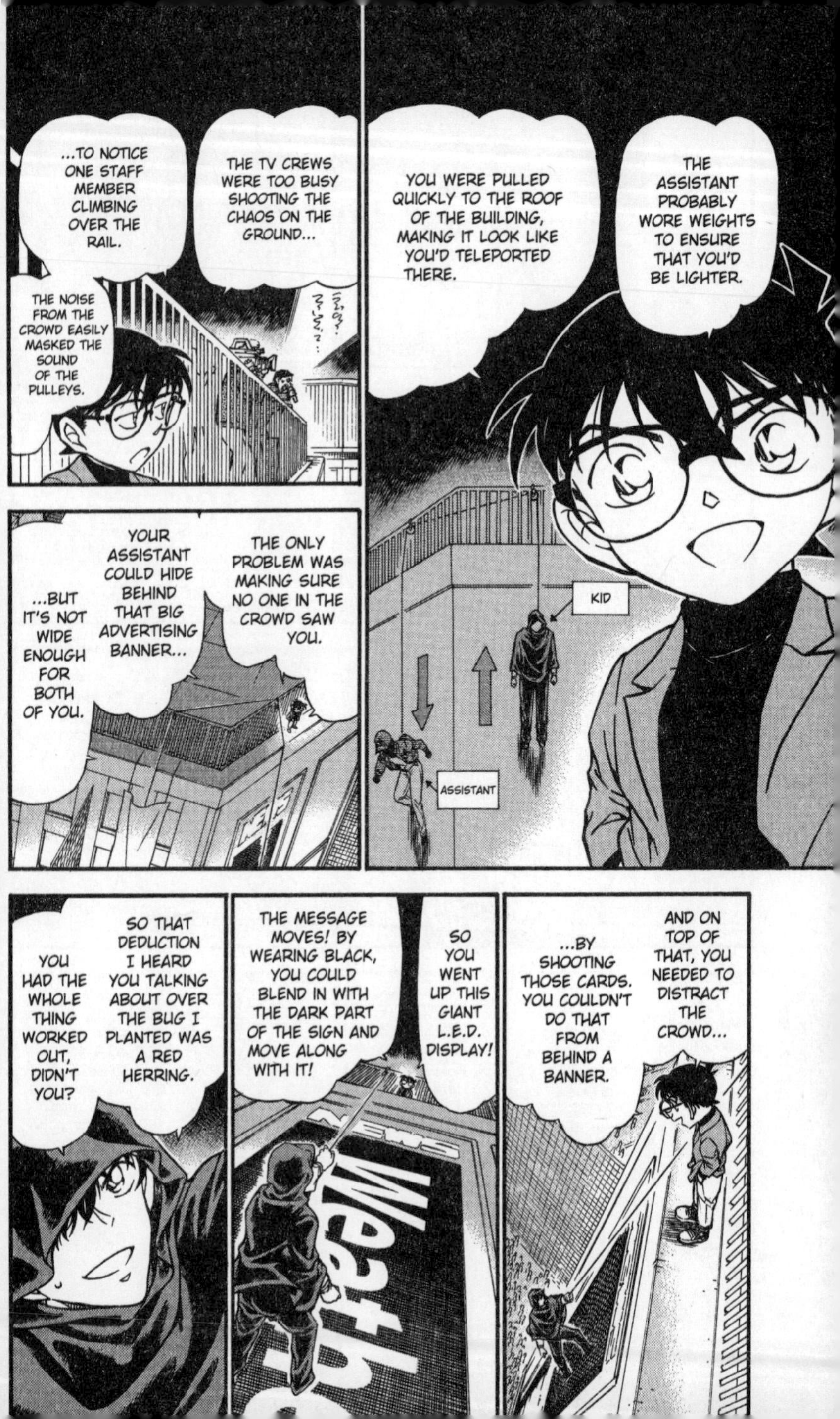
THE ASSISTANT PROBABLY WORE WEIGHTS TO ENSURE THAT YOU'D BE LIGHTER.
YOU WERE PULLED QUICKLY TO THE ROOF OF THE BUILDING, MAKING IT LOOK LIKE YOU'D TELEPORTED THERE.
KID
ASSISTANT
THE TV CREWS WERE TOO BUSY SHOOTING THE CHAOS ON THE GROUND...
...TO NOTICE ONE STAFF MEMBER CLIMBING OVER THE RAIL.
THE NOISE FROM THE CROWD EASILY MASKED THE SOUND OF THE PULLEYS.
THE ONLY PROBLEM WAS MAKING SURE NO ONE IN THE CROWD SAW YOU.
YOUR ASSISTANT COULD HIDE BEHIND THAT BIG ADVERTISING BANNER...
...BUT IT'S NOT WIDE ENOUGH FOR BOTH OF YOU.
AND ON TOP OF THAT, YOU NEEDED TO DISTRACT THE CROWD...
...BY SHOOTING THOSE CARDS. YOU COULDN'T DO THAT FROM BEHIND A BANNER.
SO YOU WENT UP THIS GIANT L.E.D. DISPLAY!
THE MESSAGE MOVES! BY WEARING BLACK, YOU COULD BLEND IN WITH THE DARK PART OF THE SIGN AND MOVE ALONG WITH IT!
SO THAT DEDUCTION I HEARD YOU TALKING ABOUT OVER THE BUG I PLANTED WAS A RED HERRING.
YOU HAD THE WHOLE THING WORKED OUT, DIDN'T YOU?

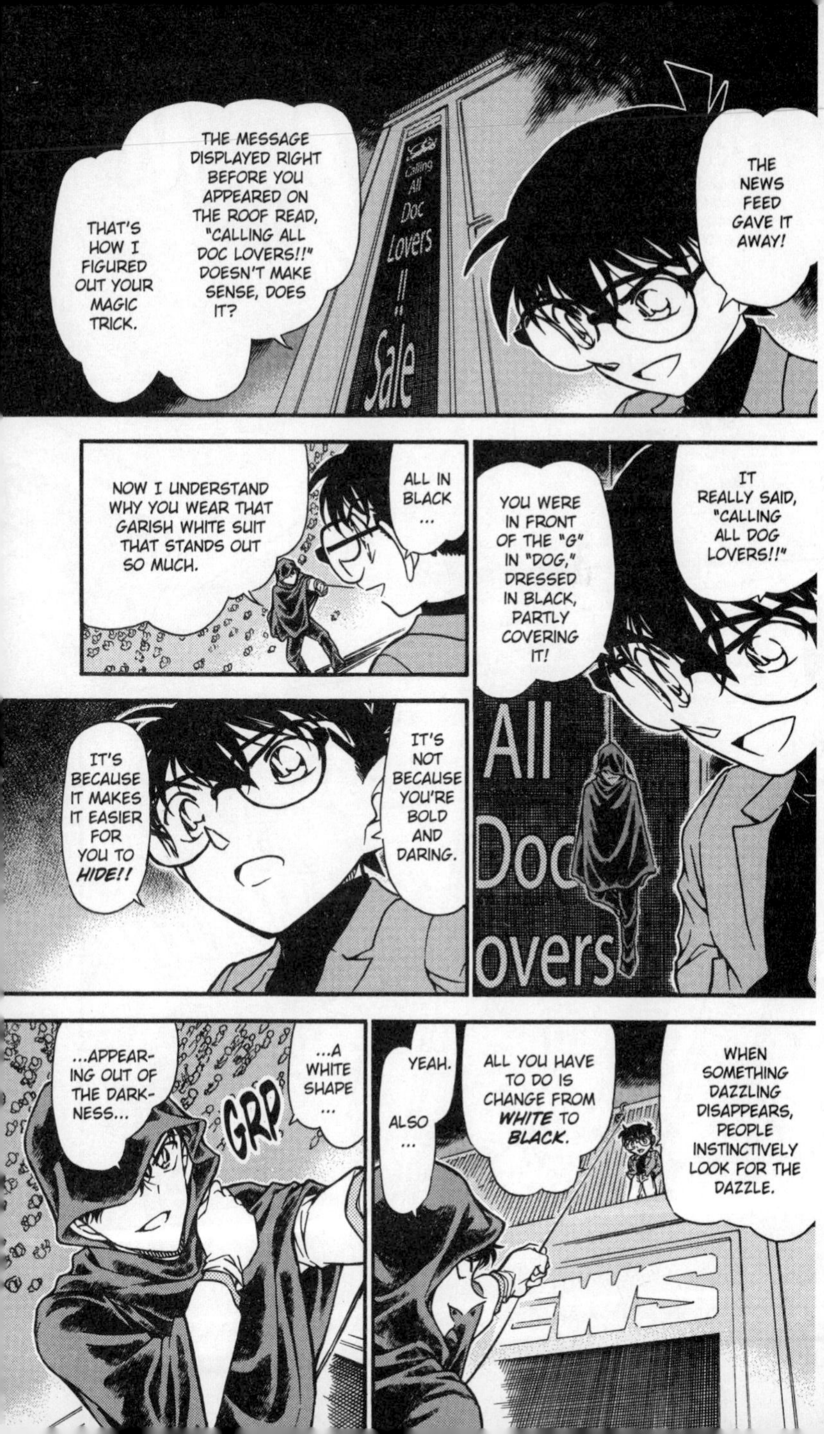
THE NEWS FEED GAVE IT AWAY!
Calling All Doc Lovers !! Sale
THE MESSAGE DISPLAYED RIGHT BEFORE YOU APPEARED ON THE ROOF READ, "CALLING ALL DOC LOVERS!!" DOESN'T MAKE SENSE, DOES IT?
THAT'S HOW I FIGURED OUT YOUR MAGIC TRICK.
IT REALLY SAID, "CALLING ALL DOG LOVERS!!"
YOU WERE IN FRONT OF THE "G" IN "DOG," DRESSED IN BLACK, PARTLY COVERING IT!
All Doc overs
ALL IN BLACK ...
NOW I UNDERSTAND WHY YOU WEAR THAT GARISH WHITE SUIT THAT STANDS OUT SO MUCH.
IT'S NOT BECAUSE YOU'RE BOLD AND DARING.
IT'S BECAUSE IT MAKES IT EASIER FOR YOU TO *HIDE!!*
WHEN SOMETHING DAZZLING DISAPPEARS, PEOPLE INSTINCTIVELY LOOK FOR THE DAZZLE.
ALL YOU HAVE TO DO IS CHANGE FROM *WHITE* TO *BLACK*.
YEAH.
ALSO ...
EWS
...A WHITE SHAPE ...
GRP
...APPEARING OUT OF THE DARKNESS...

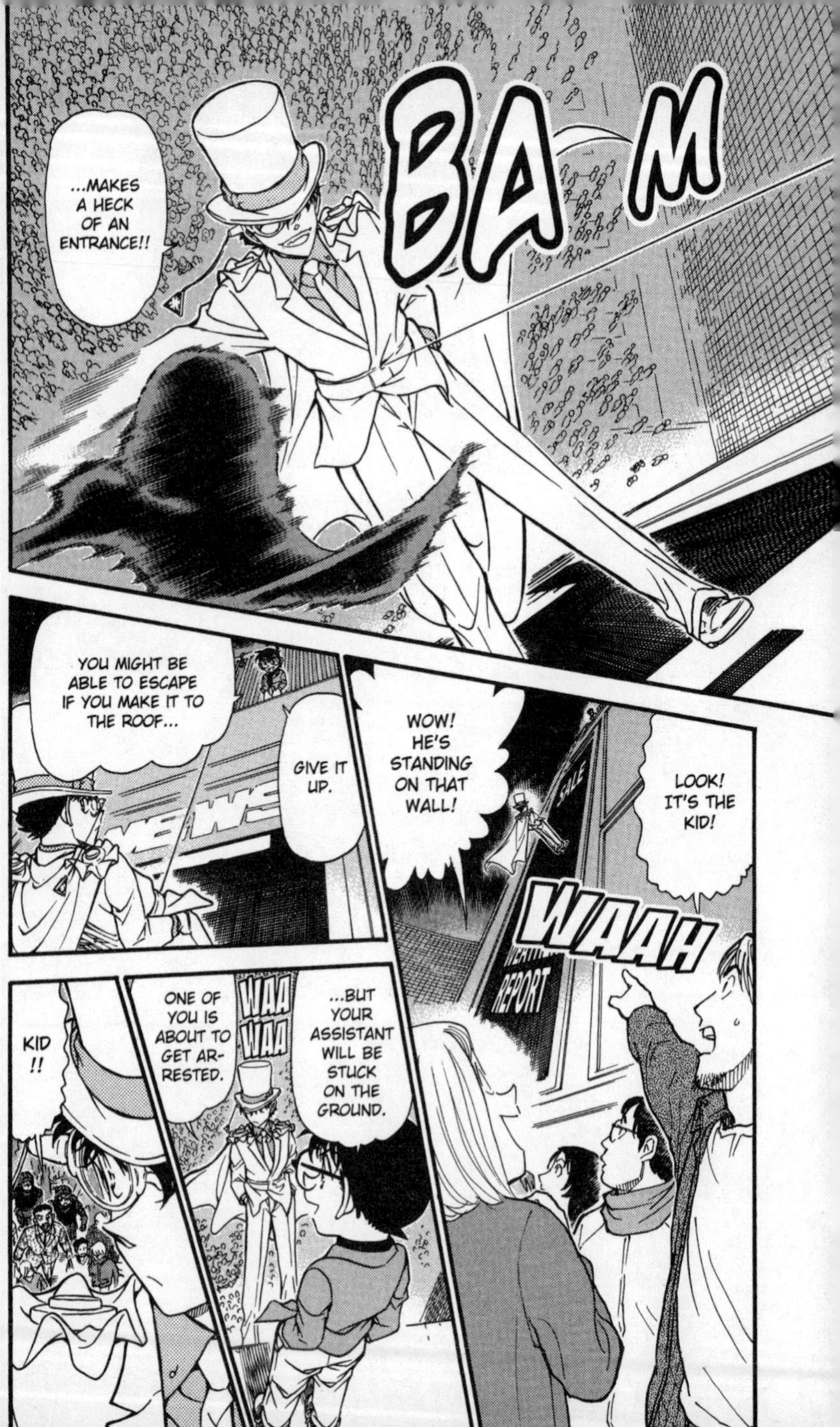
BAM
...MAKES A HECK OF AN ENTRANCE!!
LOOK! IT'S THE KID!
WOW! HE'S STANDING ON THAT WALL!
WAAH
GIVE IT UP.
YOU MIGHT BE ABLE TO ESCAPE IF YOU MAKE IT TO THE ROOF...
...BUT YOUR ASSISTANT WILL BE STUCK ON THE GROUND.
WAA WAA
ONE OF YOU IS ABOUT TO GET AR- RESTED.
KID !!

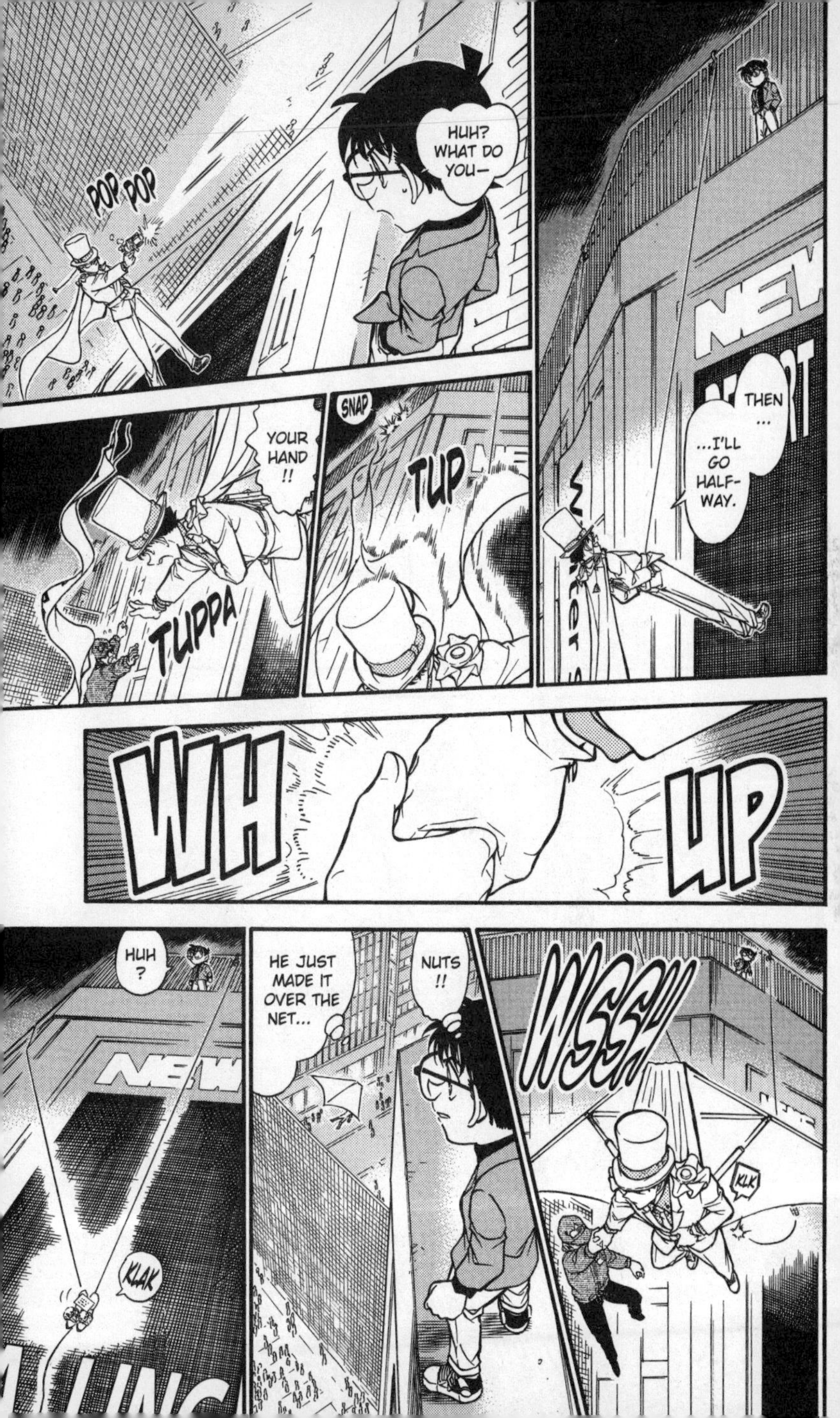
THEN...
...I'LL GO HALFWAY.
HUH? WHAT DO YOU—
POP POP
SNAP
TUP
YOUR HAND!!
TUPPA
WH
UP
WSSH
KLK
NUTS!!
HE JUST MADE IT OVER THE NET...
HUH?
KLAK

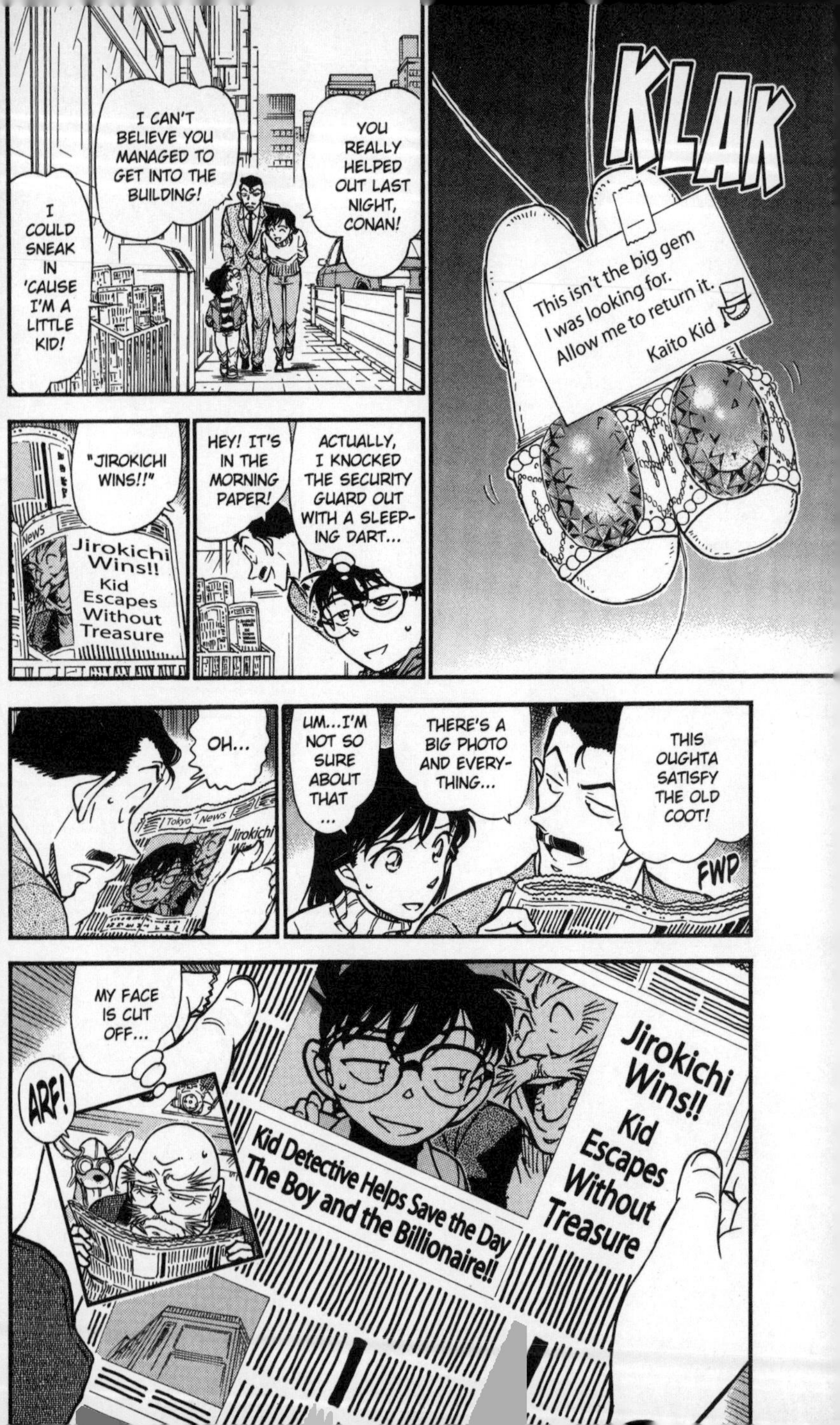
KLAK
This isn't the big gem
I was looking for.
Allow me to return it.
Kaito Kid
YOU REALLY HELPED OUT LAST NIGHT, CONAN!
I CAN'T BELIEVE YOU MANAGED TO GET INTO THE BUILDING!
I COULD SNEAK IN 'CAUSE I'M A LITTLE KID!
ACTUALLY, I KNOCKED THE SECURITY GUARD OUT WITH A SLEEP-ING DART...
HEY! IT'S IN THE MORNING PAPER!
"JIROKICHI WINS!!"
News
Jirokichi Wins!! Kid Escapes Without Treasure
THIS OUGHTA SATISFY THE OLD COOT!
FWP
THERE'S A BIG PHOTO AND EVERY-THING...
UM...I'M NOT SO SURE ABOUT THAT...
OH...
Tokyo News
Jirokichi Wins!! Kid Escapes Without Treasure
Kid Detective Helps Save the Day
The Boy and the Billionaire!!
MY FACE IS CUT OFF...
ARF!

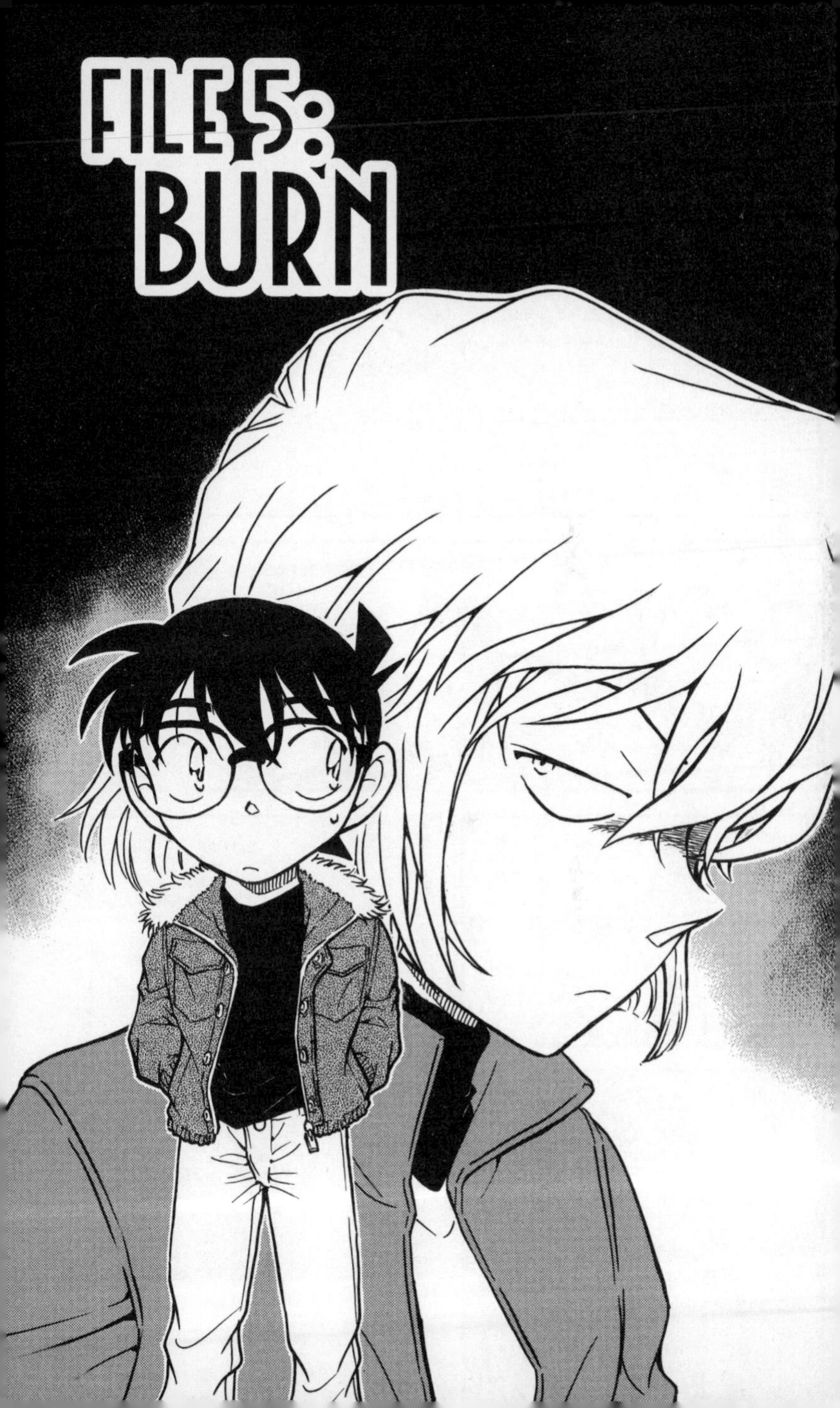
FILE 5:
BURN

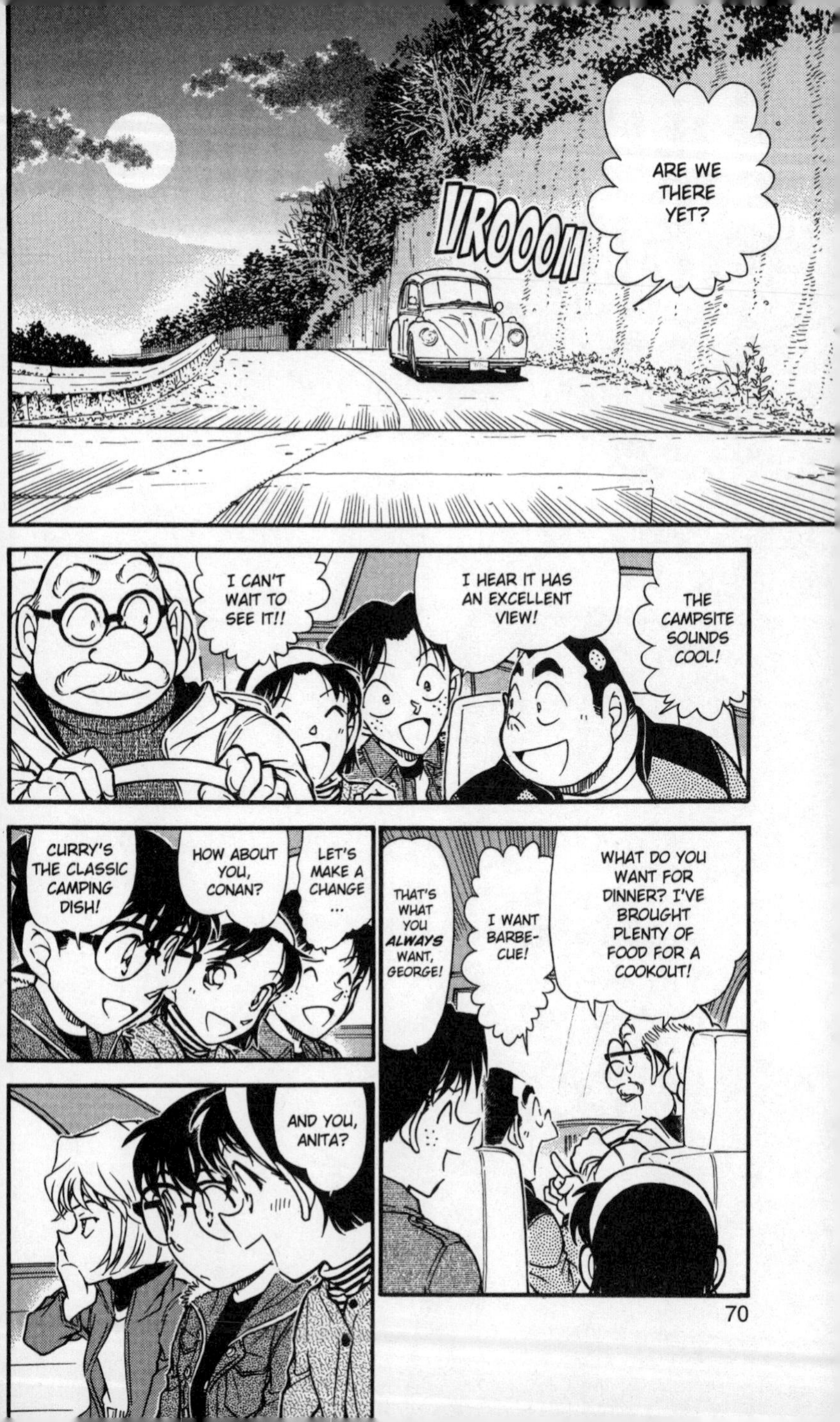
VROOOM
ARE WE THERE YET?
THE CAMPSITE SOUNDS COOL!
I HEAR IT HAS AN EXCELLENT VIEW!
I CAN'T WAIT TO SEE IT!!
WHAT DO YOU WANT FOR DINNER? I'VE BROUGHT PLENTY OF FOOD FOR A COOKOUT!
I WANT BARBECUE!
THAT'S WHAT YOU *ALWAYS* WANT, GEORGE!
LET'S MAKE A CHANGE ...
HOW ABOUT YOU, CONAN?
CURRY'S THE CLASSIC CAMPING DISH!
AND YOU, ANITA?

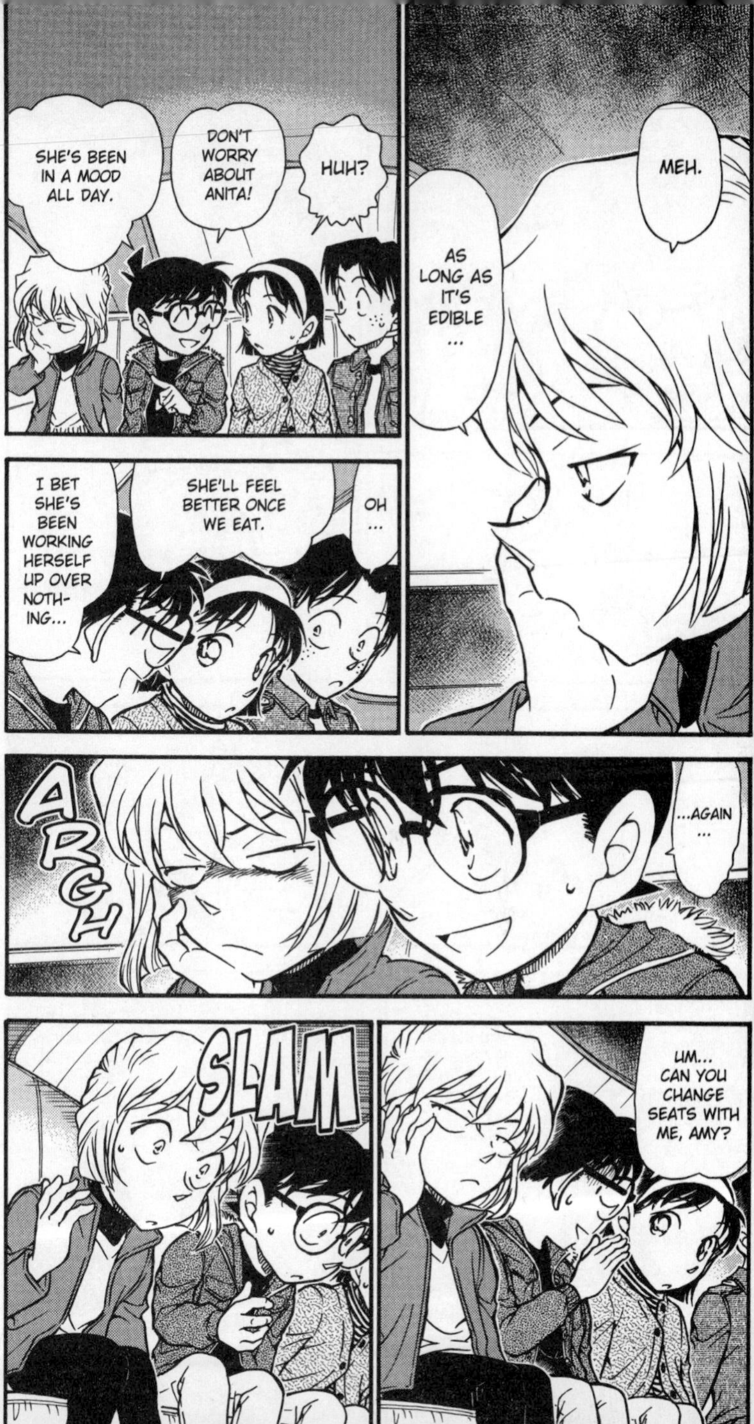
MEH.
AS LONG AS IT'S EDIBLE ...
HUH?
DON'T WORRY ABOUT ANITA!
SHE'S BEEN IN A MOOD ALL DAY.
OH ...
SHE'LL FEEL BETTER ONCE WE EAT.
I BET SHE'S BEEN WORKING HERSELF UP OVER NOTH-ING...
...AGAIN ...
ARGH
UM... CAN YOU CHANGE SEATS WITH ME, AMY?
SLAM

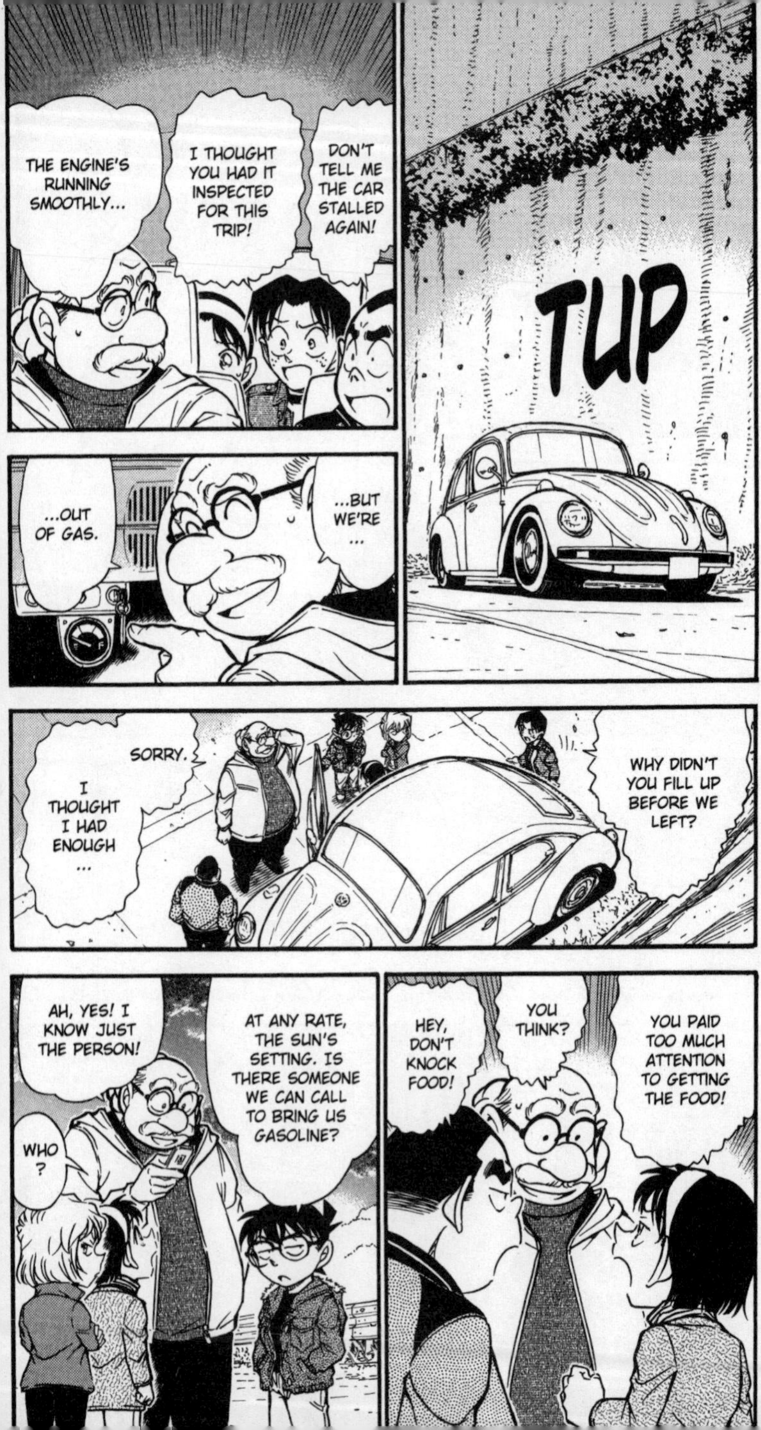

TUP
DON'T TELL ME THE CAR STALLED AGAIN!
I THOUGHT YOU HAD IT INSPECTED FOR THIS TRIP!
THE ENGINE'S RUNNING SMOOTHLY...
...BUT WE'RE ...
...OUT OF GAS.
WHY DIDN'T YOU FILL UP BEFORE WE LEFT?
SORRY.
I THOUGHT I HAD ENOUGH ...
YOU PAID TOO MUCH ATTENTION TO GETTING THE FOOD!
YOU THINK?
HEY, DON'T KNOCK FOOD!
AT ANY RATE, THE SUN'S SETTING. IS THERE SOMEONE WE CAN CALL TO BRING US GASOLINE?
AH, YES! I KNOW JUST THE PERSON!
WHO ?

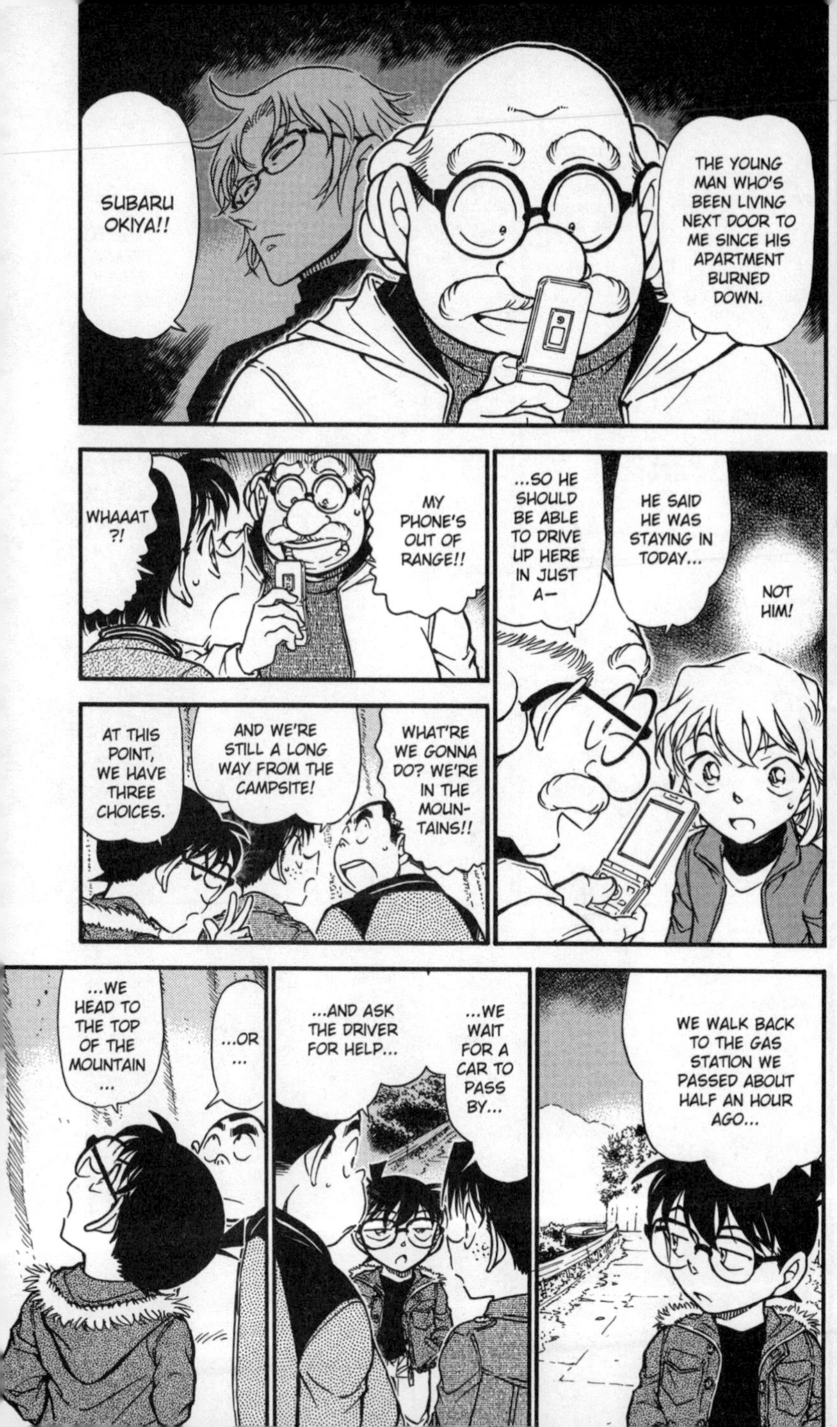
THE YOUNG MAN WHO'S BEEN LIVING NEXT DOOR TO ME SINCE HIS APARTMENT BURNED DOWN.
SUBARU OKIYA!!
HE SAID HE WAS STAYING IN TODAY...
...SO HE SHOULD BE ABLE TO DRIVE UP HERE IN JUST A—
NOT HIM!
MY PHONE'S OUT OF RANGE!!
WHAAAT?!
WHAT'RE WE GONNA DO? WE'RE IN THE MOUNTAINS!!
AND WE'RE STILL A LONG WAY FROM THE CAMPSITE!
AT THIS POINT, WE HAVE THREE CHOICES.
WE WALK BACK TO THE GAS STATION WE PASSED ABOUT HALF AN HOUR AGO...
...WE WAIT FOR A CAR TO PASS BY...
...AND ASK THE DRIVER FOR HELP...
...OR ...
...WE HEAD TO THE TOP OF THE MOUNTAIN ...

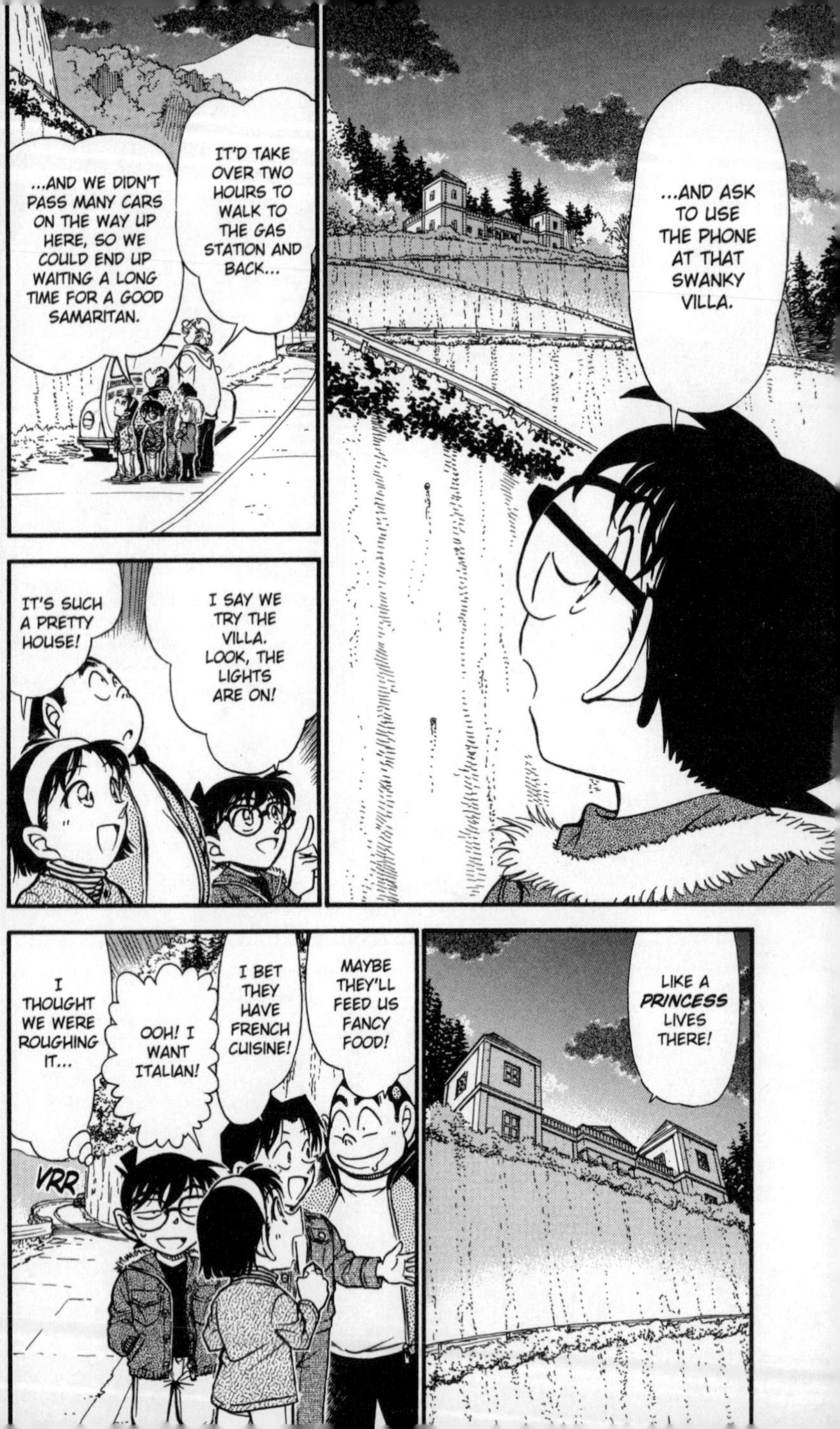
...AND ASK TO USE THE PHONE AT THAT SWANKY VILLA.
IT'D TAKE OVER TWO HOURS TO WALK TO THE GAS STATION AND BACK...
...AND WE DIDN'T PASS MANY CARS ON THE WAY UP HERE, SO WE COULD END UP WAITING A LONG TIME FOR A GOOD SAMARITAN.
I SAY WE TRY THE VILLA. LOOK, THE LIGHTS ARE ON!
IT'S SUCH A PRETTY HOUSE!
LIKE A *PRINCESS* LIVES THERE!
MAYBE THEY'LL FEED US FANCY FOOD!
I BET THEY HAVE FRENCH CUISINE!
OOH! I WANT ITALIAN!
I THOUGHT WE WERE ROUGHING IT...
VRR

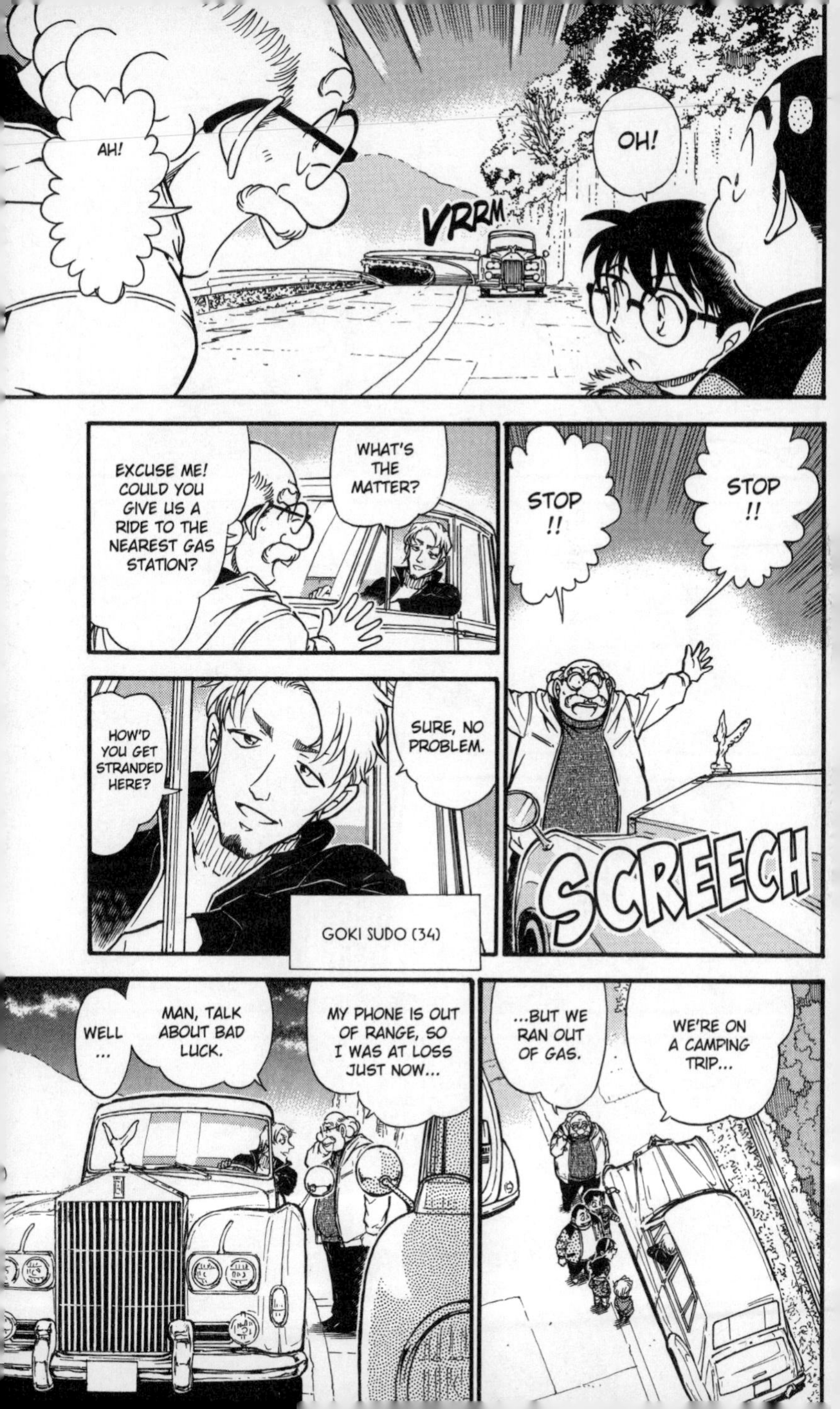
OH!
VRRM
AH!
STOP !!
STOP !!
SCREECH
WHAT'S THE MATTER?
EXCUSE ME! COULD YOU GIVE US A RIDE TO THE NEAREST GAS STATION?
SURE, NO PROBLEM.
HOW'D YOU GET STRANDED HERE?
GOKI SUDO (34)
WE'RE ON A CAMPING TRIP...
...BUT WE RAN OUT OF GAS.
MY PHONE IS OUT OF RANGE, SO I WAS AT LOSS JUST NOW...
MAN, TALK ABOUT BAD LUCK.
WELL ...

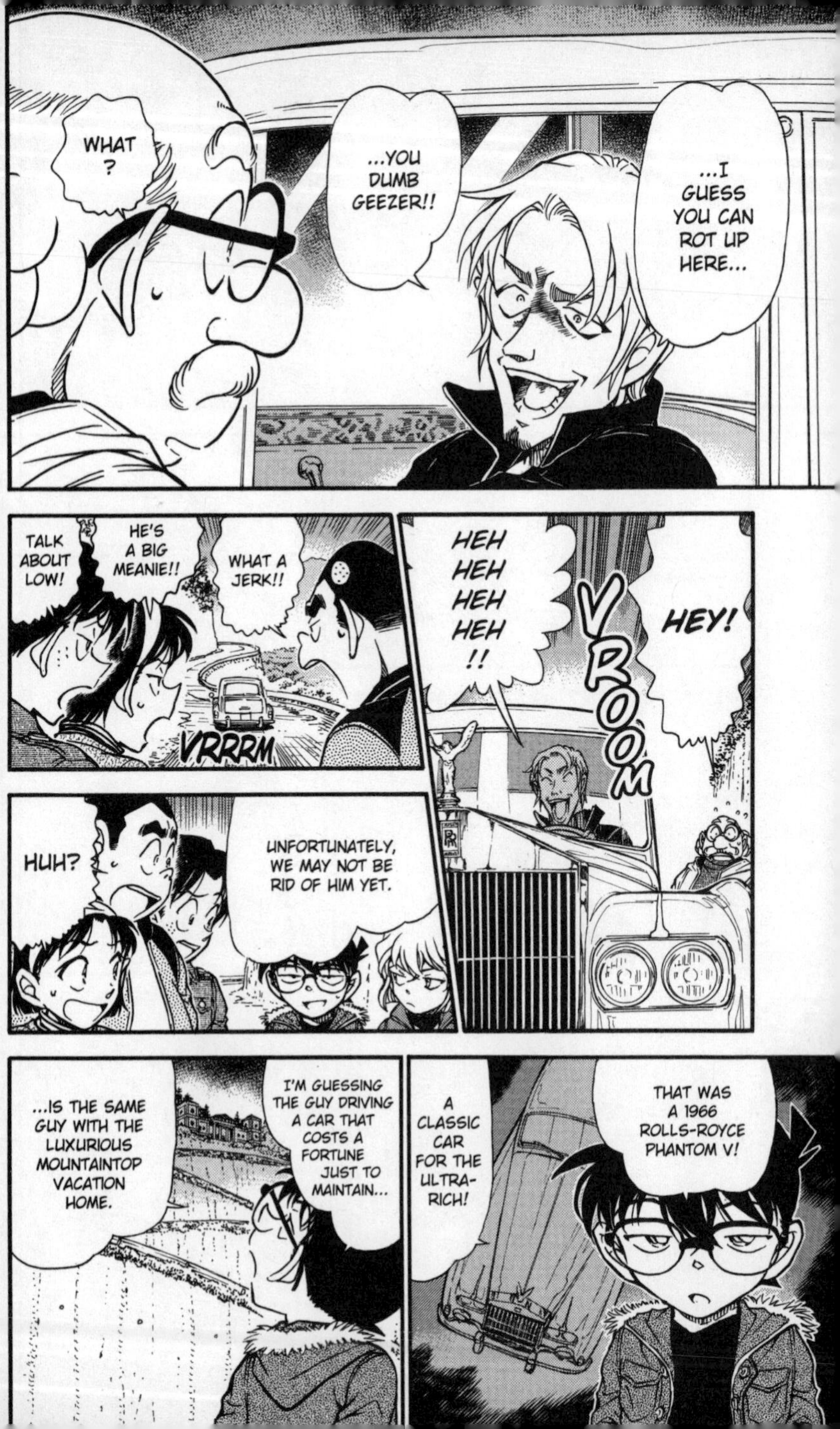
...I GUESS YOU CAN ROT UP HERE...
...YOU DUMB GEEZER!!
WHAT?
HEY!
HEH HEH HEH HEH!!
VROOM
WHAT A JERK!!
HE'S A BIG MEANIE!!
TALK ABOUT LOW!
VRRRM
UNFORTUNATELY, WE MAY NOT BE RID OF HIM YET.
HUH?
THAT WAS A 1966 ROLLS-ROYCE PHANTOM V!
A CLASSIC CAR FOR THE ULTRA-RICH!
I'M GUESSING THE GUY DRIVING A CAR THAT COSTS A FORTUNE JUST TO MAINTAIN...
...IS THE SAME GUY WITH THE LUXURIOUS MOUNTAINTOP VACATION HOME.

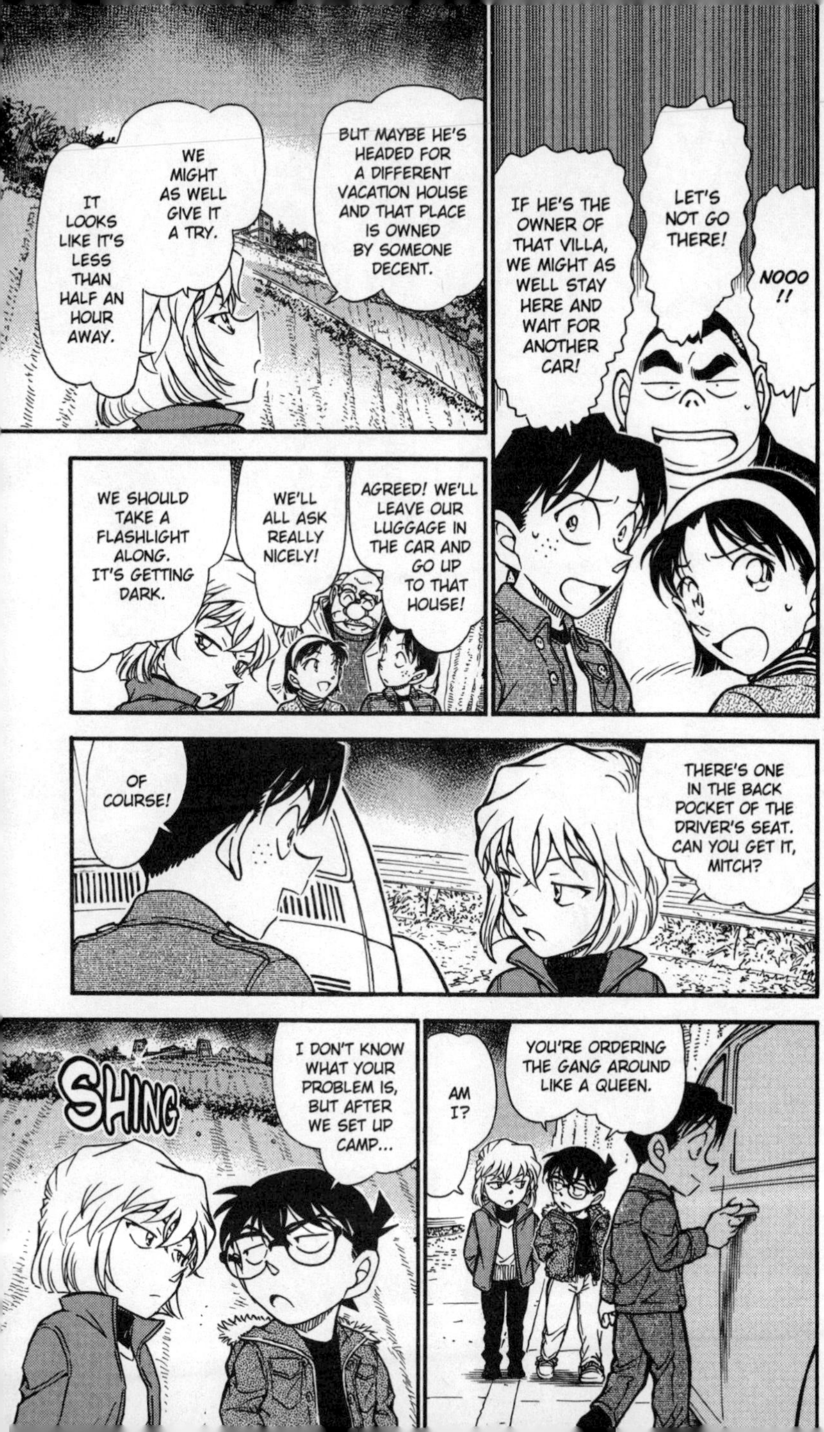
NOOO!!
LET'S NOT GO THERE!
IF HE'S THE OWNER OF THAT VILLA, WE MIGHT AS WELL STAY HERE AND WAIT FOR ANOTHER CAR!
BUT MAYBE HE'S HEADED FOR A DIFFERENT VACATION HOUSE AND THAT PLACE IS OWNED BY SOMEONE DECENT.
WE MIGHT AS WELL GIVE IT A TRY.
IT LOOKS LIKE IT'S LESS THAN HALF AN HOUR AWAY.
AGREED! WE'LL LEAVE OUR LUGGAGE IN THE CAR AND GO UP TO THAT HOUSE!
WE'LL ALL ASK REALLY NICELY!
WE SHOULD TAKE A FLASHLIGHT ALONG. IT'S GETTING DARK.
THERE'S ONE IN THE BACK POCKET OF THE DRIVER'S SEAT. CAN YOU GET IT, MITCH?
OF COURSE!
YOU'RE ORDERING THE GANG AROUND LIKE A QUEEN.
AM I?
I DON'T KNOW WHAT YOUR PROBLEM IS, BUT AFTER WE SET UP CAMP...
SHING

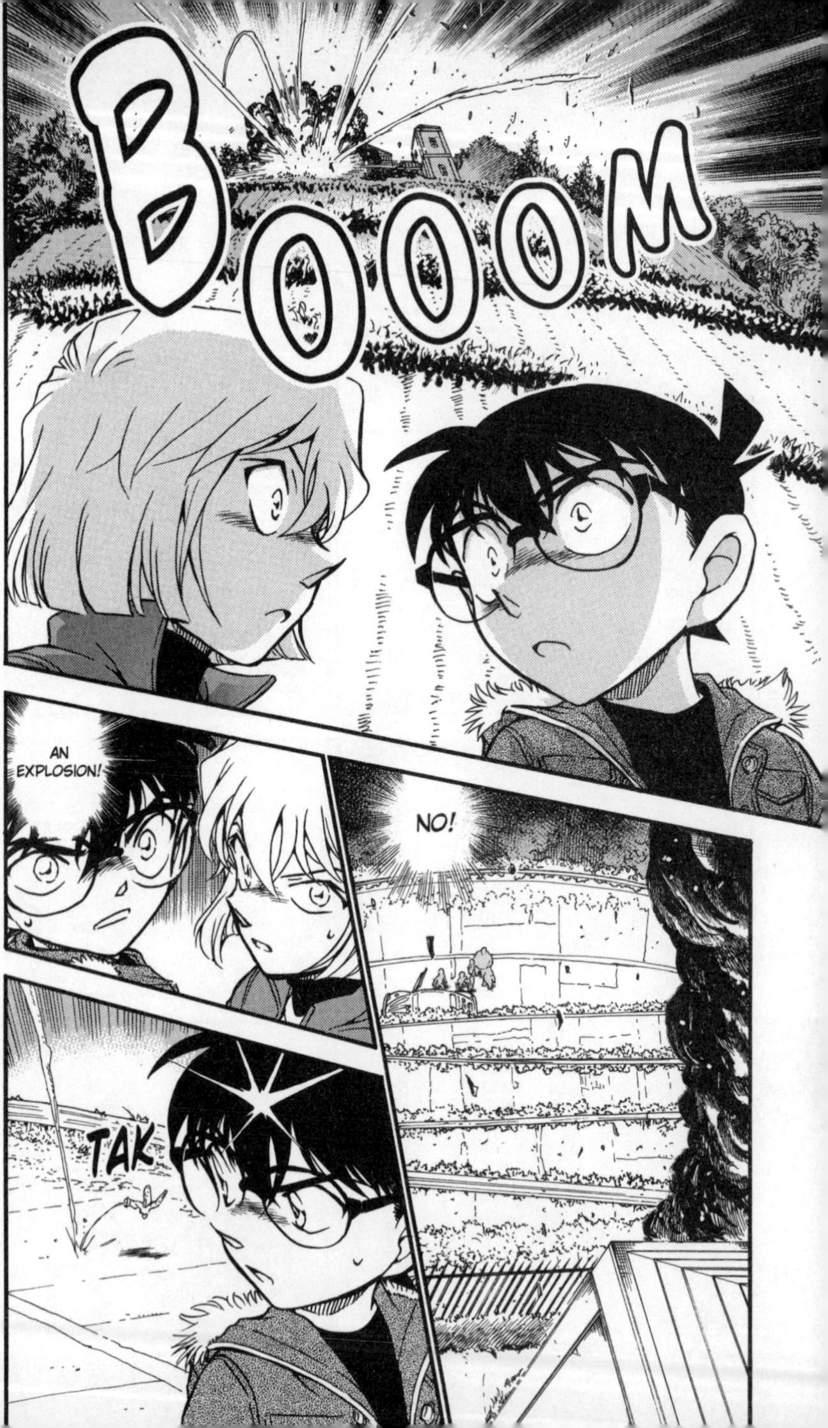
BOOOM
NO!
AN EXPLOSION!
TAK

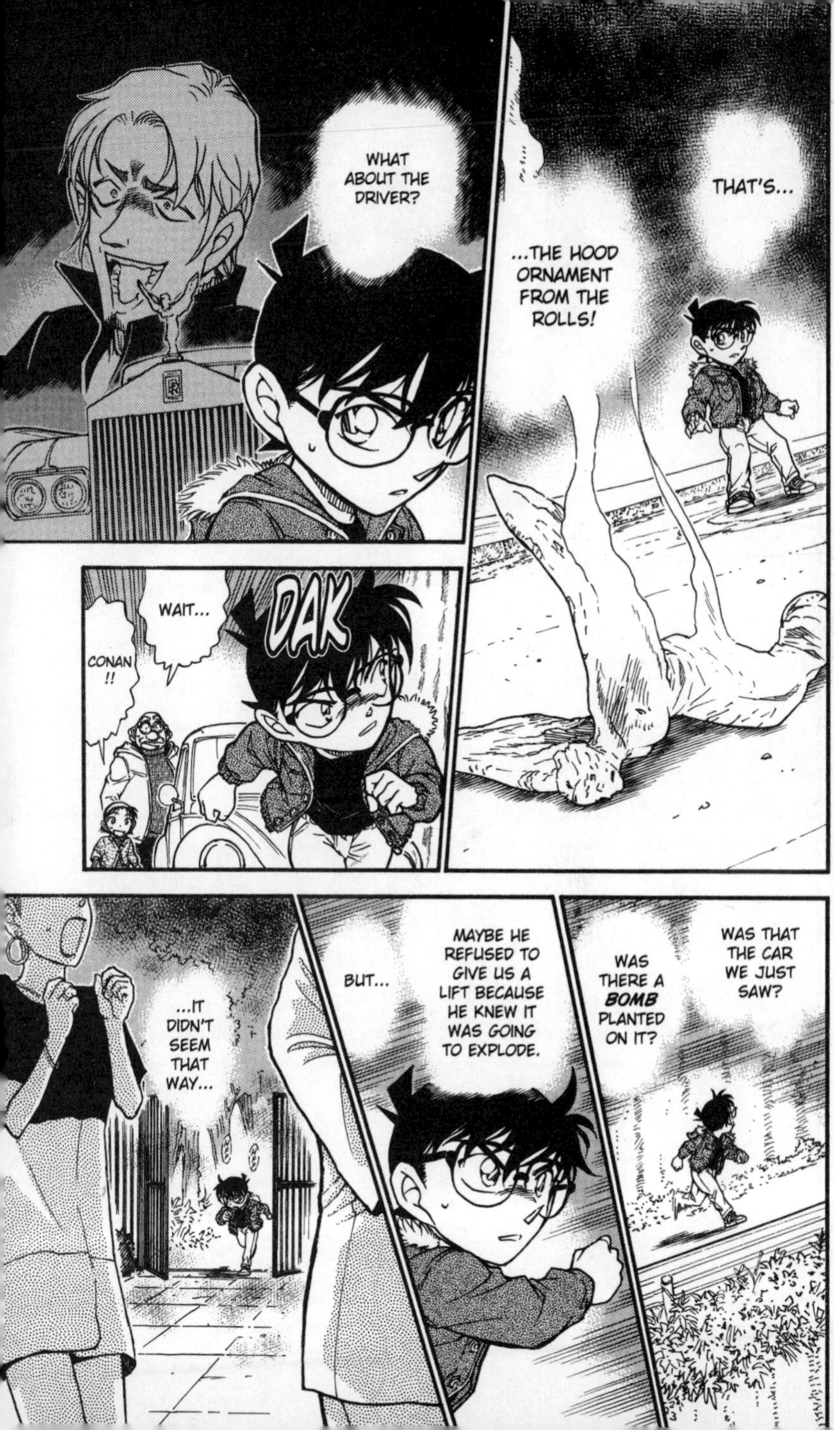
THAT'S...
...THE HOOD ORNAMENT FROM THE ROLLS!
WHAT ABOUT THE DRIVER?
DAK
WAIT...
CONAN!!
WAS THAT THE CAR WE JUST SAW?
WAS THERE A BOMB PLANTED ON IT?
MAYBE HE REFUSED TO GIVE US A LIFT BECAUSE HE KNEW IT WAS GOING TO EXPLODE.
BUT...
...IT DIDN'T SEEM THAT WAY...

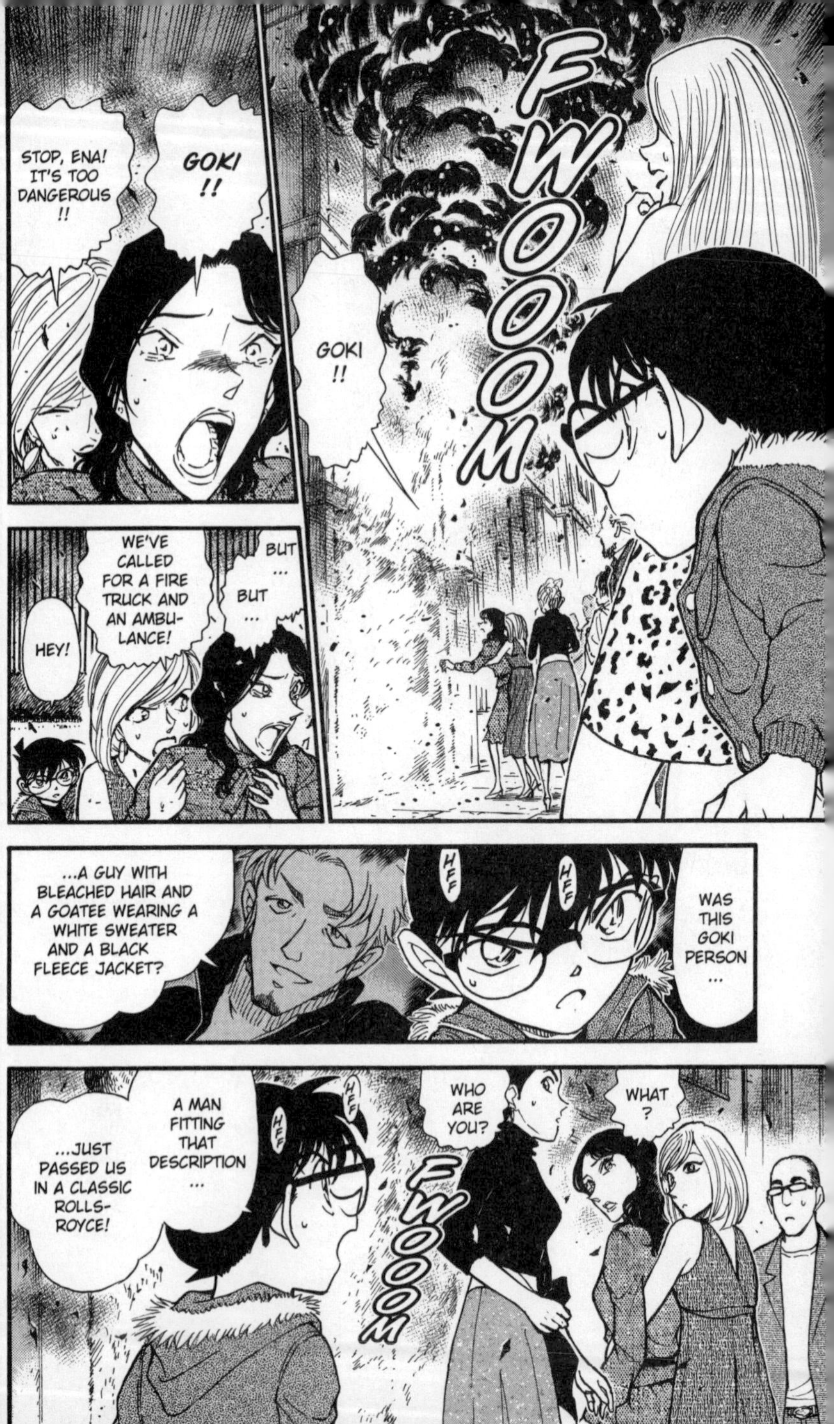
FWOOOOM
GOKI !!
GOKI !!
STOP, ENA! IT'S TOO DANGEROUS !!
BUT ... BUT ...
WE'VE CALLED FOR A FIRE TRUCK AND AN AMBULANCE!
HEY!
WAS THIS GOKI PERSON ...
HFF HFF
...A GUY WITH BLEACHED HAIR AND A GOATEE WEARING A WHITE SWEATER AND A BLACK FLEECE JACKET?
WHAT ?
WHO ARE YOU?
FWOOOOM
HFF HFF
A MAN FITTING THAT DESCRIPTION ...
...JUST PASSED US IN A CLASSIC ROLLS-ROYCE!

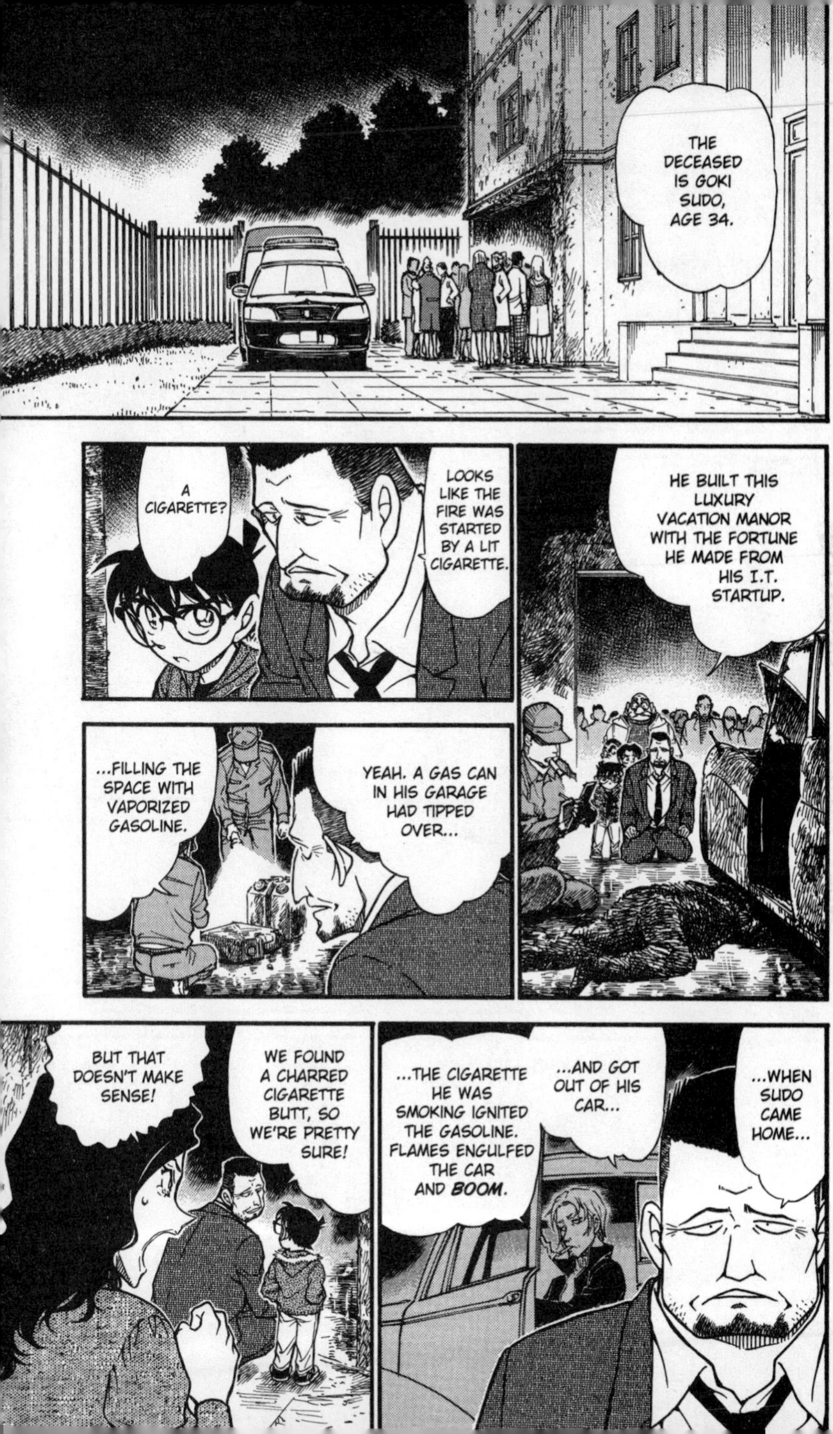
THE DECEASED IS GOKI SUDO, AGE 34.
HE BUILT THIS LUXURY VACATION MANOR WITH THE FORTUNE HE MADE FROM HIS I.T. STARTUP.
LOOKS LIKE THE FIRE WAS STARTED BY A LIT CIGARETTE.
A CIGARETTE?
YEAH. A GAS CAN IN HIS GARAGE HAD TIPPED OVER...
...FILLING THE SPACE WITH VAPORIZED GASOLINE.
...WHEN SUDO CAME HOME...
...AND GOT OUT OF HIS CAR...
...THE CIGARETTE HE WAS SMOKING IGNITED THE GASOLINE. FLAMES ENGULFED THE CAR AND ***BOOM***.
WE FOUND A CHARRED CIGARETTE BUTT, SO WE'RE PRETTY SURE!
BUT THAT DOESN'T MAKE SENSE!

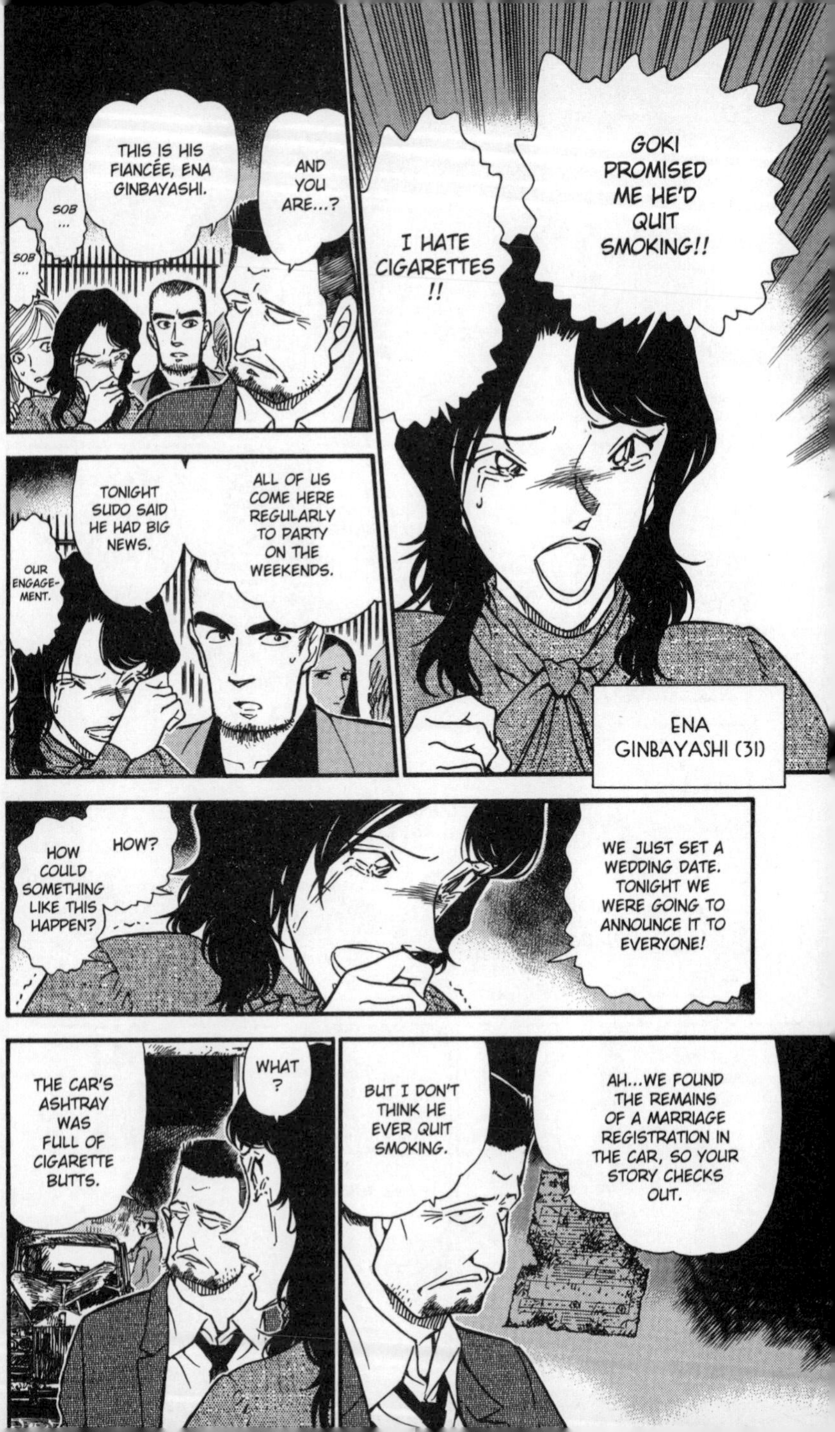
GOKI PROMISED ME HE'D QUIT SMOKING!!
I HATE CIGARETTES !!
ENA GINBAYASHI (31)
AND YOU ARE...?
THIS IS HIS FIANCÉE, ENA GINBAYASHI.
SOB ...
SOB ...
ALL OF US COME HERE REGULARLY TO PARTY ON THE WEEKENDS.
TONIGHT SUDO SAID HE HAD BIG NEWS.
OUR ENGAGE-MENT.
WE JUST SET A WEDDING DATE. TONIGHT WE WERE GOING TO ANNOUNCE IT TO EVERYONE!
HOW?
HOW COULD SOMETHING LIKE THIS HAPPEN?
AH...WE FOUND THE REMAINS OF A MARRIAGE REGISTRATION IN THE CAR, SO YOUR STORY CHECKS OUT.
BUT I DON'T THINK HE EVER QUIT SMOKING.
WHAT ?
THE CAR'S ASHTRAY WAS FULL OF CIGARETTE BUTTS.

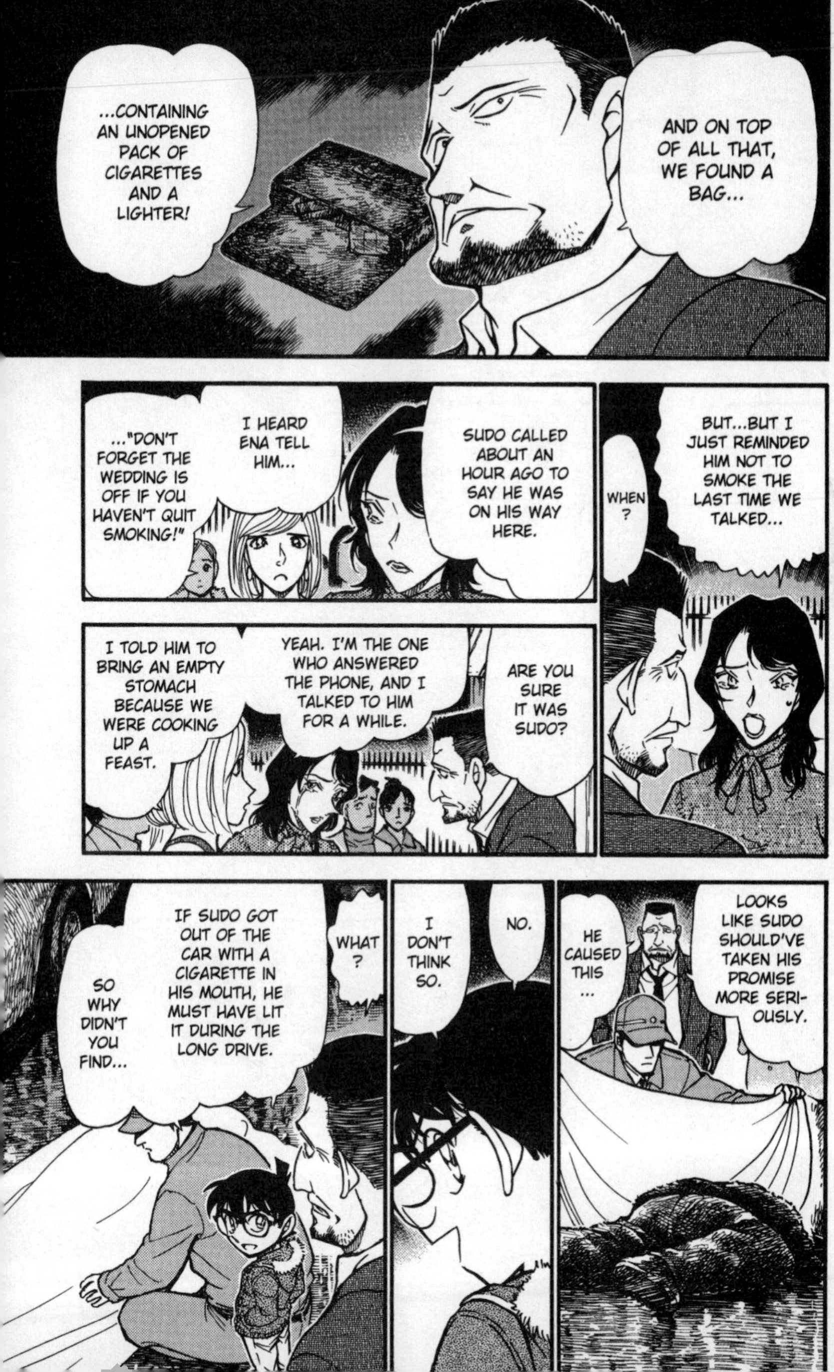
AND ON TOP OF ALL THAT, WE FOUND A BAG...
...CONTAINING AN UNOPENED PACK OF CIGARETTES AND A LIGHTER!
BUT...BUT I JUST REMINDED HIM NOT TO SMOKE THE LAST TIME WE TALKED...
WHEN?
SUDO CALLED ABOUT AN HOUR AGO TO SAY HE WAS ON HIS WAY HERE.
I HEARD ENA TELL HIM...
..."DON'T FORGET THE WEDDING IS OFF IF YOU HAVEN'T QUIT SMOKING!"
ARE YOU SURE IT WAS SUDO?
YEAH. I'M THE ONE WHO ANSWERED THE PHONE, AND I TALKED TO HIM FOR A WHILE.
I TOLD HIM TO BRING AN EMPTY STOMACH BECAUSE WE WERE COOKING UP A FEAST.
LOOKS LIKE SUDO SHOULD'VE TAKEN HIS PROMISE MORE SERI-OUSLY.
HE CAUSED THIS...
NO.
I DON'T THINK SO.
WHAT?
IF SUDO GOT OUT OF THE CAR WITH A CIGARETTE IN HIS MOUTH, HE MUST HAVE LIT IT DURING THE LONG DRIVE.
SO WHY DIDN'T YOU FIND...

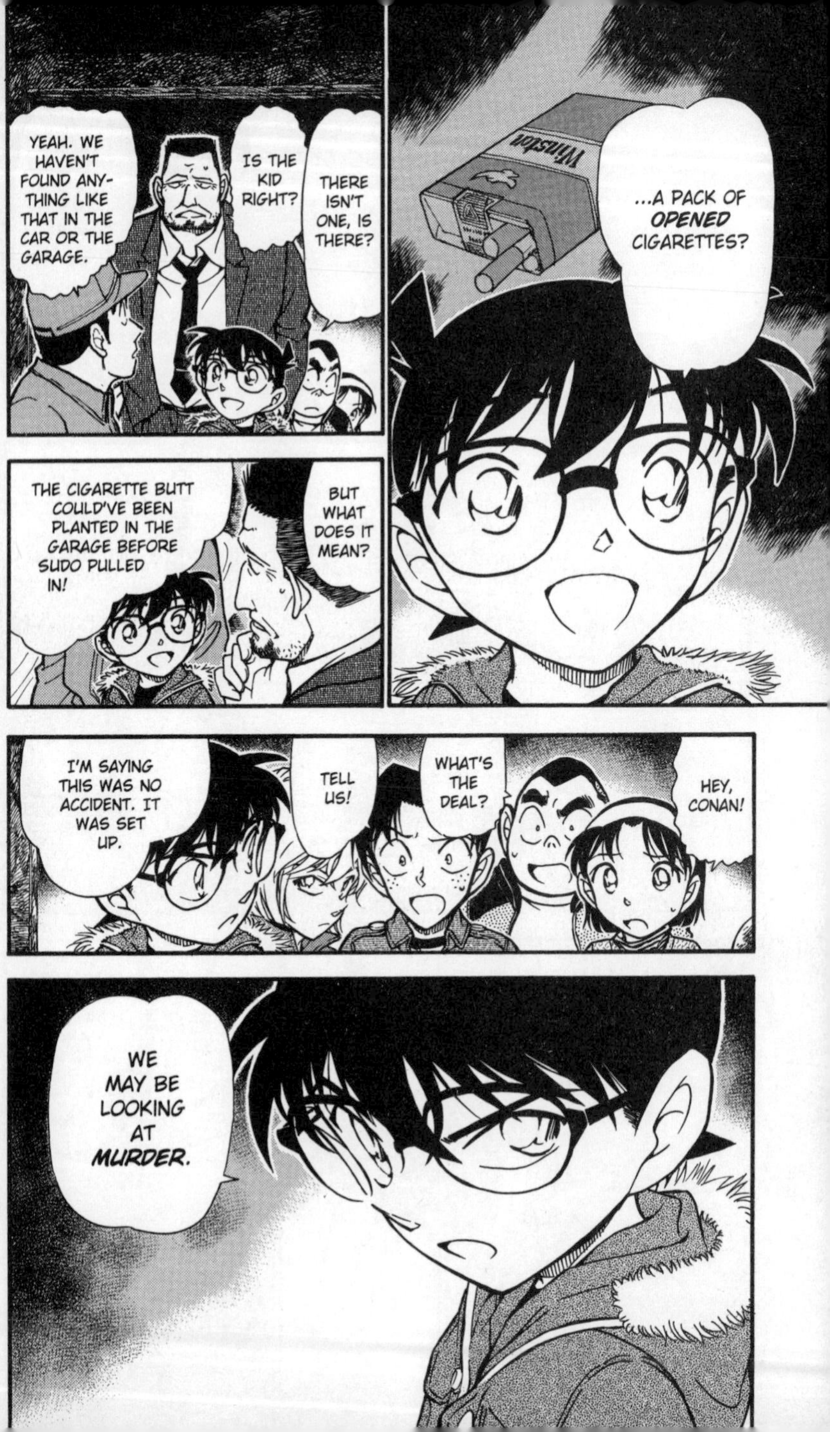
Winston
...A PACK OF OPENED CIGARETTES?
THERE ISN'T ONE, IS THERE?
IS THE KID RIGHT?
YEAH. WE HAVEN'T FOUND ANYTHING LIKE THAT IN THE CAR OR THE GARAGE.
BUT WHAT DOES IT MEAN?
THE CIGARETTE BUTT COULD'VE BEEN PLANTED IN THE GARAGE BEFORE SUDO PULLED IN!
HEY, CONAN!
WHAT'S THE DEAL?
TELL US!
I'M SAYING THIS WAS NO ACCIDENT. IT WAS SET UP.
WE MAY BE LOOKING AT MURDER.

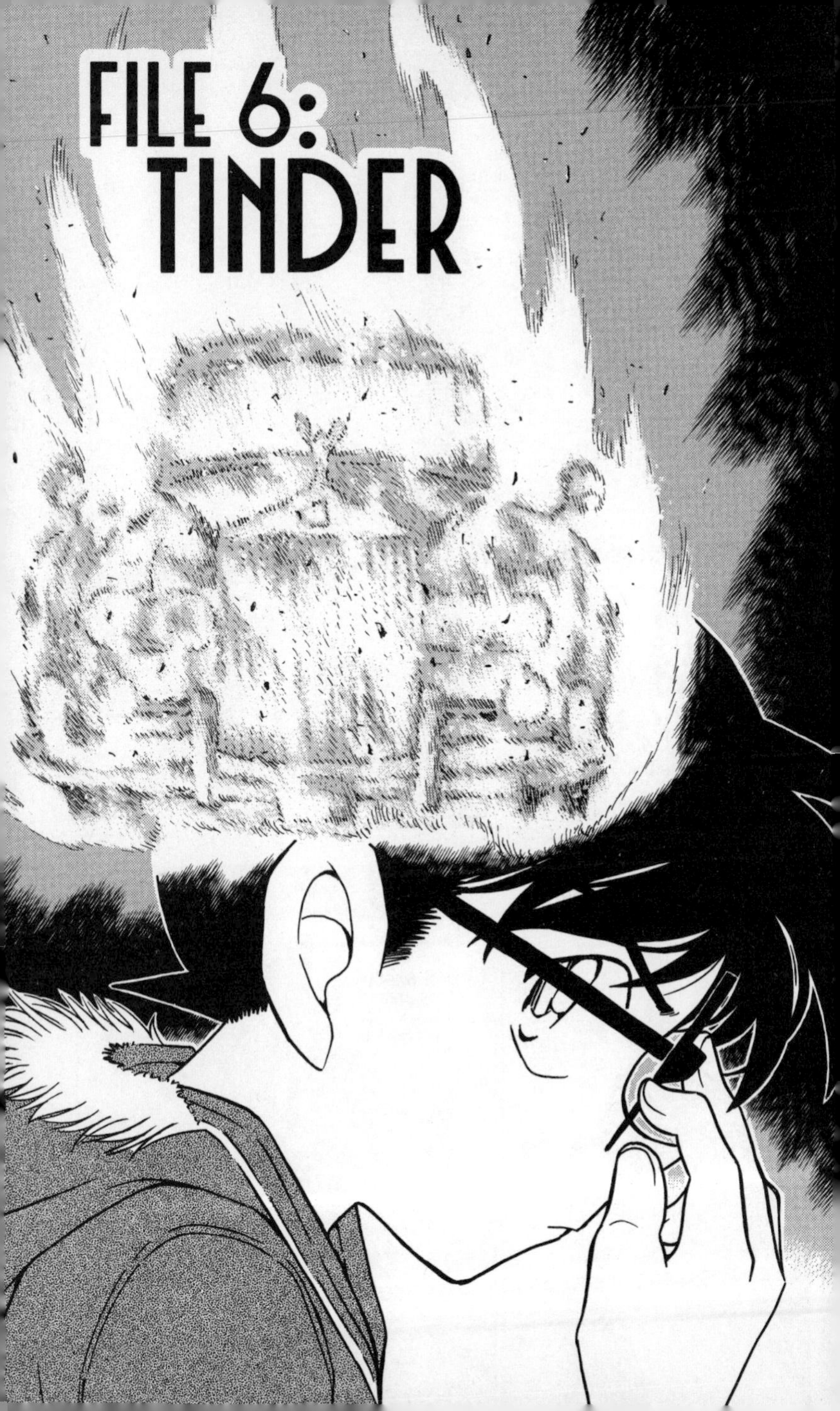
FILE 6:
TINDER

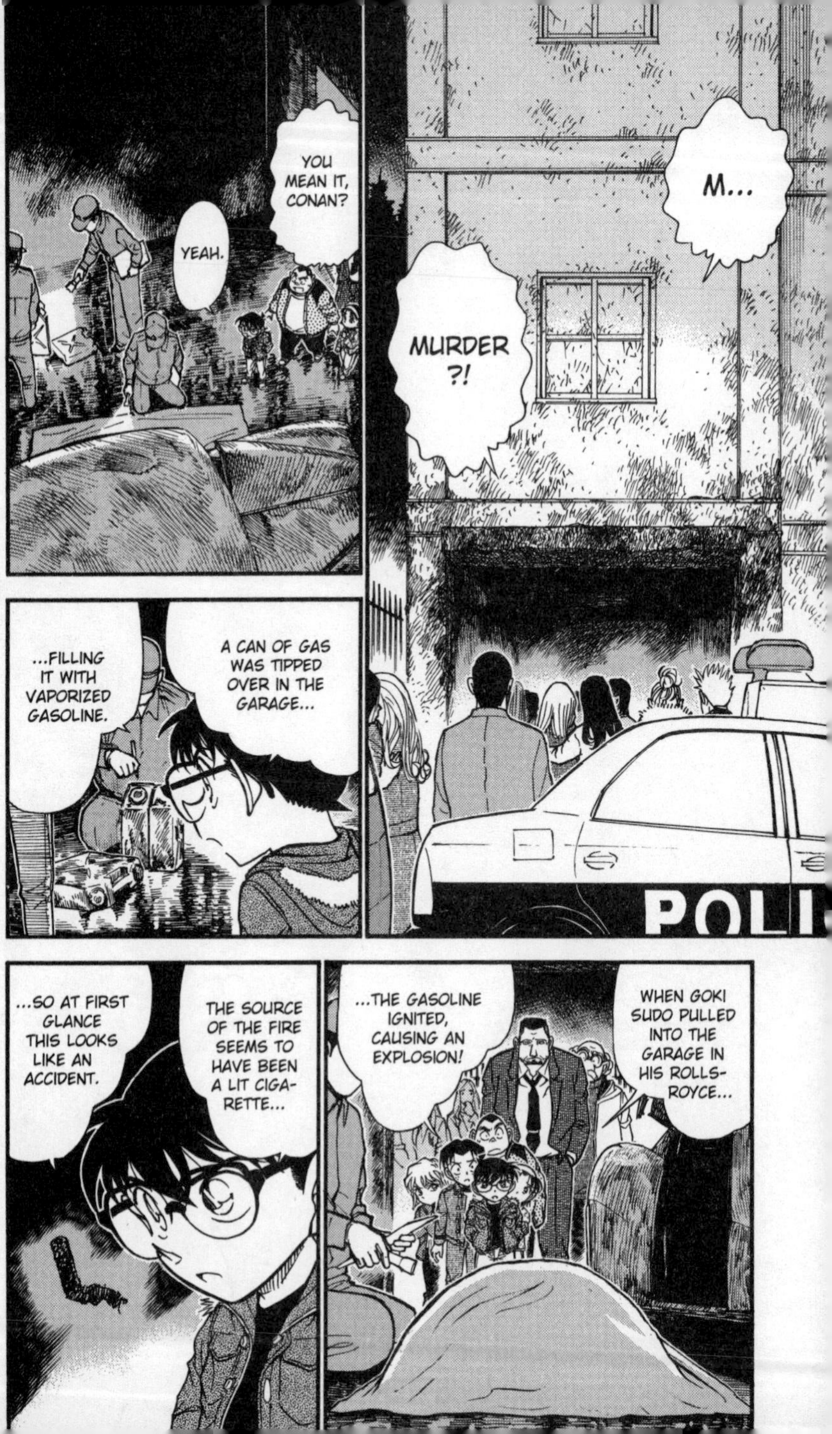
M...
MURDER ?!
POLI
YOU MEAN IT, CONAN?
YEAH.
A CAN OF GAS WAS TIPPED OVER IN THE GARAGE...
...FILLING IT WITH VAPORIZED GASOLINE.
WHEN GOKI SUDO PULLED INTO THE GARAGE IN HIS ROLLS-ROYCE...
...THE GASOLINE IGNITED, CAUSING AN EXPLOSION!
THE SOURCE OF THE FIRE SEEMS TO HAVE BEEN A LIT CIGA-RETTE...
...SO AT FIRST GLANCE THIS LOOKS LIKE AN ACCIDENT.

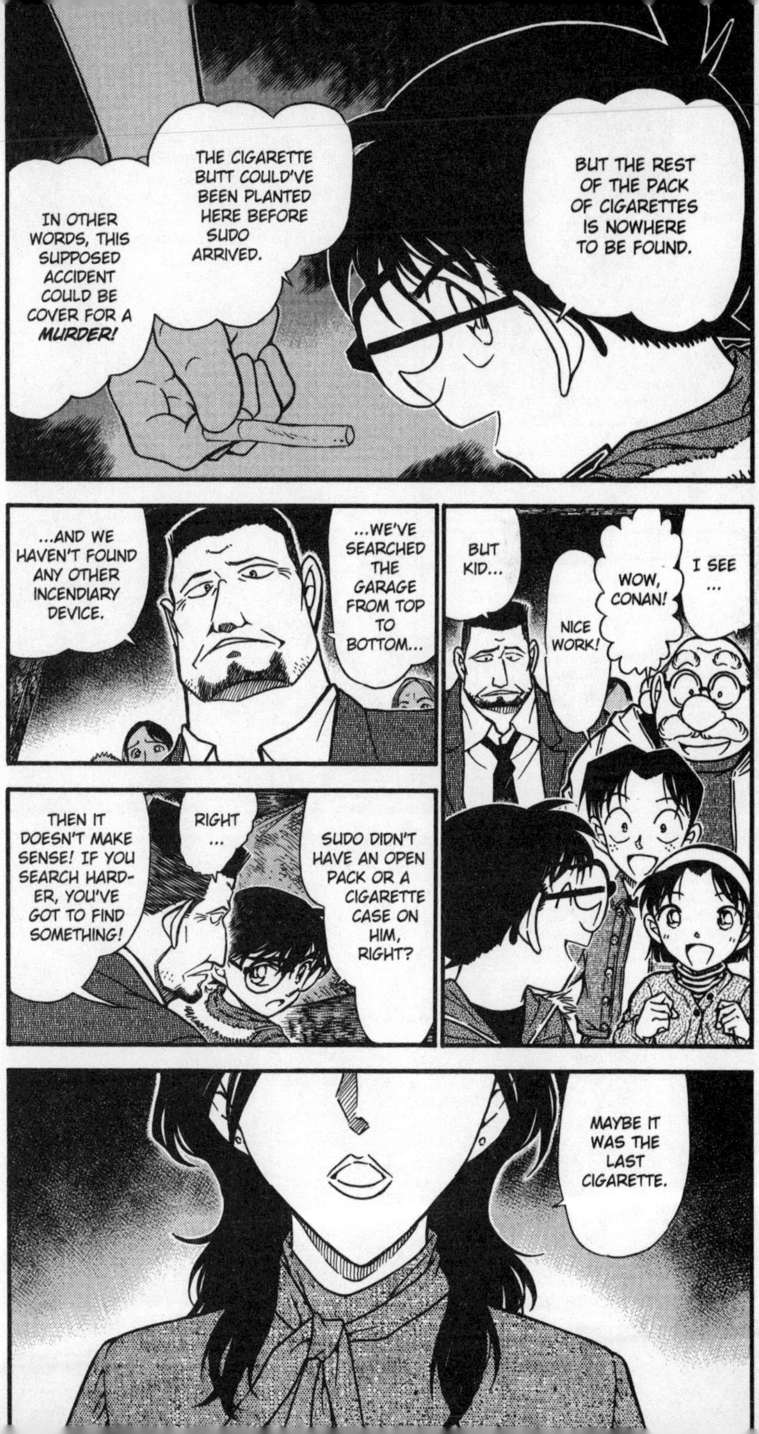

BUT THE REST OF THE PACK OF CIGARETTES IS NOWHERE TO BE FOUND.
THE CIGARETTE BUTT COULD'VE BEEN PLANTED HERE BEFORE SUDO ARRIVED.
IN OTHER WORDS, THIS SUPPOSED ACCIDENT COULD BE COVER FOR A ***MURDER!***
I SEE ...
WOW, CONAN!
NICE WORK!
BUT KID...
...WE'VE SEARCHED THE GARAGE FROM TOP TO BOTTOM...
...AND WE HAVEN'T FOUND ANY OTHER INCENDIARY DEVICE.
SUDO DIDN'T HAVE AN OPEN PACK OR A CIGARETTE CASE ON HIM, RIGHT?
RIGHT ...
THEN IT DOESN'T MAKE SENSE! IF YOU SEARCH HARD-ER, YOU'VE GOT TO FIND SOMETHING!
MAYBE IT WAS THE LAST CIGARETTE.

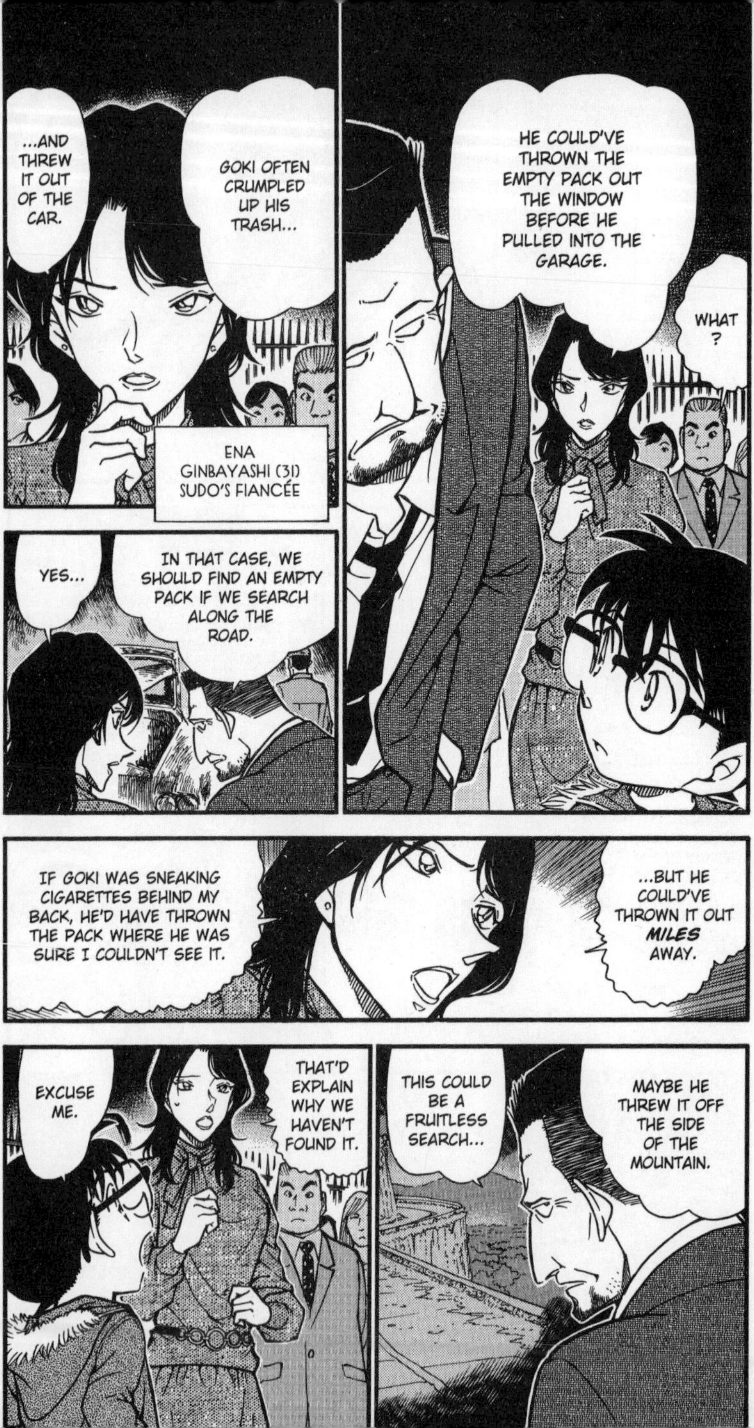

HE COULD'VE THROWN THE EMPTY PACK OUT THE WINDOW BEFORE HE PULLED INTO THE GARAGE.
WHAT?
GOKI OFTEN CRUMPLED UP HIS TRASH...
...AND THREW IT OUT OF THE CAR.
ENA GINBAYASHI (31) SUDO'S FIANCÉE
IN THAT CASE, WE SHOULD FIND AN EMPTY PACK IF WE SEARCH ALONG THE ROAD.
YES...
...BUT HE COULD'VE THROWN IT OUT *MILES* AWAY.
IF GOKI WAS SNEAKING CIGARETTES BEHIND MY BACK, HE'D HAVE THROWN THE PACK WHERE HE WAS SURE I COULDN'T SEE IT.
MAYBE HE THREW IT OFF THE SIDE OF THE MOUNTAIN.
THIS COULD BE A FRUITLESS SEARCH...
THAT'D EXPLAIN WHY WE HAVEN'T FOUND IT.
EXCUSE ME.

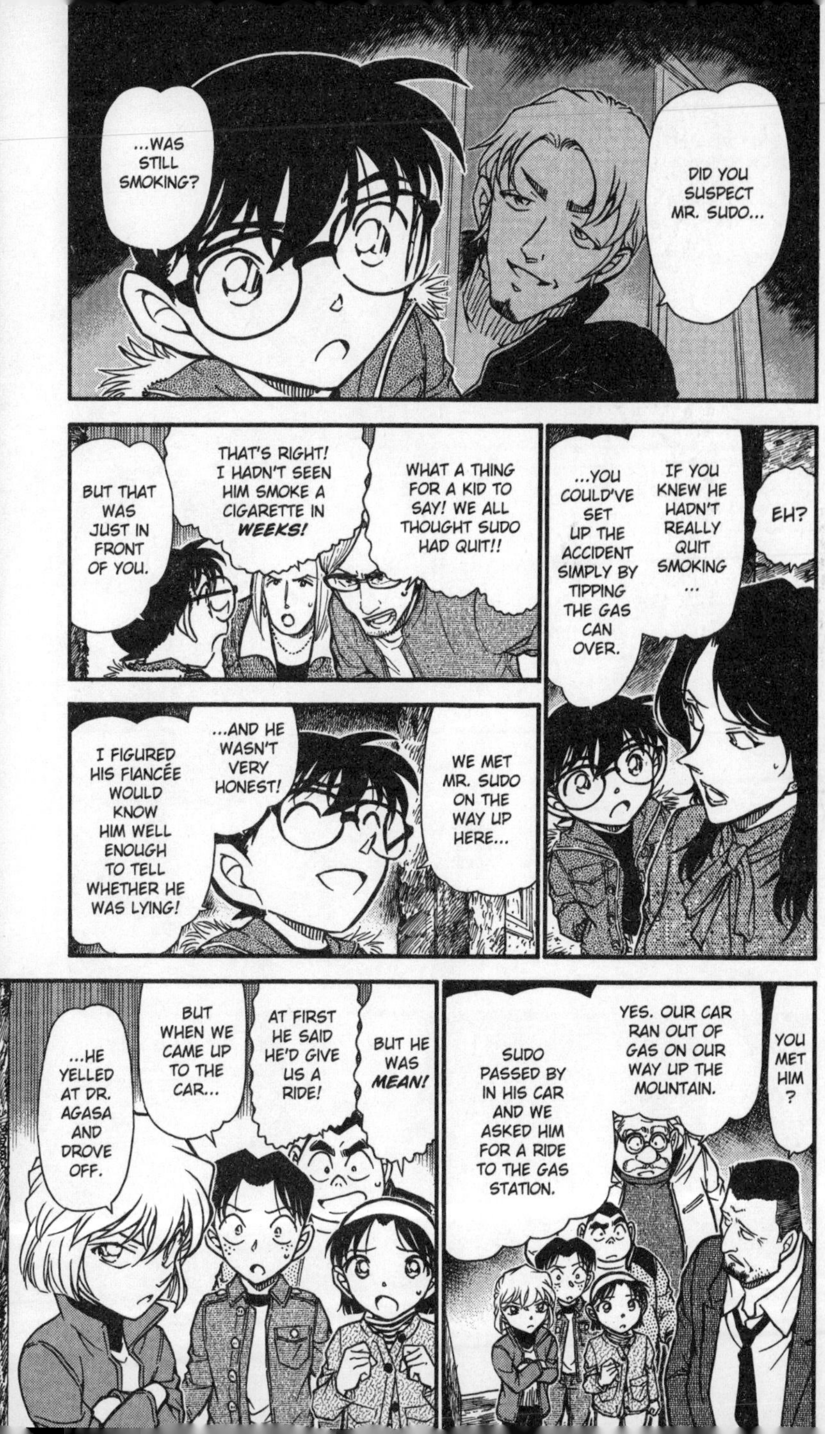
DID YOU SUSPECT MR. SUDO...
...WAS STILL SMOKING?
EH?
IF YOU KNEW HE HADN'T REALLY QUIT SMOKING...
...YOU COULD'VE SET UP THE ACCIDENT SIMPLY BY TIPPING THE GAS CAN OVER.
WHAT A THING FOR A KID TO SAY! WE ALL THOUGHT SUDO HAD QUIT!!
THAT'S RIGHT! I HADN'T SEEN HIM SMOKE A CIGARETTE IN *WEEKS!*
BUT THAT WAS JUST IN FRONT OF YOU.
WE MET MR. SUDO ON THE WAY UP HERE...
...AND HE WASN'T VERY HONEST!
I FIGURED HIS FIANCÉE WOULD KNOW HIM WELL ENOUGH TO TELL WHETHER HE WAS LYING!
YOU MET HIM?
YES. OUR CAR RAN OUT OF GAS ON OUR WAY UP THE MOUNTAIN.
SUDO PASSED BY IN HIS CAR AND WE ASKED HIM FOR A RIDE TO THE GAS STATION.
BUT HE WAS *MEAN!*
AT FIRST HE SAID HE'D GIVE US A RIDE!
BUT WHEN WE CAME UP TO THE CAR...
...HE YELLED AT DR. AGASA AND DROVE OFF.

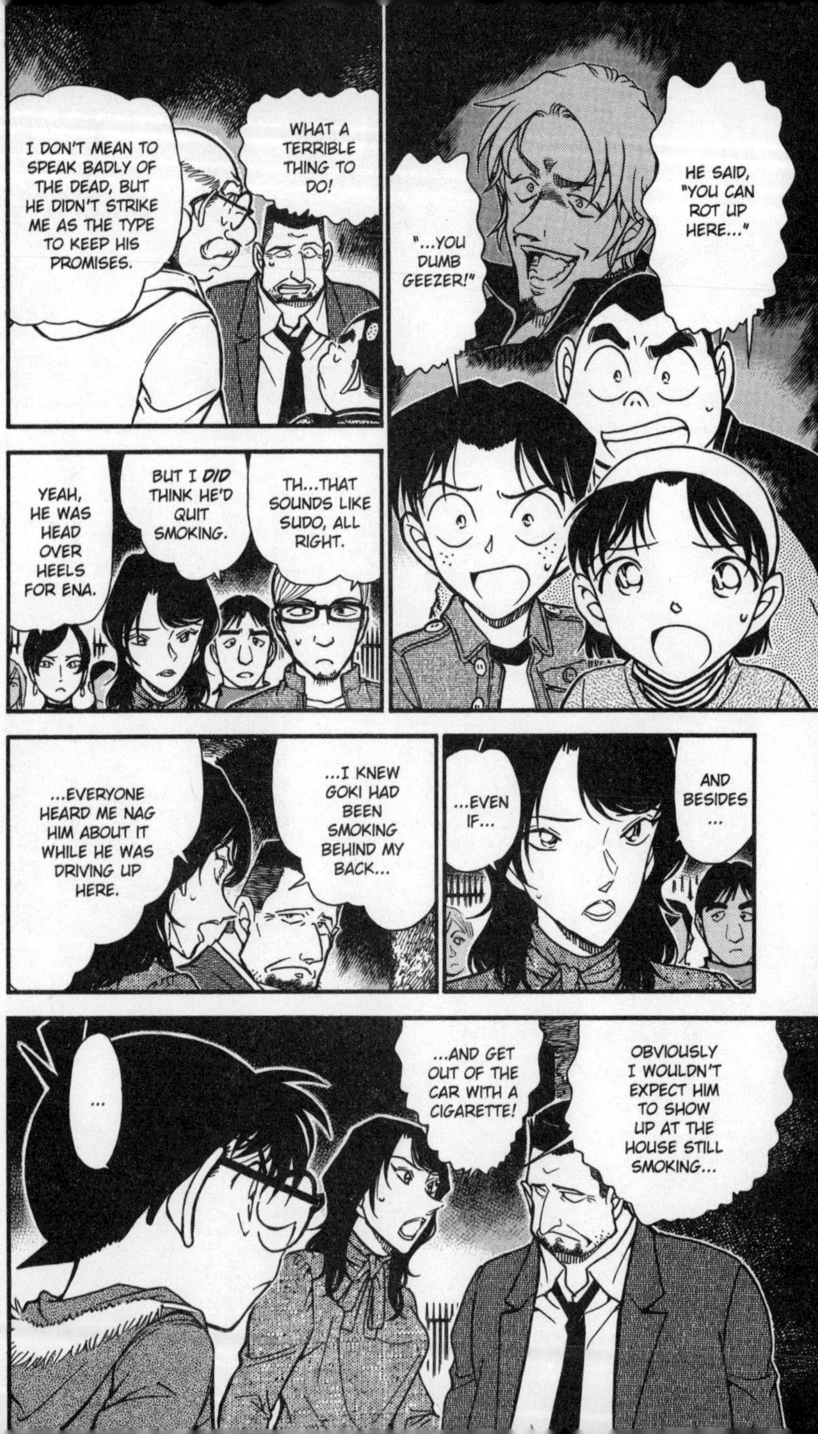
HE SAID, "YOU CAN ROT UP HERE..."
"...YOU DUMB GEEZER!"
WHAT A TERRIBLE THING TO DO!
I DON'T MEAN TO SPEAK BADLY OF THE DEAD, BUT HE DIDN'T STRIKE ME AS THE TYPE TO KEEP HIS PROMISES.
TH...THAT SOUNDS LIKE SUDO, ALL RIGHT.
BUT I *DID* THINK HE'D QUIT SMOKING.
YEAH, HE WAS HEAD OVER HEELS FOR ENA.
AND BESIDES...
...EVEN IF...
...I KNEW GOKI HAD BEEN SMOKING BEHIND MY BACK...
...EVERYONE HEARD ME NAG HIM ABOUT IT WHILE HE WAS DRIVING UP HERE.
OBVIOUSLY I WOULDN'T EXPECT HIM TO SHOW UP AT THE HOUSE STILL SMOKING...
...AND GET OUT OF THE CAR WITH A CIGARETTE!
...

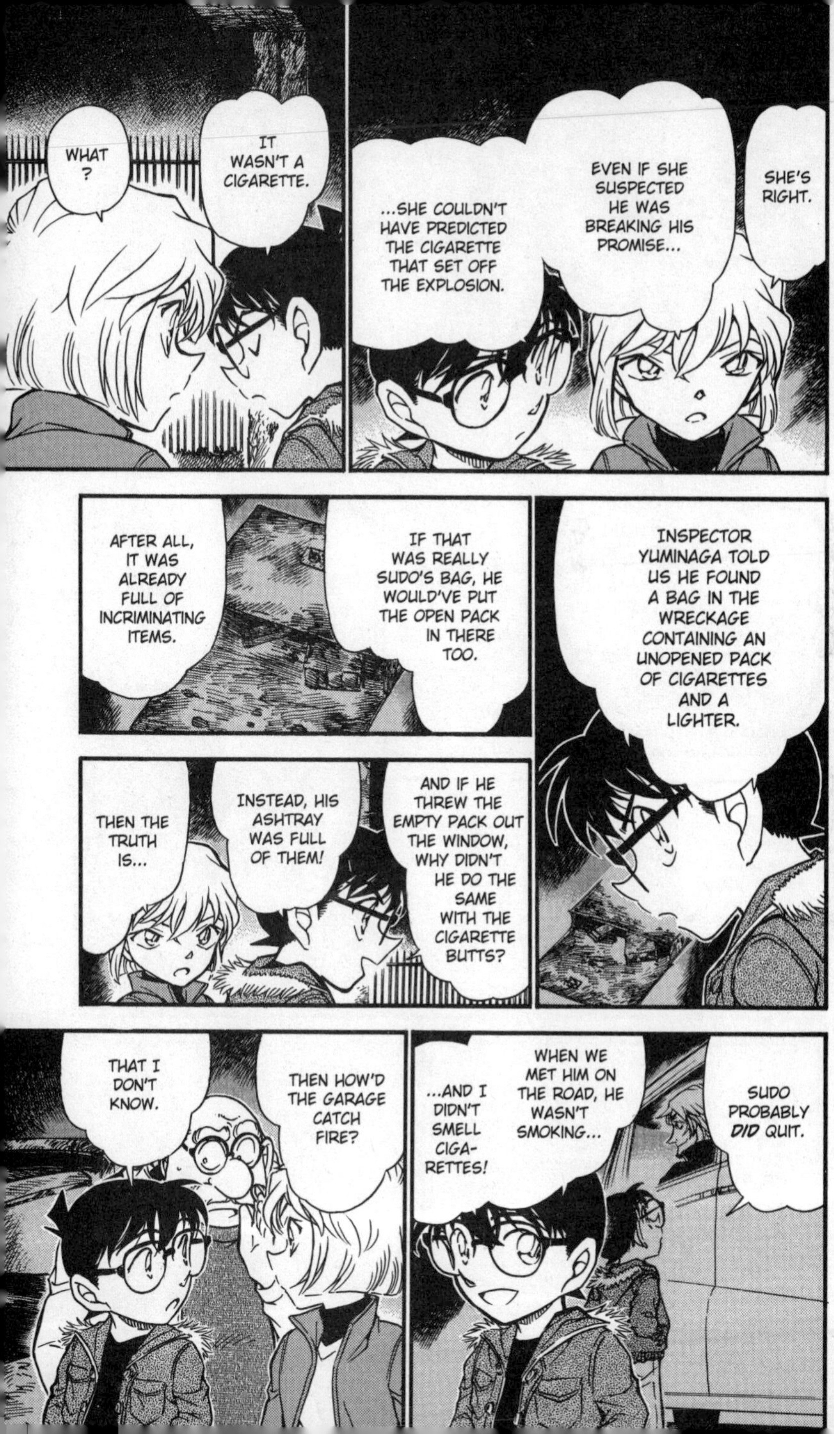
SHE'S RIGHT.
EVEN IF SHE SUSPECTED HE WAS BREAKING HIS PROMISE...
...SHE COULDN'T HAVE PREDICTED THE CIGARETTE THAT SET OFF THE EXPLOSION.
IT WASN'T A CIGARETTE.
WHAT?
INSPECTOR YUMINAGA TOLD US HE FOUND A BAG IN THE WRECKAGE CONTAINING AN UNOPENED PACK OF CIGARETTES AND A LIGHTER.
IF THAT WAS REALLY SUDO'S BAG, HE WOULD'VE PUT THE OPEN PACK IN THERE TOO.
AFTER ALL, IT WAS ALREADY FULL OF INCRIMINATING ITEMS.
AND IF HE THREW THE EMPTY PACK OUT THE WINDOW, WHY DIDN'T HE DO THE SAME WITH THE CIGARETTE BUTTS?
INSTEAD, HIS ASHTRAY WAS FULL OF THEM!
THEN THE TRUTH IS...
SUDO PROBABLY *DID* QUIT.
WHEN WE MET HIM ON THE ROAD, HE WASN'T SMOKING...
...AND I DIDN'T SMELL CIGA-RETTES!
THEN HOW'D THE GARAGE CATCH FIRE?
THAT I DON'T KNOW.

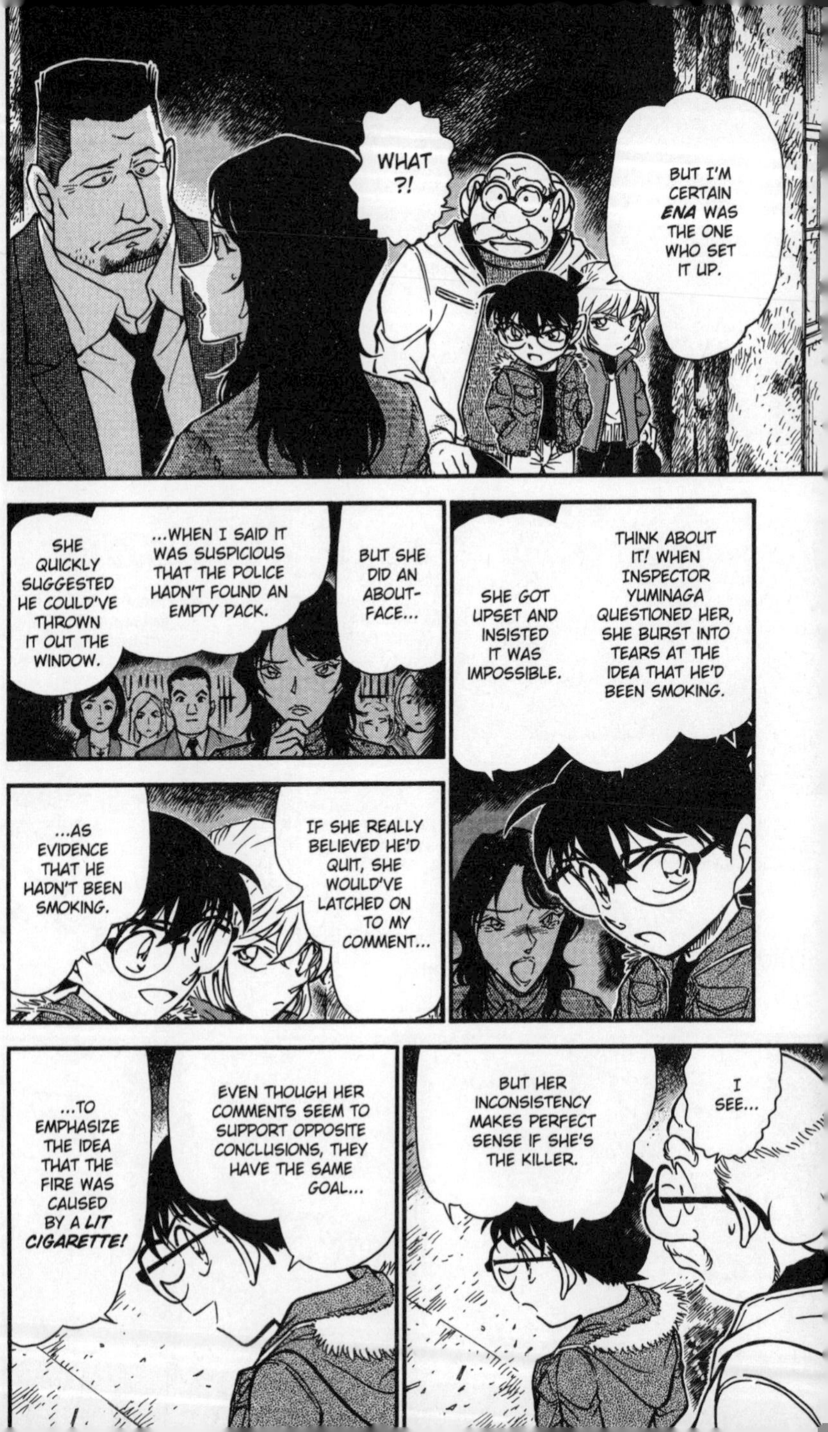
BUT I'M CERTAIN *ENA* WAS THE ONE WHO SET IT UP.
WHAT ?!
THINK ABOUT IT! WHEN INSPECTOR YUMINAGA QUESTIONED HER, SHE BURST INTO TEARS AT THE IDEA THAT HE'D BEEN SMOKING.
SHE GOT UPSET AND INSISTED IT WAS IMPOSSIBLE.
BUT SHE DID AN ABOUT-FACE...
...WHEN I SAID IT WAS SUSPICIOUS THAT THE POLICE HADN'T FOUND AN EMPTY PACK.
SHE QUICKLY SUGGESTED HE COULD'VE THROWN IT OUT THE WINDOW.
IF SHE REALLY BELIEVED HE'D QUIT, SHE WOULD'VE LATCHED ON TO MY COMMENT...
...AS EVIDENCE THAT HE HADN'T BEEN SMOKING.
I SEE...
BUT HER INCONSISTENCY MAKES PERFECT SENSE IF SHE'S THE KILLER.
EVEN THOUGH HER COMMENTS SEEM TO SUPPORT OPPOSITE CONCLUSIONS, THEY HAVE THE SAME GOAL...
...TO EMPHASIZE THE IDEA THAT THE FIRE WAS CAUSED BY A *LIT CIGARETTE!*

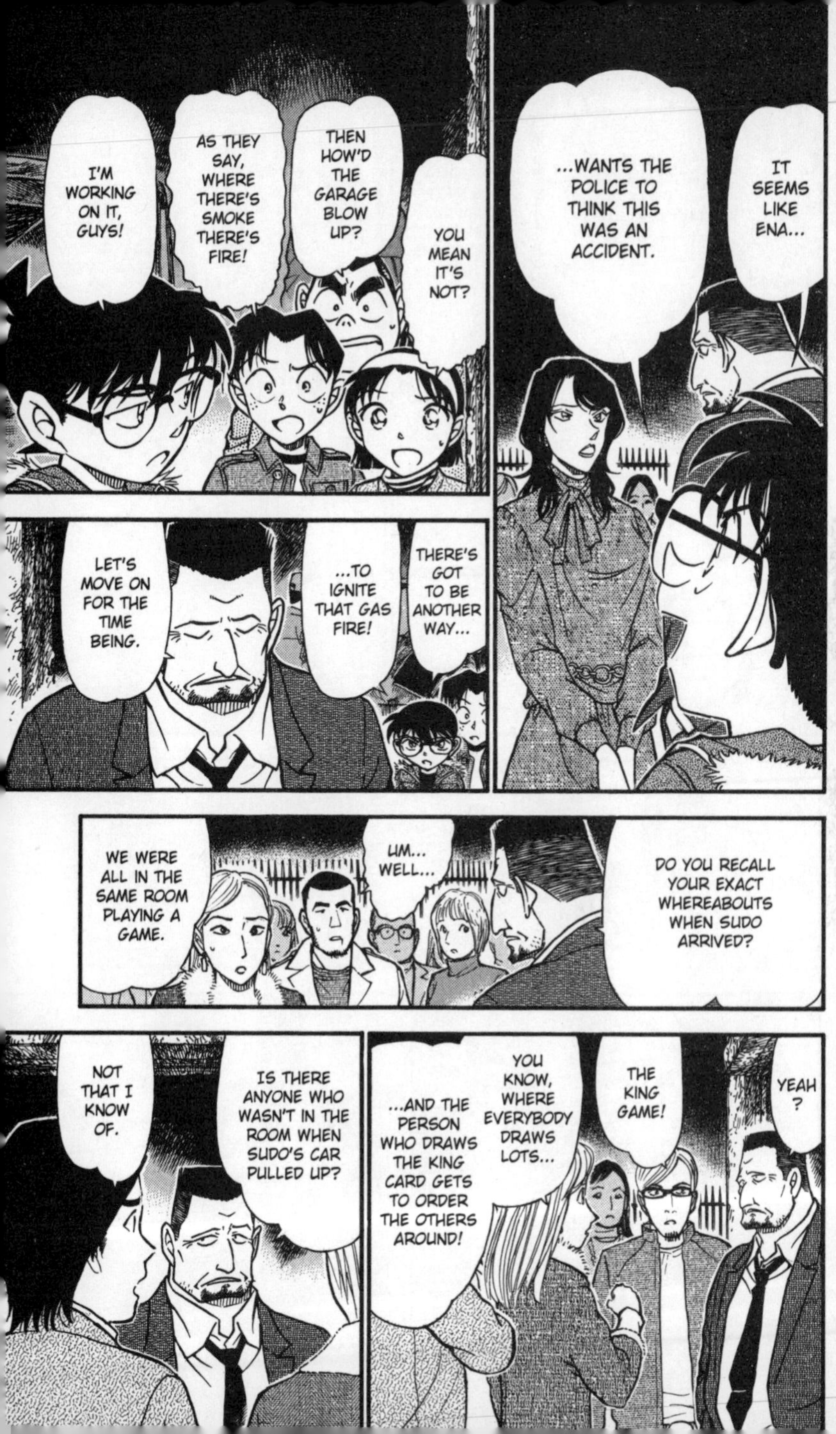
IT SEEMS LIKE ENA...
...WANTS THE POLICE TO THINK THIS WAS AN ACCIDENT.
YOU MEAN IT'S NOT?
THEN HOW'D THE GARAGE BLOW UP?
AS THEY SAY, WHERE THERE'S SMOKE THERE'S FIRE!
I'M WORKING ON IT, GUYS!
THERE'S GOT TO BE ANOTHER WAY...
...TO IGNITE THAT GAS FIRE!
LET'S MOVE ON FOR THE TIME BEING.
DO YOU RECALL YOUR EXACT WHEREABOUTS WHEN SUDO ARRIVED?
UM... WELL...
WE WERE ALL IN THE SAME ROOM PLAYING A GAME.
YEAH?
THE KING GAME!
YOU KNOW, WHERE EVERYBODY DRAWS LOTS...
...AND THE PERSON WHO DRAWS THE KING CARD GETS TO ORDER THE OTHERS AROUND!
IS THERE ANYONE WHO WASN'T IN THE ROOM WHEN SUDO'S CAR PULLED UP?
NOT THAT I KNOW OF.

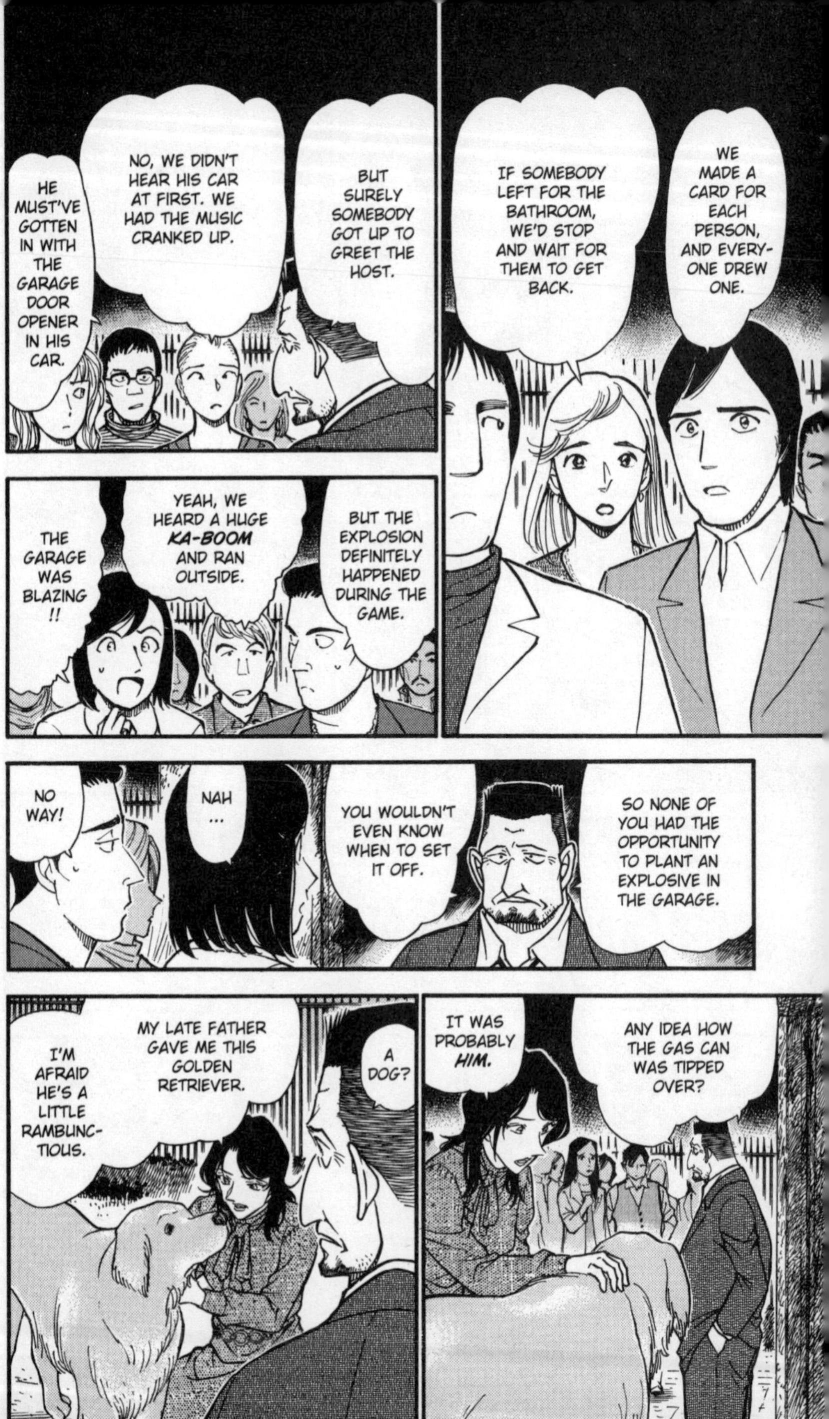
WE MADE A CARD FOR EACH PERSON, AND EVERY-ONE DREW ONE.
IF SOMEBODY LEFT FOR THE BATHROOM, WE'D STOP AND WAIT FOR THEM TO GET BACK.
BUT SURELY SOMEBODY GOT UP TO GREET THE HOST.
NO, WE DIDN'T HEAR HIS CAR AT FIRST. WE HAD THE MUSIC CRANKED UP.
HE MUST'VE GOTTEN IN WITH THE GARAGE DOOR OPENER IN HIS CAR.
BUT THE EXPLOSION DEFINITELY HAPPENED DURING THE GAME.
YEAH, WE HEARD A HUGE ***KA-BOOM*** AND RAN OUTSIDE.
THE GARAGE WAS BLAZING!!
SO NONE OF YOU HAD THE OPPORTUNITY TO PLANT AN EXPLOSIVE IN THE GARAGE.
YOU WOULDN'T EVEN KNOW WHEN TO SET IT OFF.
NAH...
NO WAY!
ANY IDEA HOW THE GAS CAN WAS TIPPED OVER?
IT WAS PROBABLY ***HIM.***
A DOG?
MY LATE FATHER GAVE ME THIS GOLDEN RETRIEVER.
I'M AFRAID HE'S A LITTLE RAMBUNC-TIOUS.

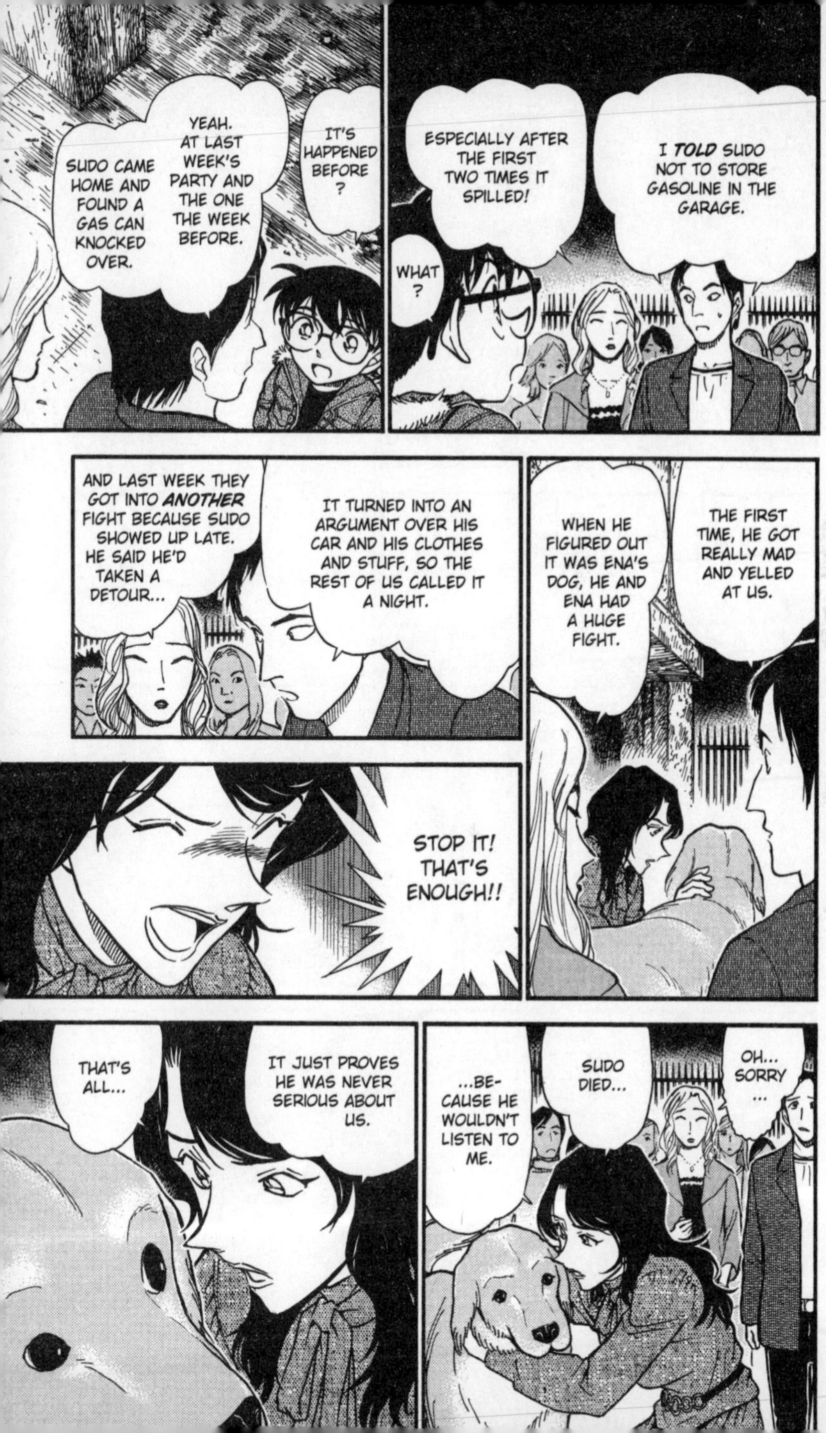

I *TOLD* SUDO NOT TO STORE GASOLINE IN THE GARAGE.
ESPECIALLY AFTER THE FIRST TWO TIMES IT SPILLED!
WHAT?
IT'S HAPPENED BEFORE?
YEAH. AT LAST WEEK'S PARTY AND THE ONE THE WEEK BEFORE.
SUDO CAME HOME AND FOUND A GAS CAN KNOCKED OVER.
THE FIRST TIME, HE GOT REALLY MAD AND YELLED AT US.
WHEN HE FIGURED OUT IT WAS ENA'S DOG, HE AND ENA HAD A HUGE FIGHT.
IT TURNED INTO AN ARGUMENT OVER HIS CAR AND HIS CLOTHES AND STUFF, SO THE REST OF US CALLED IT A NIGHT.
AND LAST WEEK THEY GOT INTO *ANOTHER* FIGHT BECAUSE SUDO SHOWED UP LATE. HE SAID HE'D TAKEN A DETOUR...
STOP IT! THAT'S ENOUGH!!
OH... SORRY...
SUDO DIED...
...BE-CAUSE HE WOULDN'T LISTEN TO ME.
IT JUST PROVES HE WAS NEVER SERIOUS ABOUT US.
THAT'S ALL...

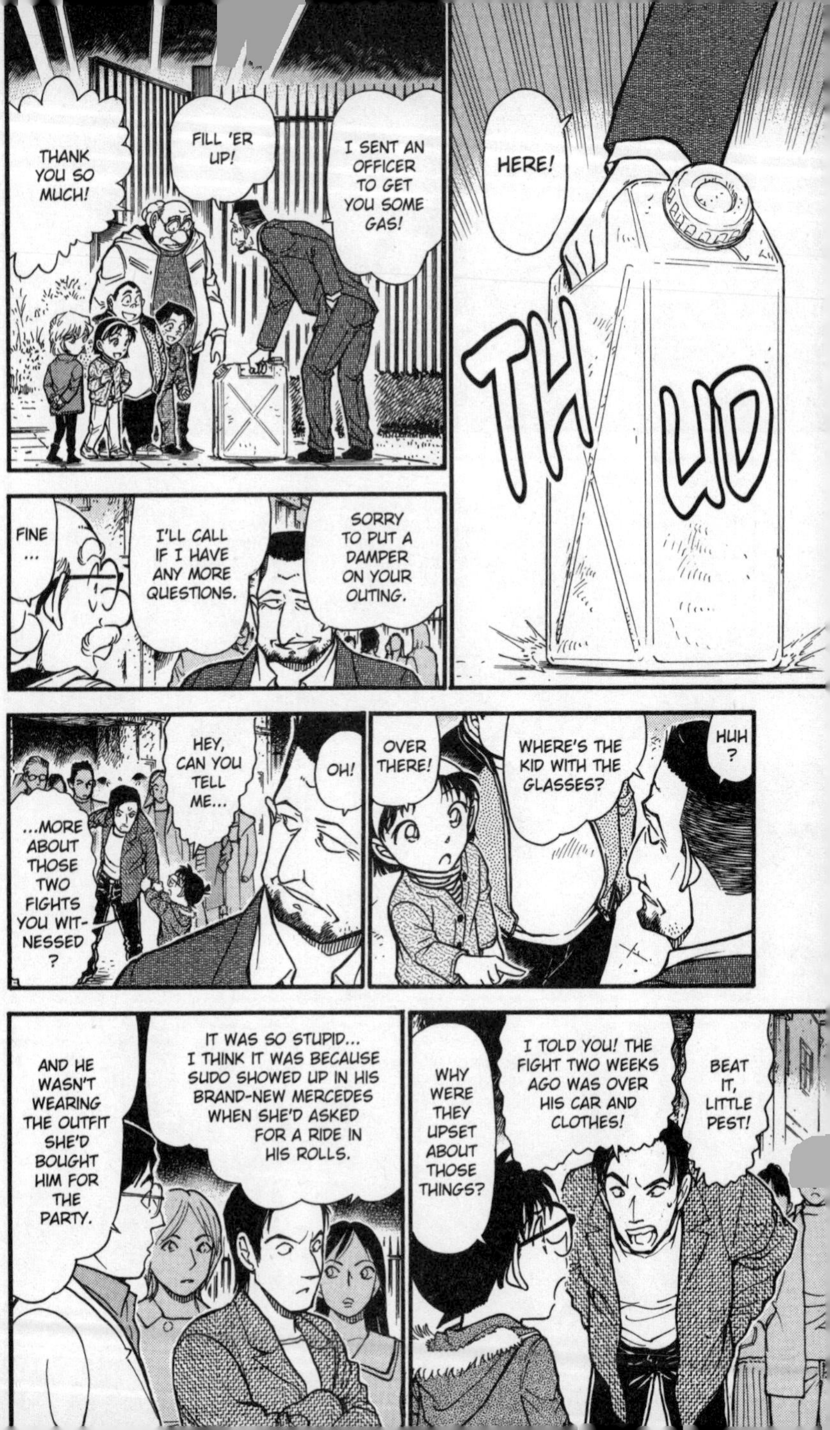
HERE!
THUD
I SENT AN OFFICER TO GET YOU SOME GAS!
FILL 'ER UP!
THANK YOU SO MUCH!
SORRY TO PUT A DAMPER ON YOUR OUTING.
I'LL CALL IF I HAVE ANY MORE QUESTIONS.
FINE...
HUH?
WHERE'S THE KID WITH THE GLASSES?
OVER THERE!
OH!
HEY, CAN YOU TELL ME...
...MORE ABOUT THOSE TWO FIGHTS YOU WITNESSED?
BEAT IT, LITTLE PEST!
I TOLD YOU! THE FIGHT TWO WEEKS AGO WAS OVER HIS CAR AND CLOTHES!
WHY WERE THEY UPSET ABOUT THOSE THINGS?
IT WAS SO STUPID... I THINK IT WAS BECAUSE SUDO SHOWED UP IN HIS BRAND-NEW MERCEDES WHEN SHE'D ASKED FOR A RIDE IN HIS ROLLS.
AND HE WASN'T WEARING THE OUTFIT SHE'D BOUGHT HIM FOR THE PARTY.

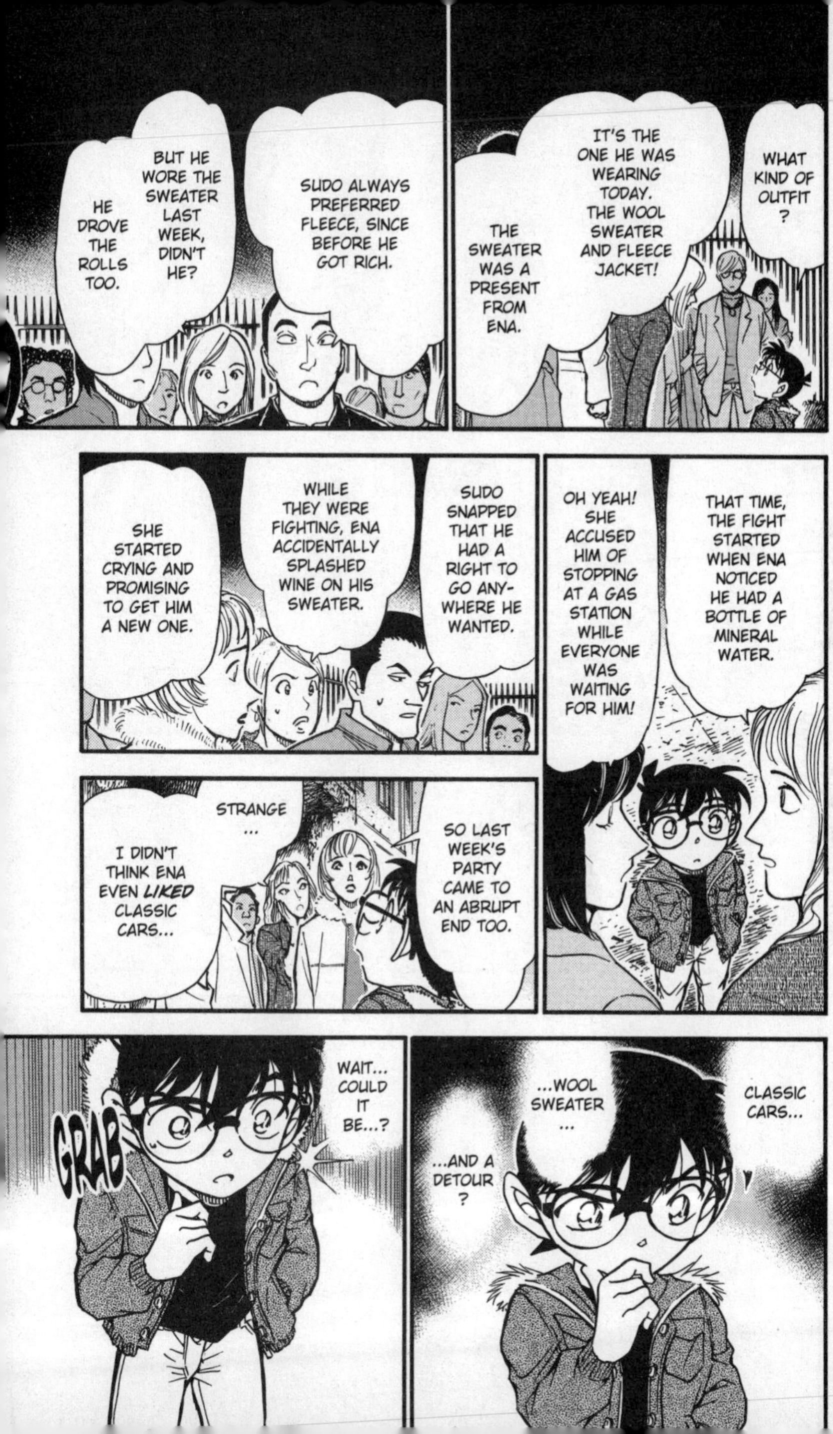
WHAT KIND OF OUTFIT?
IT'S THE ONE HE WAS WEARING TODAY. THE WOOL SWEATER AND FLEECE JACKET!
THE SWEATER WAS A PRESENT FROM ENA.
SUDO ALWAYS PREFERRED FLEECE, SINCE BEFORE HE GOT RICH.
BUT HE WORE THE SWEATER LAST WEEK, DIDN'T HE?
HE DROVE THE ROLLS TOO.
THAT TIME, THE FIGHT STARTED WHEN ENA NOTICED HE HAD A BOTTLE OF MINERAL WATER.
OH YEAH! SHE ACCUSED HIM OF STOPPING AT A GAS STATION WHILE EVERYONE WAS WAITING FOR HIM!
SUDO SNAPPED THAT HE HAD A RIGHT TO GO ANY-WHERE HE WANTED.
WHILE THEY WERE FIGHTING, ENA ACCIDENTALLY SPLASHED WINE ON HIS SWEATER.
SHE STARTED CRYING AND PROMISING TO GET HIM A NEW ONE.
SO LAST WEEK'S PARTY CAME TO AN ABRUPT END TOO.
STRANGE...
I DIDN'T THINK ENA EVEN *LIKED* CLASSIC CARS...
CLASSIC CARS...
...WOOL SWEATER...
...AND A DETOUR?
WAIT... COULD IT BE...?
GRAB

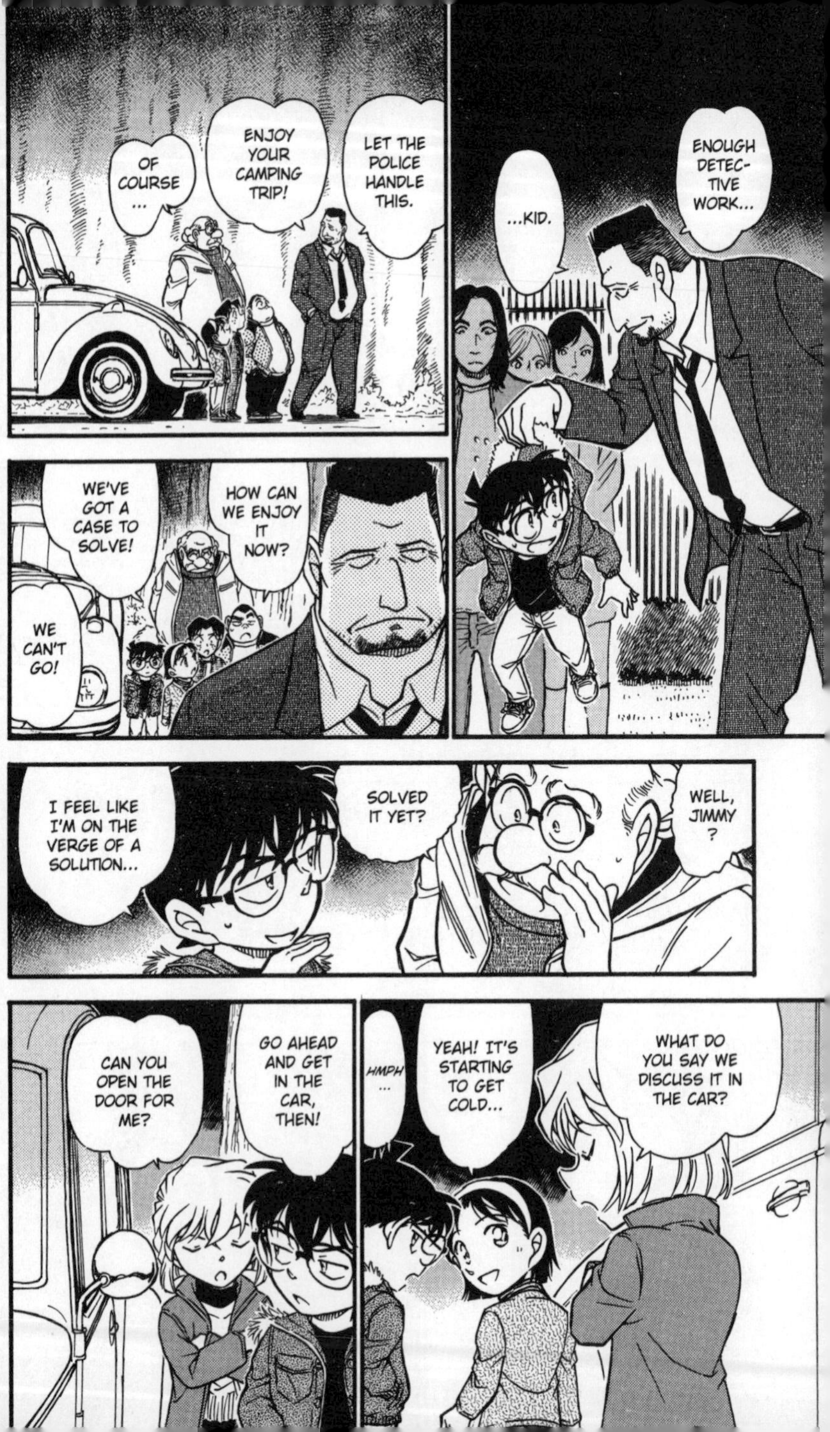
ENOUGH DETECTIVE WORK...
...KID.
LET THE POLICE HANDLE THIS.
ENJOY YOUR CAMPING TRIP!
OF COURSE ...
HOW CAN WE ENJOY IT NOW?
WE'VE GOT A CASE TO SOLVE!
WE CAN'T GO!
WELL, JIMMY?
SOLVED IT YET?
I FEEL LIKE I'M ON THE VERGE OF A SOLUTION...
WHAT DO YOU SAY WE DISCUSS IT IN THE CAR?
YEAH! IT'S STARTING TO GET COLD...
HMPH ...
GO AHEAD AND GET IN THE CAR, THEN!
CAN YOU OPEN THE DOOR FOR ME?

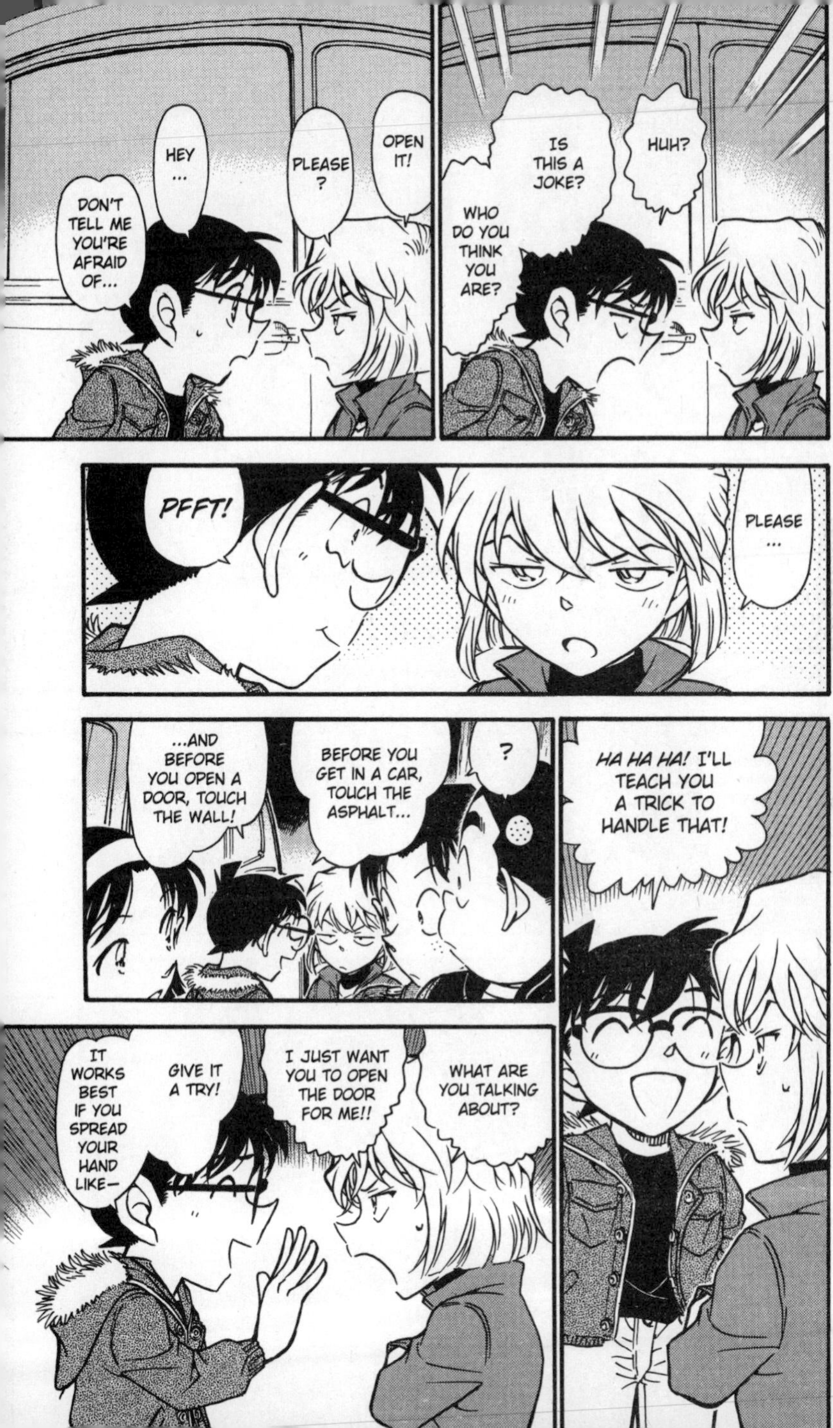
HUH?
IS THIS A JOKE?
WHO DO YOU THINK YOU ARE?
OPEN IT!
PLEASE ?
HEY ...
DON'T TELL ME YOU'RE AFRAID OF...
PLEASE ...
PFFT!
HA HA HA! I'LL TEACH YOU A TRICK TO HANDLE THAT!
?
BEFORE YOU GET IN A CAR, TOUCH THE ASPHALT...
...AND BEFORE YOU OPEN A DOOR, TOUCH THE WALL!
WHAT ARE YOU TALKING ABOUT?
I JUST WANT YOU TO OPEN THE DOOR FOR ME!!
GIVE IT A TRY!
IT WORKS BEST IF YOU SPREAD YOUR HAND LIKE—

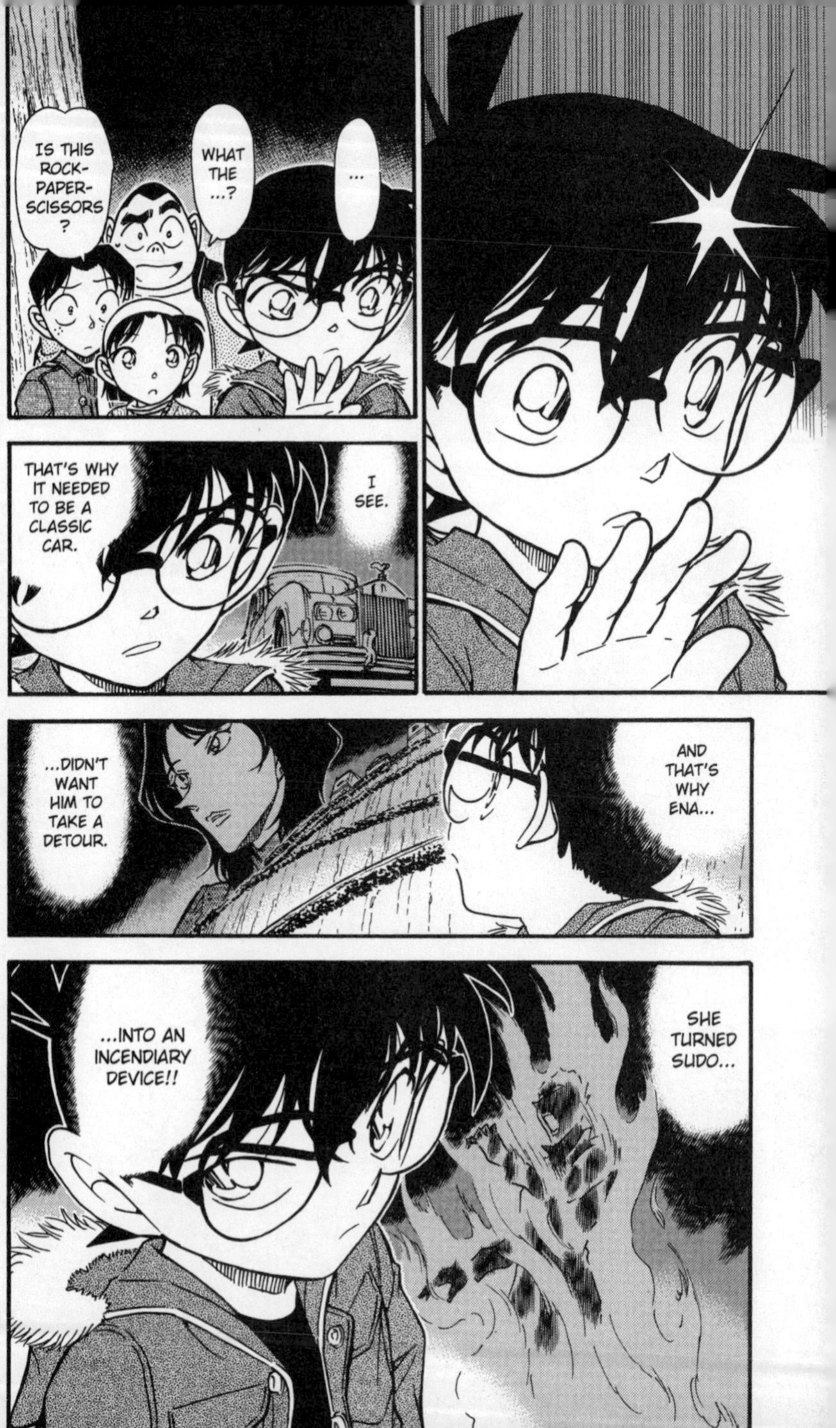
...
WHAT THE ...?
IS THIS ROCK-PAPER-SCISSORS?
I SEE.
THAT'S WHY IT NEEDED TO BE A CLASSIC CAR.
AND THAT'S WHY ENA...
...DIDN'T WANT HIM TO TAKE A DETOUR.
SHE TURNED SUDO...
...INTO AN INCENDIARY DEVICE!!

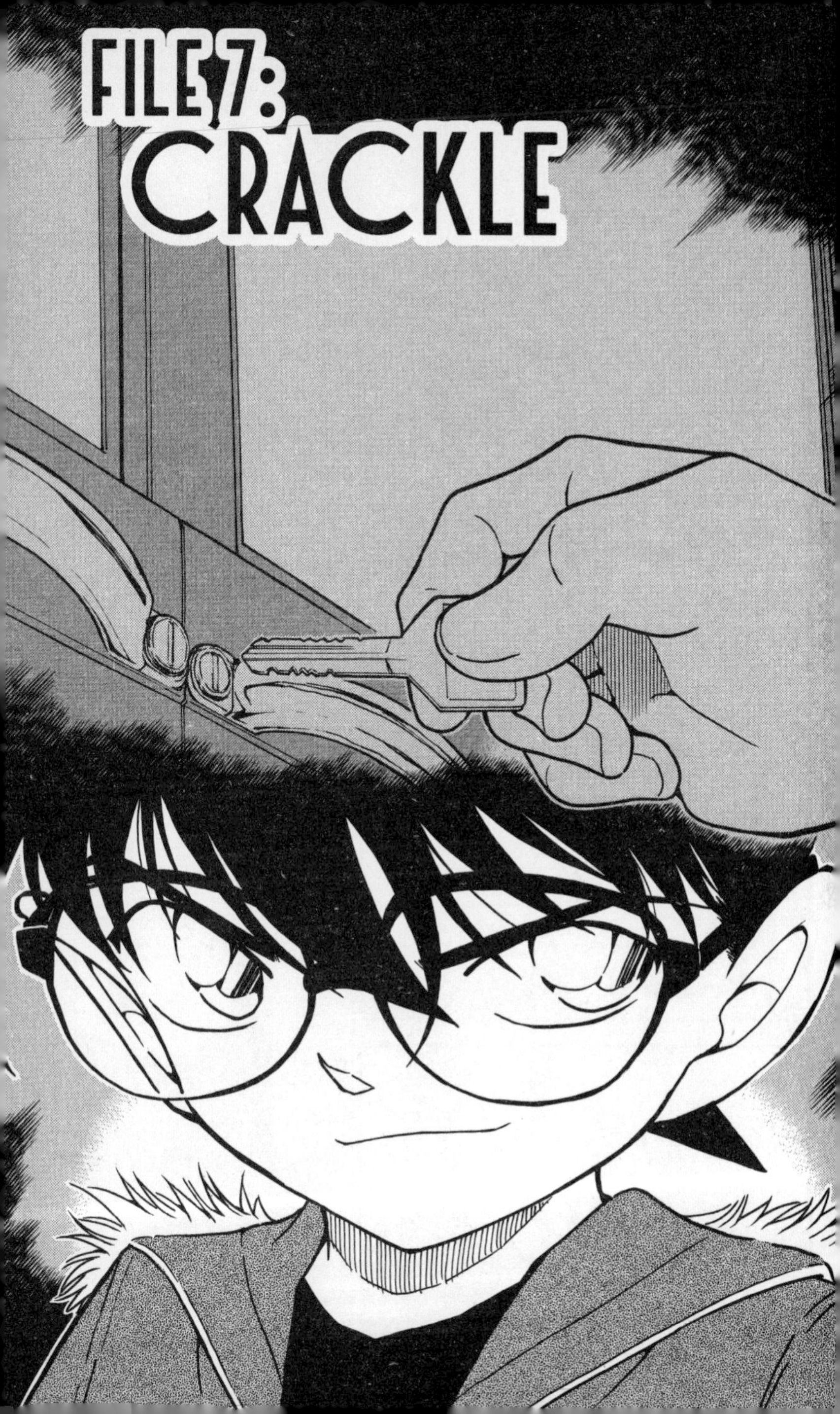
FILE 7:
CRACKLE

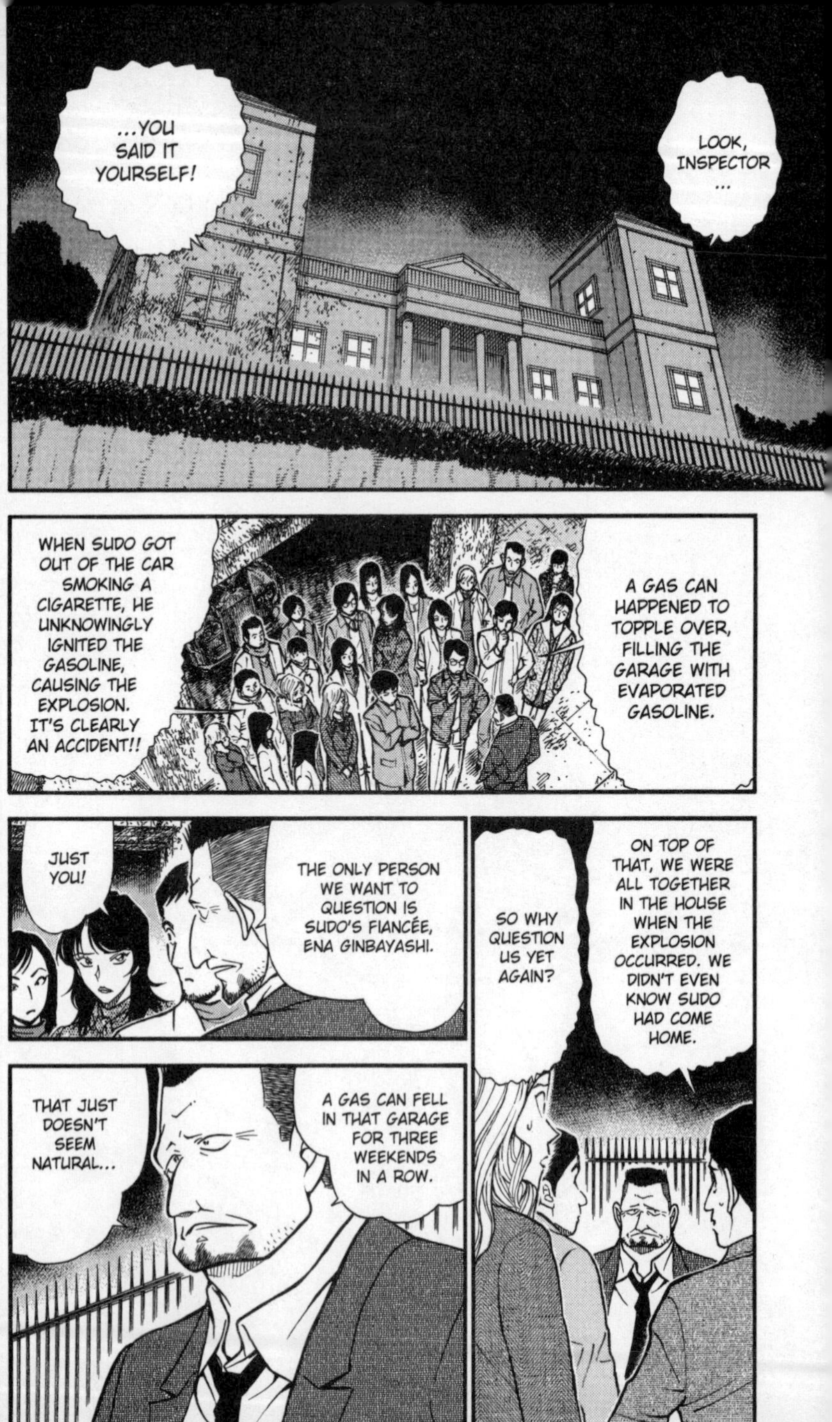
LOOK, INSPECTOR ...
...YOU SAID IT YOURSELF!
A GAS CAN HAPPENED TO TOPPLE OVER, FILLING THE GARAGE WITH EVAPORATED GASOLINE.
WHEN SUDO GOT OUT OF THE CAR SMOKING A CIGARETTE, HE UNKNOWINGLY IGNITED THE GASOLINE, CAUSING THE EXPLOSION. IT'S CLEARLY AN ACCIDENT!!
ON TOP OF THAT, WE WERE ALL TOGETHER IN THE HOUSE WHEN THE EXPLOSION OCCURRED. WE DIDN'T EVEN KNOW SUDO HAD COME HOME.
SO WHY QUESTION US YET AGAIN?
THE ONLY PERSON WE WANT TO QUESTION IS SUDO'S FIANCÉE, ENA GINBAYASHI.
JUST YOU!
A GAS CAN FELL IN THAT GARAGE FOR THREE WEEKENDS IN A ROW.
THAT JUST DOESN'T SEEM NATURAL...

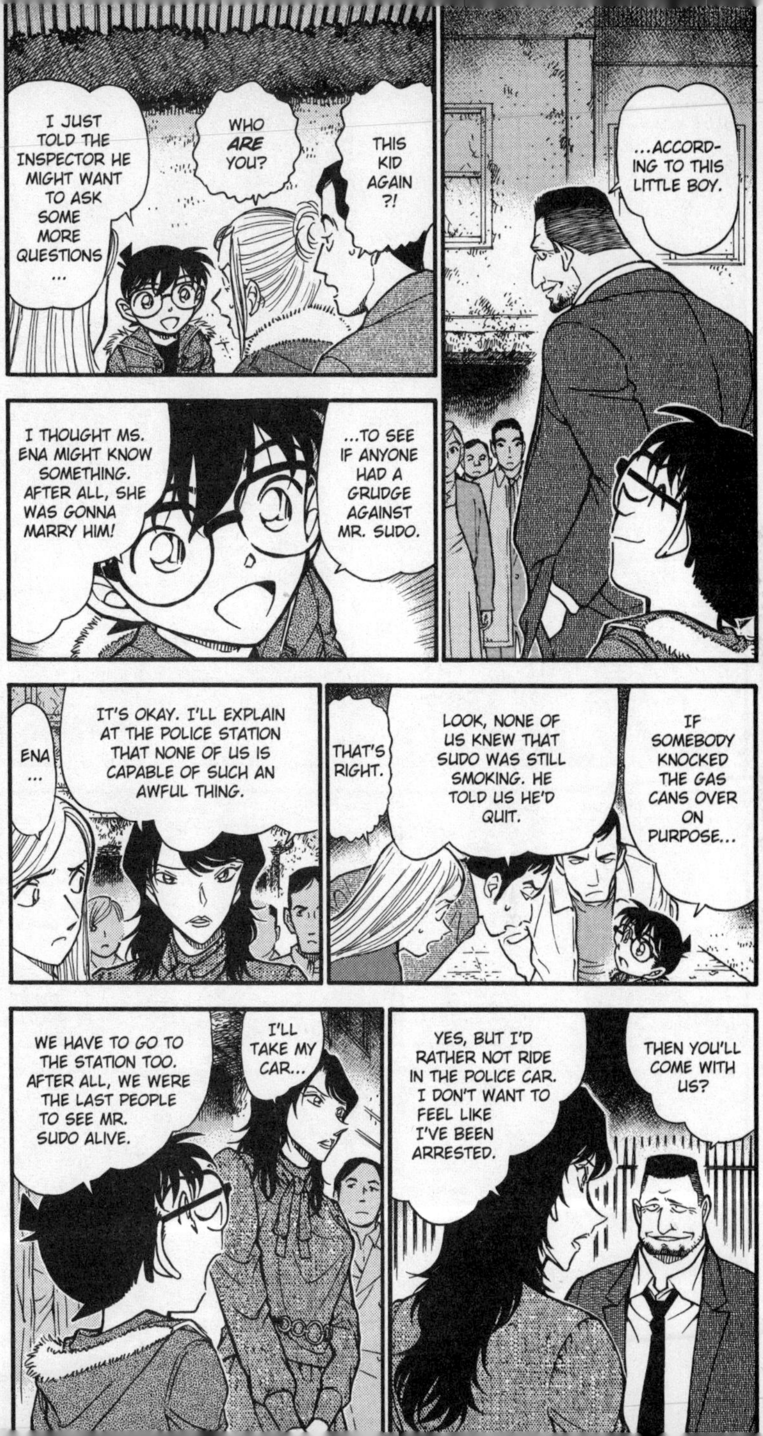
...ACCORDING TO THIS LITTLE BOY.
THIS KID AGAIN?!
WHO *ARE* YOU?
I JUST TOLD THE INSPECTOR HE MIGHT WANT TO ASK SOME MORE QUESTIONS ...
...TO SEE IF ANYONE HAD A GRUDGE AGAINST MR. SUDO.
I THOUGHT MS. ENA MIGHT KNOW SOMETHING. AFTER ALL, SHE WAS GONNA MARRY HIM!
IF SOMEBODY KNOCKED THE GAS CANS OVER ON PURPOSE...
LOOK, NONE OF US KNEW THAT SUDO WAS STILL SMOKING. HE TOLD US HE'D QUIT.
THAT'S RIGHT.
IT'S OKAY. I'LL EXPLAIN AT THE POLICE STATION THAT NONE OF US IS CAPABLE OF SUCH AN AWFUL THING.
ENA ...
THEN YOU'LL COME WITH US?
YES, BUT I'D RATHER NOT RIDE IN THE POLICE CAR. I DON'T WANT TO FEEL LIKE I'VE BEEN ARRESTED.
I'LL TAKE MY CAR...
WE HAVE TO GO TO THE STATION TOO. AFTER ALL, WE WERE THE LAST PEOPLE TO SEE MR. SUDO ALIVE.

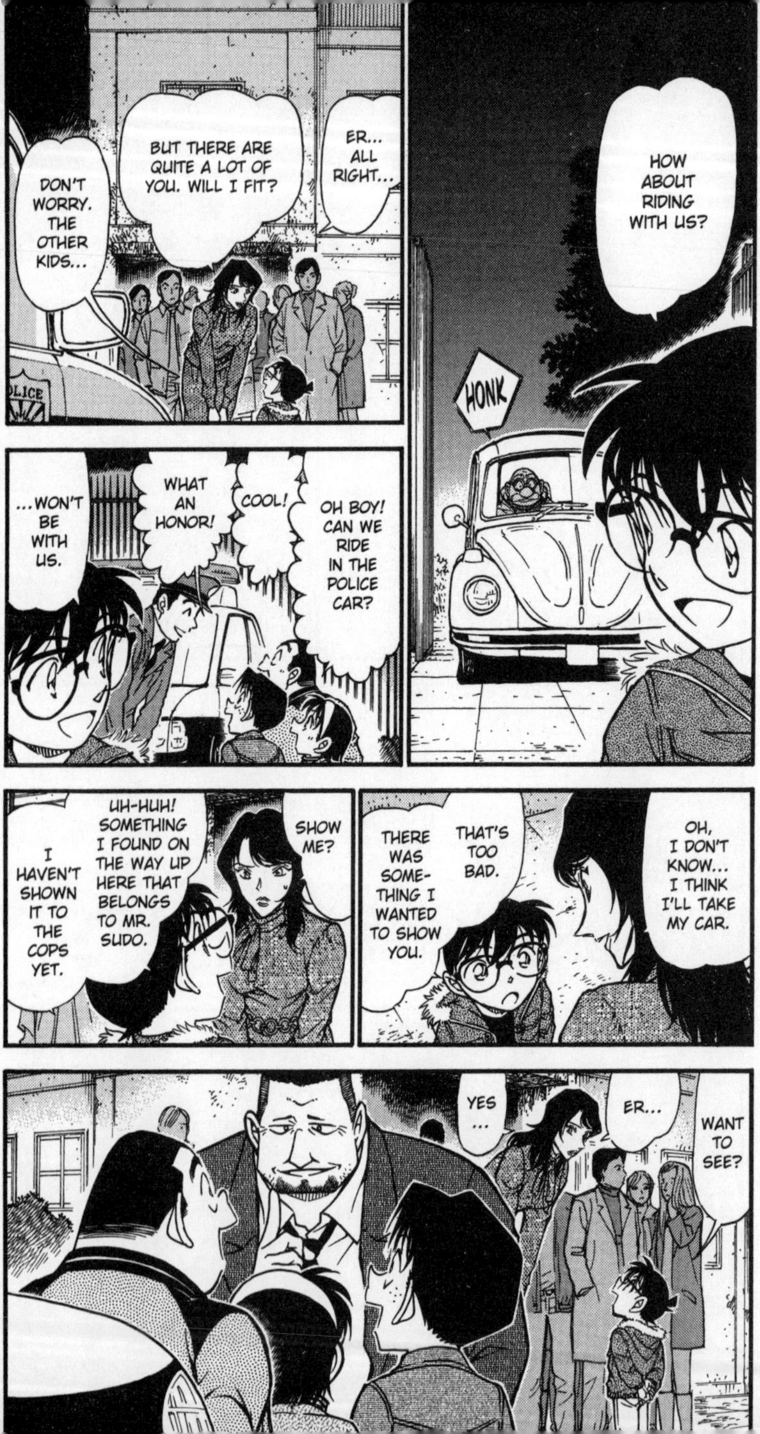
HOW ABOUT RIDING WITH US?
HONK
ER... ALL RIGHT...
BUT THERE ARE QUITE A LOT OF YOU. WILL I FIT?
DON'T WORRY. THE OTHER KIDS...
OH BOY! CAN WE RIDE IN THE POLICE CAR?
COOL!
WHAT AN HONOR!
...WON'T BE WITH US.
OH, I DON'T KNOW... I THINK I'LL TAKE MY CAR.
THAT'S TOO BAD.
THERE WAS SOME-THING I WANTED TO SHOW YOU.
SHOW ME?
UH-HUH! SOMETHING I FOUND ON THE WAY UP HERE THAT BELONGS TO MR. SUDO.
I HAVEN'T SHOWN IT TO THE COPS YET.
WANT TO SEE?
ER...
YES...

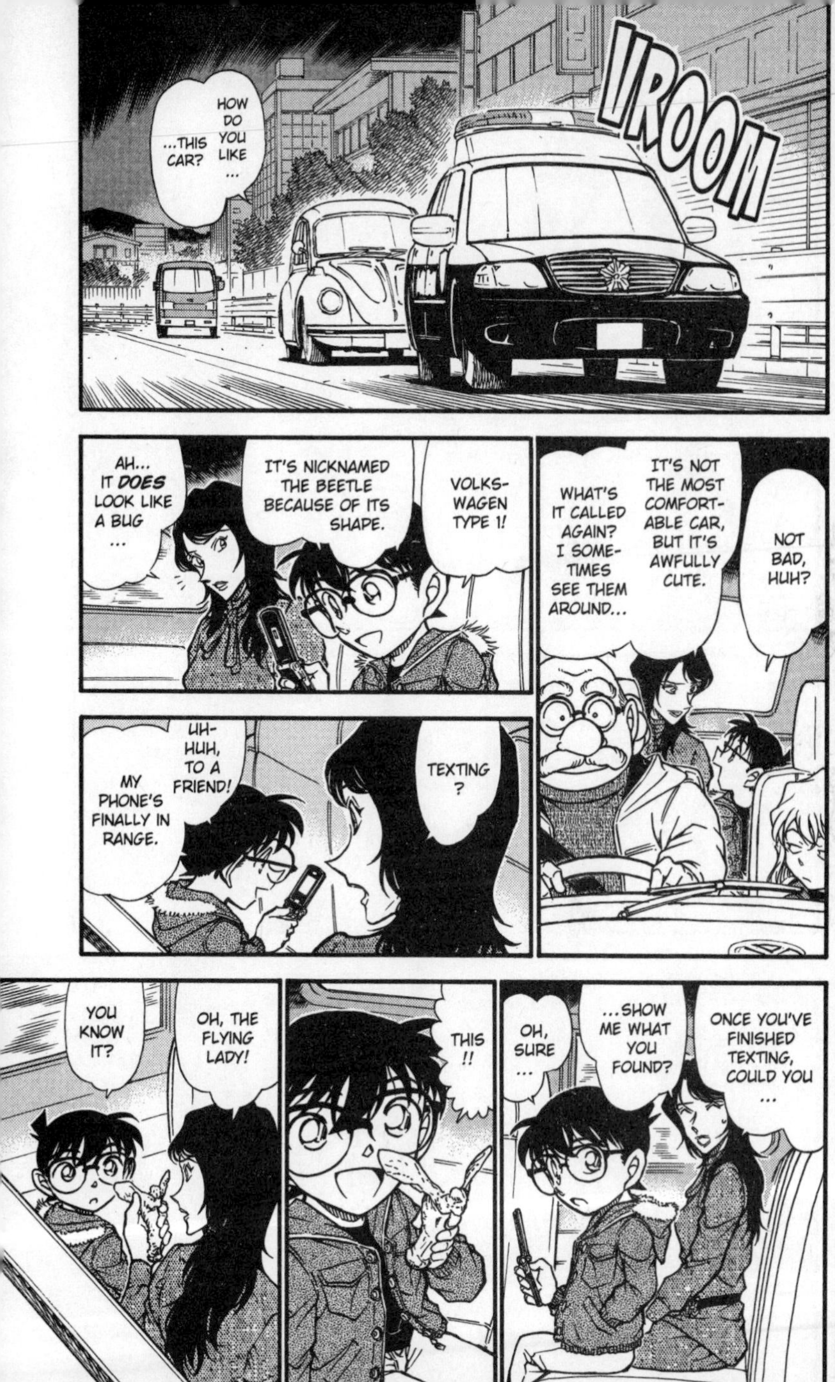
VROOM
HOW DO YOU LIKE ...
...THIS CAR?
NOT BAD, HUH?
IT'S NOT THE MOST COMFORTABLE CAR, BUT IT'S AWFULLY CUTE.
WHAT'S IT CALLED AGAIN? I SOMETIMES SEE THEM AROUND...
VOLKSWAGEN TYPE 1!
IT'S NICKNAMED THE BEETLE BECAUSE OF ITS SHAPE.
AH... IT *DOES* LOOK LIKE A BUG ...
TEXTING?
UH-HUH, TO A FRIEND!
MY PHONE'S FINALLY IN RANGE.
ONCE YOU'VE FINISHED TEXTING, COULD YOU ...
...SHOW ME WHAT YOU FOUND?
OH, SURE ...
THIS!!
OH, THE FLYING LADY!
YOU KNOW IT?

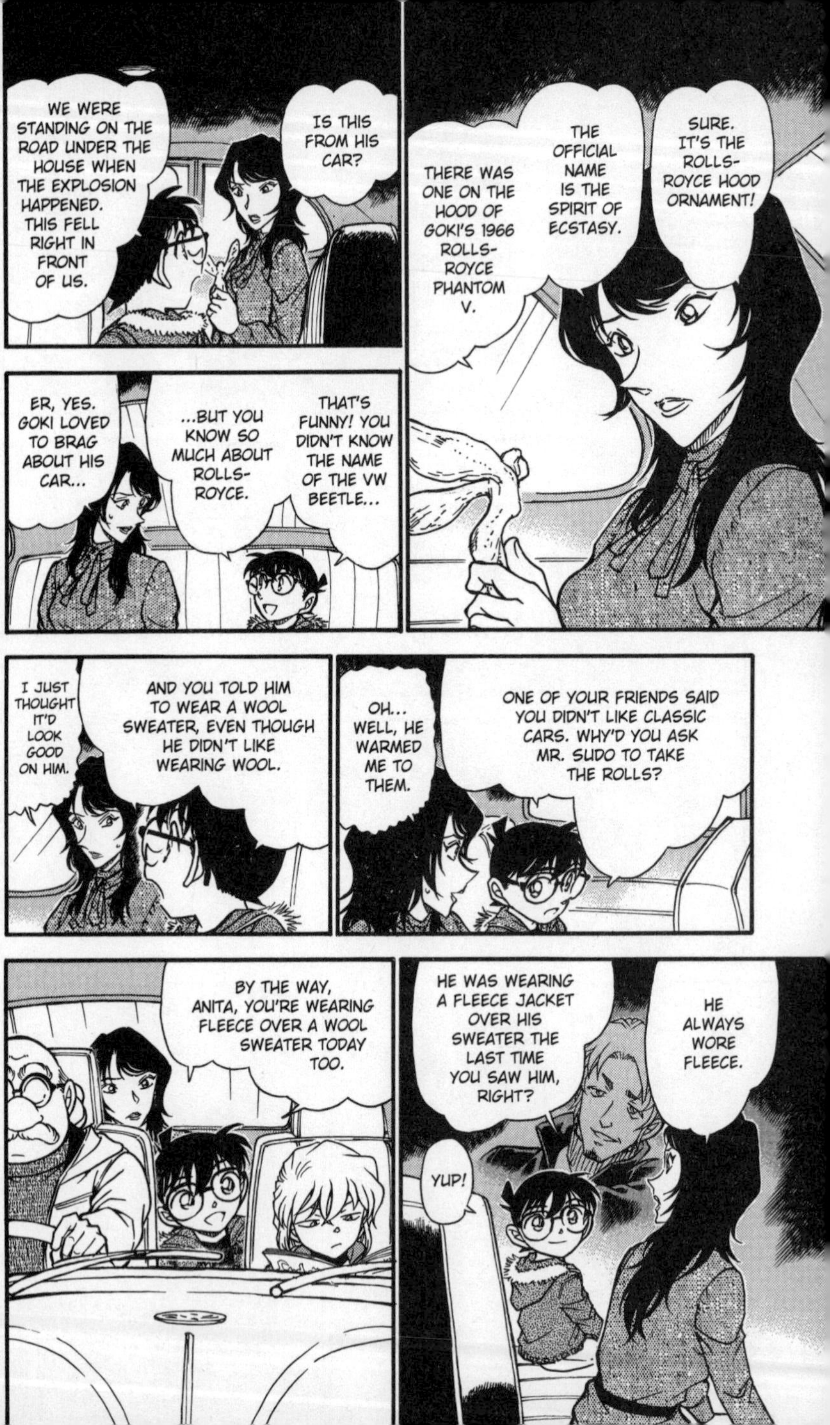
SURE. IT'S THE ROLLS-ROYCE HOOD ORNAMENT!
THE OFFICIAL NAME IS THE SPIRIT OF ECSTASY.
THERE WAS ONE ON THE HOOD OF GOKI'S 1966 ROLLS-ROYCE PHANTOM V.
IS THIS FROM HIS CAR?
WE WERE STANDING ON THE ROAD UNDER THE HOUSE WHEN THE EXPLOSION HAPPENED. THIS FELL RIGHT IN FRONT OF US.
THAT'S FUNNY! YOU DIDN'T KNOW THE NAME OF THE VW BEETLE...
...BUT YOU KNOW SO MUCH ABOUT ROLLS-ROYCE.
ER, YES. GOKI LOVED TO BRAG ABOUT HIS CAR...
ONE OF YOUR FRIENDS SAID YOU DIDN'T LIKE CLASSIC CARS. WHY'D YOU ASK MR. SUDO TO TAKE THE ROLLS?
OH... WELL, HE WARMED ME TO THEM.
AND YOU TOLD HIM TO WEAR A WOOL SWEATER, EVEN THOUGH HE DIDN'T LIKE WEARING WOOL.
I JUST THOUGHT IT'D LOOK GOOD ON HIM.
HE ALWAYS WORE FLEECE.
HE WAS WEARING A FLEECE JACKET OVER HIS SWEATER THE LAST TIME YOU SAW HIM, RIGHT?
YUP!
BY THE WAY, ANITA, YOU'RE WEARING FLEECE OVER A WOOL SWEATER TODAY TOO.

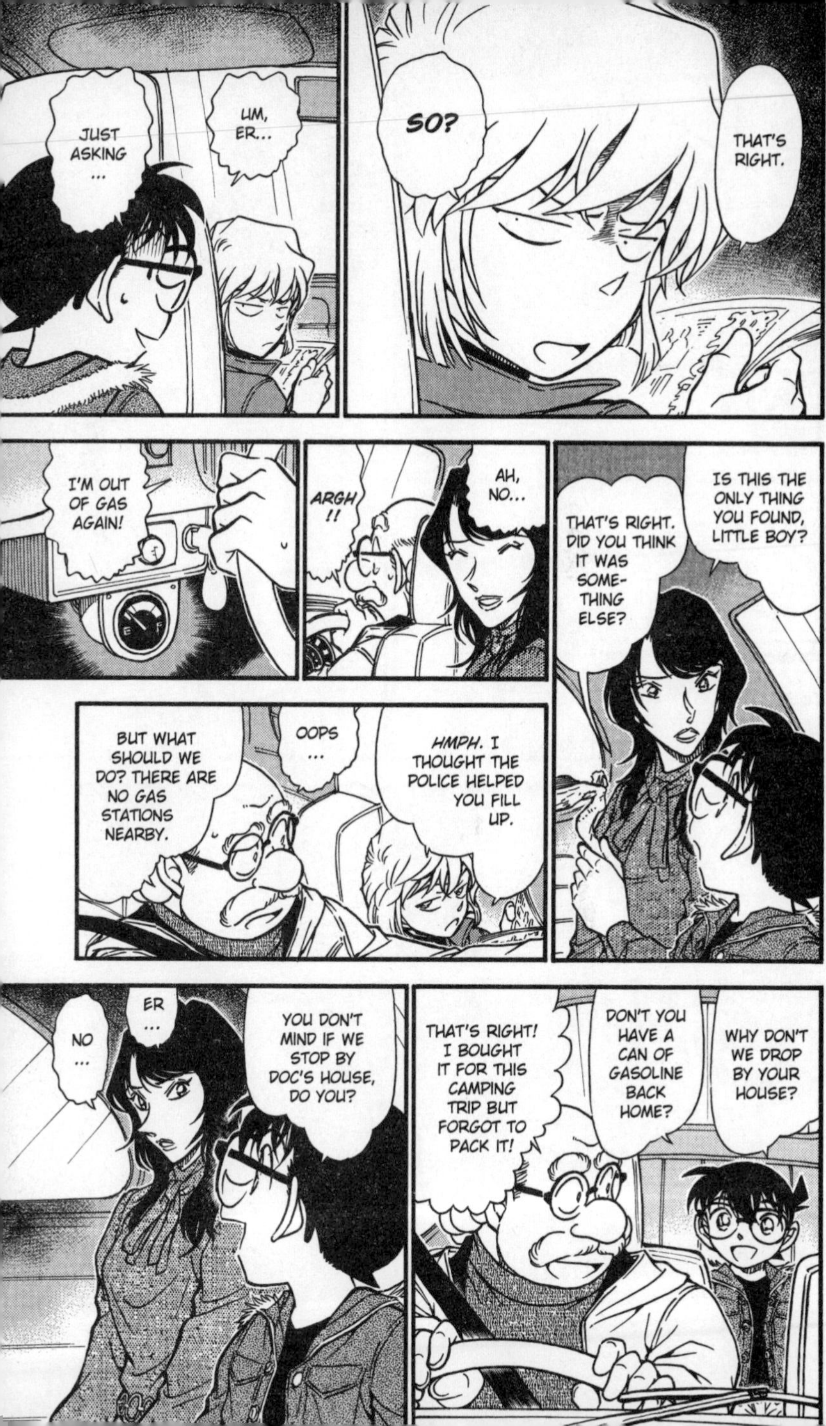
THAT'S RIGHT.
SO?
UM, ER...
JUST ASKING ...
IS THIS THE ONLY THING YOU FOUND, LITTLE BOY?
THAT'S RIGHT. DID YOU THINK IT WAS SOME-THING ELSE?
AH, NO...
ARGH !!
I'M OUT OF GAS AGAIN!
HMPH. I THOUGHT THE POLICE HELPED YOU FILL UP.
OOPS ...
BUT WHAT SHOULD WE DO? THERE ARE NO GAS STATIONS NEARBY.
WHY DON'T WE DROP BY YOUR HOUSE?
DON'T YOU HAVE A CAN OF GASOLINE BACK HOME?
THAT'S RIGHT! I BOUGHT IT FOR THIS CAMPING TRIP BUT FORGOT TO PACK IT!
YOU DON'T MIND IF WE STOP BY DOC'S HOUSE, DO YOU?
ER ...
NO ...

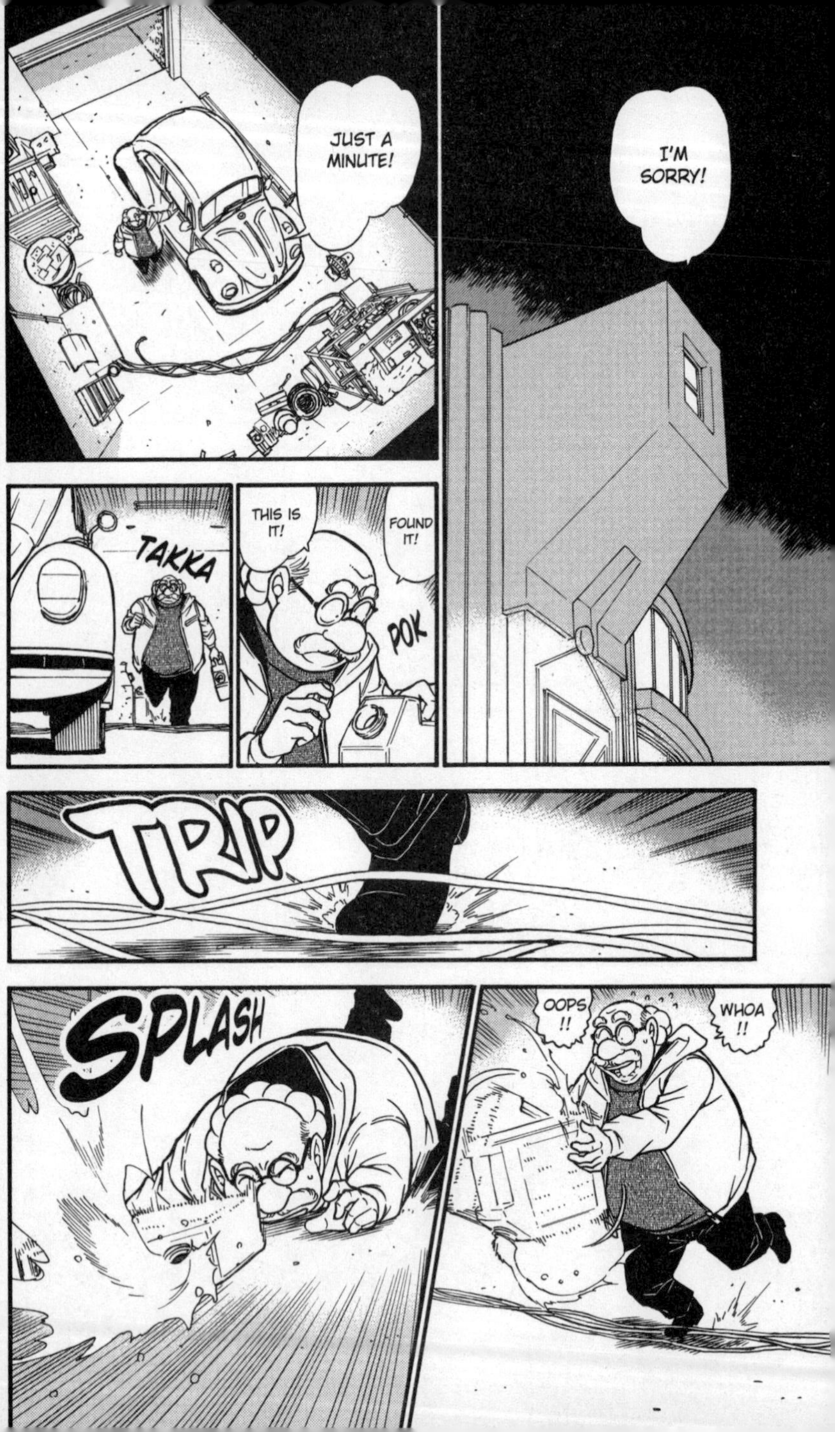
I'M SORRY!
JUST A MINUTE!
FOUND IT!
THIS IS IT!
POK
TAKKA
TRIP
WHOA !!
OOPS !!
SPLASH

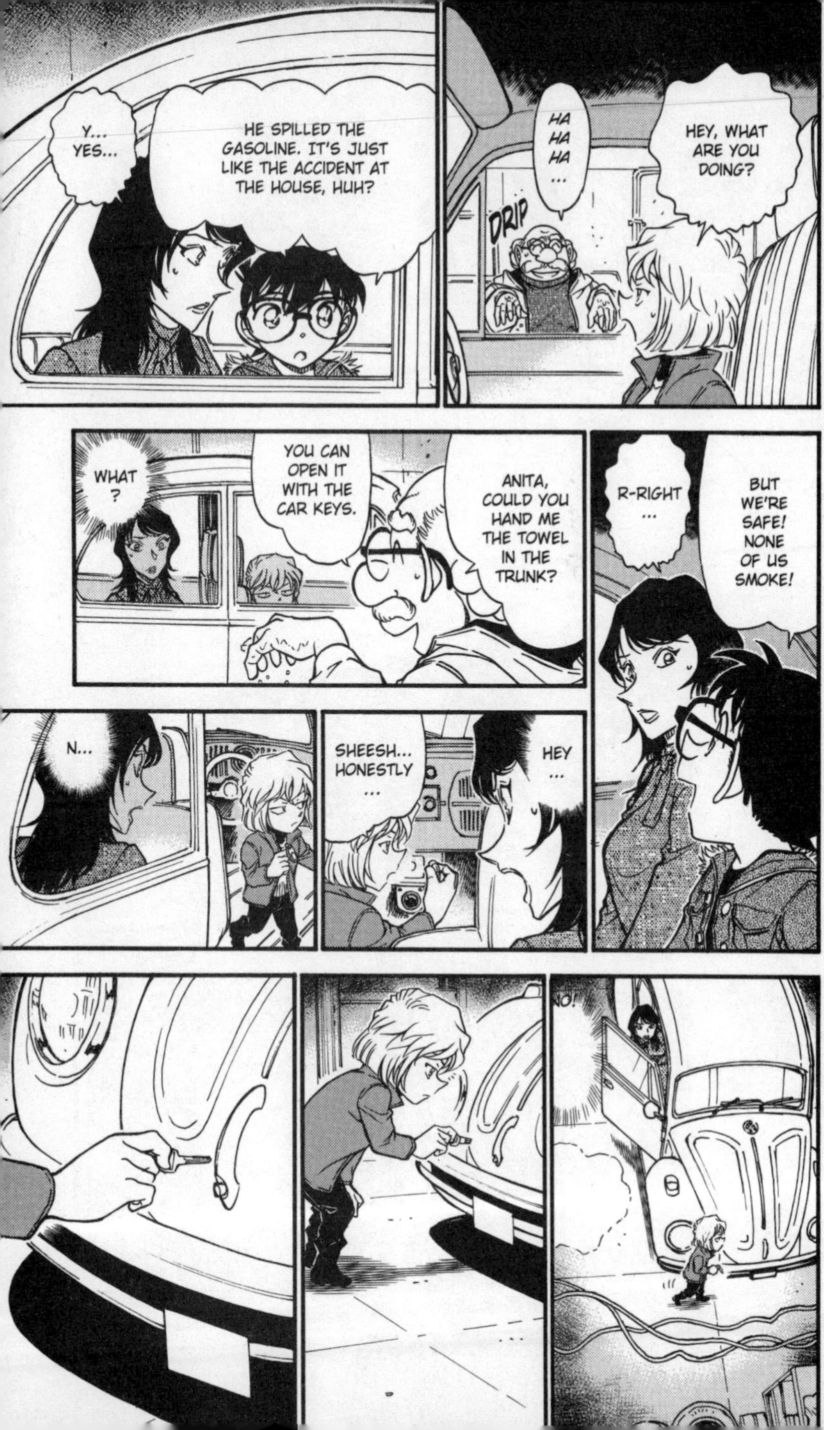
HEY, WHAT ARE YOU DOING?
HA HA HA ...
DRIP
HE SPILLED THE GASOLINE. IT'S JUST LIKE THE ACCIDENT AT THE HOUSE, HUH?
Y... YES...
BUT WE'RE SAFE! NONE OF US SMOKE!
R-RIGHT ...
ANITA, COULD YOU HAND ME THE TOWEL IN THE TRUNK?
YOU CAN OPEN IT WITH THE CAR KEYS.
WHAT ?
HEY ...
SHEESH... HONESTLY ...
N...
NO!

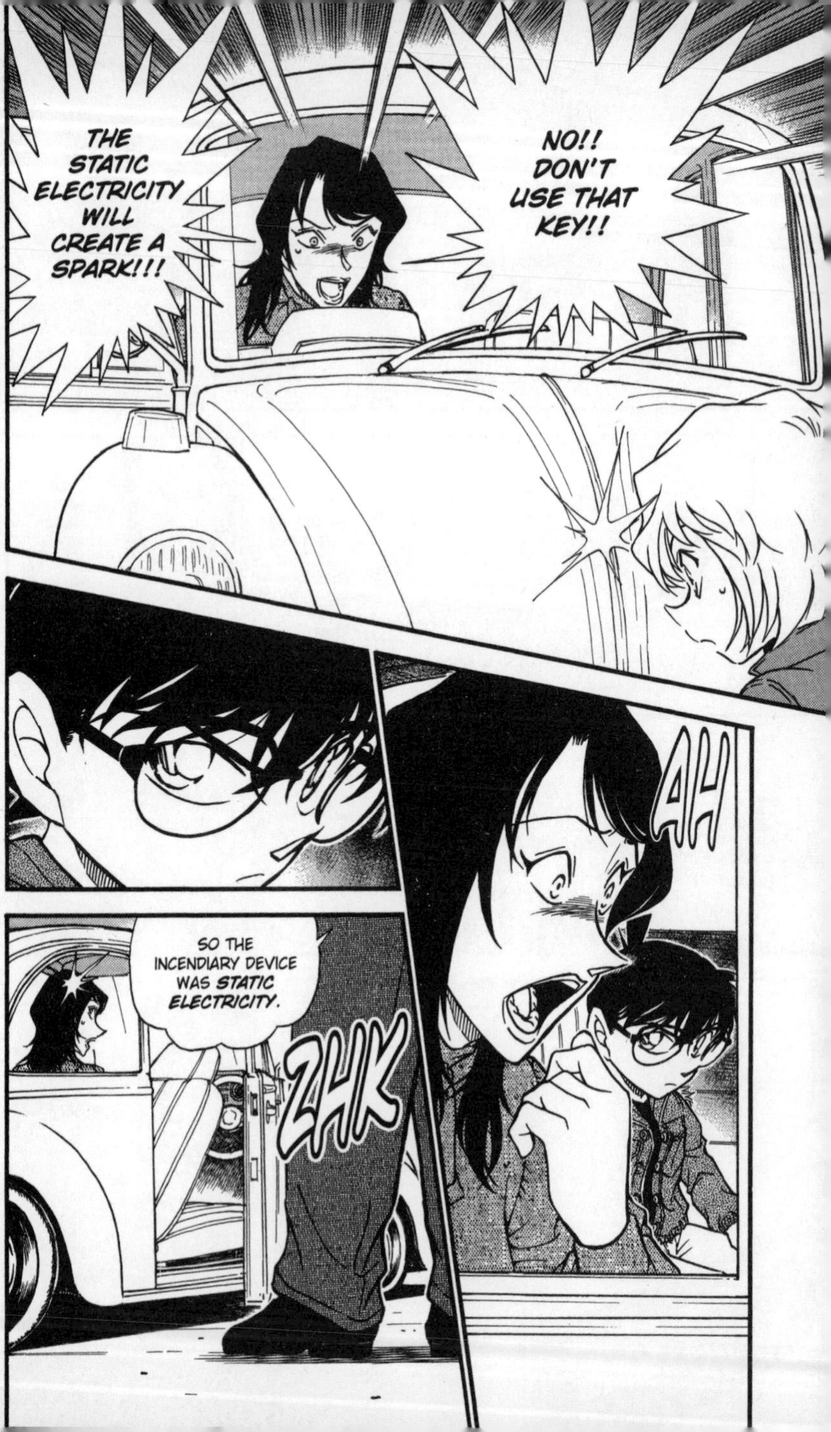
NO!! DON'T USE THAT KEY!!
THE STATIC ELECTRICITY WILL CREATE A SPARK!!!
AH
SO THE INCENDIARY DEVICE WAS *STATIC ELECTRICITY*.
ZHK

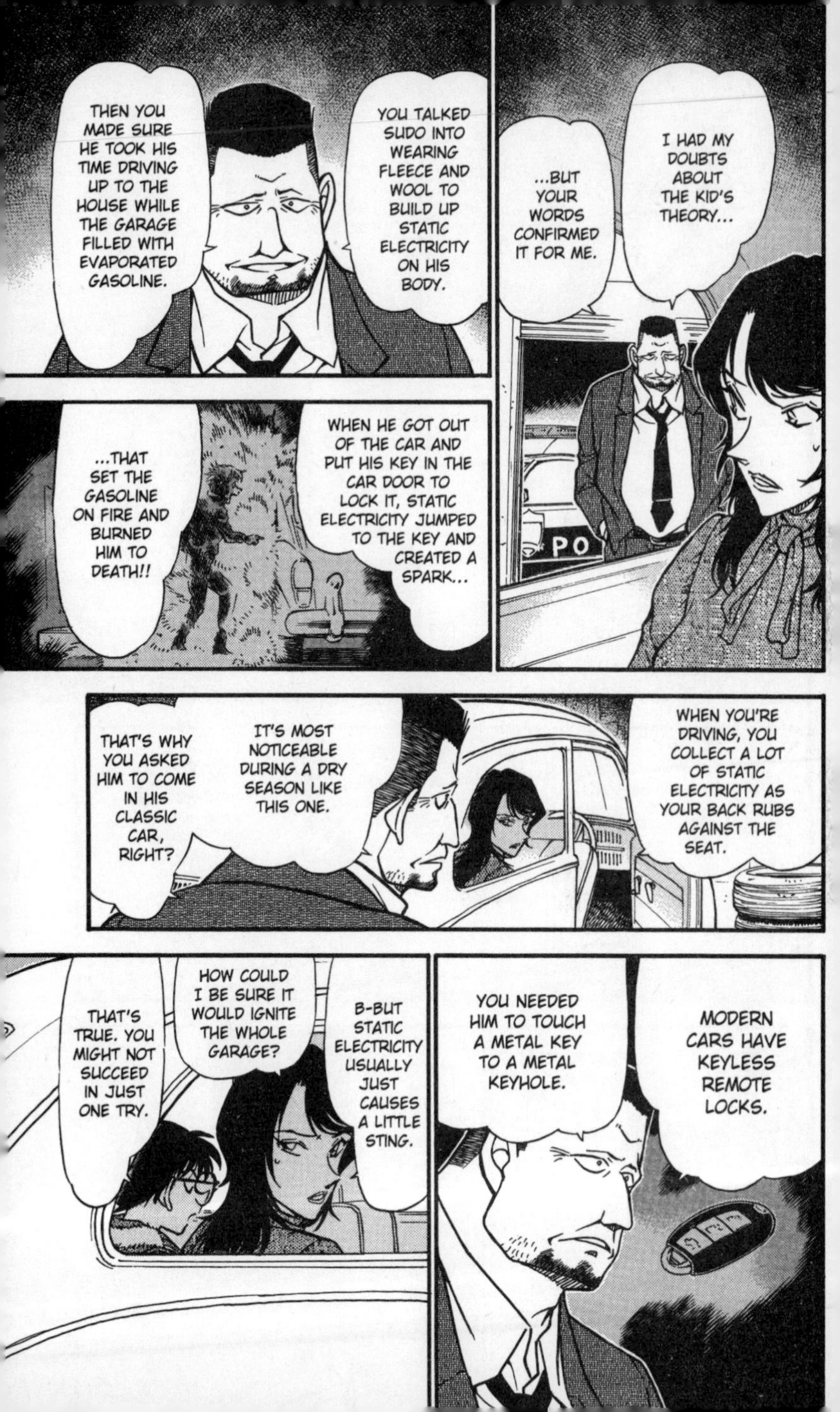
I HAD MY DOUBTS ABOUT THE KID'S THEORY...
...BUT YOUR WORDS CONFIRMED IT FOR ME.
YOU TALKED SUDO INTO WEARING FLEECE AND WOOL TO BUILD UP STATIC ELECTRICITY ON HIS BODY.
THEN YOU MADE SURE HE TOOK HIS TIME DRIVING UP TO THE HOUSE WHILE THE GARAGE FILLED WITH EVAPORATED GASOLINE.
WHEN HE GOT OUT OF THE CAR AND PUT HIS KEY IN THE CAR DOOR TO LOCK IT, STATIC ELECTRICITY JUMPED TO THE KEY AND CREATED A SPARK...
...THAT SET THE GASOLINE ON FIRE AND BURNED HIM TO DEATH!!
WHEN YOU'RE DRIVING, YOU COLLECT A LOT OF STATIC ELECTRICITY AS YOUR BACK RUBS AGAINST THE SEAT.
IT'S MOST NOTICEABLE DURING A DRY SEASON LIKE THIS ONE.
THAT'S WHY YOU ASKED HIM TO COME IN HIS CLASSIC CAR, RIGHT?
MODERN CARS HAVE KEYLESS REMOTE LOCKS.
YOU NEEDED HIM TO TOUCH A METAL KEY TO A METAL KEYHOLE.
B-BUT STATIC ELECTRICITY USUALLY JUST CAUSES A LITTLE STING.
HOW COULD I BE SURE IT WOULD IGNITE THE WHOLE GARAGE?
THAT'S TRUE. YOU MIGHT NOT SUCCEED IN JUST ONE TRY.

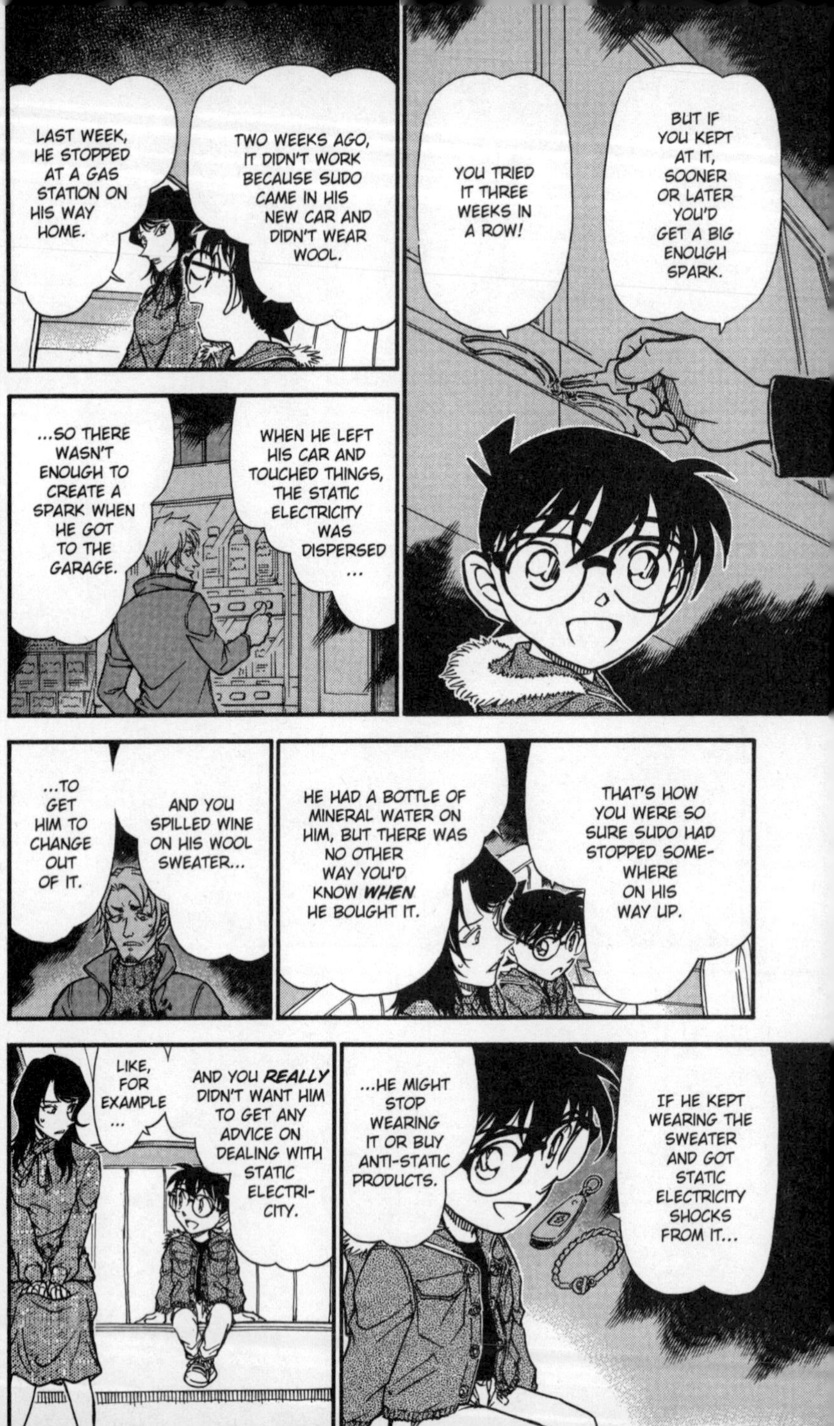
BUT IF YOU KEPT AT IT, SOONER OR LATER YOU'D GET A BIG ENOUGH SPARK.
YOU TRIED IT THREE WEEKS IN A ROW!
TWO WEEKS AGO, IT DIDN'T WORK BECAUSE SUDO CAME IN HIS NEW CAR AND DIDN'T WEAR WOOL.
LAST WEEK, HE STOPPED AT A GAS STATION ON HIS WAY HOME.
WHEN HE LEFT HIS CAR AND TOUCHED THINGS, THE STATIC ELECTRICITY WAS DISPERSED...
...SO THERE WASN'T ENOUGH TO CREATE A SPARK WHEN HE GOT TO THE GARAGE.
THAT'S HOW YOU WERE SO SURE SUDO HAD STOPPED SOMEWHERE ON HIS WAY UP.
HE HAD A BOTTLE OF MINERAL WATER ON HIM, BUT THERE WAS NO OTHER WAY YOU'D KNOW ***WHEN*** HE BOUGHT IT.
AND YOU SPILLED WINE ON HIS WOOL SWEATER...
...TO GET HIM TO CHANGE OUT OF IT.
IF HE KEPT WEARING THE SWEATER AND GOT STATIC ELECTRICITY SHOCKS FROM IT...
...HE MIGHT STOP WEARING IT OR BUY ANTI-STATIC PRODUCTS.
AND YOU ***REALLY*** DIDN'T WANT HIM TO GET ANY ADVICE ON DEALING WITH STATIC ELECTRICITY.
LIKE, FOR EXAMPLE...

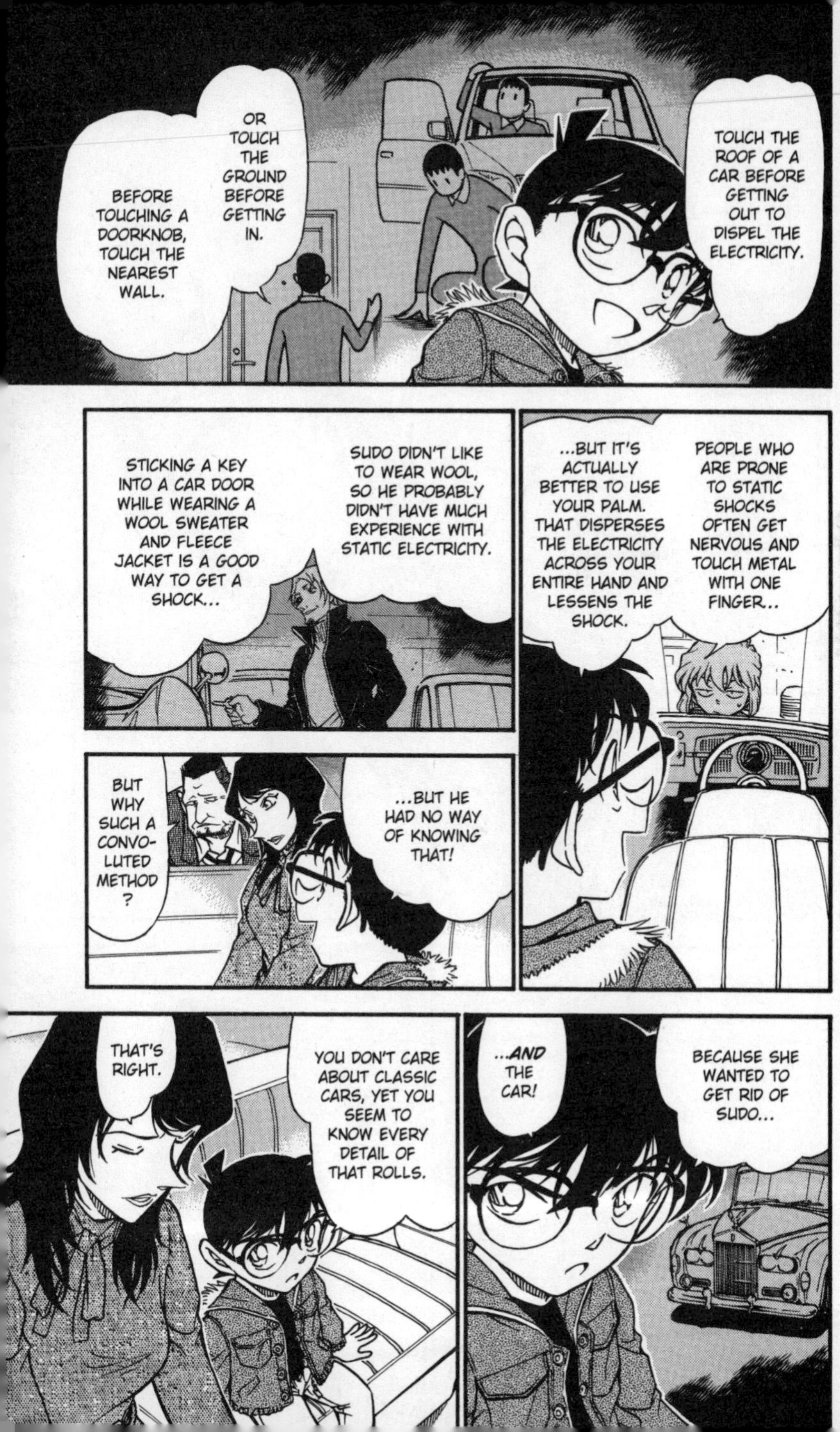
TOUCH THE ROOF OF A CAR BEFORE GETTING OUT TO DISPEL THE ELECTRICITY.
OR TOUCH THE GROUND BEFORE GETTING IN.
BEFORE TOUCHING A DOORKNOB, TOUCH THE NEAREST WALL.
PEOPLE WHO ARE PRONE TO STATIC SHOCKS OFTEN GET NERVOUS AND TOUCH METAL WITH ONE FINGER...
...BUT IT'S ACTUALLY BETTER TO USE YOUR PALM. THAT DISPERSES THE ELECTRICITY ACROSS YOUR ENTIRE HAND AND LESSENS THE SHOCK.
SUDO DIDN'T LIKE TO WEAR WOOL, SO HE PROBABLY DIDN'T HAVE MUCH EXPERIENCE WITH STATIC ELECTRICITY.
STICKING A KEY INTO A CAR DOOR WHILE WEARING A WOOL SWEATER AND FLEECE JACKET IS A GOOD WAY TO GET A SHOCK...
...BUT HE HAD NO WAY OF KNOWING THAT!
BUT WHY SUCH A CONVOLUTED METHOD?
BECAUSE SHE WANTED TO GET RID OF SUDO...
...*AND* THE CAR!
YOU DON'T CARE ABOUT CLASSIC CARS, YET YOU SEEM TO KNOW EVERY DETAIL OF THAT ROLLS.
THAT'S RIGHT.

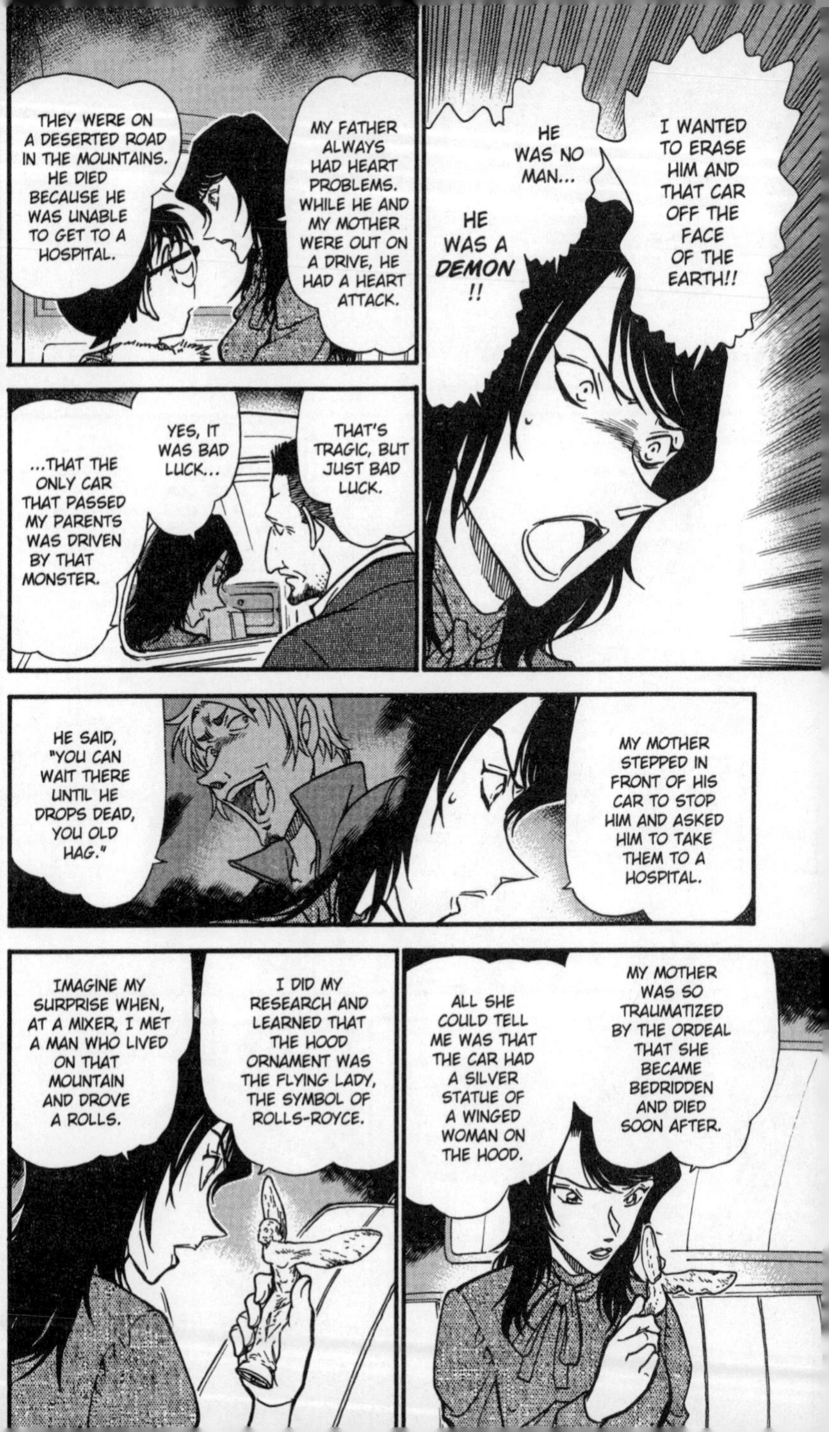

MY FATHER ALWAYS HAD HEART PROBLEMS. WHILE HE AND MY MOTHER WERE OUT ON A DRIVE, HE HAD A HEART ATTACK.
THEY WERE ON A DESERTED ROAD IN THE MOUNTAINS. HE DIED BECAUSE HE WAS UNABLE TO GET TO A HOSPITAL.
THAT'S TRAGIC, BUT JUST BAD LUCK.
YES, IT WAS BAD LUCK...
...THAT THE ONLY CAR THAT PASSED MY PARENTS WAS DRIVEN BY THAT MONSTER.
HE WAS NO MAN...
HE WAS A *DEMON* !!
I WANTED TO ERASE HIM AND THAT CAR OFF THE FACE OF THE EARTH!!
MY MOTHER STEPPED IN FRONT OF HIS CAR TO STOP HIM AND ASKED HIM TO TAKE THEM TO A HOSPITAL.
HE SAID, "YOU CAN WAIT THERE UNTIL HE DROPS DEAD, YOU OLD HAG."
MY MOTHER WAS SO TRAUMATIZED BY THE ORDEAL THAT SHE BECAME BEDRIDDEN AND DIED SOON AFTER.
ALL SHE COULD TELL ME WAS THAT THE CAR HAD A SILVER STATUE OF A WINGED WOMAN ON THE HOOD.
I DID MY RESEARCH AND LEARNED THAT THE HOOD ORNAMENT WAS THE FLYING LADY, THE SYMBOL OF ROLLS-ROYCE.
IMAGINE MY SURPRISE WHEN, AT A MIXER, I MET A MAN WHO LIVED ON THAT MOUNTAIN AND DROVE A ROLLS.

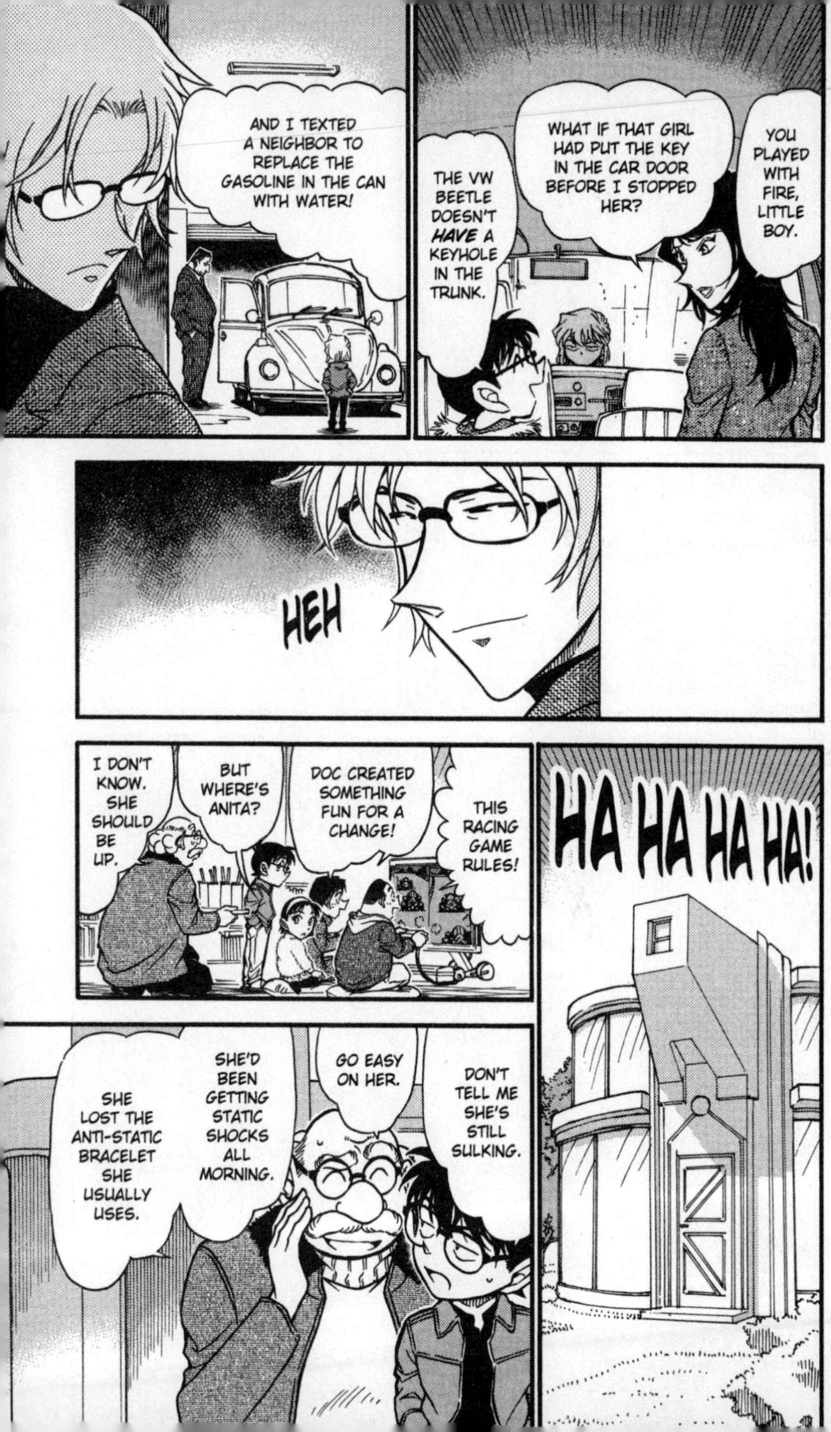
YOU PLAYED WITH FIRE, LITTLE BOY.
WHAT IF THAT GIRL HAD PUT THE KEY IN THE CAR DOOR BEFORE I STOPPED HER?
THE VW BEETLE DOESN'T *HAVE* A KEYHOLE IN THE TRUNK.
AND I TEXTED A NEIGHBOR TO REPLACE THE GASOLINE IN THE CAN WITH WATER!
HEH
HA HA HA HA HA!
THIS RACING GAME RULES!
DOC CREATED SOMETHING FUN FOR A CHANGE!
BUT WHERE'S ANITA?
I DON'T KNOW. SHE SHOULD BE UP.
DON'T TELL ME SHE'S STILL SULKING.
GO EASY ON HER.
SHE'D BEEN GETTING STATIC SHOCKS ALL MORNING.
SHE LOST THE ANTI-STATIC BRACELET SHE USUALLY USES.

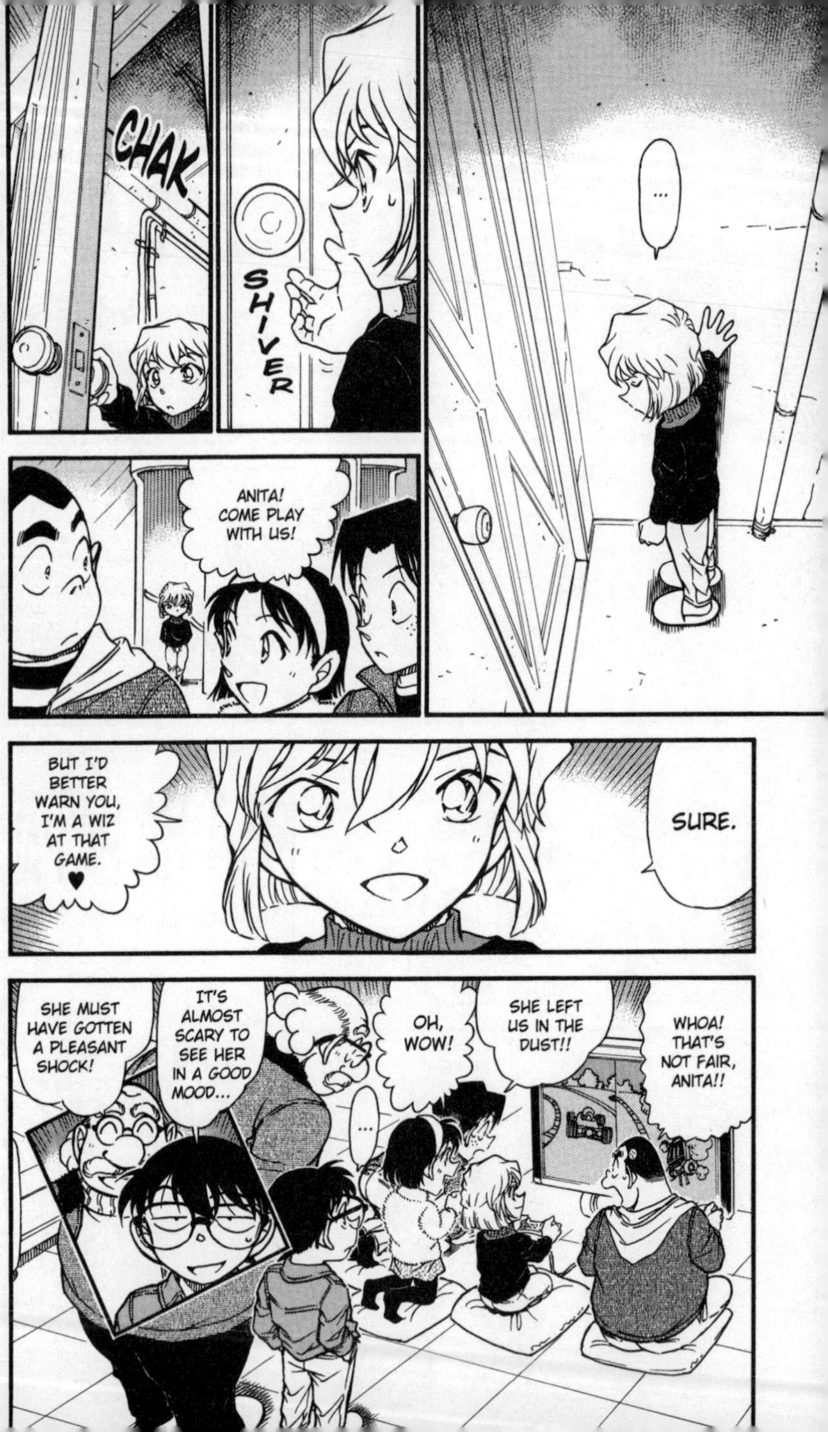
...
SHIVER
CHAK
ANITA! COME PLAY WITH US!
SURE.
BUT I'D BETTER WARN YOU, I'M A WIZ AT THAT GAME. ♥
WHOA! THAT'S NOT FAIR, ANITA!!
SHE LEFT US IN THE DUST!!
OH, WOW!
...
IT'S ALMOST SCARY TO SEE HER IN A GOOD MOOD...
SHE MUST HAVE GOTTEN A PLEASANT SHOCK!

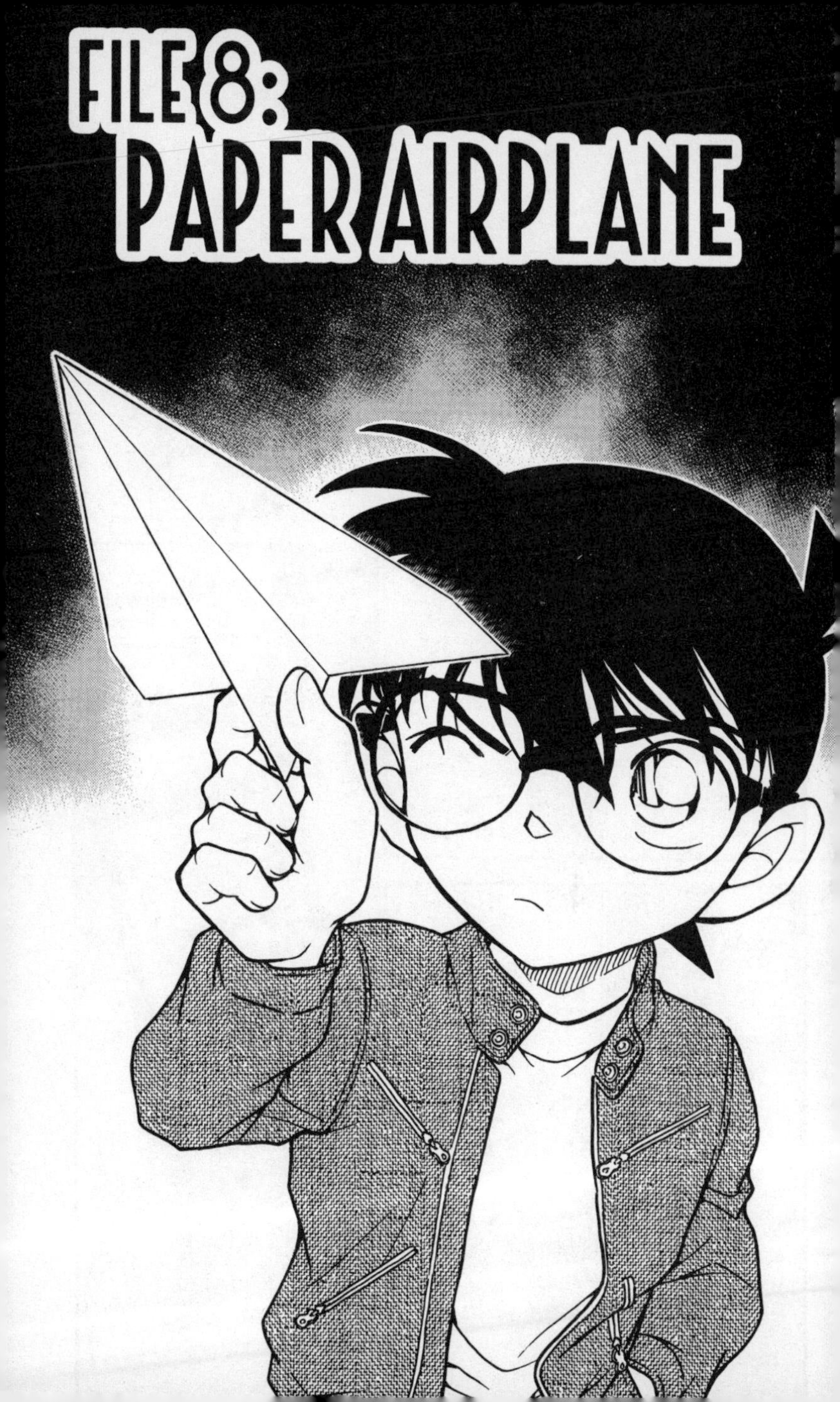
FILE 8:
PAPER AIRPLANE

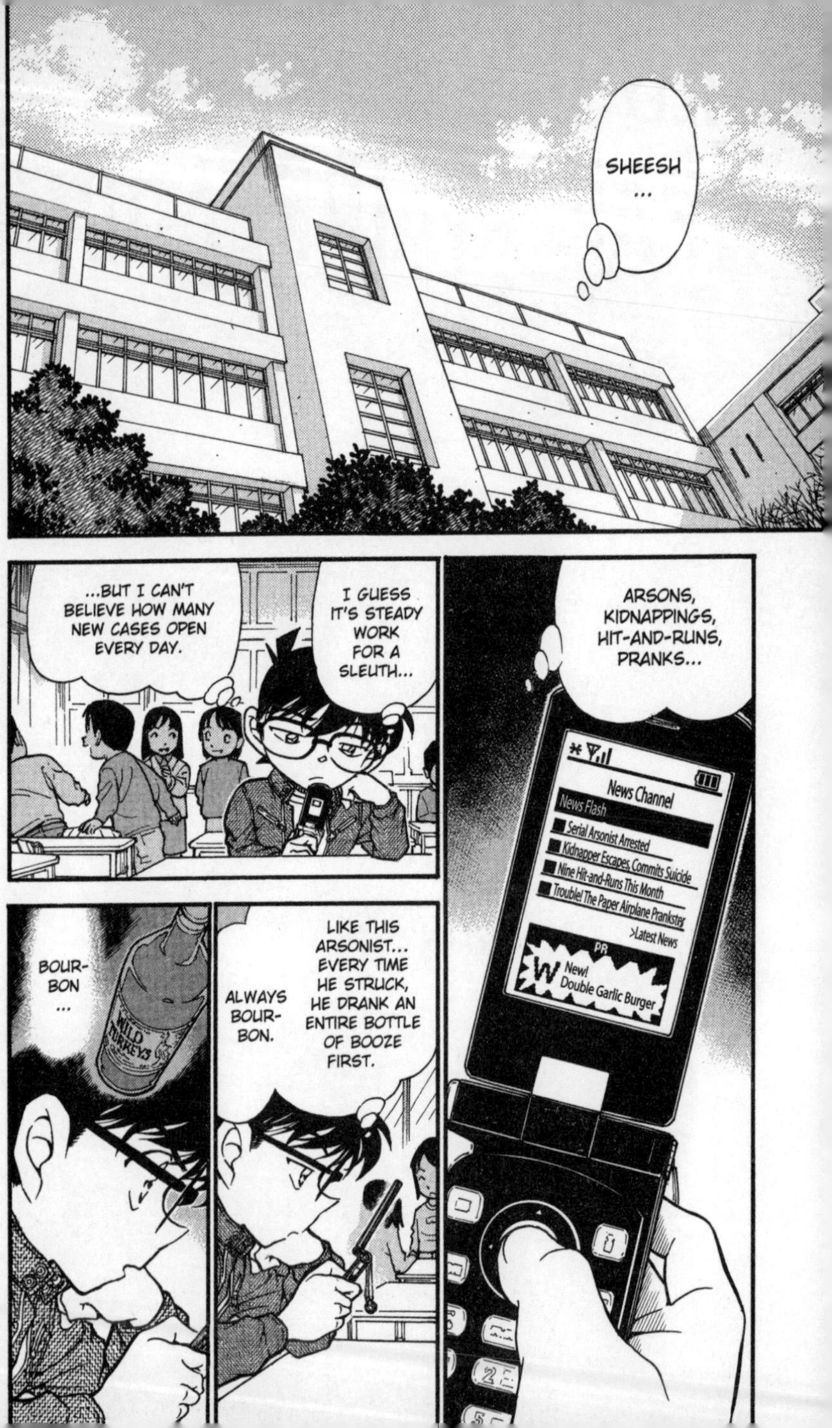
SHEESH ...
ARSONS, KIDNAPPINGS, HIT-AND-RUNS, PRANKS...
News Channel
News Flash
Serial Arsonist Arrested
Kidnapper Escapes, Commits Suicide
Nine Hit-and-Runs This Month
Trouble! The Paper Airplane Prankster
>Latest News
PR
W New! Double Garlic Burger
I GUESS IT'S STEADY WORK FOR A SLEUTH...
...BUT I CAN'T BELIEVE HOW MANY NEW CASES OPEN EVERY DAY.
LIKE THIS ARSONIST... EVERY TIME HE STRUCK, HE DRANK AN ENTIRE BOTTLE OF BOOZE FIRST.
ALWAYS BOURBON.
BOURBON ...
WILD TURKEY

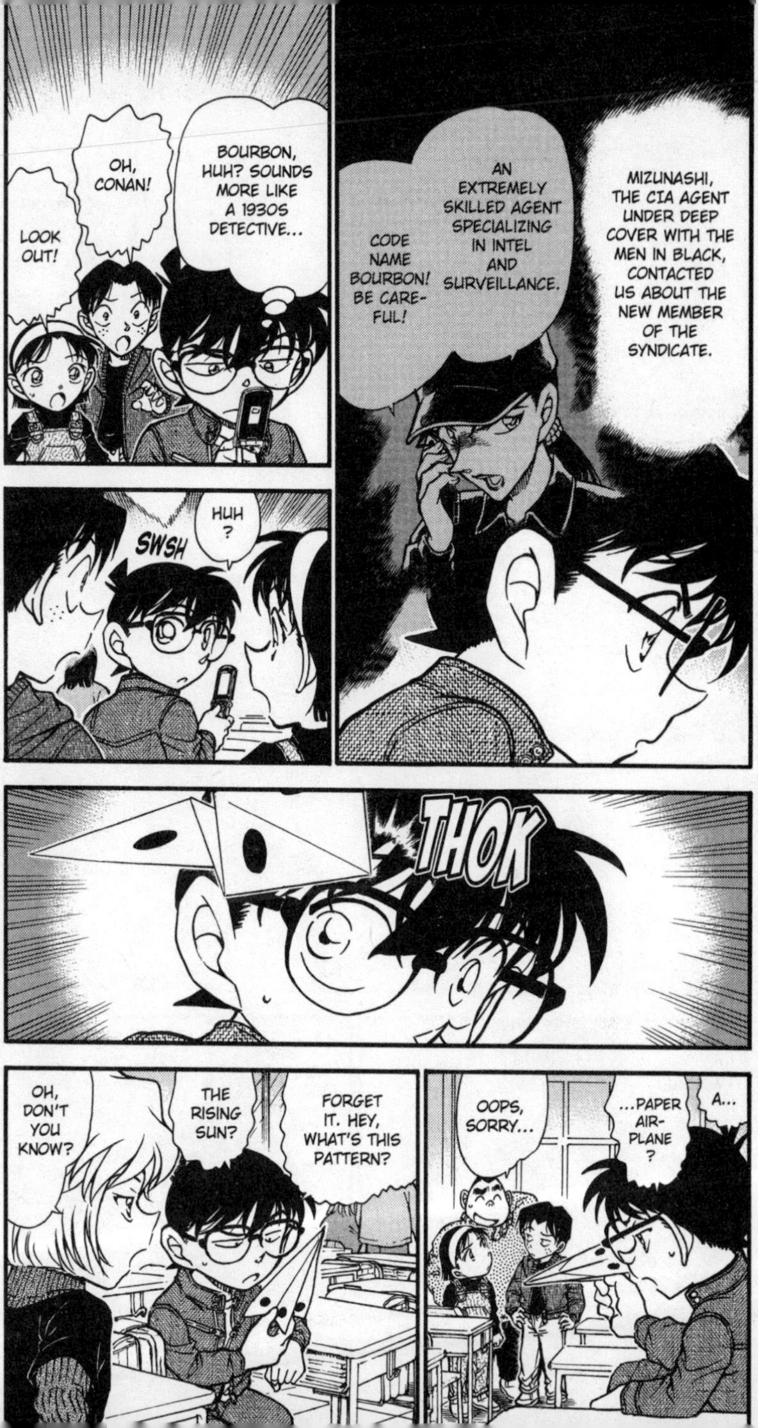
MIZUNASHI, THE CIA AGENT UNDER DEEP COVER WITH THE MEN IN BLACK, CONTACTED US ABOUT THE NEW MEMBER OF THE SYNDICATE.
AN EXTREMELY SKILLED AGENT SPECIALIZING IN INTEL AND SURVEILLANCE.
CODE NAME BOURBON! BE CARE-FUL!
BOURBON, HUH? SOUNDS MORE LIKE A 1930S DETECTIVE...
OH, CONAN!
LOOK OUT!
HUH?
SWSH
THOK
A...
...PAPER AIR-PLANE?
OOPS, SORRY...
FORGET IT. HEY, WHAT'S THIS PATTERN?
THE RISING SUN?
OH, DON'T YOU KNOW?

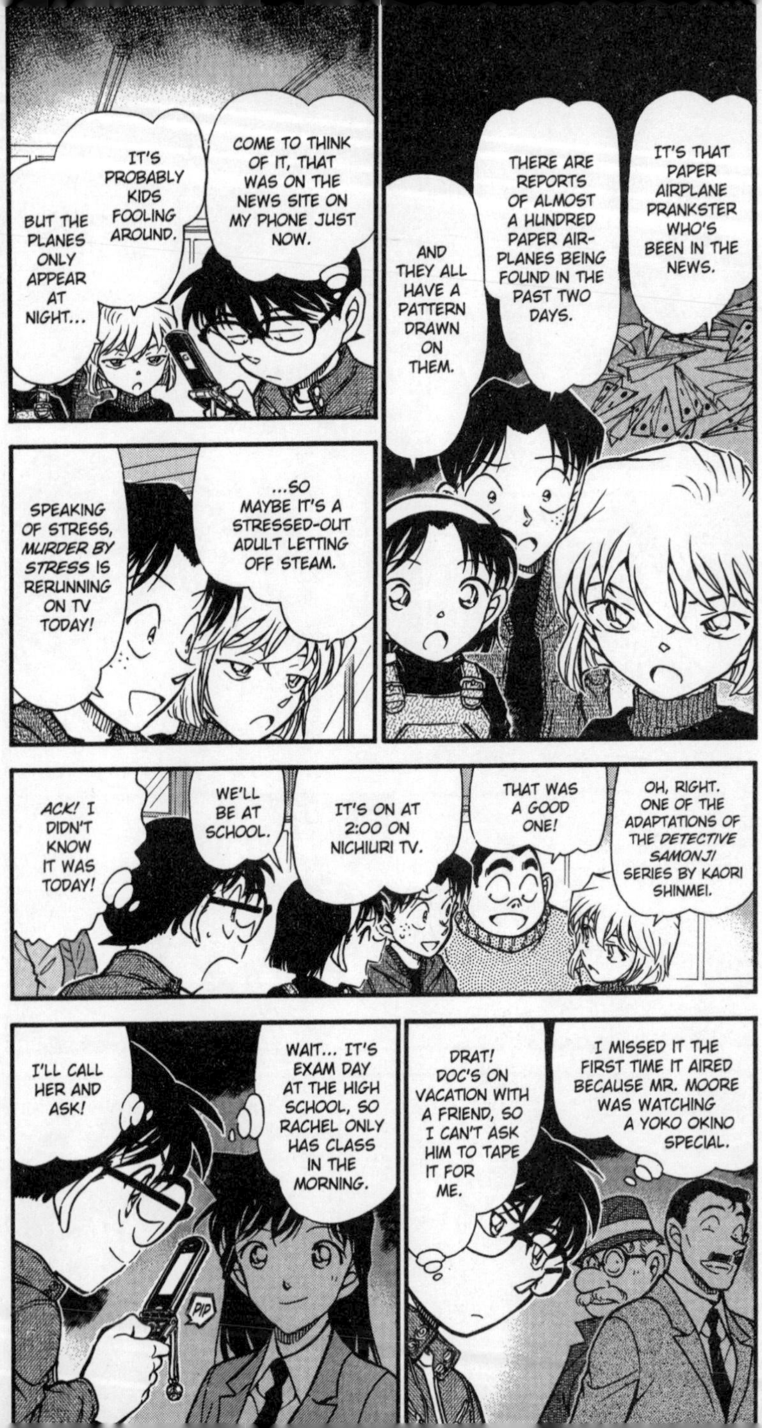

IT'S THAT PAPER AIRPLANE PRANKSTER WHO'S BEEN IN THE NEWS.
THERE ARE REPORTS OF ALMOST A HUNDRED PAPER AIR-PLANES BEING FOUND IN THE PAST TWO DAYS.
AND THEY ALL HAVE A PATTERN DRAWN ON THEM.
COME TO THINK OF IT, THAT WAS ON THE NEWS SITE ON MY PHONE JUST NOW.
IT'S PROBABLY KIDS FOOLING AROUND.
BUT THE PLANES ONLY APPEAR AT NIGHT...
...SO MAYBE IT'S A STRESSED-OUT ADULT LETTING OFF STEAM.
SPEAKING OF STRESS, *MURDER BY STRESS* IS RERUNNING ON TV TODAY!
OH, RIGHT. ONE OF THE ADAPTATIONS OF THE *DETECTIVE SAMONJI* SERIES BY KAORI SHINMEI.
THAT WAS A GOOD ONE!
IT'S ON AT 2:00 ON NICHIURI TV.
WE'LL BE AT SCHOOL.
*ACK!* I DIDN'T KNOW IT WAS TODAY!
I MISSED IT THE FIRST TIME IT AIRED BECAUSE MR. MOORE WAS WATCHING A YOKO OKINO SPECIAL.
DRAT! DOC'S ON VACATION WITH A FRIEND, SO I CAN'T ASK HIM TO TAPE IT FOR ME.
WAIT... IT'S EXAM DAY AT THE HIGH SCHOOL, SO RACHEL ONLY HAS CLASS IN THE MORNING.
I'LL CALL HER AND ASK!
PIP

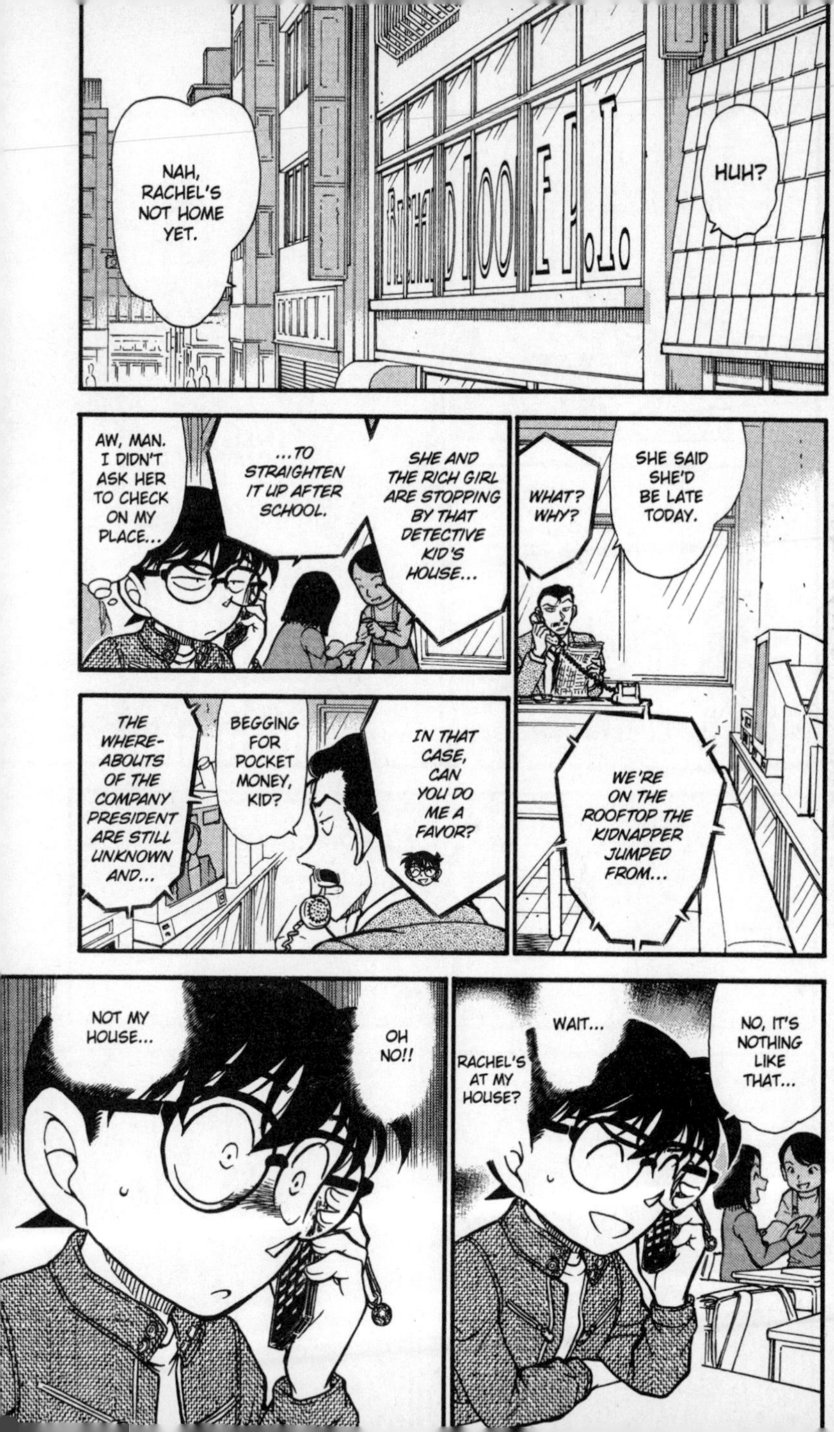
HUH?
NAH, RACHEL'S NOT HOME YET.
SHE SAID SHE'D BE LATE TODAY.
WHAT? WHY?
WE'RE ON THE ROOFTOP THE KIDNAPPER JUMPED FROM...
SHE AND THE RICH GIRL ARE STOPPING BY THAT DETECTIVE KID'S HOUSE...
...TO STRAIGHTEN IT UP AFTER SCHOOL.
AW, MAN. I DIDN'T ASK HER TO CHECK ON MY PLACE...
IN THAT CASE, CAN YOU DO ME A FAVOR?
BEGGING FOR POCKET MONEY, KID?
THE WHERE-ABOUTS OF THE COMPANY PRESIDENT ARE STILL UNKNOWN AND...
NO, IT'S NOTHING LIKE THAT...
WAIT...
RACHEL'S AT MY HOUSE?
OH NO!!
NOT MY HOUSE...

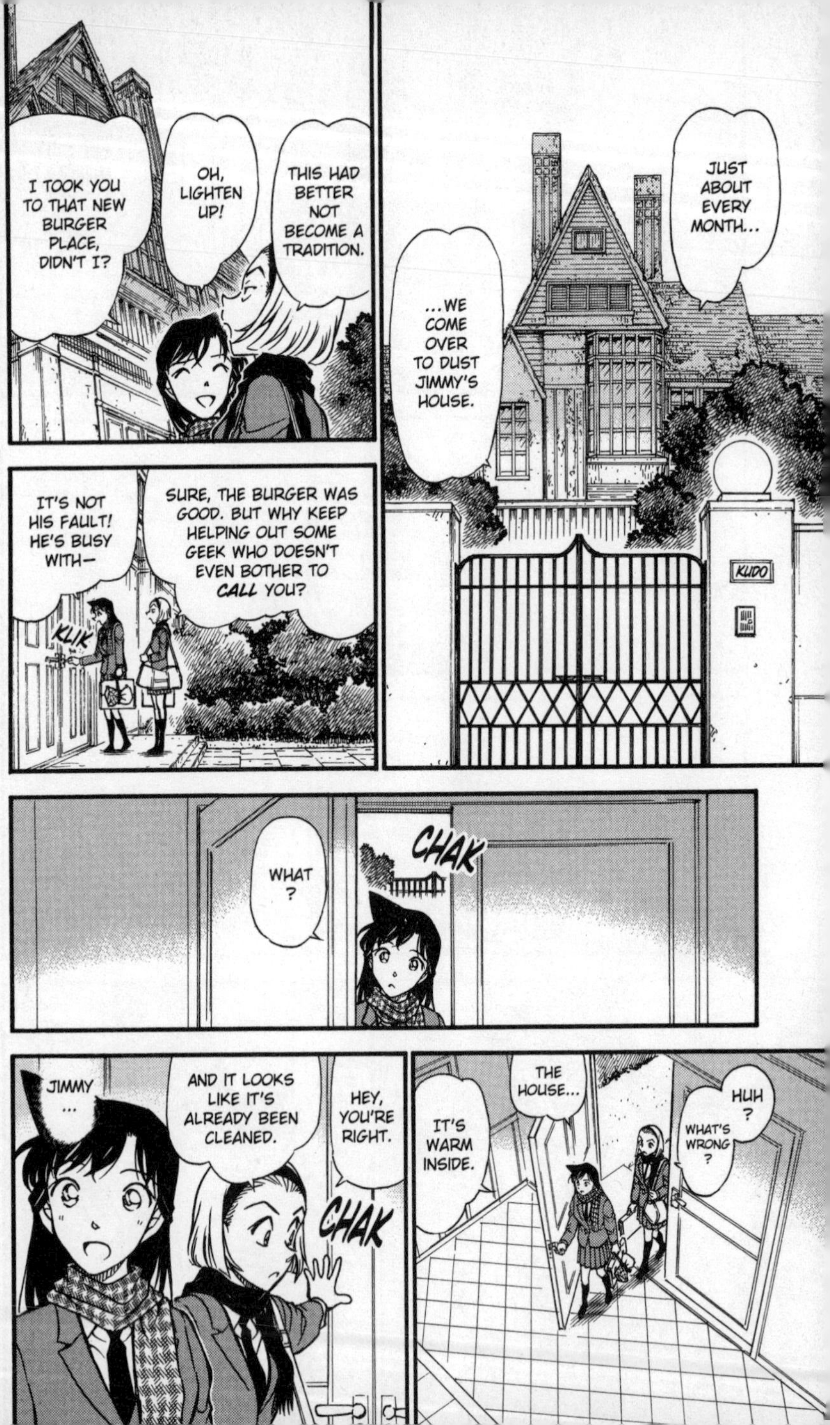
JUST ABOUT EVERY MONTH...
...WE COME OVER TO DUST JIMMY'S HOUSE.
KUDO
THIS HAD BETTER NOT BECOME A TRADITION.
OH, LIGHTEN UP!
I TOOK YOU TO THAT NEW BURGER PLACE, DIDN'T I?
SURE, THE BURGER WAS GOOD. BUT WHY KEEP HELPING OUT SOME GEEK WHO DOESN'T EVEN BOTHER TO CALL YOU?
IT'S NOT HIS FAULT! HE'S BUSY WITH—
KLIK
CHAK
WHAT?
HUH?
WHAT'S WRONG?
THE HOUSE...
IT'S WARM INSIDE.
HEY, YOU'RE RIGHT.
CHAK
AND IT LOOKS LIKE IT'S ALREADY BEEN CLEANED.
JIMMY...

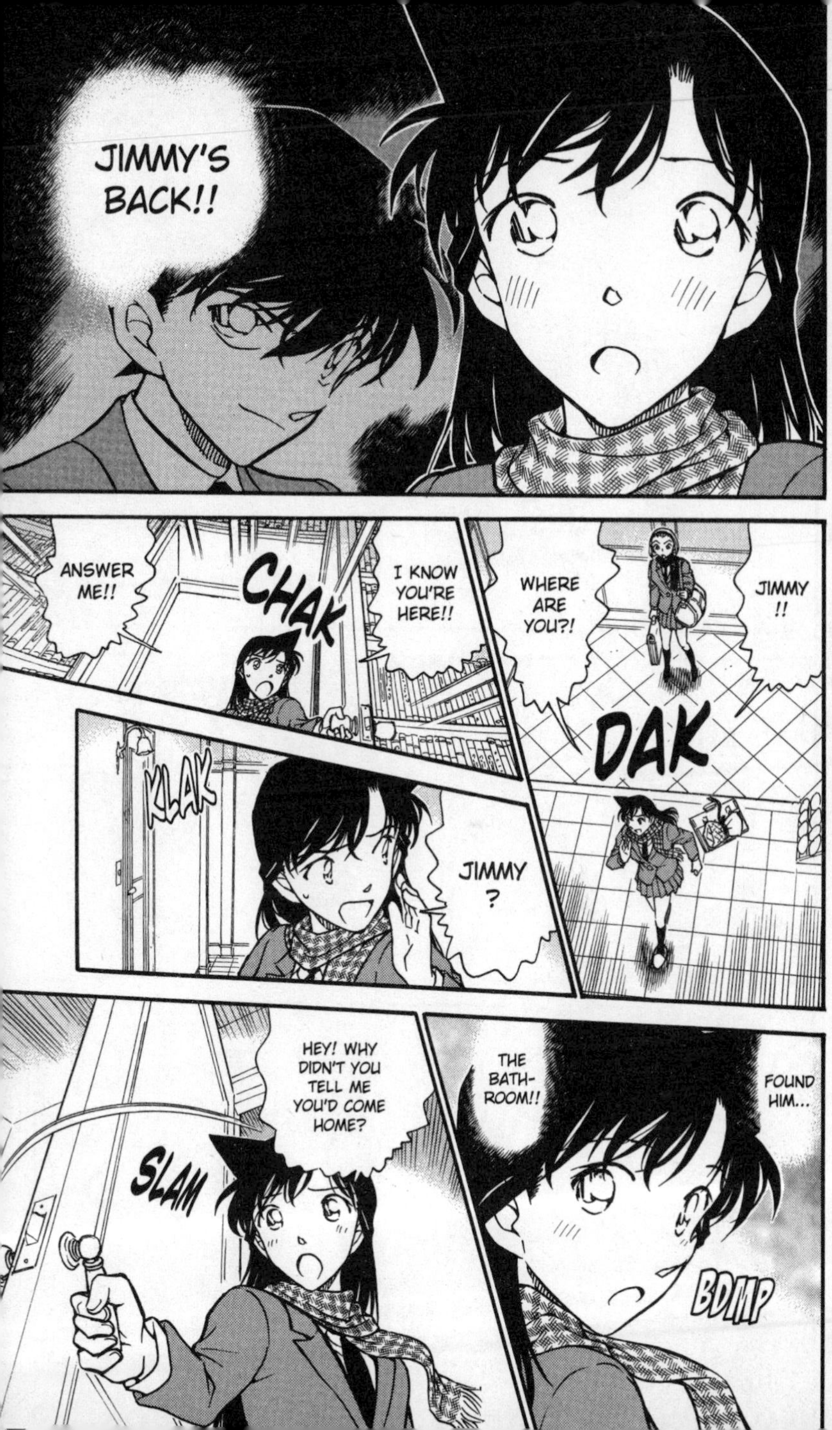
JIMMY'S BACK!!
JIMMY !!
WHERE ARE YOU?!
DAK
I KNOW YOU'RE HERE!!
CHAK
ANSWER ME!!
JIMMY ?
KLAK
FOUND HIM...
THE BATH-ROOM!!
BDMP
HEY! WHY DIDN'T YOU TELL ME YOU'D COME HOME?
SLAM

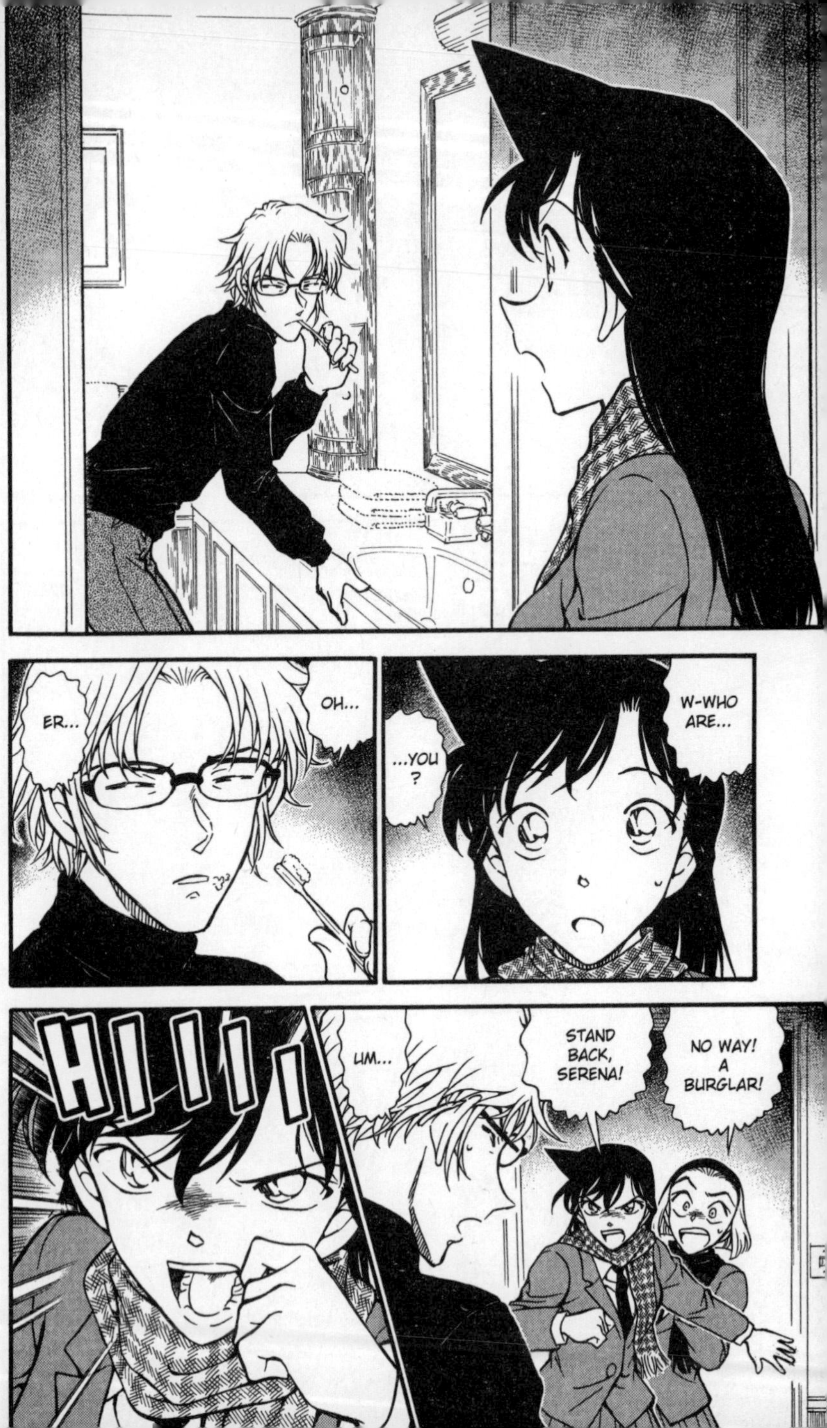
W-WHO ARE...
...YOU?
OH...
ER...
NO WAY! A BURGLAR!
STAND BACK, SERENA!
UM...
HIIII

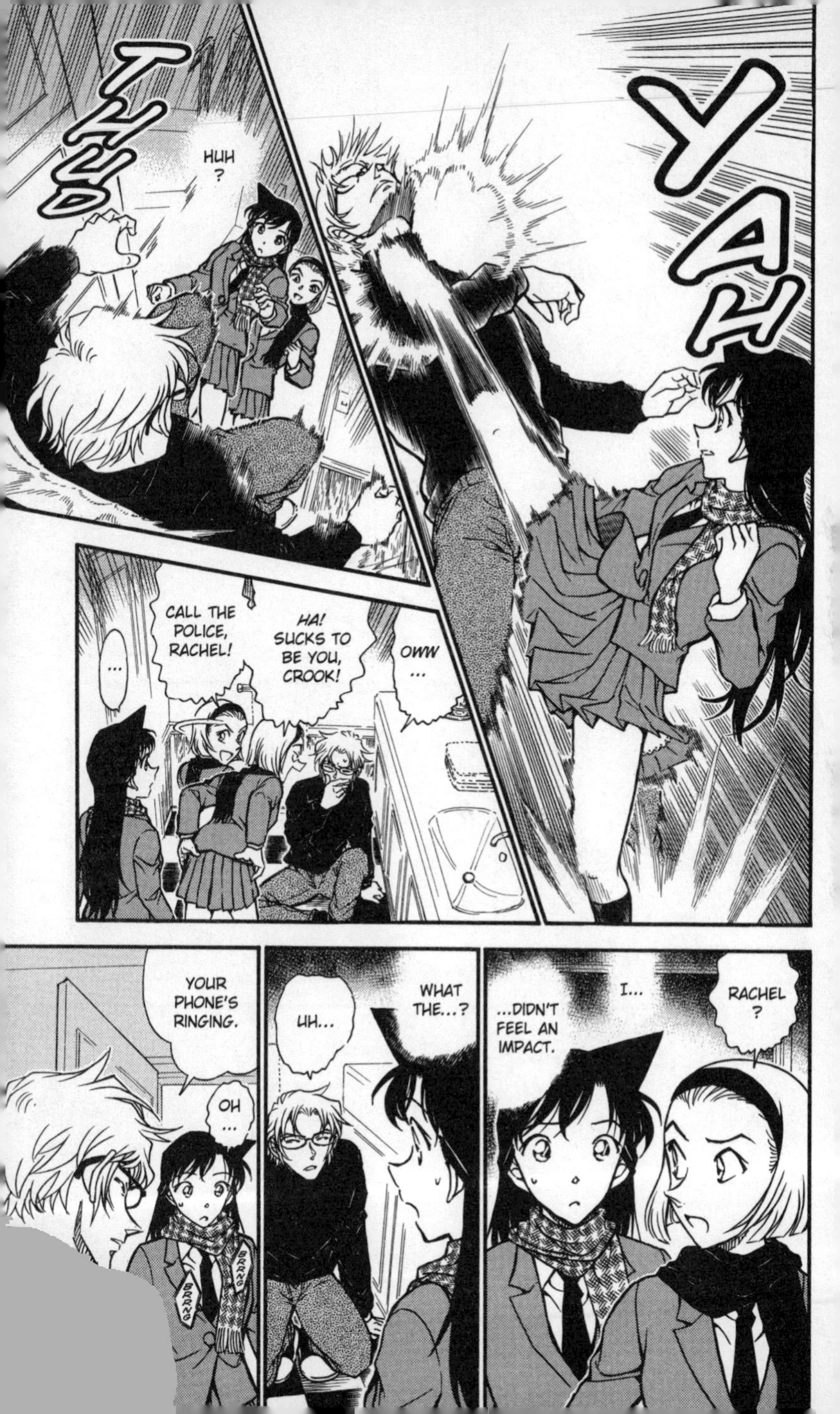
YAH
THUD
HUH?
OWW...
HA! SUCKS TO BE YOU, CROOK!
CALL THE POLICE, RACHEL!
...
RACHEL?
I...
...DIDN'T FEEL AN IMPACT.
WHAT THE...?
UH...
YOUR PHONE'S RINGING.
OH...
BRRNG
BRRNG

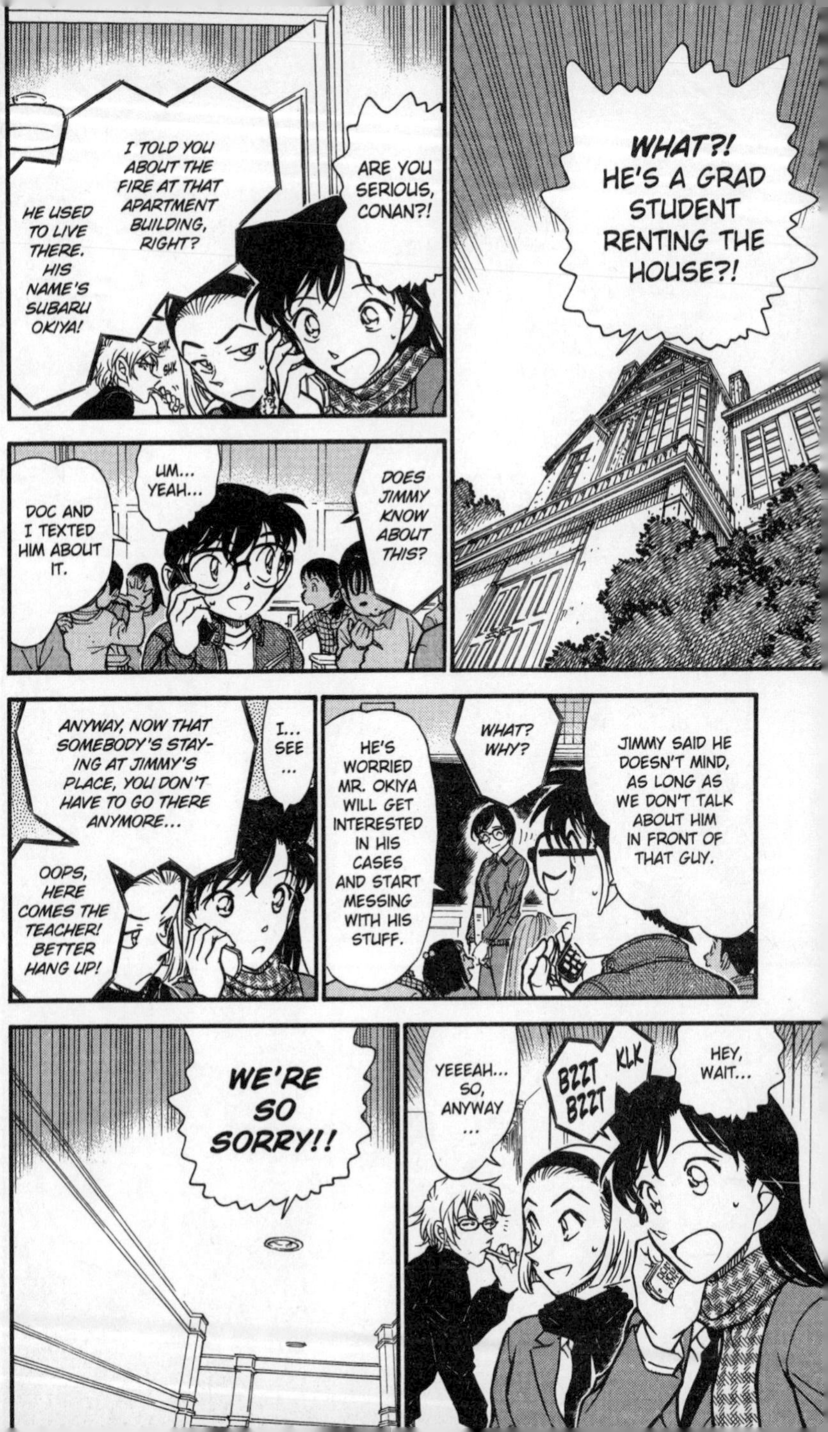
WHAT?! HE'S A GRAD STUDENT RENTING THE HOUSE?!
ARE YOU SERIOUS, CONAN?!
I TOLD YOU ABOUT THE FIRE AT THAT APARTMENT BUILDING, RIGHT?
HE USED TO LIVE THERE. HIS NAME'S SUBARU OKIYA!
SHK
SHK
DOES JIMMY KNOW ABOUT THIS?
UM... YEAH...
DOC AND I TEXTED HIM ABOUT IT.
JIMMY SAID HE DOESN'T MIND, AS LONG AS WE DON'T TALK ABOUT HIM IN FRONT OF THAT GUY.
WHAT? WHY?
HE'S WORRIED MR. OKIYA WILL GET INTERESTED IN HIS CASES AND START MESSING WITH HIS STUFF.
I... SEE ...
ANYWAY, NOW THAT SOMEBODY'S STAY-ING AT JIMMY'S PLACE, YOU DON'T HAVE TO GO THERE ANYMORE...
OOPS, HERE COMES THE TEACHER! BETTER HANG UP!
HEY, WAIT...
KLK
BZZT BZZT
YEEEAH... SO, ANYWAY ...
WE'RE SO SORRY!!

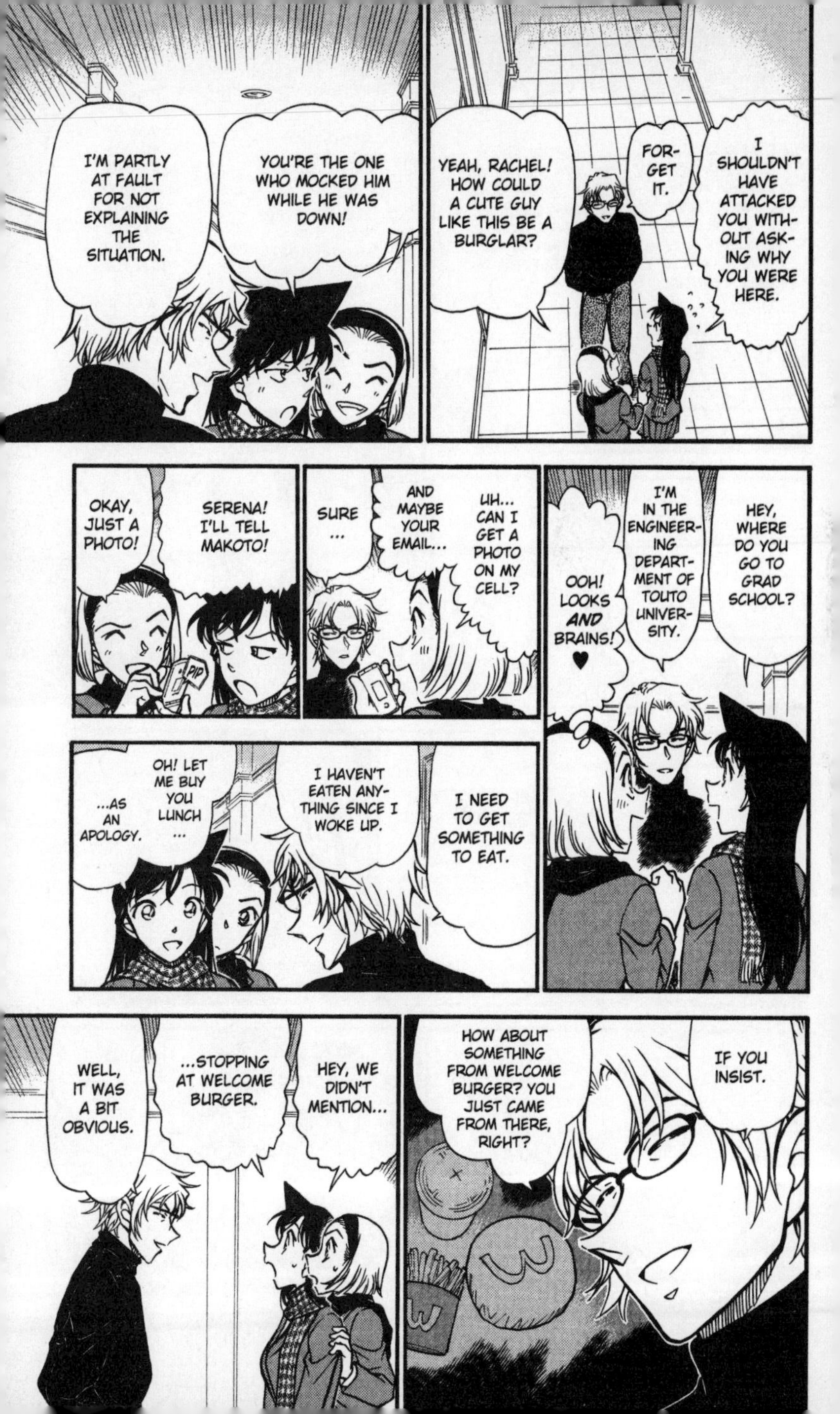
I SHOULDN'T HAVE ATTACKED YOU WITHOUT ASKING WHY YOU WERE HERE.
FORGET IT.
YEAH, RACHEL! HOW COULD A CUTE GUY LIKE THIS BE A BURGLAR?
YOU'RE THE ONE WHO MOCKED HIM WHILE HE WAS DOWN!
I'M PARTLY AT FAULT FOR NOT EXPLAINING THE SITUATION.
HEY, WHERE DO YOU GO TO GRAD SCHOOL?
I'M IN THE ENGINEERING DEPARTMENT OF TOUTO UNIVERSITY.
OOH! LOOKS **AND** BRAINS! ♥
UH... CAN I GET A PHOTO ON MY CELL?
AND MAYBE YOUR EMAIL...
SURE ...
SERENA! I'LL TELL MAKOTO!
OKAY, JUST A PHOTO!
PIP
I NEED TO GET SOMETHING TO EAT.
I HAVEN'T EATEN ANYTHING SINCE I WOKE UP.
OH! LET ME BUY YOU LUNCH ...
...AS AN APOLOGY.
IF YOU INSIST.
HOW ABOUT SOMETHING FROM WELCOME BURGER? YOU JUST CAME FROM THERE, RIGHT?
HEY, WE DIDN'T MENTION...
...STOPPING AT WELCOME BURGER.
WELL, IT WAS A BIT OBVIOUS.

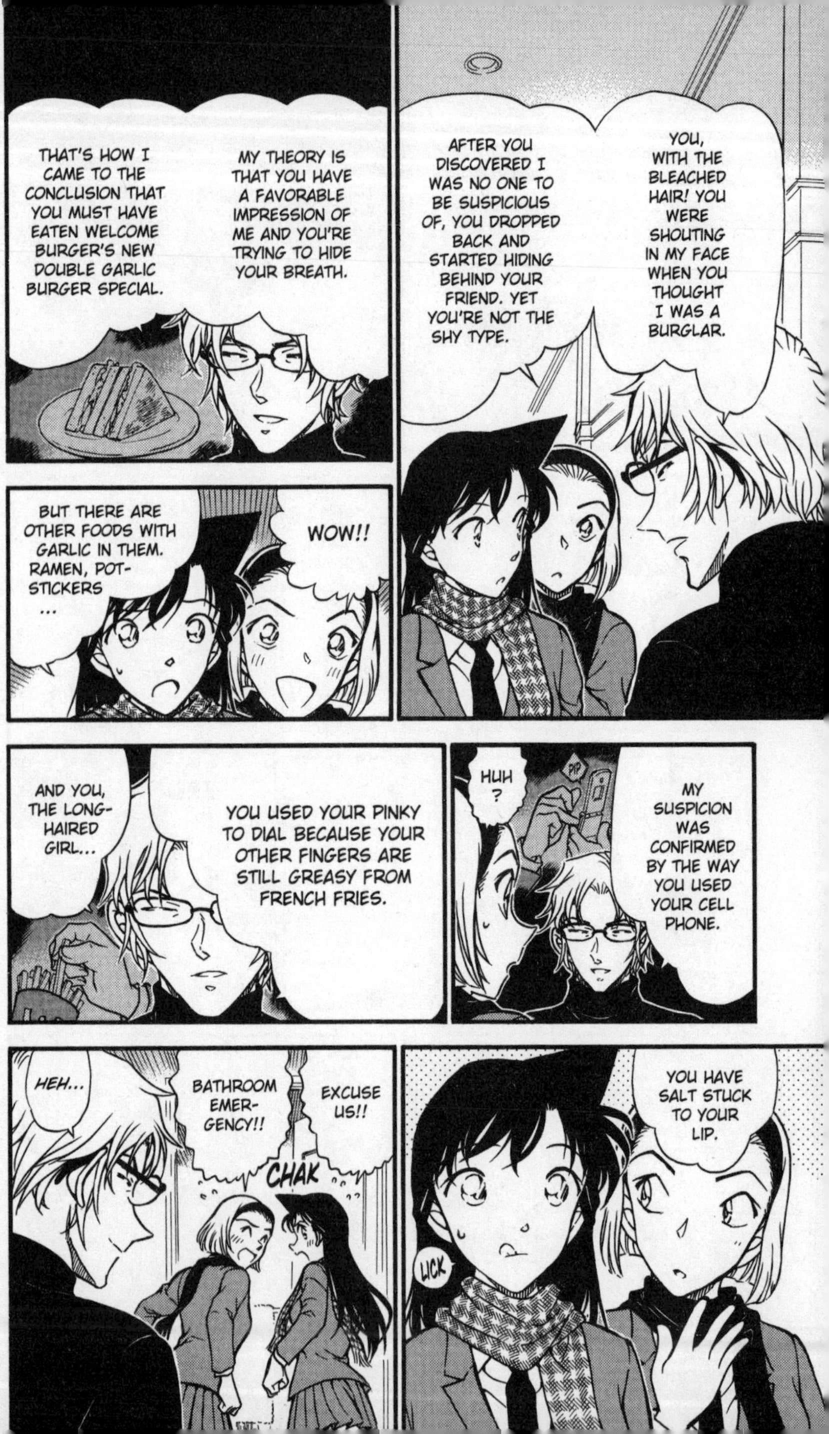
YOU, WITH THE BLEACHED HAIR! YOU WERE SHOUTING IN MY FACE WHEN YOU THOUGHT I WAS A BURGLAR.
AFTER YOU DISCOVERED I WAS NO ONE TO BE SUSPICIOUS OF, YOU DROPPED BACK AND STARTED HIDING BEHIND YOUR FRIEND. YET YOU'RE NOT THE SHY TYPE.
MY THEORY IS THAT YOU HAVE A FAVORABLE IMPRESSION OF ME AND YOU'RE TRYING TO HIDE YOUR BREATH.
THAT'S HOW I CAME TO THE CONCLUSION THAT YOU MUST HAVE EATEN WELCOME BURGER'S NEW DOUBLE GARLIC BURGER SPECIAL.
WOW!!
BUT THERE ARE OTHER FOODS WITH GARLIC IN THEM. RAMEN, POT-STICKERS ...
HUH ?
PIP
MY SUSPICION WAS CONFIRMED BY THE WAY YOU USED YOUR CELL PHONE.
AND YOU, THE LONG-HAIRED GIRL...
YOU USED YOUR PINKY TO DIAL BECAUSE YOUR OTHER FINGERS ARE STILL GREASY FROM FRENCH FRIES.
YOU HAVE SALT STUCK TO YOUR LIP.
LICK
EXCUSE US!!
BATHROOM EMERGENCY!!
CHAK
HEH...

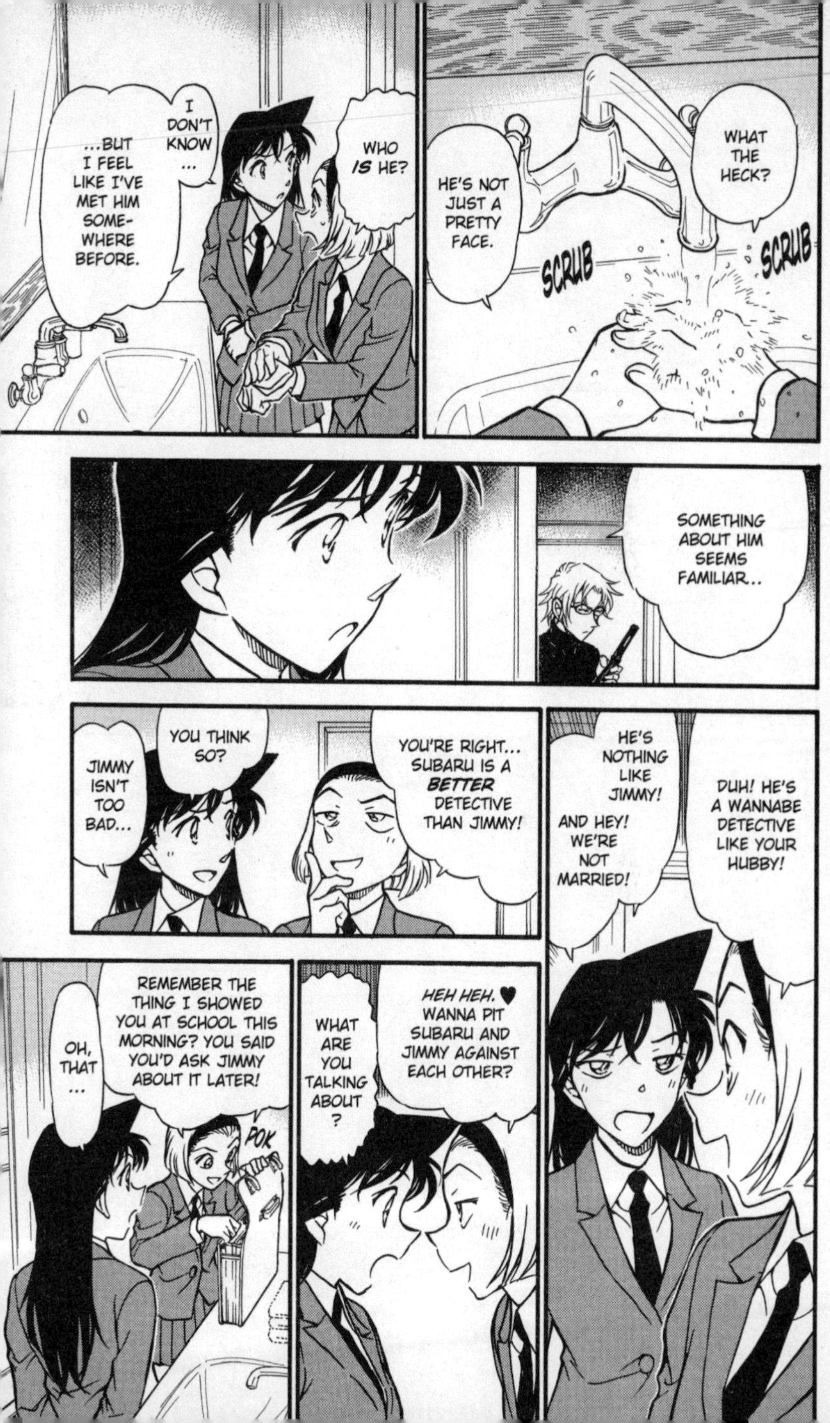
WHAT THE HECK?
HE'S NOT JUST A PRETTY FACE.
SCRUB
SCRUB
WHO *IS* HE?
I DON'T KNOW...
...BUT I FEEL LIKE I'VE MET HIM SOME-WHERE BEFORE.
SOMETHING ABOUT HIM SEEMS FAMILIAR...
DUH! HE'S A WANNABE DETECTIVE LIKE YOUR HUBBY!
HE'S NOTHING LIKE JIMMY!
AND HEY! WE'RE NOT MARRIED!
YOU'RE RIGHT... SUBARU IS A ***BETTER*** DETECTIVE THAN JIMMY!
YOU THINK SO?
JIMMY ISN'T TOO BAD...
*HEH HEH.* ♥ WANNA PIT SUBARU AND JIMMY AGAINST EACH OTHER?
WHAT ARE YOU TALKING ABOUT?
REMEMBER THE THING I SHOWED YOU AT SCHOOL THIS MORNING? YOU SAID YOU'D ASK JIMMY ABOUT IT LATER!
OH, THAT...
POK

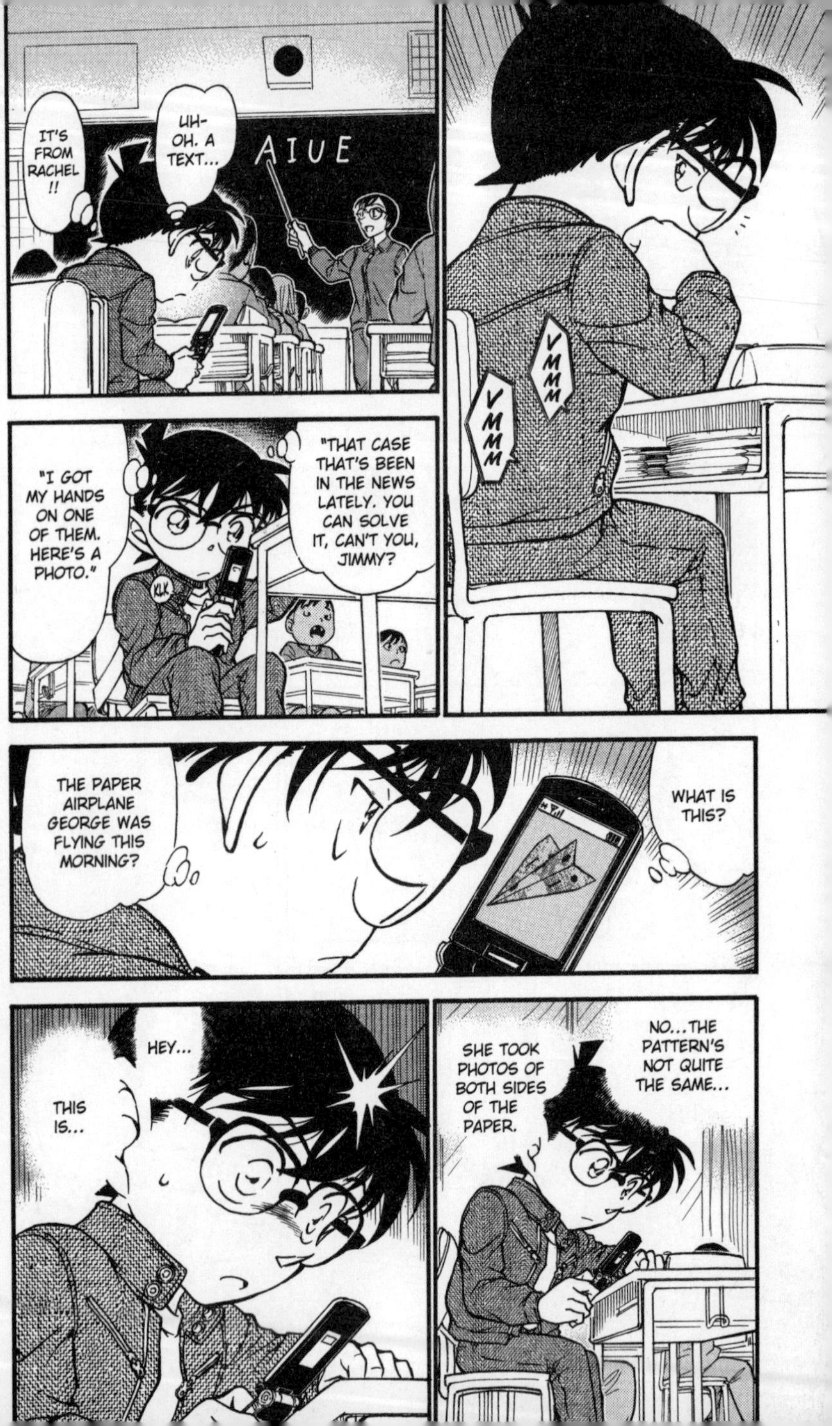
VMMM
VMMM
UH-OH. A TEXT...
IT'S FROM RACHEL !!
AIUE
"THAT CASE THAT'S BEEN IN THE NEWS LATELY. YOU CAN SOLVE IT, CAN'T YOU, JIMMY?
"I GOT MY HANDS ON ONE OF THEM. HERE'S A PHOTO."
KLK
WHAT IS THIS?
THE PAPER AIRPLANE GEORGE WAS FLYING THIS MORNING?
NO...THE PATTERN'S NOT QUITE THE SAME...
SHE TOOK PHOTOS OF BOTH SIDES OF THE PAPER.
HEY...
THIS IS...

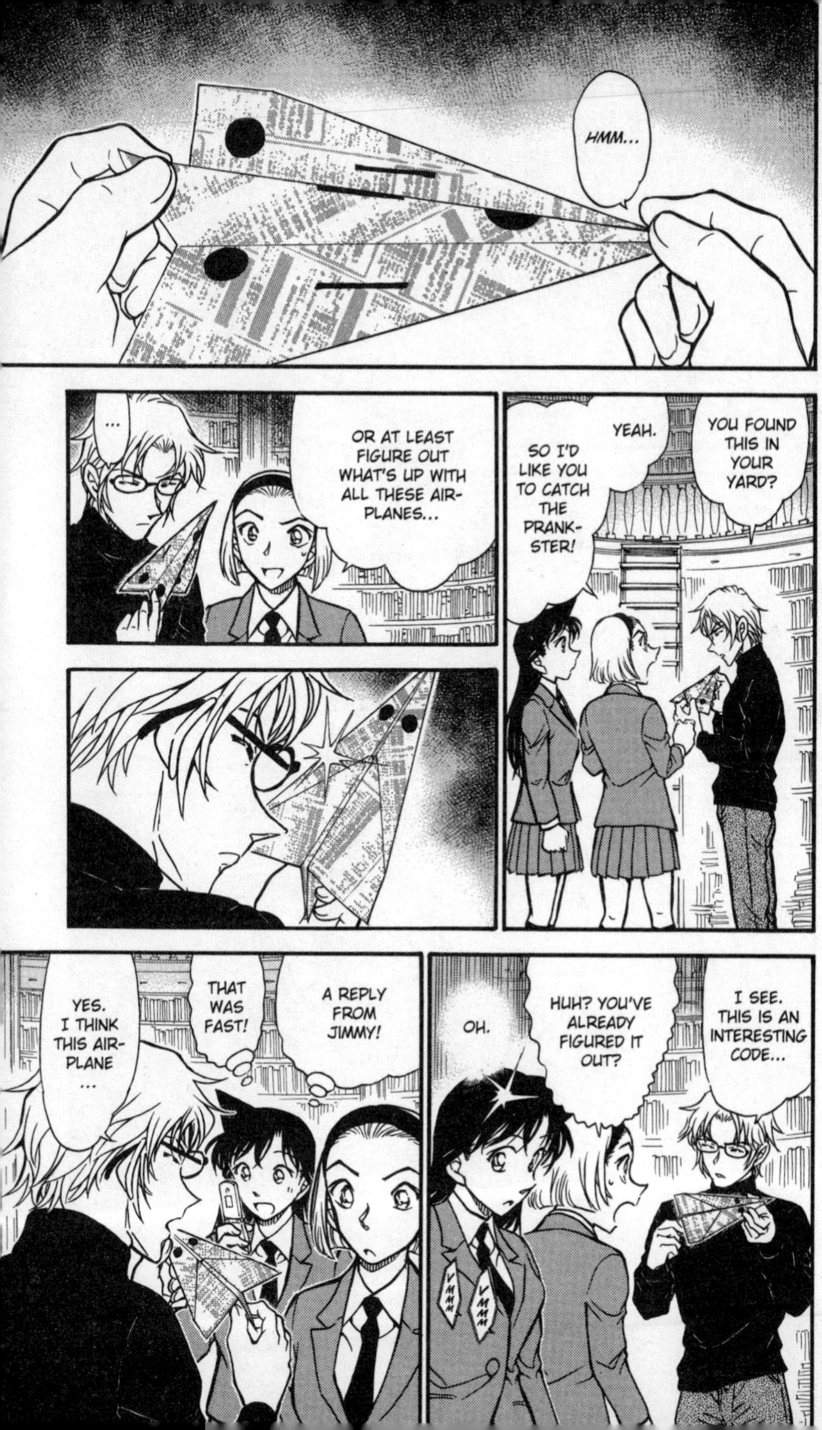
HMM...
YOU FOUND THIS IN YOUR YARD?
YEAH.
SO I'D LIKE YOU TO CATCH THE PRANK-STER!
OR AT LEAST FIGURE OUT WHAT'S UP WITH ALL THESE AIR-PLANES...
...
I SEE. THIS IS AN INTERESTING CODE...
HUH? YOU'VE ALREADY FIGURED IT OUT?
OH.
VMMM
VMMM
A REPLY FROM JIMMY!
THAT WAS FAST!
YES. I THINK THIS AIR-PLANE ...

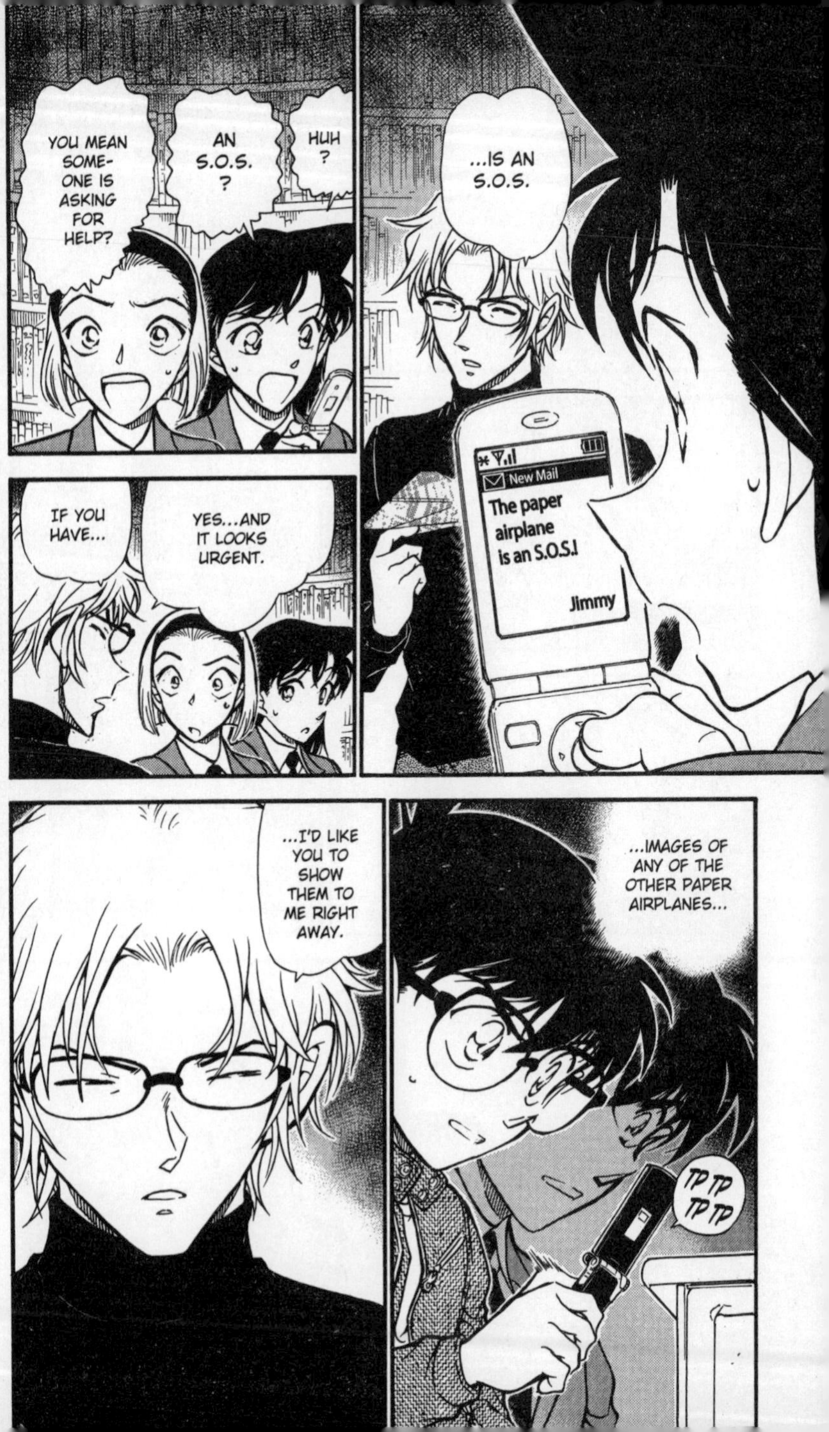
...IS AN S.O.S.
New Mail
The paper airplane is an S.O.S.!
Jimmy
HUH?
AN S.O.S.?
YOU MEAN SOME-ONE IS ASKING FOR HELP?
YES...AND IT LOOKS URGENT.
IF YOU HAVE...
...IMAGES OF ANY OF THE OTHER PAPER AIRPLANES...
TP TP TP TP
...I'D LIKE YOU TO SHOW THEM TO ME RIGHT AWAY.

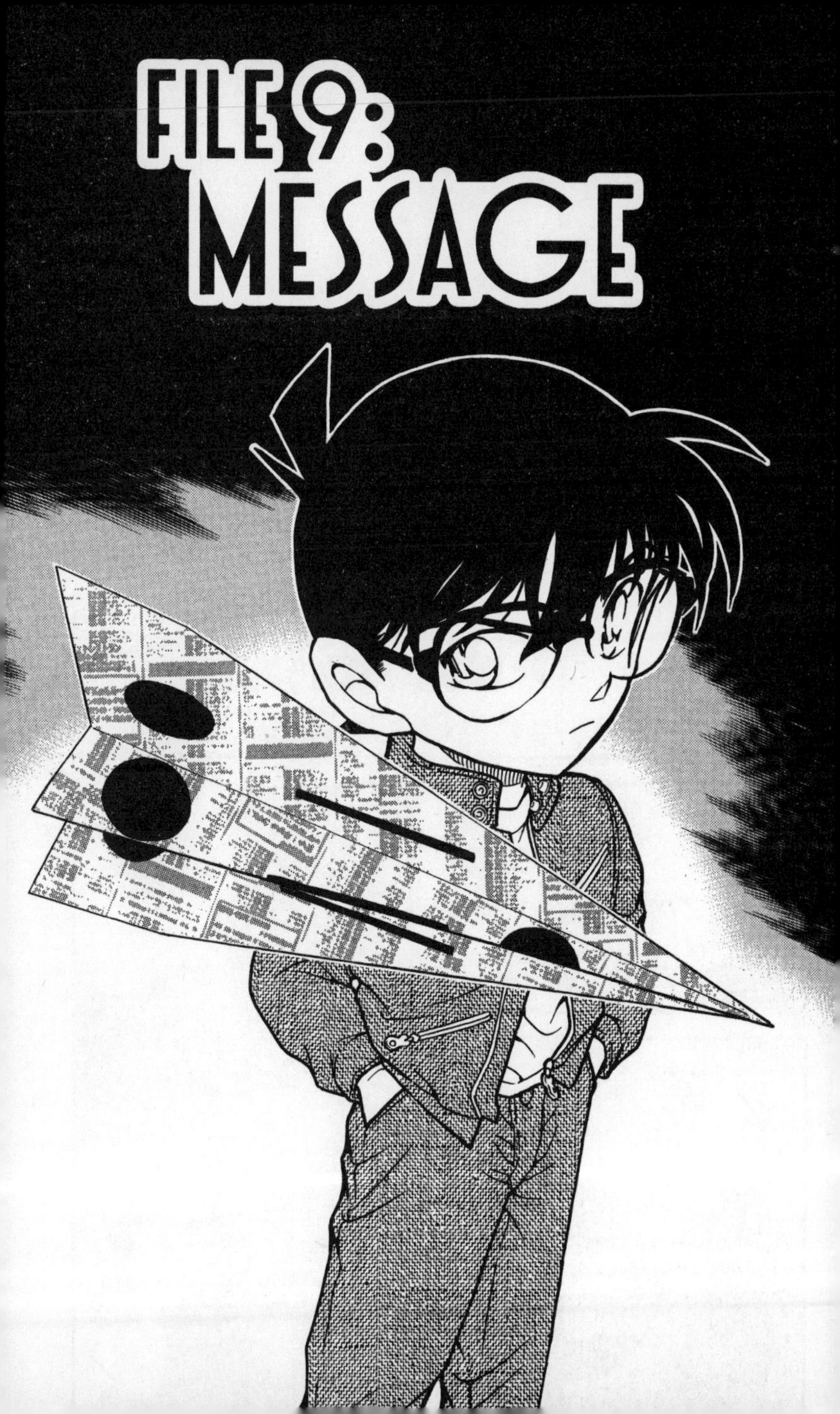
FILE 9:
MESSAGE

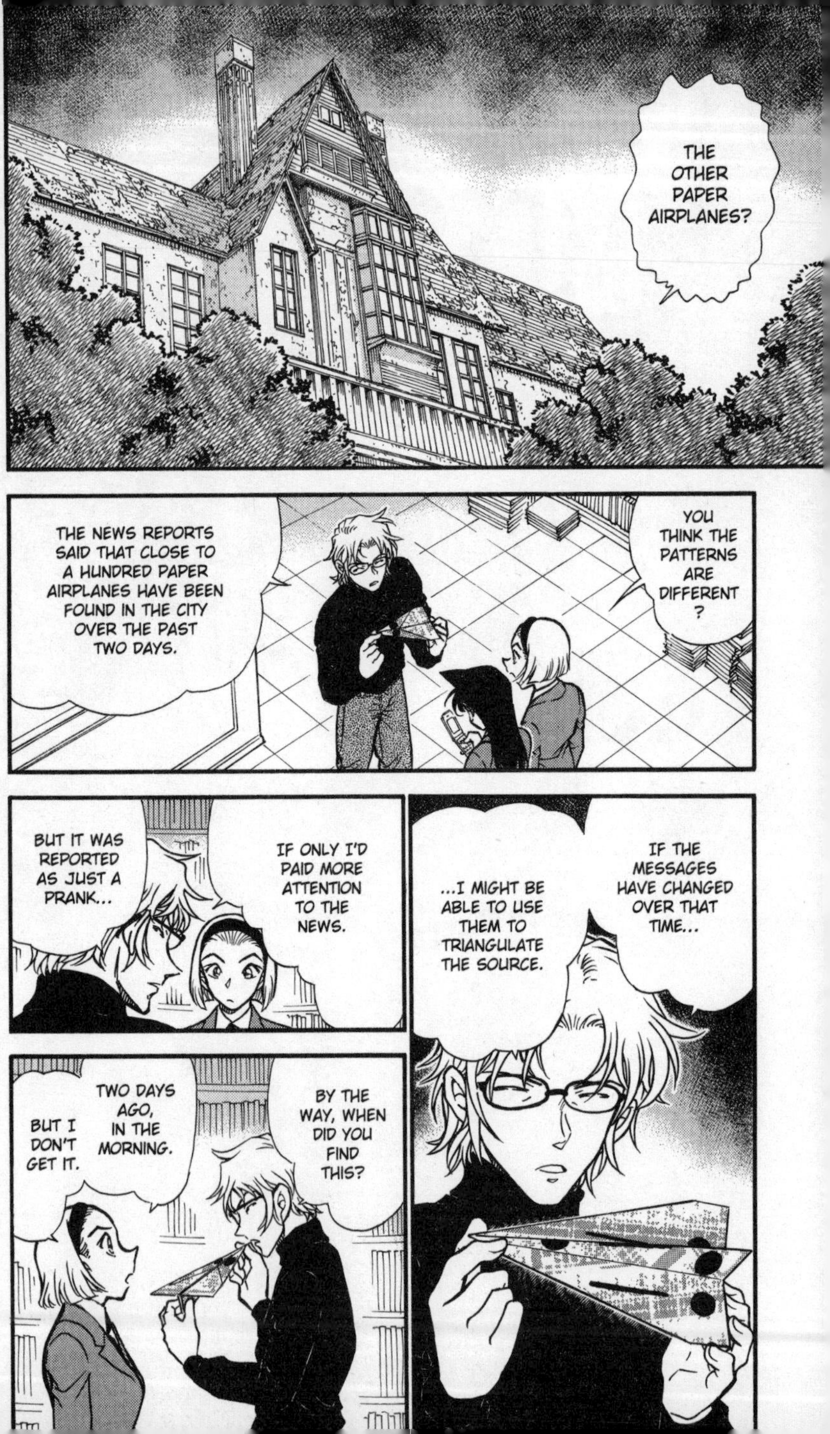
THE OTHER PAPER AIRPLANES?
YOU THINK THE PATTERNS ARE DIFFERENT?
THE NEWS REPORTS SAID THAT CLOSE TO A HUNDRED PAPER AIRPLANES HAVE BEEN FOUND IN THE CITY OVER THE PAST TWO DAYS.
IF THE MESSAGES HAVE CHANGED OVER THAT TIME...
...I MIGHT BE ABLE TO USE THEM TO TRIANGULATE THE SOURCE.
IF ONLY I'D PAID MORE ATTENTION TO THE NEWS.
BUT IT WAS REPORTED AS JUST A PRANK...
BY THE WAY, WHEN DID YOU FIND THIS?
TWO DAYS AGO, IN THE MORNING.
BUT I DON'T GET IT.

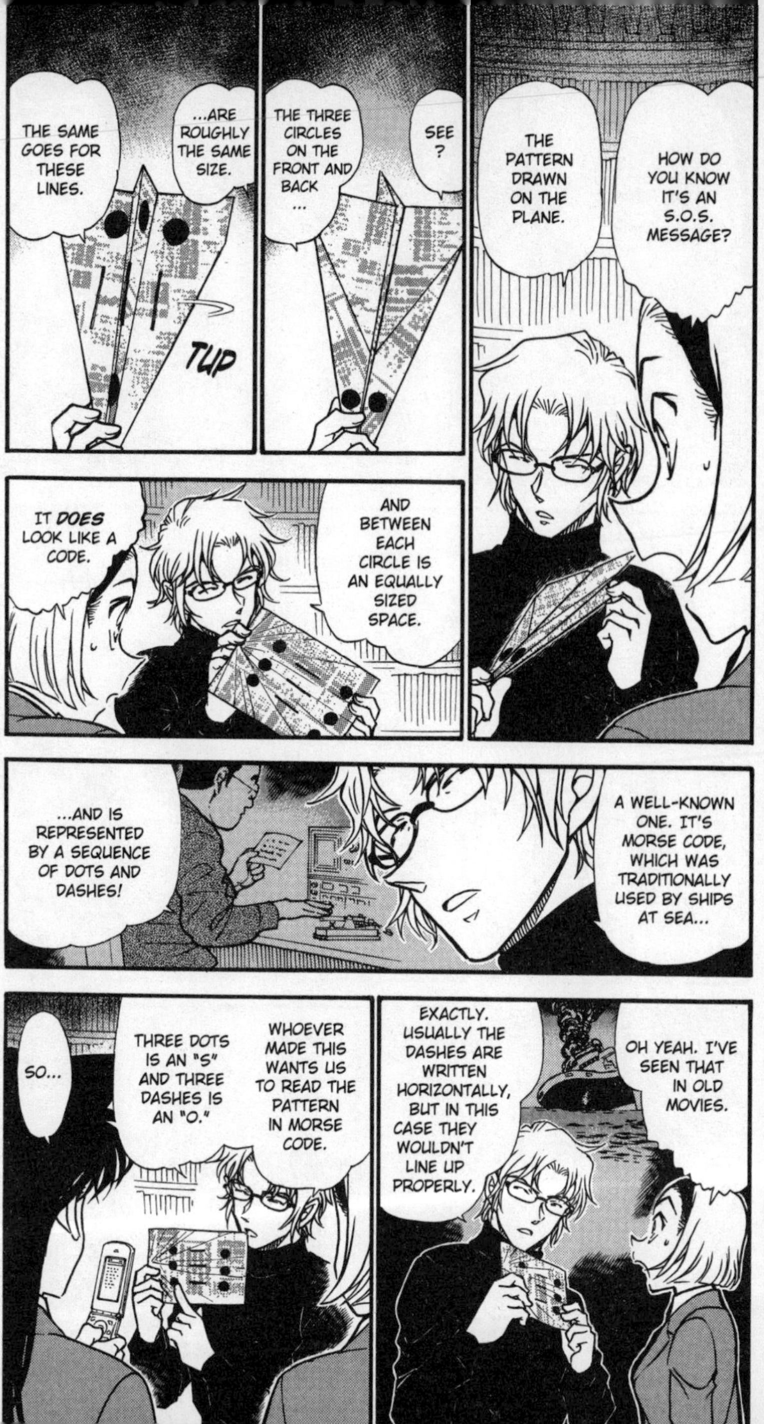
HOW DO YOU KNOW IT'S AN S.O.S. MESSAGE?
THE PATTERN DRAWN ON THE PLANE.
SEE?
THE THREE CIRCLES ON THE FRONT AND BACK ...
...ARE ROUGHLY THE SAME SIZE.
THE SAME GOES FOR THESE LINES.
TUP
AND BETWEEN EACH CIRCLE IS AN EQUALLY SIZED SPACE.
IT DOES LOOK LIKE A CODE.
A WELL-KNOWN ONE. IT'S MORSE CODE, WHICH WAS TRADITIONALLY USED BY SHIPS AT SEA...
...AND IS REPRESENTED BY A SEQUENCE OF DOTS AND DASHES!
OH YEAH. I'VE SEEN THAT IN OLD MOVIES.
EXACTLY. USUALLY THE DASHES ARE WRITTEN HORIZONTALLY, BUT IN THIS CASE THEY WOULDN'T LINE UP PROPERLY.
WHOEVER MADE THIS WANTS US TO READ THE PATTERN IN MORSE CODE.
THREE DOTS IS AN "S" AND THREE DASHES IS AN "O."
SO...

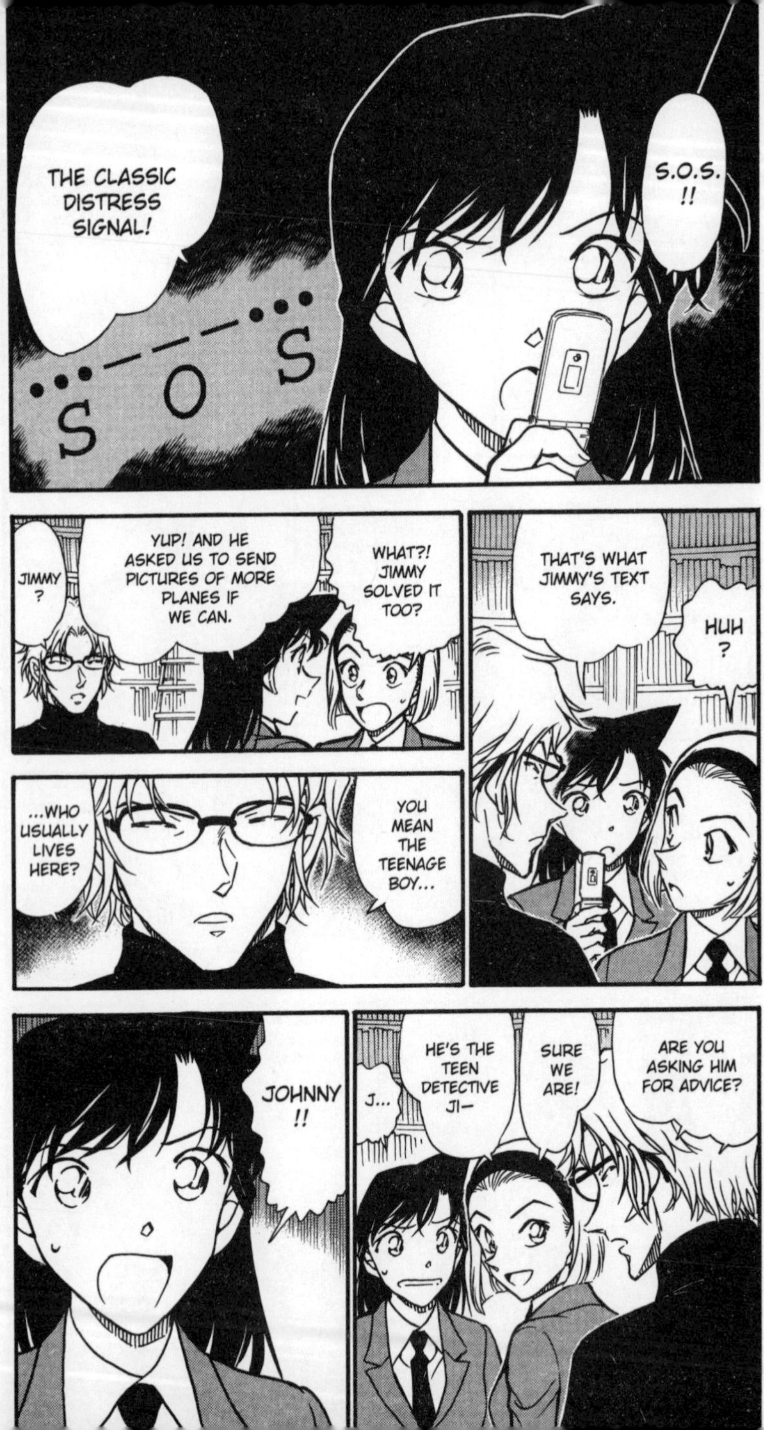
S.O.S. !!
THE CLASSIC DISTRESS SIGNAL!
S O S
THAT'S WHAT JIMMY'S TEXT SAYS.
HUH ?
WHAT?! JIMMY SOLVED IT TOO?
YUP! AND HE ASKED US TO SEND PICTURES OF MORE PLANES IF WE CAN.
JIMMY ?
YOU MEAN THE TEENAGE BOY...
...WHO USUALLY LIVES HERE?
ARE YOU ASKING HIM FOR ADVICE?
SURE WE ARE!
HE'S THE TEEN DETECTIVE JI—
J...
JOHNNY !!

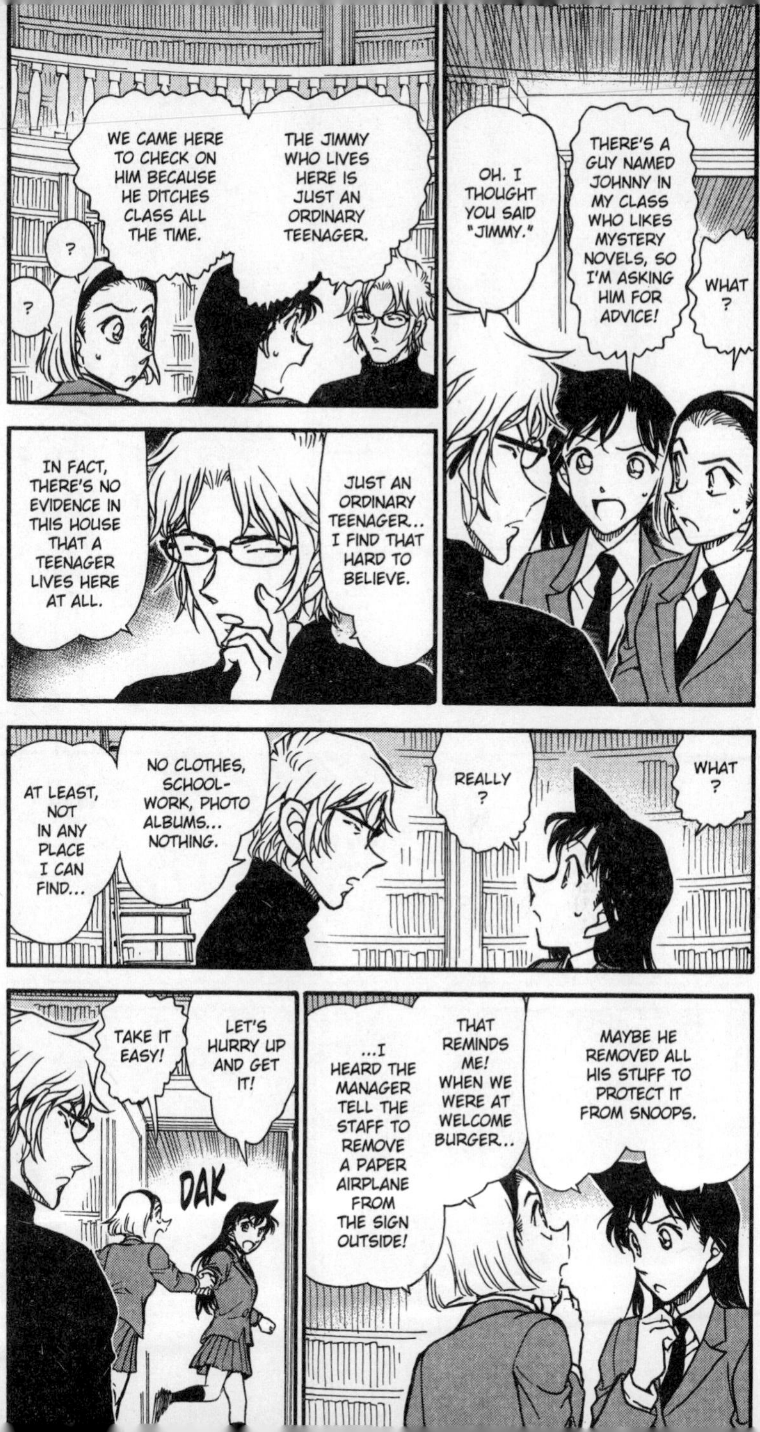
WHAT?
THERE'S A GUY NAMED JOHNNY IN MY CLASS WHO LIKES MYSTERY NOVELS, SO I'M ASKING HIM FOR ADVICE!
OH. I THOUGHT YOU SAID "JIMMY."
THE JIMMY WHO LIVES HERE IS JUST AN ORDINARY TEENAGER.
WE CAME HERE TO CHECK ON HIM BECAUSE HE DITCHES CLASS ALL THE TIME.
?
?
JUST AN ORDINARY TEENAGER... I FIND THAT HARD TO BELIEVE.
IN FACT, THERE'S NO EVIDENCE IN THIS HOUSE THAT A TEENAGER LIVES HERE AT ALL.
WHAT?
REALLY?
NO CLOTHES, SCHOOL-WORK, PHOTO ALBUMS... NOTHING.
AT LEAST, NOT IN ANY PLACE I CAN FIND...
MAYBE HE REMOVED ALL HIS STUFF TO PROTECT IT FROM SNOOPS.
THAT REMINDS ME! WHEN WE WERE AT WELCOME BURGER...
...I HEARD THE MANAGER TELL THE STAFF TO REMOVE A PAPER AIRPLANE FROM THE SIGN OUTSIDE!
LET'S HURRY UP AND GET IT!
TAKE IT EASY!
DAK

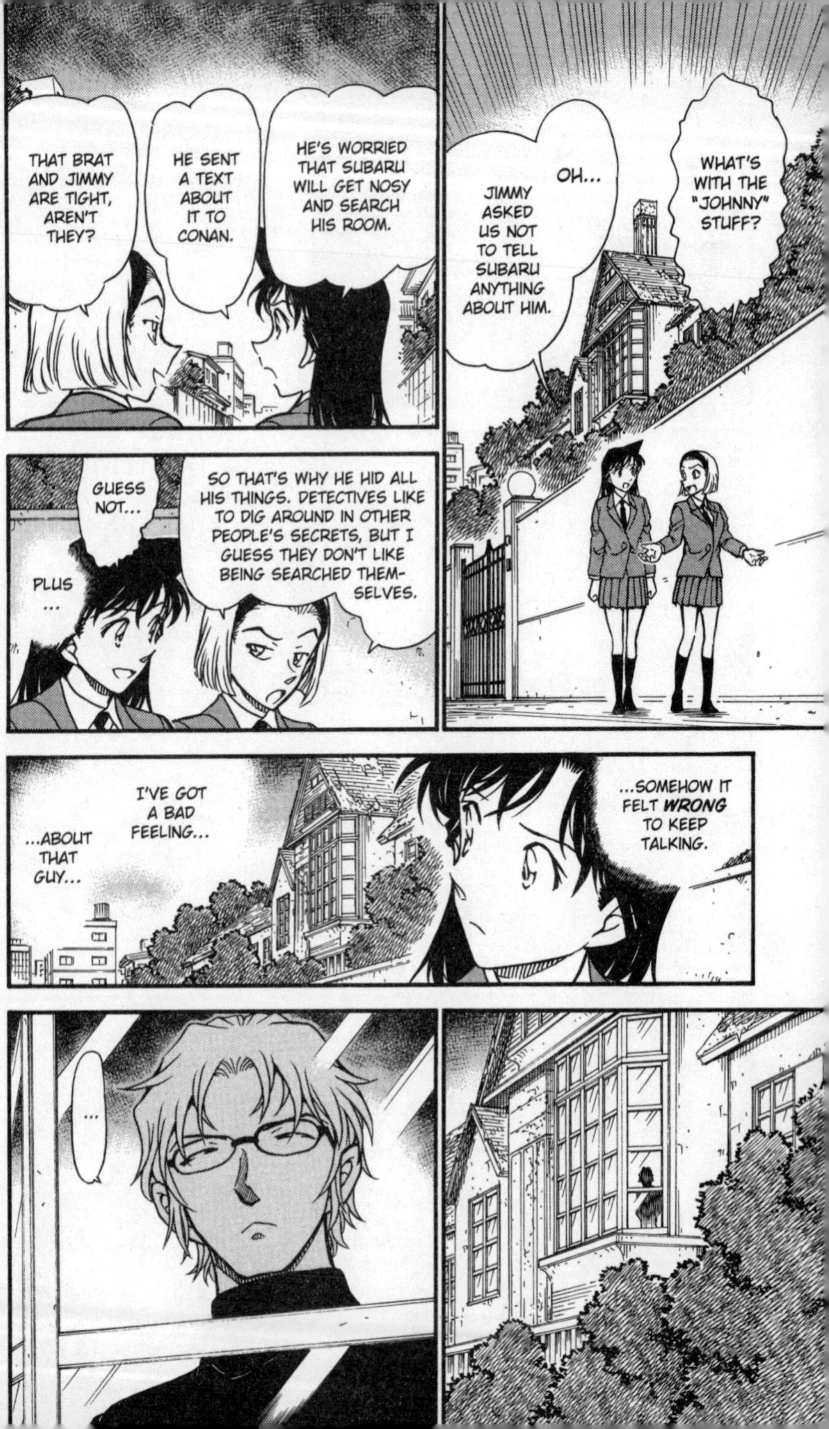
WHAT'S WITH THE "JOHNNY" STUFF?
OH...
JIMMY ASKED US NOT TO TELL SUBARU ANYTHING ABOUT HIM.
HE'S WORRIED THAT SUBARU WILL GET NOSY AND SEARCH HIS ROOM.
HE SENT A TEXT ABOUT IT TO CONAN.
THAT BRAT AND JIMMY ARE TIGHT, AREN'T THEY?
SO THAT'S WHY HE HID ALL HIS THINGS. DETECTIVES LIKE TO DIG AROUND IN OTHER PEOPLE'S SECRETS, BUT I GUESS THEY DON'T LIKE BEING SEARCHED THEMSELVES.
GUESS NOT...
PLUS ...
...SOMEHOW IT FELT **WRONG** TO KEEP TALKING.
I'VE GOT A BAD FEELING...
...ABOUT THAT GUY...
...

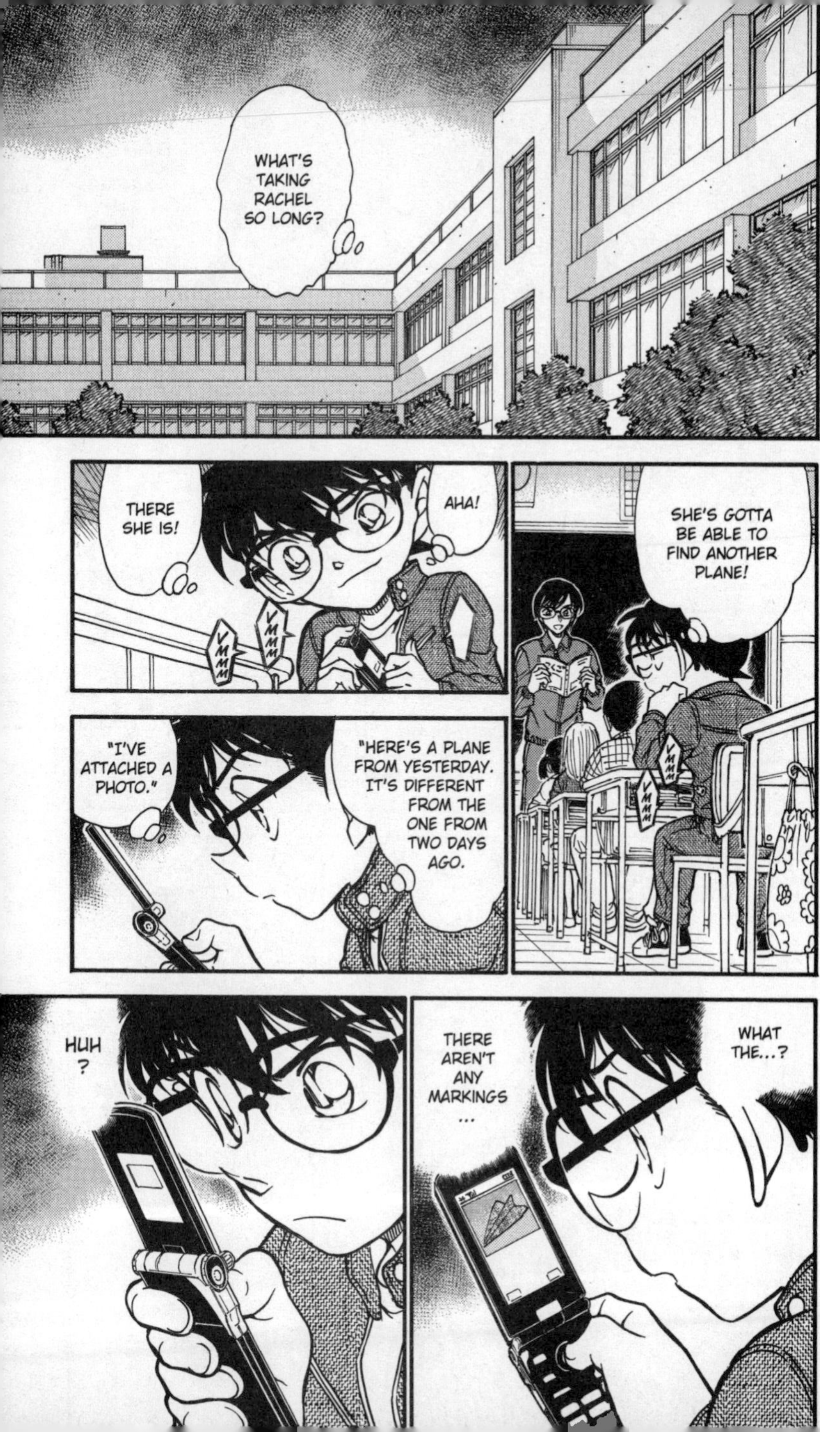
WHAT'S TAKING RACHEL SO LONG?
SHE'S GOTTA BE ABLE TO FIND ANOTHER PLANE!
VMMM
VMMM
AHA!
THERE SHE IS!
VMMM
VMMM
"HERE'S A PLANE FROM YESTERDAY. IT'S DIFFERENT FROM THE ONE FROM TWO DAYS AGO.
"I'VE ATTACHED A PHOTO."
WHAT THE...?
THERE AREN'T ANY MARKINGS...
HUH?

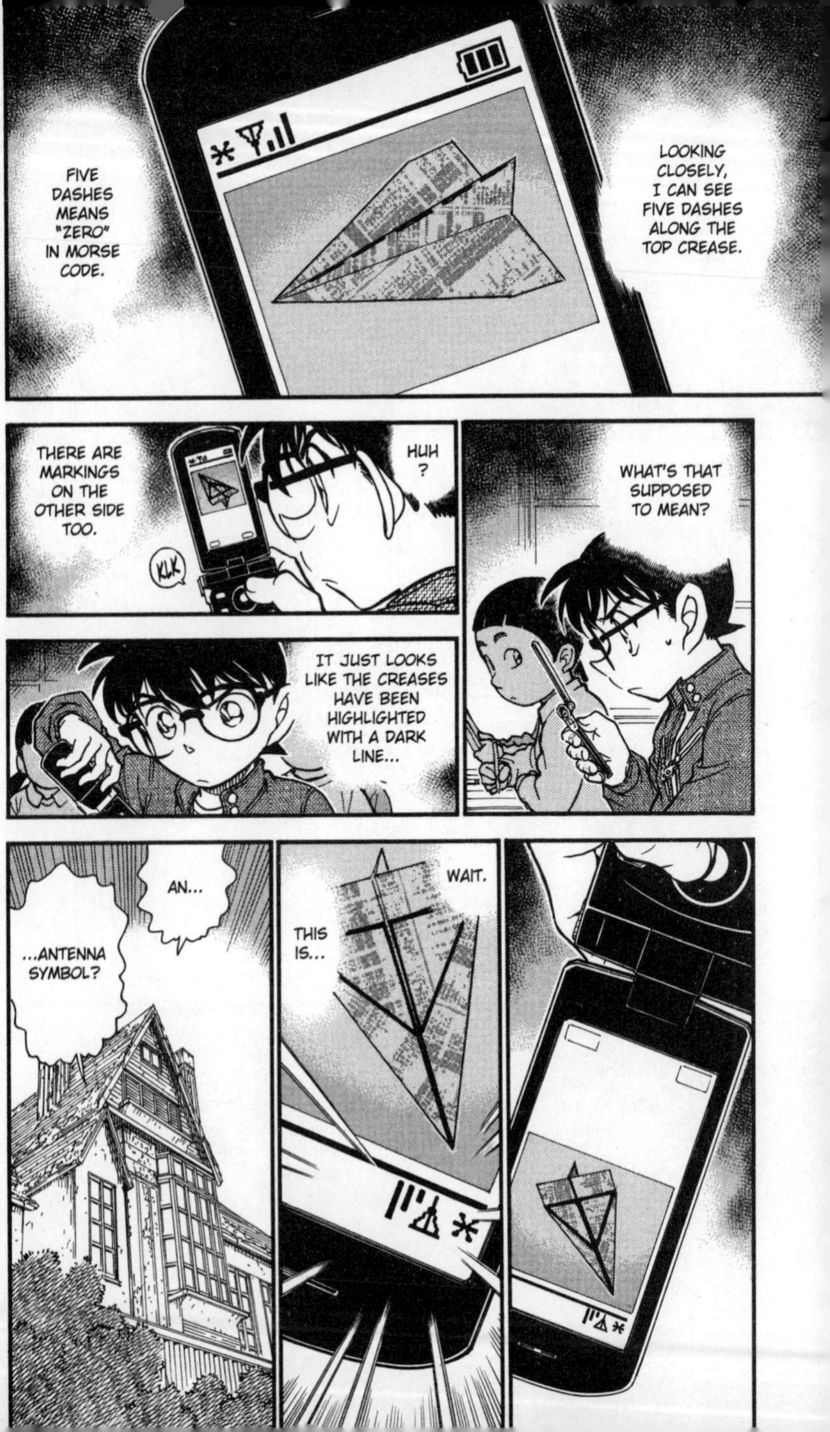
LOOKING CLOSELY, I CAN SEE FIVE DASHES ALONG THE TOP CREASE.
FIVE DASHES MEANS "ZERO" IN MORSE CODE.
WHAT'S THAT SUPPOSED TO MEAN?
HUH?
THERE ARE MARKINGS ON THE OTHER SIDE TOO.
KLK
IT JUST LOOKS LIKE THE CREASES HAVE BEEN HIGHLIGHTED WITH A DARK LINE...
WAIT.
THIS IS...
AN...
...ANTENNA SYMBOL?

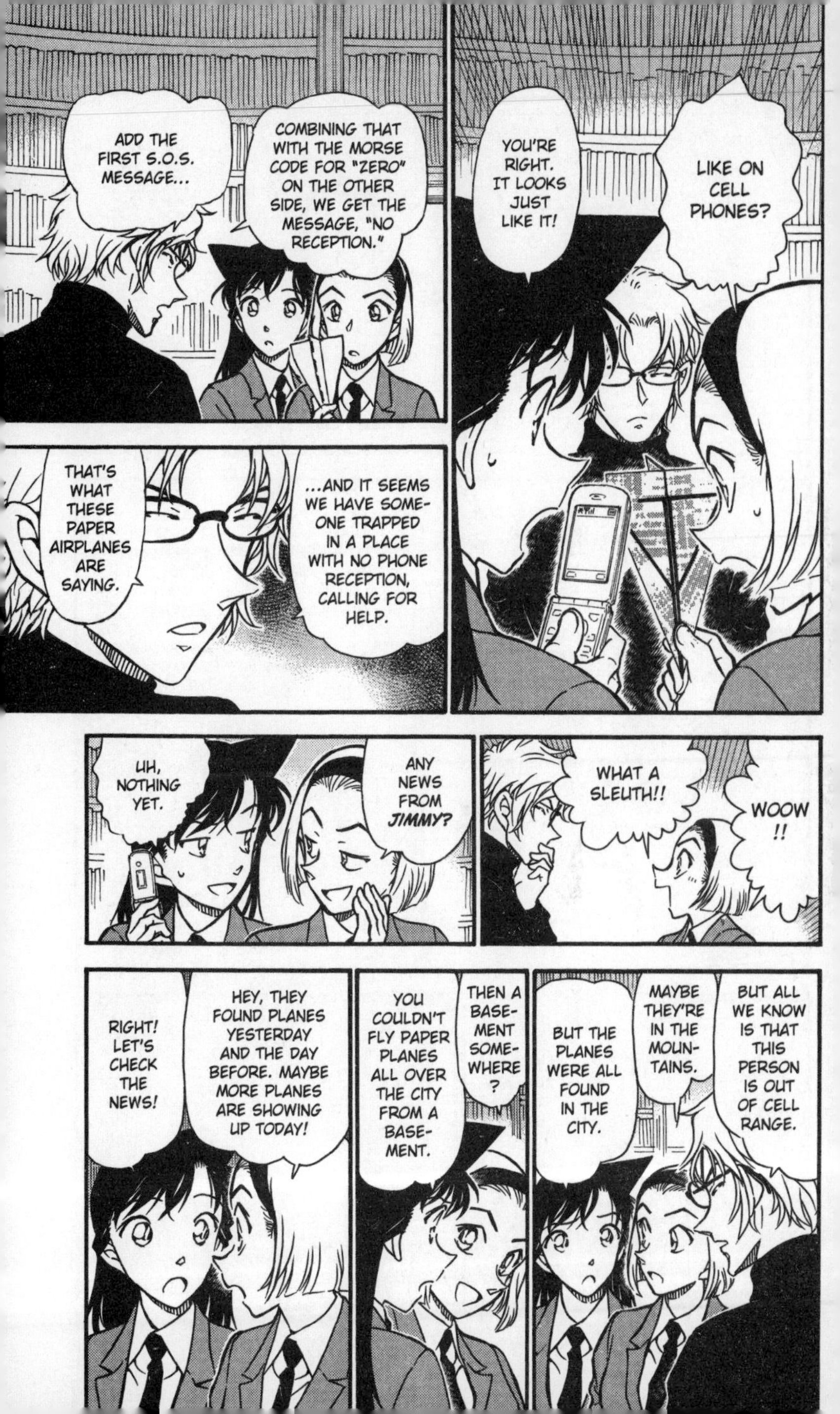
LIKE ON CELL PHONES?
YOU'RE RIGHT. IT LOOKS JUST LIKE IT!
COMBINING THAT WITH THE MORSE CODE FOR "ZERO" ON THE OTHER SIDE, WE GET THE MESSAGE, "NO RECEPTION."
ADD THE FIRST S.O.S. MESSAGE...
THAT'S WHAT THESE PAPER AIRPLANES ARE SAYING.
...AND IT SEEMS WE HAVE SOME-ONE TRAPPED IN A PLACE WITH NO PHONE RECEPTION, CALLING FOR HELP.
WOOW!!
WHAT A SLEUTH!!
ANY NEWS FROM *JIMMY?*
UH, NOTHING YET.
BUT ALL WE KNOW IS THAT THIS PERSON IS OUT OF CELL RANGE.
MAYBE THEY'RE IN THE MOUN-TAINS.
BUT THE PLANES WERE ALL FOUND IN THE CITY.
THEN A BASE-MENT SOME-WHERE?
YOU COULDN'T FLY PAPER PLANES ALL OVER THE CITY FROM A BASE-MENT.
HEY, THEY FOUND PLANES YESTERDAY AND THE DAY BEFORE. MAYBE MORE PLANES ARE SHOWING UP TODAY!
RIGHT! LET'S CHECK THE NEWS!

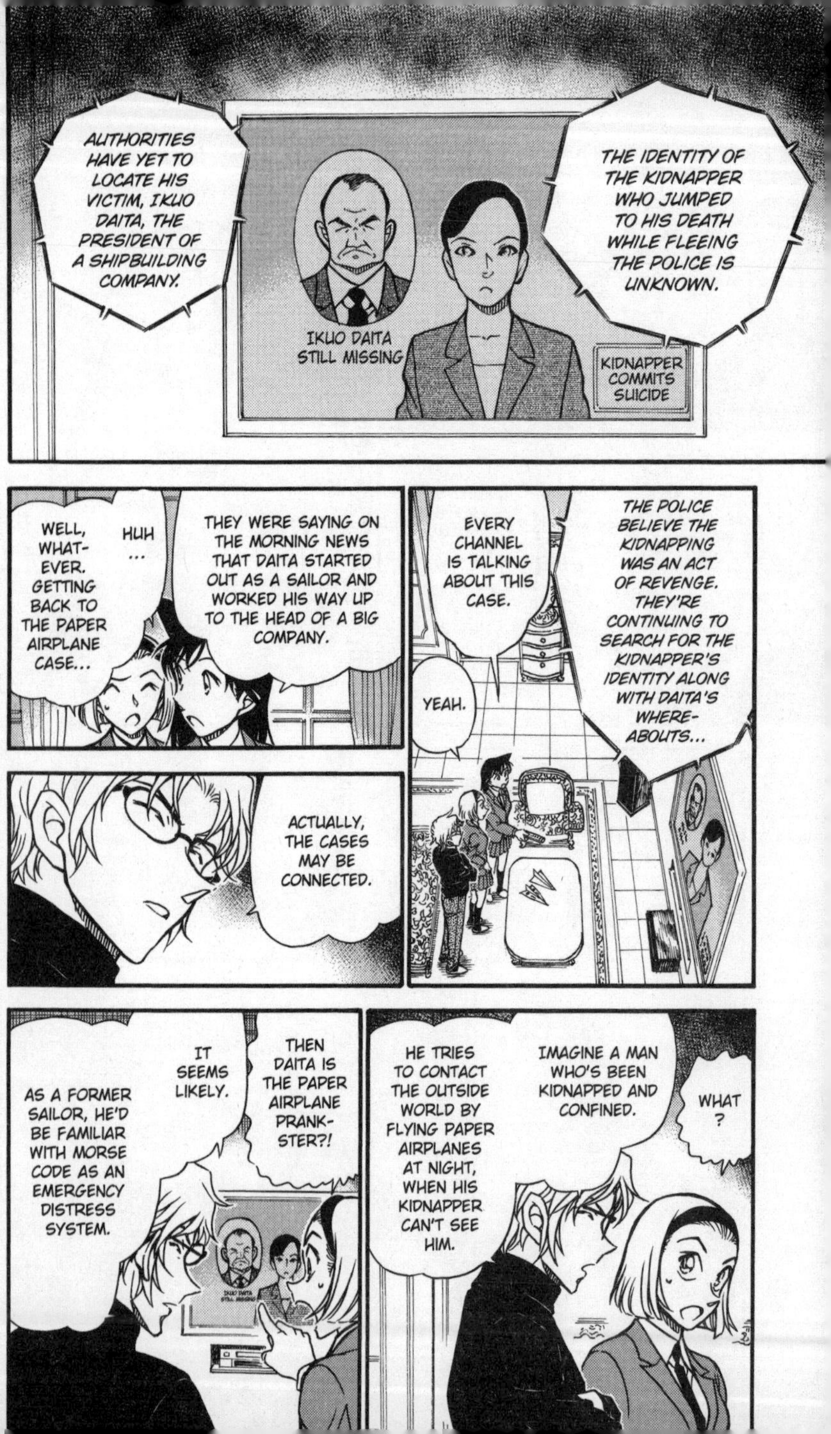
THE IDENTITY OF THE KIDNAPPER WHO JUMPED TO HIS DEATH WHILE FLEEING THE POLICE IS UNKNOWN.
AUTHORITIES HAVE YET TO LOCATE HIS VICTIM, IKUO DAITA, THE PRESIDENT OF A SHIPBUILDING COMPANY.
KIDNAPPER COMMITS SUICIDE
IKUO DAITA STILL MISSING
THE POLICE BELIEVE THE KIDNAPPING WAS AN ACT OF REVENGE. THEY'RE CONTINUING TO SEARCH FOR THE KIDNAPPER'S IDENTITY ALONG WITH DAITA'S WHERE-ABOUTS...
EVERY CHANNEL IS TALKING ABOUT THIS CASE.
YEAH.
THEY WERE SAYING ON THE MORNING NEWS THAT DAITA STARTED OUT AS A SAILOR AND WORKED HIS WAY UP TO THE HEAD OF A BIG COMPANY.
HUH ...
WELL, WHAT-EVER. GETTING BACK TO THE PAPER AIRPLANE CASE...
ACTUALLY, THE CASES MAY BE CONNECTED.
WHAT ?
IMAGINE A MAN WHO'S BEEN KIDNAPPED AND CONFINED.
HE TRIES TO CONTACT THE OUTSIDE WORLD BY FLYING PAPER AIRPLANES AT NIGHT, WHEN HIS KIDNAPPER CAN'T SEE HIM.
THEN DAITA IS THE PAPER AIRPLANE PRANK-STER?!
IT SEEMS LIKELY.
AS A FORMER SAILOR, HE'D BE FAMILIAR WITH MORSE CODE AS AN EMERGENCY DISTRESS SYSTEM.

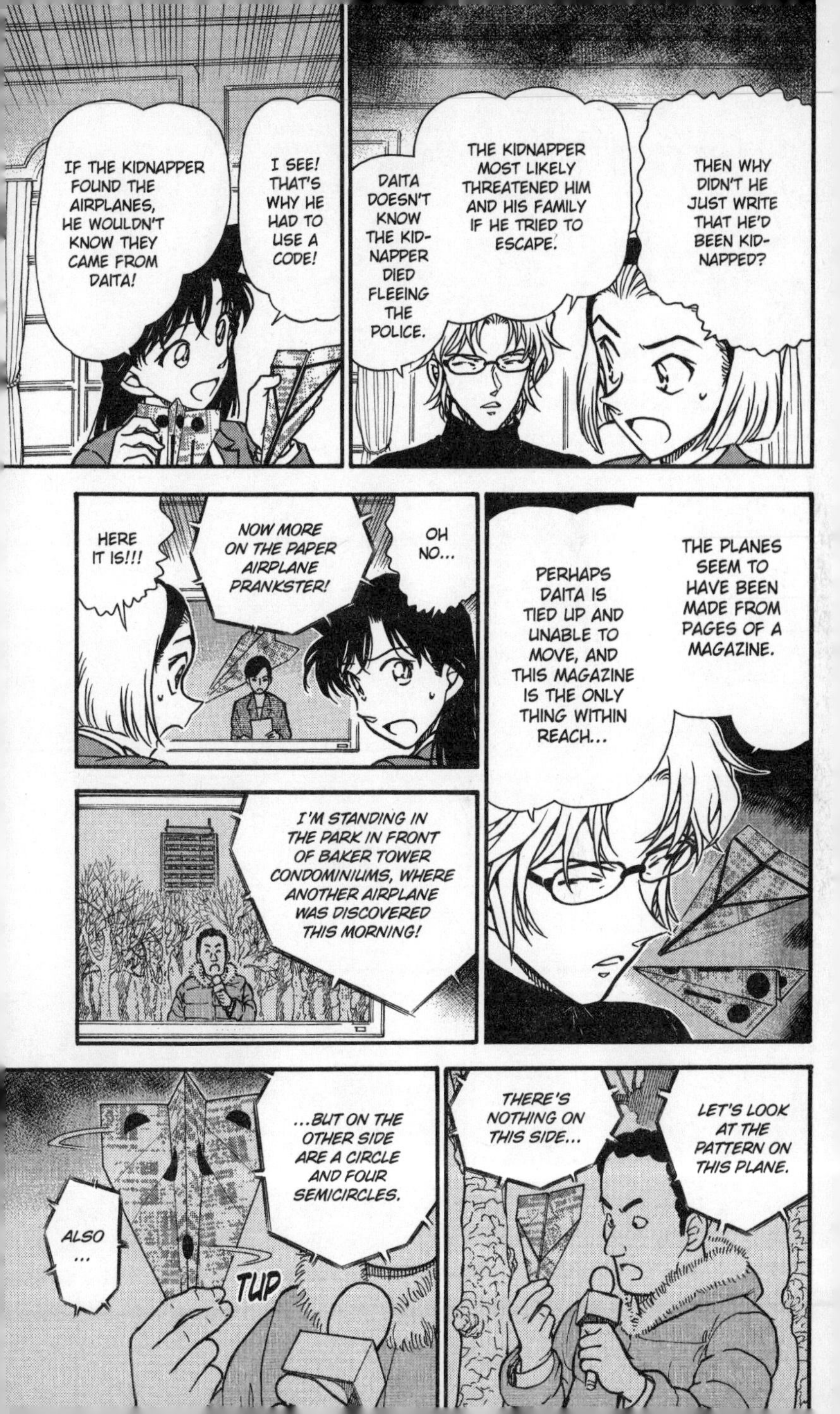
THEN WHY DIDN'T HE JUST WRITE THAT HE'D BEEN KIDNAPPED?
THE KIDNAPPER MOST LIKELY THREATENED HIM AND HIS FAMILY IF HE TRIED TO ESCAPE.
DAITA DOESN'T KNOW THE KIDNAPPER DIED FLEEING THE POLICE.
I SEE! THAT'S WHY HE HAD TO USE A CODE!
IF THE KIDNAPPER FOUND THE AIRPLANES, HE WOULDN'T KNOW THEY CAME FROM DAITA!
THE PLANES SEEM TO HAVE BEEN MADE FROM PAGES OF A MAGAZINE.
PERHAPS DAITA IS TIED UP AND UNABLE TO MOVE, AND THIS MAGAZINE IS THE ONLY THING WITHIN REACH...
OH NO...
NOW MORE ON THE PAPER AIRPLANE PRANKSTER!
HERE IT IS!!!
I'M STANDING IN THE PARK IN FRONT OF BAKER TOWER CONDOMINIUMS, WHERE ANOTHER AIRPLANE WAS DISCOVERED THIS MORNING!
LET'S LOOK AT THE PATTERN ON THIS PLANE.
THERE'S NOTHING ON THIS SIDE...
...BUT ON THE OTHER SIDE ARE A CIRCLE AND FOUR SEMICIRCLES.
TUP
ALSO ...

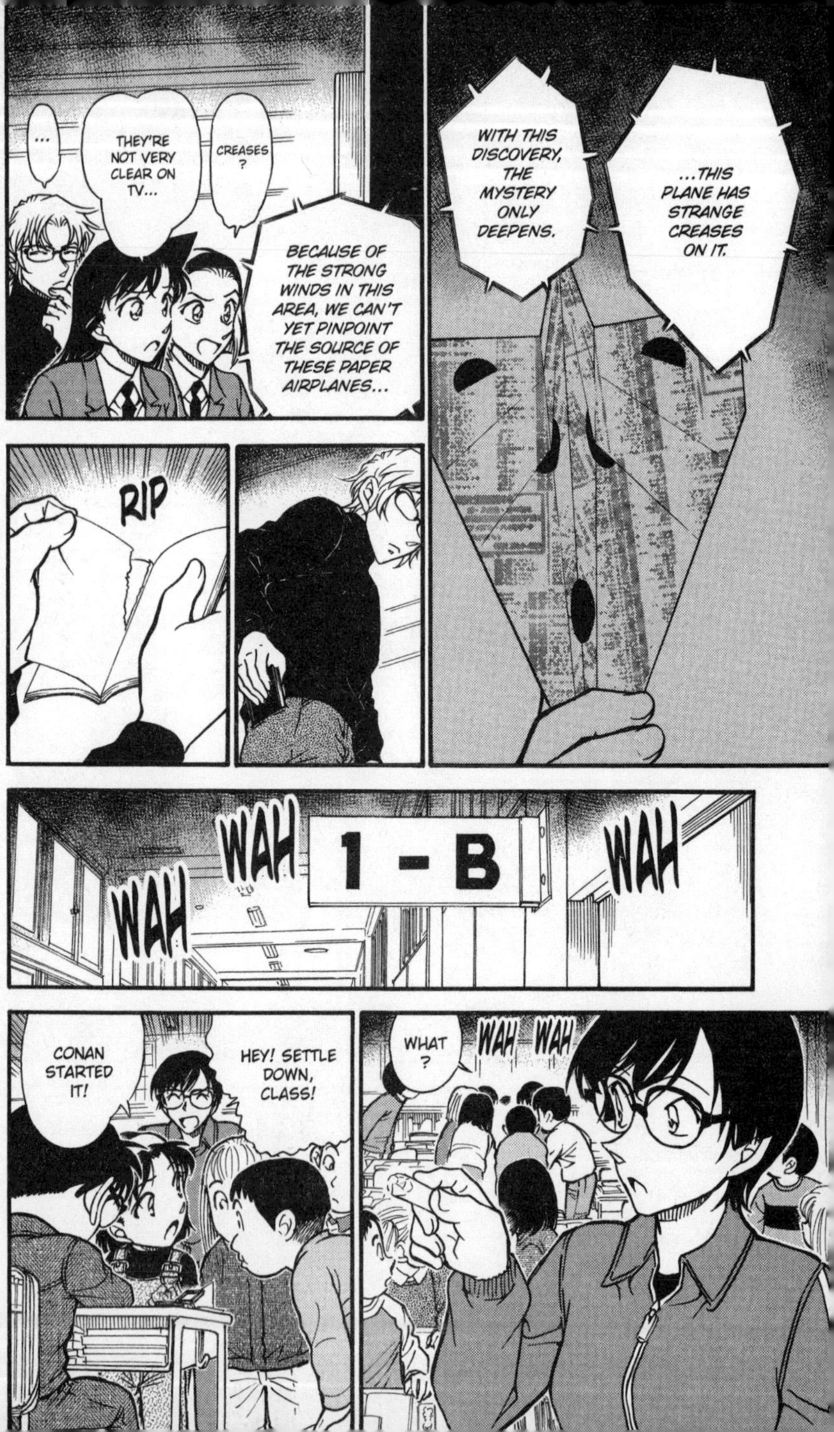
...THIS PLANE HAS STRANGE CREASES ON IT.
WITH THIS DISCOVERY, THE MYSTERY ONLY DEEPENS.
BECAUSE OF THE STRONG WINDS IN THIS AREA, WE CAN'T YET PINPOINT THE SOURCE OF THESE PAPER AIRPLANES...
CREASES?
THEY'RE NOT VERY CLEAR ON TV...
...
RIP
WAH
1 - B
WAH
WAH
WAH WAH
WHAT?
HEY! SETTLE DOWN, CLASS!
CONAN STARTED IT!

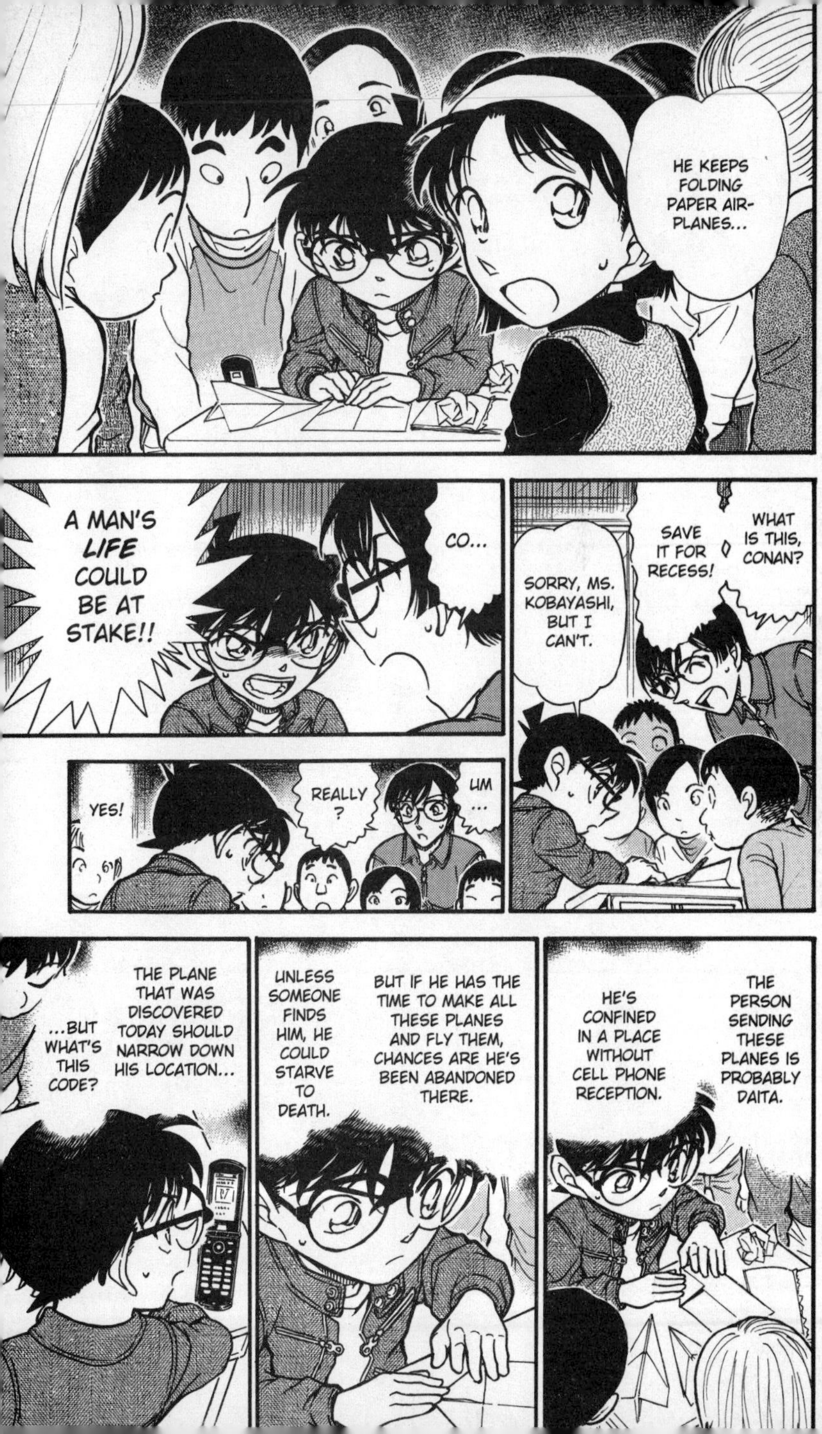
HE KEEPS FOLDING PAPER AIR-PLANES...
WHAT IS THIS, CONAN?
SAVE IT FOR RECESS!
SORRY, MS. KOBAYASHI, BUT I CAN'T.
CO...
A MAN'S *LIFE* COULD BE AT STAKE!!
UM...
REALLY?
YES!
THE PERSON SENDING THESE PLANES IS PROBABLY DAITA.
HE'S CONFINED IN A PLACE WITHOUT CELL PHONE RECEPTION.
BUT IF HE HAS THE TIME TO MAKE ALL THESE PLANES AND FLY THEM, CHANCES ARE HE'S BEEN ABANDONED THERE.
UNLESS SOMEONE FINDS HIM, HE COULD STARVE TO DEATH.
THE PLANE THAT WAS DISCOVERED TODAY SHOULD NARROW DOWN HIS LOCATION...
...BUT WHAT'S THIS CODE?

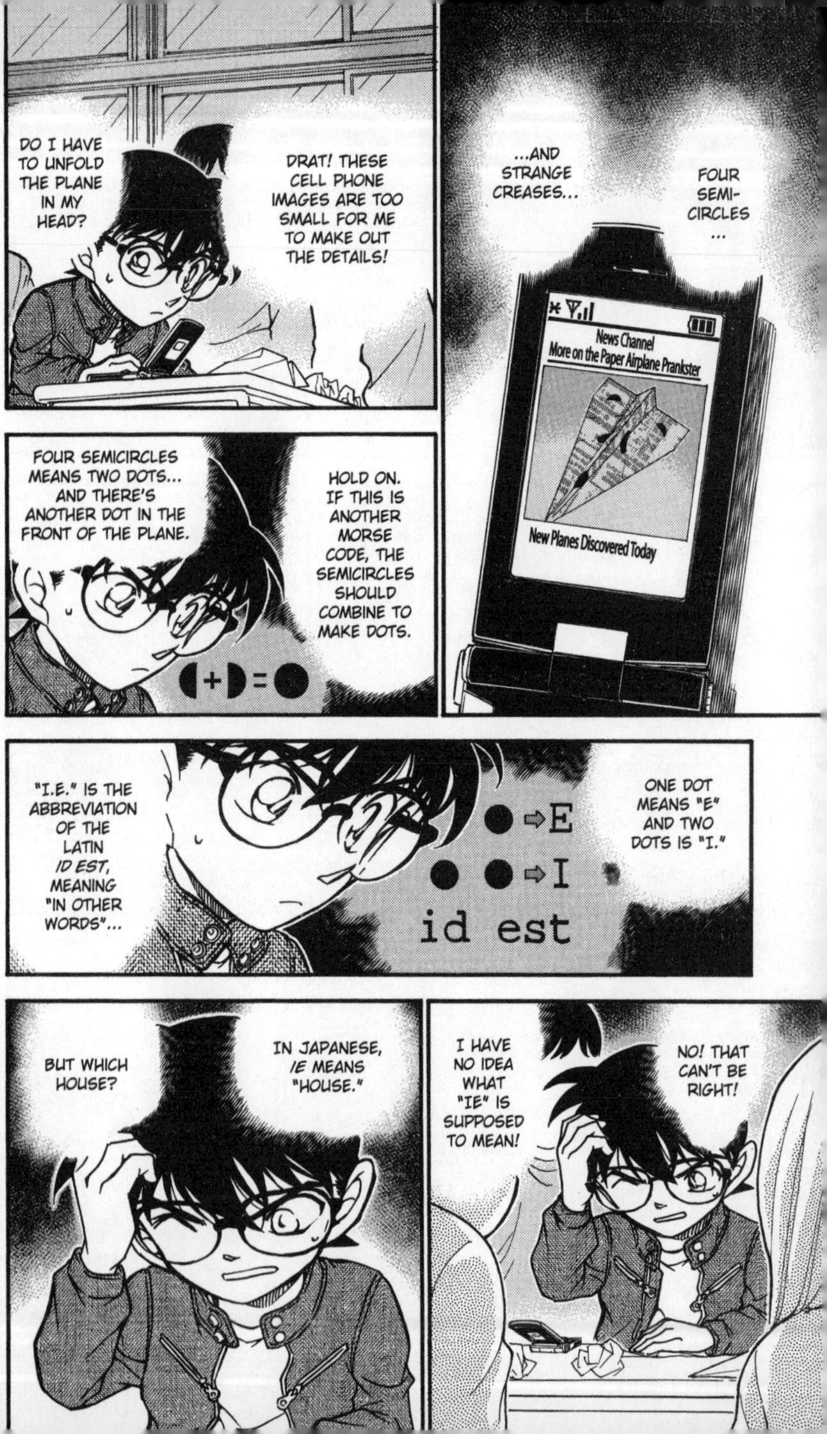

FOUR SEMI-CIRCLES ...
...AND STRANGE CREASES...
News Channel
More on the Paper Airplane Prankster
New Planes Discovered Today
DRAT! THESE CELL PHONE IMAGES ARE TOO SMALL FOR ME TO MAKE OUT THE DETAILS!
DO I HAVE TO UNFOLD THE PLANE IN MY HEAD?
HOLD ON. IF THIS IS ANOTHER MORSE CODE, THE SEMICIRCLES SHOULD COMBINE TO MAKE DOTS.
FOUR SEMICIRCLES MEANS TWO DOTS... AND THERE'S ANOTHER DOT IN THE FRONT OF THE PLANE.
ONE DOT MEANS "E" AND TWO DOTS IS "I."
E
I
id est
"I.E." IS THE ABBREVIATION OF THE LATIN *ID EST*, MEANING "IN OTHER WORDS"...
NO! THAT CAN'T BE RIGHT!
I HAVE NO IDEA WHAT "IE" IS SUPPOSED TO MEAN!
IN JAPANESE, *IE* MEANS "HOUSE."
BUT WHICH HOUSE?

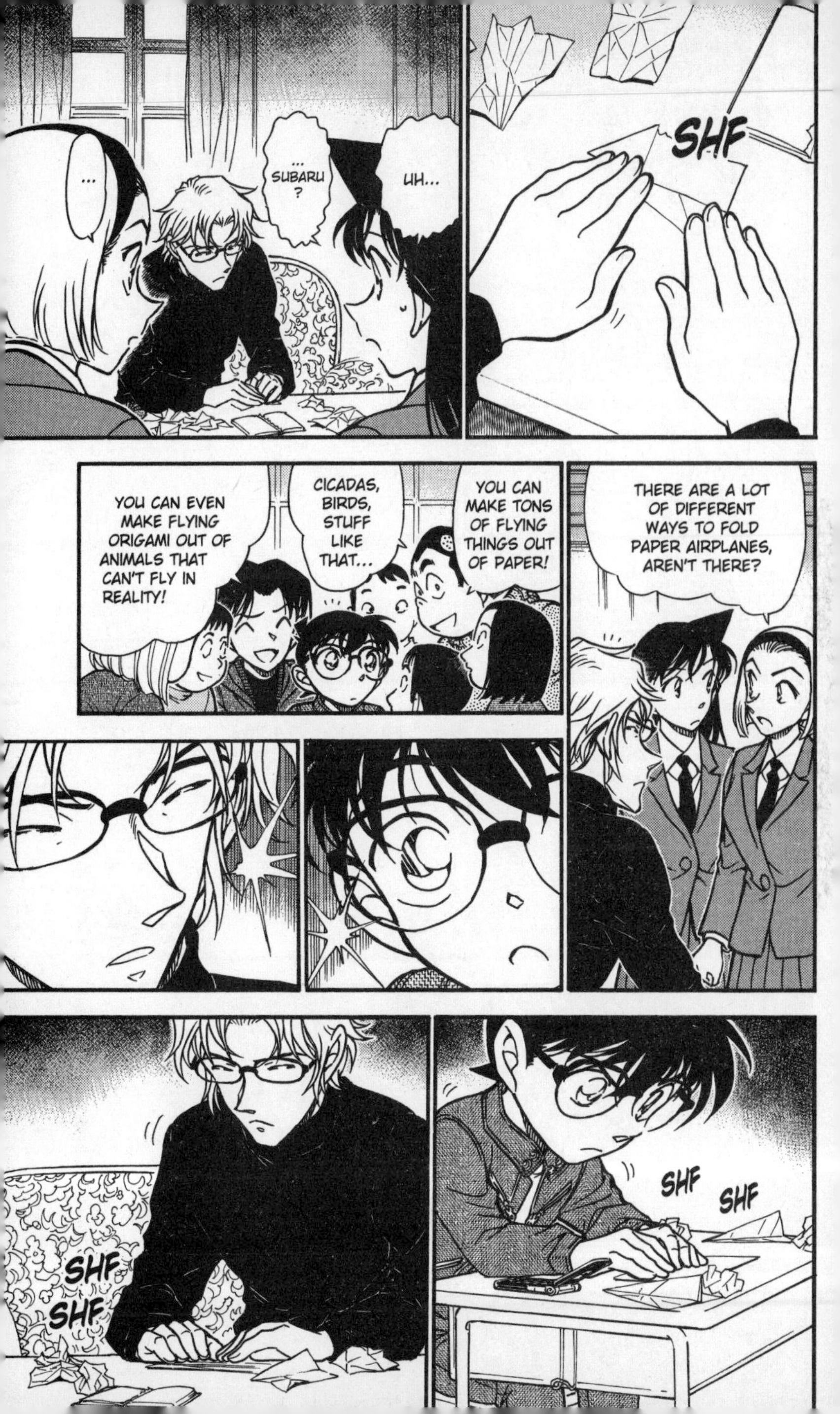
SHF
UH...
... SUBARU ?
...
THERE ARE A LOT OF DIFFERENT WAYS TO FOLD PAPER AIRPLANES, AREN'T THERE?
YOU CAN MAKE TONS OF FLYING THINGS OUT OF PAPER!
CICADAS, BIRDS, STUFF LIKE THAT...
YOU CAN EVEN MAKE FLYING ORIGAMI OUT OF ANIMALS THAT CAN'T FLY IN REALITY!
SHF
SHF
SHF
SHF

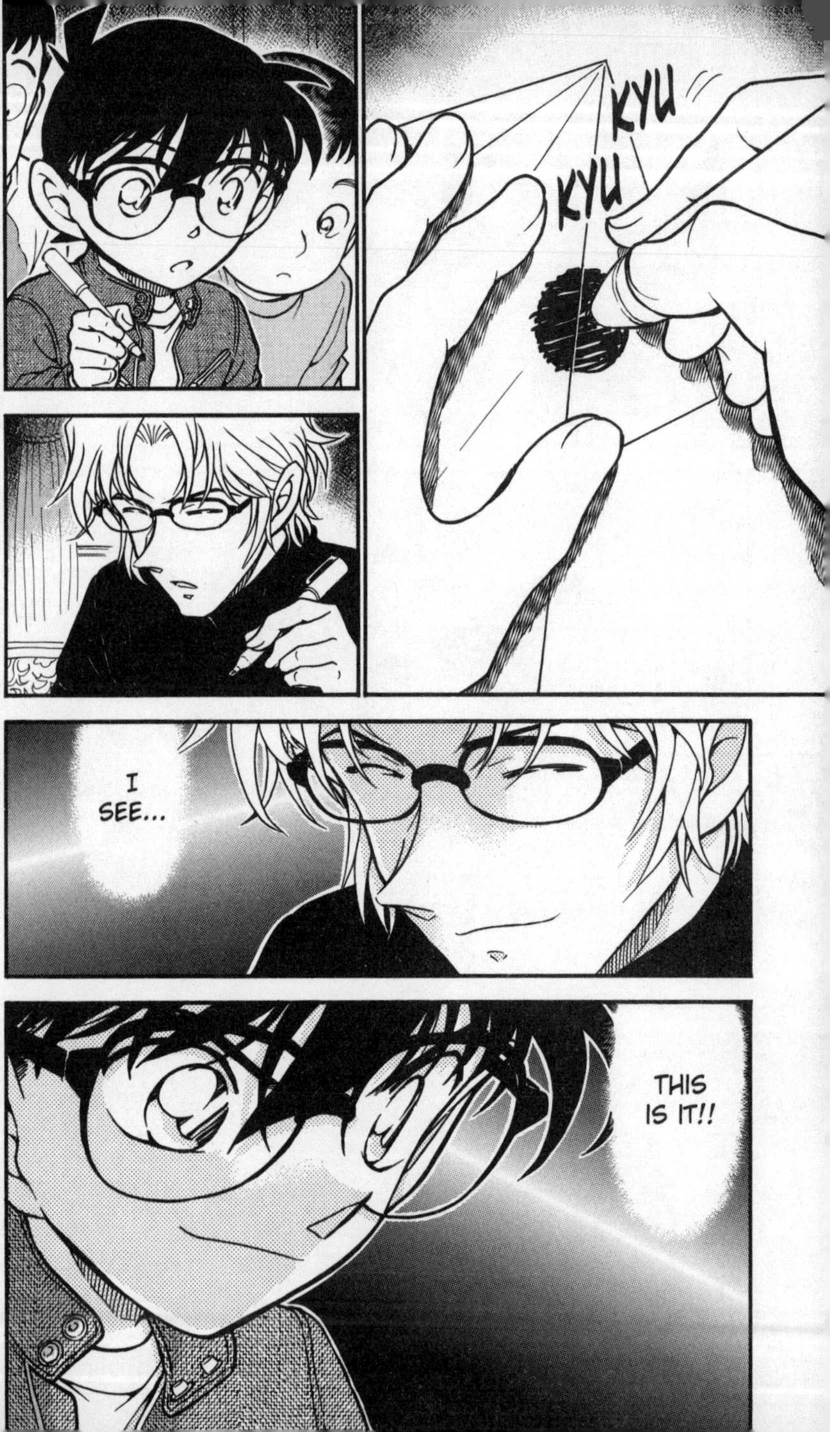
KYU
KYU
I SEE...
THIS IS IT!!

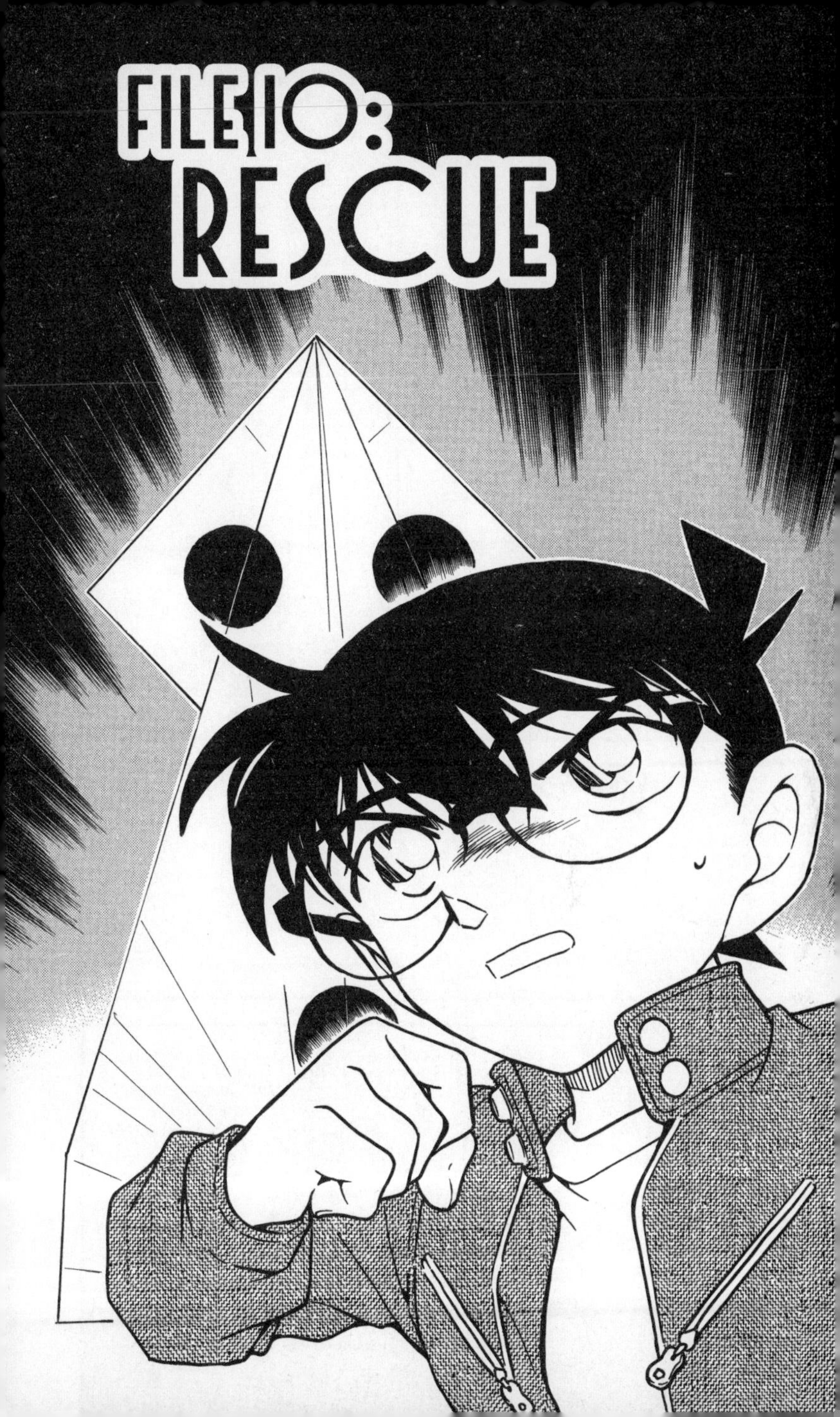
FILE 10:
RESCUE

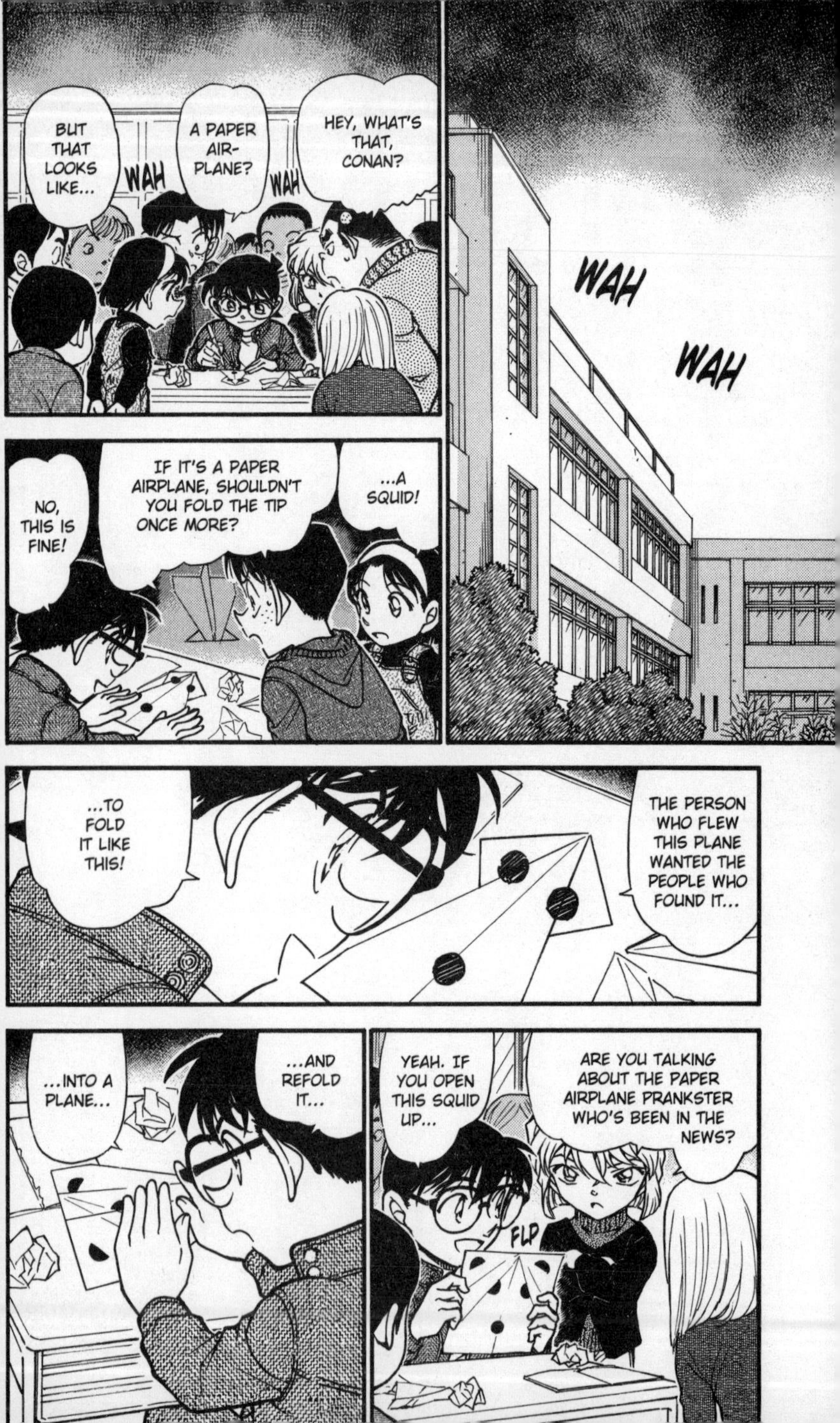
WAH
WAH
HEY, WHAT'S THAT, CONAN?
WAH
A PAPER AIRPLANE?
WAH
BUT THAT LOOKS LIKE...
...A SQUID!
IF IT'S A PAPER AIRPLANE, SHOULDN'T YOU FOLD THE TIP ONCE MORE?
NO, THIS IS FINE!
THE PERSON WHO FLEW THIS PLANE WANTED THE PEOPLE WHO FOUND IT...
...TO FOLD IT LIKE THIS!
ARE YOU TALKING ABOUT THE PAPER AIRPLANE PRANKSTER WHO'S BEEN IN THE NEWS?
YEAH. IF YOU OPEN THIS SQUID UP...
FLP
...AND REFOLD IT...
...INTO A PLANE...

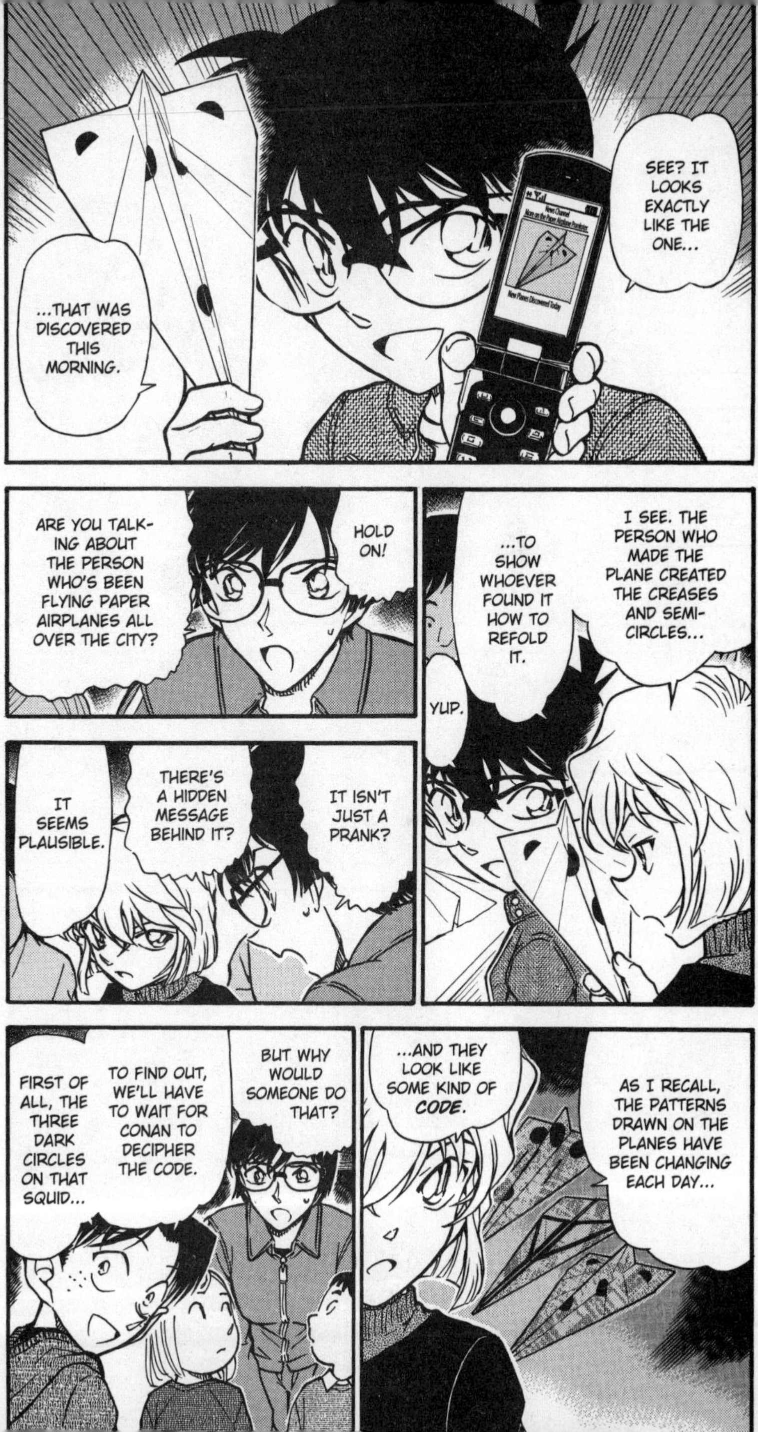
SEE? IT LOOKS EXACTLY LIKE THE ONE...
...THAT WAS DISCOVERED THIS MORNING.
I SEE. THE PERSON WHO MADE THE PLANE CREATED THE CREASES AND SEMI-CIRCLES...
...TO SHOW WHOEVER FOUND IT HOW TO REFOLD IT.
YUP.
HOLD ON!
ARE YOU TALK-ING ABOUT THE PERSON WHO'S BEEN FLYING PAPER AIRPLANES ALL OVER THE CITY?
IT ISN'T JUST A PRANK?
THERE'S A HIDDEN MESSAGE BEHIND IT?
IT SEEMS PLAUSIBLE.
AS I RECALL, THE PATTERNS DRAWN ON THE PLANES HAVE BEEN CHANGING EACH DAY...
...AND THEY LOOK LIKE SOME KIND OF ***CODE***.
BUT WHY WOULD SOMEONE DO THAT?
TO FIND OUT, WE'LL HAVE TO WAIT FOR CONAN TO DECIPHER THE CODE.
FIRST OF ALL, THE THREE DARK CIRCLES ON THAT SQUID...

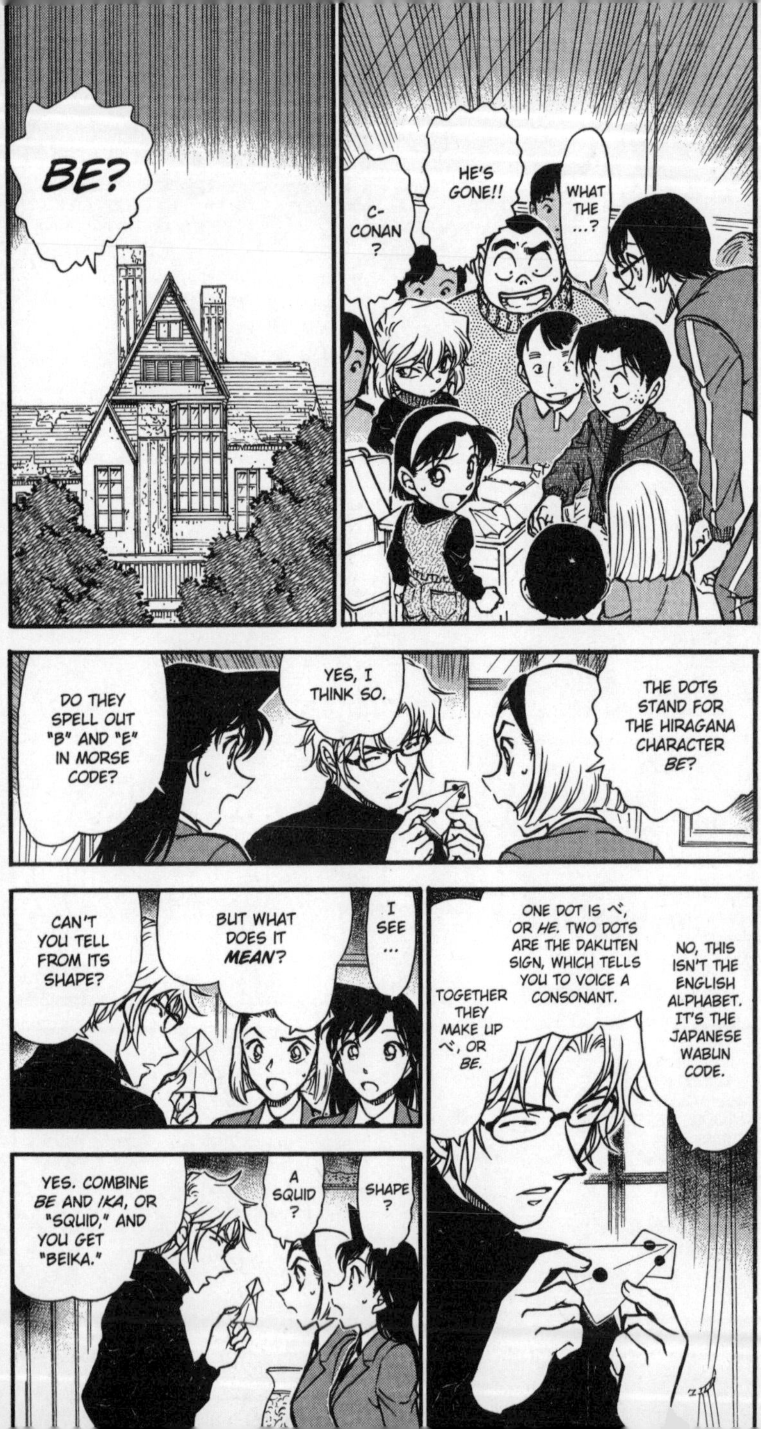
WHAT THE ...?
HE'S GONE!!
C- CONAN ?
BE?
THE DOTS STAND FOR THE HIRAGANA CHARACTER BE?
YES, I THINK SO.
DO THEY SPELL OUT "B" AND "E" IN MORSE CODE?
NO, THIS ISN'T THE ENGLISH ALPHABET. IT'S THE JAPANESE WABUN CODE.
ONE DOT IS べ, OR HE. TWO DOTS ARE THE DAKUTEN SIGN, WHICH TELLS YOU TO VOICE A CONSONANT.
TOGETHER THEY MAKE UP べ, OR BE.
I SEE ...
BUT WHAT DOES IT MEAN?
CAN'T YOU TELL FROM ITS SHAPE?
SHAPE?
A SQUID?
YES. COMBINE BE AND IKA, OR "SQUID," AND YOU GET "BEIKA."

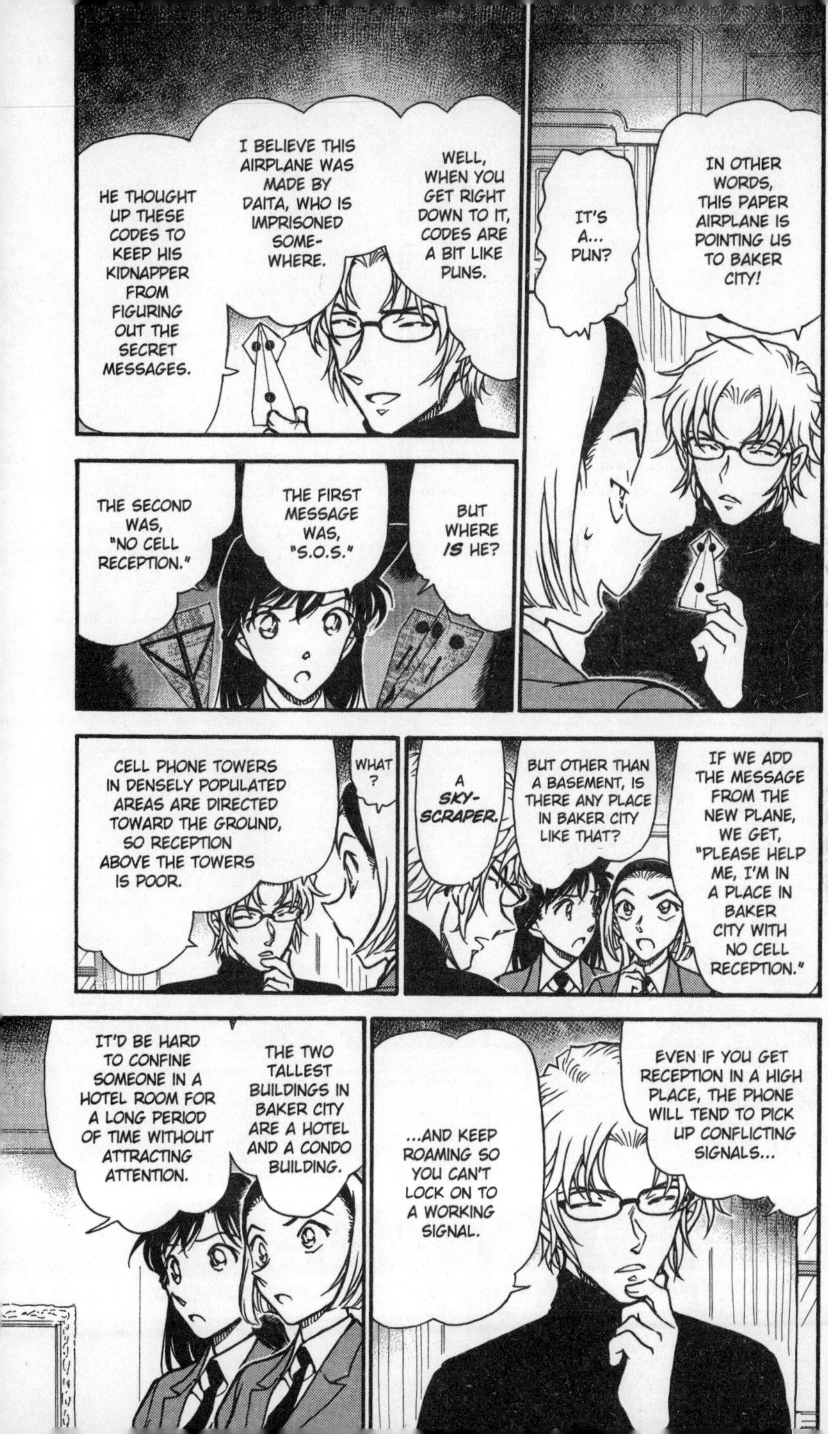
IN OTHER WORDS, THIS PAPER AIRPLANE IS POINTING US TO BAKER CITY!
IT'S A... PUN?
WELL, WHEN YOU GET RIGHT DOWN TO IT, CODES ARE A BIT LIKE PUNS.
I BELIEVE THIS AIRPLANE WAS MADE BY DAITA, WHO IS IMPRISONED SOME-WHERE.
HE THOUGHT UP THESE CODES TO KEEP HIS KIDNAPPER FROM FIGURING OUT THE SECRET MESSAGES.
BUT WHERE *IS* HE?
THE FIRST MESSAGE WAS, "S.O.S."
THE SECOND WAS, "NO CELL RECEPTION."
IF WE ADD THE MESSAGE FROM THE NEW PLANE, WE GET, "PLEASE HELP ME, I'M IN A PLACE IN BAKER CITY WITH NO CELL RECEPTION."
BUT OTHER THAN A BASEMENT, IS THERE ANY PLACE IN BAKER CITY LIKE THAT?
A ***SKY-SCRAPER.***
WHAT?
CELL PHONE TOWERS IN DENSELY POPULATED AREAS ARE DIRECTED TOWARD THE GROUND, SO RECEPTION ABOVE THE TOWERS IS POOR.
EVEN IF YOU GET RECEPTION IN A HIGH PLACE, THE PHONE WILL TEND TO PICK UP CONFLICTING SIGNALS...
...AND KEEP ROAMING SO YOU CAN'T LOCK ON TO A WORKING SIGNAL.
THE TWO TALLEST BUILDINGS IN BAKER CITY ARE A HOTEL AND A CONDO BUILDING.
IT'D BE HARD TO CONFINE SOMEONE IN A HOTEL ROOM FOR A LONG PERIOD OF TIME WITHOUT ATTRACTING ATTENTION.

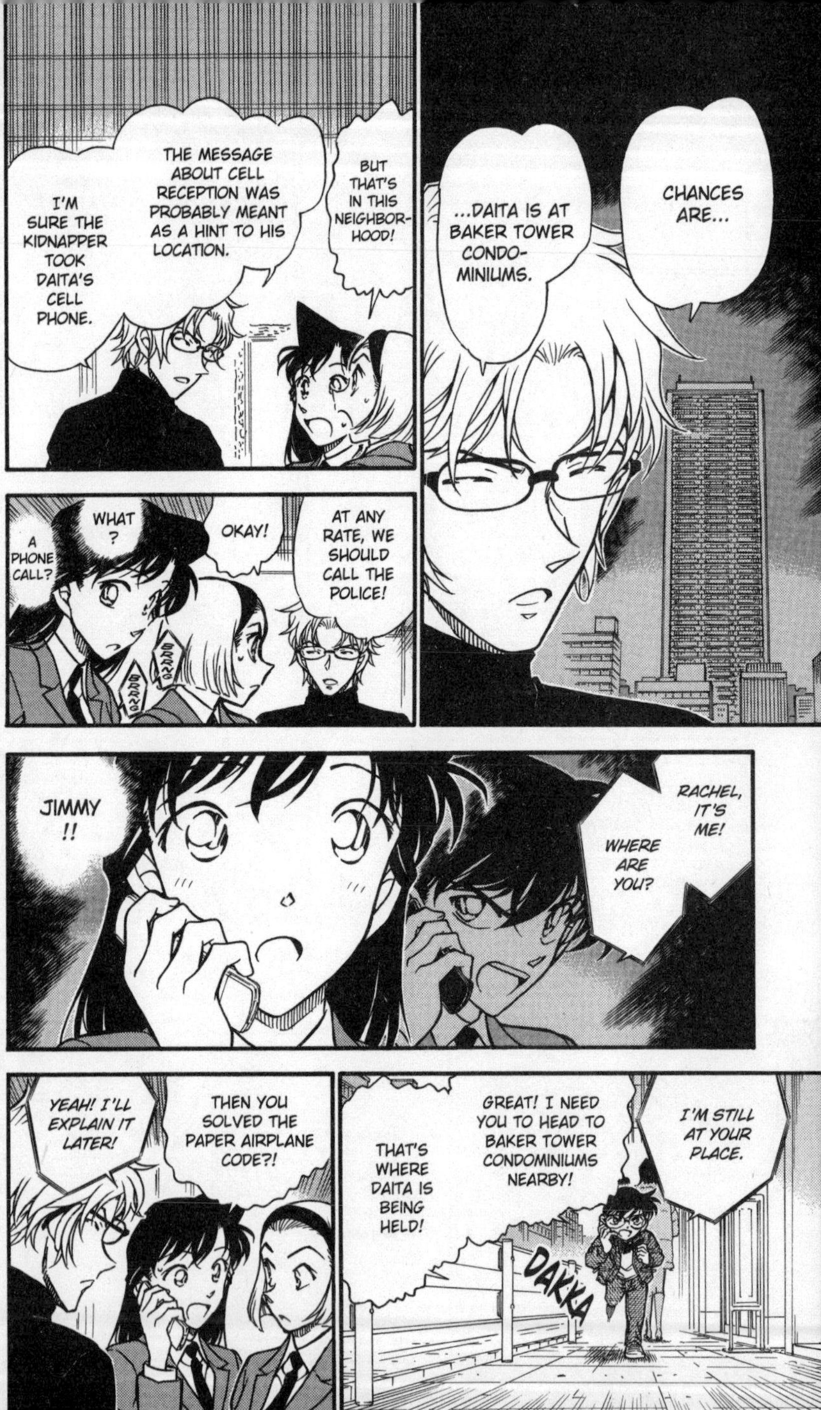
CHANCES ARE...
...DAITA IS AT BAKER TOWER CONDOMINIUMS.
BUT THAT'S IN THIS NEIGHBORHOOD!
THE MESSAGE ABOUT CELL RECEPTION WAS PROBABLY MEANT AS A HINT TO HIS LOCATION.
I'M SURE THE KIDNAPPER TOOK DAITA'S CELL PHONE.
AT ANY RATE, WE SHOULD CALL THE POLICE!
OKAY!
BRRNG
BRRNG
WHAT?
A PHONE CALL?
RACHEL, IT'S ME!
WHERE ARE YOU?
JIMMY!!
I'M STILL AT YOUR PLACE.
GREAT! I NEED YOU TO HEAD TO BAKER TOWER CONDOMINIUMS NEARBY!
THAT'S WHERE DAITA IS BEING HELD!
DAKKA
THEN YOU SOLVED THE PAPER AIRPLANE CODE?!
YEAH! I'LL EXPLAIN IT LATER!

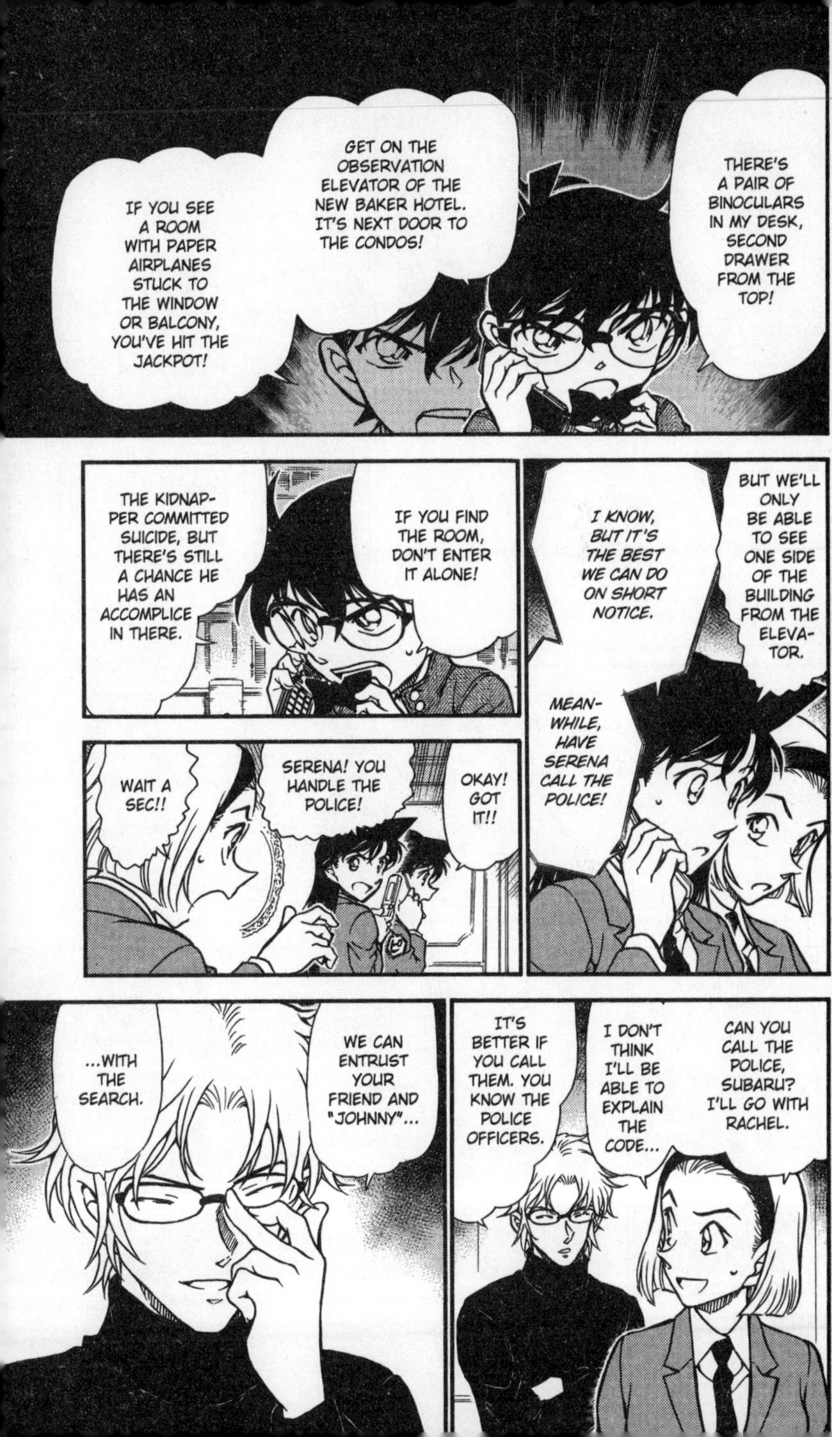
THERE'S A PAIR OF BINOCULARS IN MY DESK, SECOND DRAWER FROM THE TOP!
GET ON THE OBSERVATION ELEVATOR OF THE NEW BAKER HOTEL. IT'S NEXT DOOR TO THE CONDOS!
IF YOU SEE A ROOM WITH PAPER AIRPLANES STUCK TO THE WINDOW OR BALCONY, YOU'VE HIT THE JACKPOT!
BUT WE'LL ONLY BE ABLE TO SEE ONE SIDE OF THE BUILDING FROM THE ELEVATOR.
I KNOW, BUT IT'S THE BEST WE CAN DO ON SHORT NOTICE.
MEANWHILE, HAVE SERENA CALL THE POLICE!
IF YOU FIND THE ROOM, DON'T ENTER IT ALONE!
THE KIDNAPPER COMMITTED SUICIDE, BUT THERE'S STILL A CHANCE HE HAS AN ACCOMPLICE IN THERE.
OKAY! GOT IT!!
SERENA! YOU HANDLE THE POLICE!
WAIT A SEC!!
CAN YOU CALL THE POLICE, SUBARU? I'LL GO WITH RACHEL.
I DON'T THINK I'LL BE ABLE TO EXPLAIN THE CODE...
IT'S BETTER IF YOU CALL THEM. YOU KNOW THE POLICE OFFICERS.
WE CAN ENTRUST YOUR FRIEND AND "JOHNNY"...
...WITH THE SEARCH.

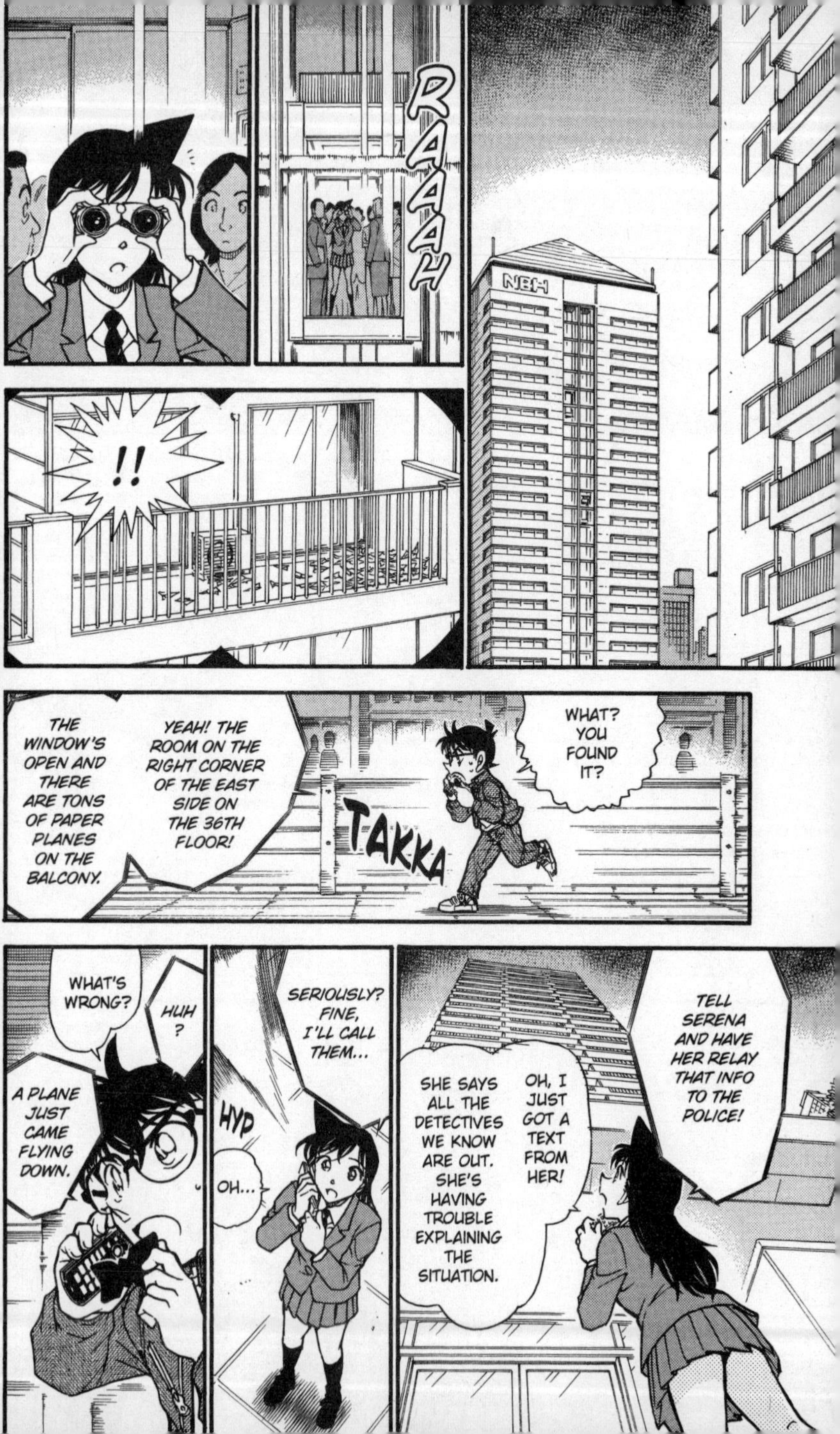
RAAAAH
!!
WHAT? YOU FOUND IT?
TAKKA
YEAH! THE ROOM ON THE RIGHT CORNER OF THE EAST SIDE ON THE 36TH FLOOR!
THE WINDOW'S OPEN AND THERE ARE TONS OF PAPER PLANES ON THE BALCONY.
TELL SERENA AND HAVE HER RELAY THAT INFO TO THE POLICE!
OH, I JUST GOT A TEXT FROM HER!
SHE SAYS ALL THE DETECTIVES WE KNOW ARE OUT. SHE'S HAVING TROUBLE EXPLAINING THE SITUATION.
SERIOUSLY? FINE, I'LL CALL THEM...
HYP
OH...
HUH ?
WHAT'S WRONG?
A PLANE JUST CAME FLYING DOWN.

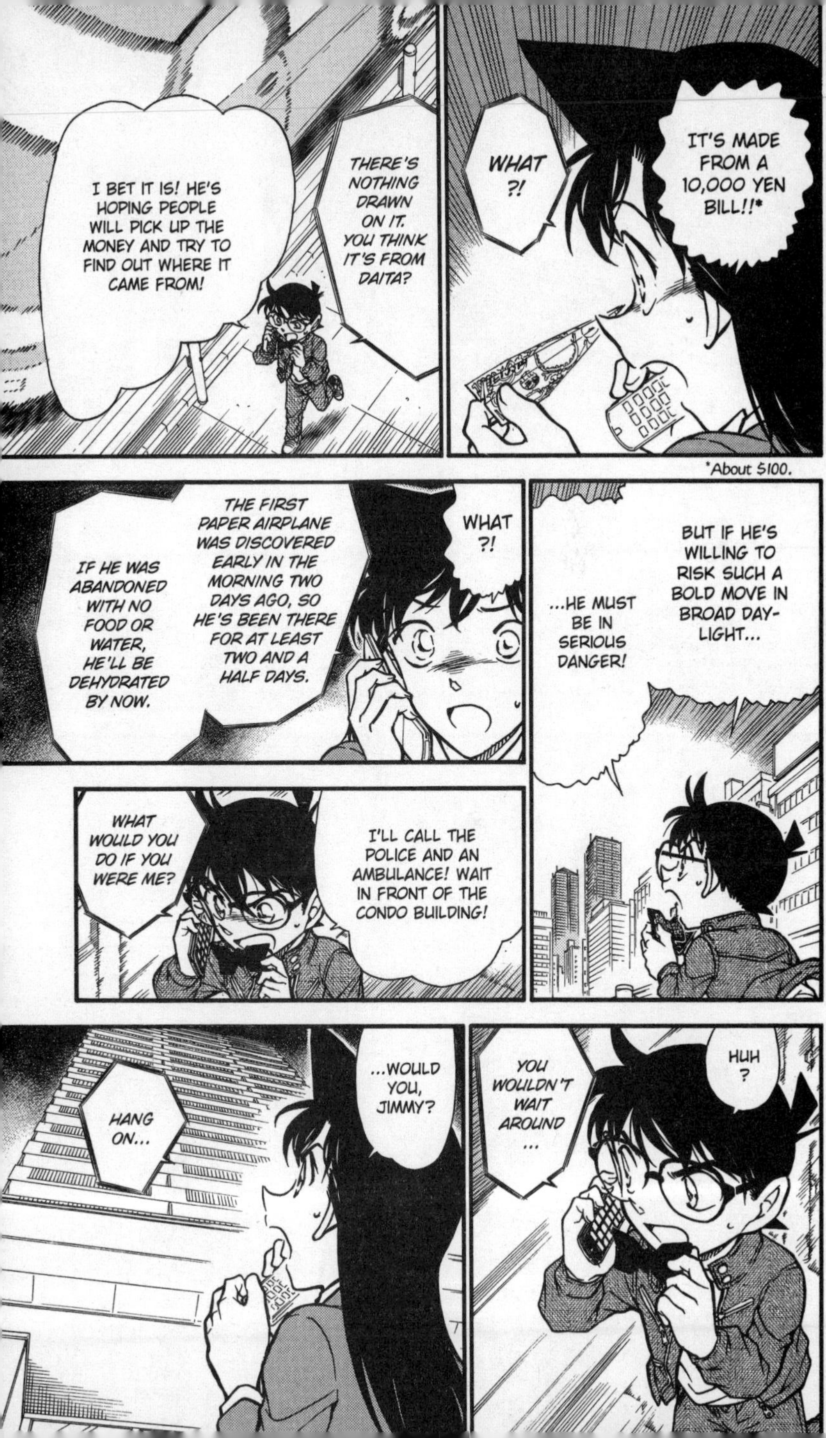
IT'S MADE FROM A 10,000 YEN BILL!!*
WHAT ?!
THERE'S NOTHING DRAWN ON IT. YOU THINK IT'S FROM DAITA?
I BET IT IS! HE'S HOPING PEOPLE WILL PICK UP THE MONEY AND TRY TO FIND OUT WHERE IT CAME FROM!
BUT IF HE'S WILLING TO RISK SUCH A BOLD MOVE IN BROAD DAY-LIGHT...
...HE MUST BE IN SERIOUS DANGER!
WHAT ?!
THE FIRST PAPER AIRPLANE WAS DISCOVERED EARLY IN THE MORNING TWO DAYS AGO, SO HE'S BEEN THERE FOR AT LEAST TWO AND A HALF DAYS.
IF HE WAS ABANDONED WITH NO FOOD OR WATER, HE'LL BE DEHYDRATED BY NOW.
I'LL CALL THE POLICE AND AN AMBULANCE! WAIT IN FRONT OF THE CONDO BUILDING!
WHAT WOULD YOU DO IF YOU WERE ME?
HUH ?
YOU WOULDN'T WAIT AROUND ...
...WOULD YOU, JIMMY?
HANG ON...
*About $100.

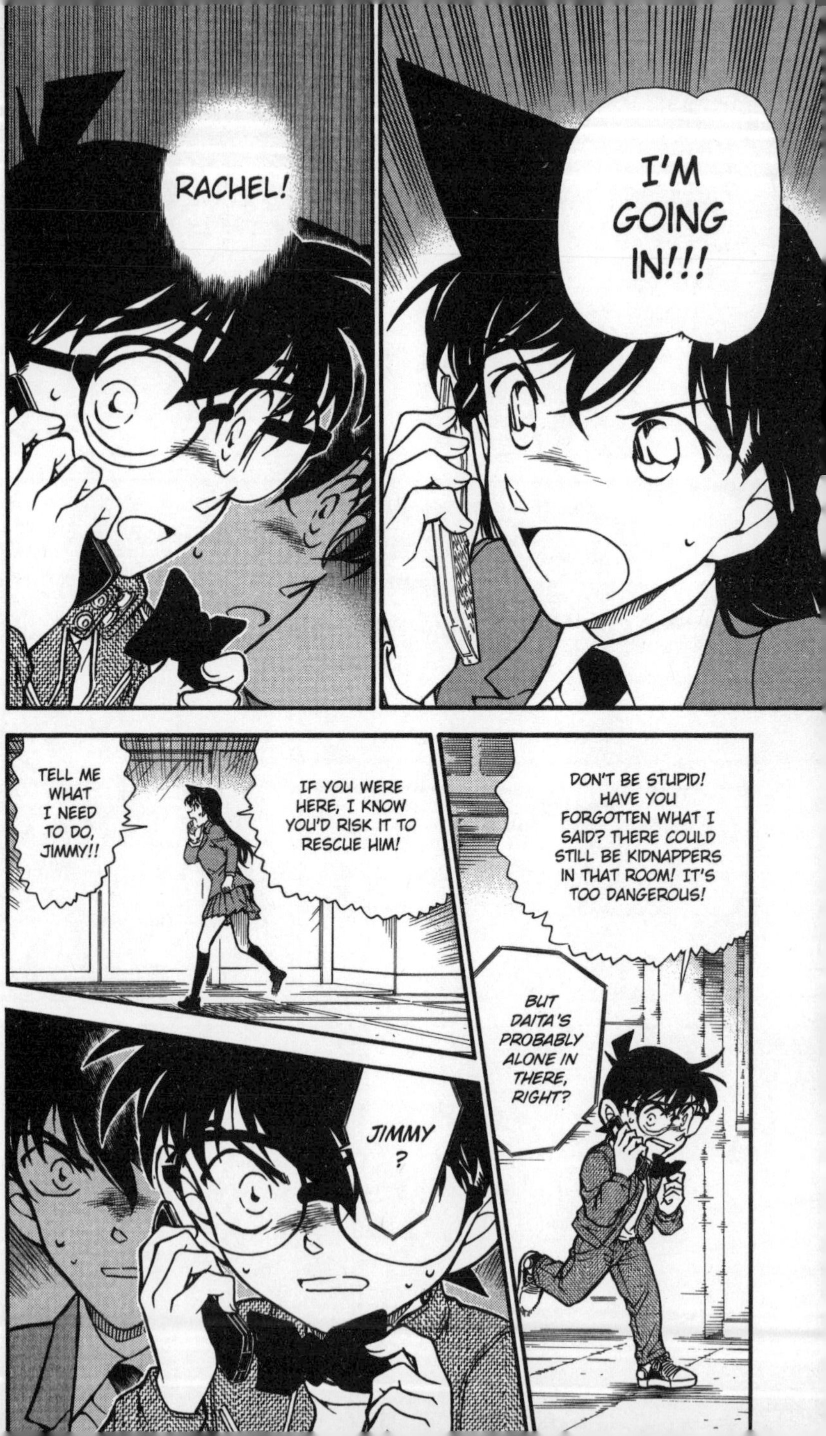
I'M GOING IN!!!
RACHEL!
DON'T BE STUPID! HAVE YOU FORGOTTEN WHAT I SAID? THERE COULD STILL BE KIDNAPPERS IN THAT ROOM! IT'S TOO DANGEROUS!
IF YOU WERE HERE, I KNOW YOU'D RISK IT TO RESCUE HIM!
TELL ME WHAT I NEED TO DO, JIMMY!!
BUT DAITA'S PROBABLY ALONE IN THERE, RIGHT?
JIMMY?

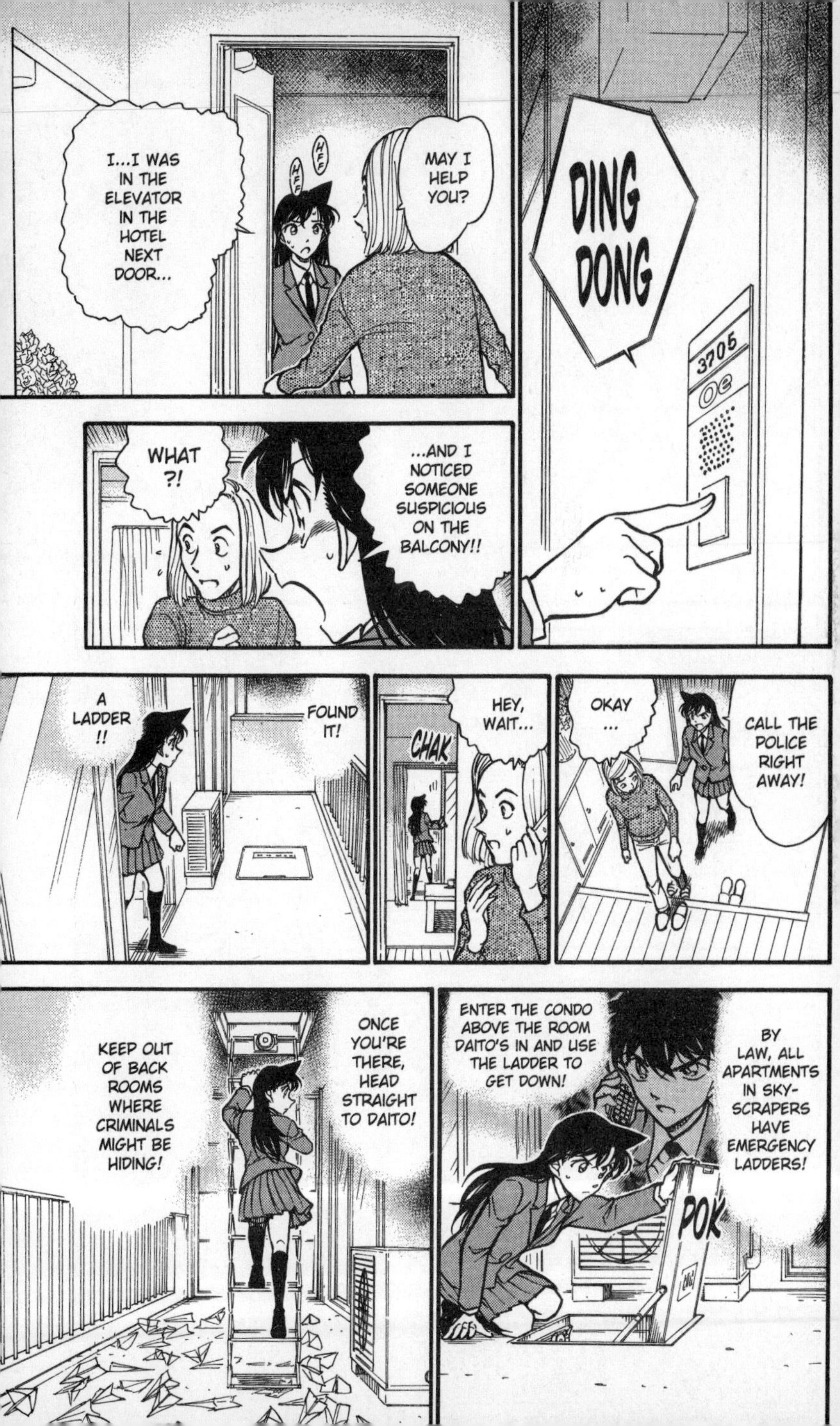
DING DONG
3705
Oe
MAY I HELP YOU?
HFF HFF
I...I WAS IN THE ELEVATOR IN THE HOTEL NEXT DOOR...
...AND I NOTICED SOMEONE SUSPICIOUS ON THE BALCONY!!
WHAT ?!
CALL THE POLICE RIGHT AWAY!
OKAY ...
HEY, WAIT...
CHAK
FOUND IT!
A LADDER !!
BY LAW, ALL APARTMENTS IN SKY-SCRAPERS HAVE EMERGENCY LADDERS!
ENTER THE CONDO ABOVE THE ROOM DAITO'S IN AND USE THE LADDER TO GET DOWN!
POK
ONCE YOU'RE THERE, HEAD STRAIGHT TO DAITO!
KEEP OUT OF BACK ROOMS WHERE CRIMINALS MIGHT BE HIDING!

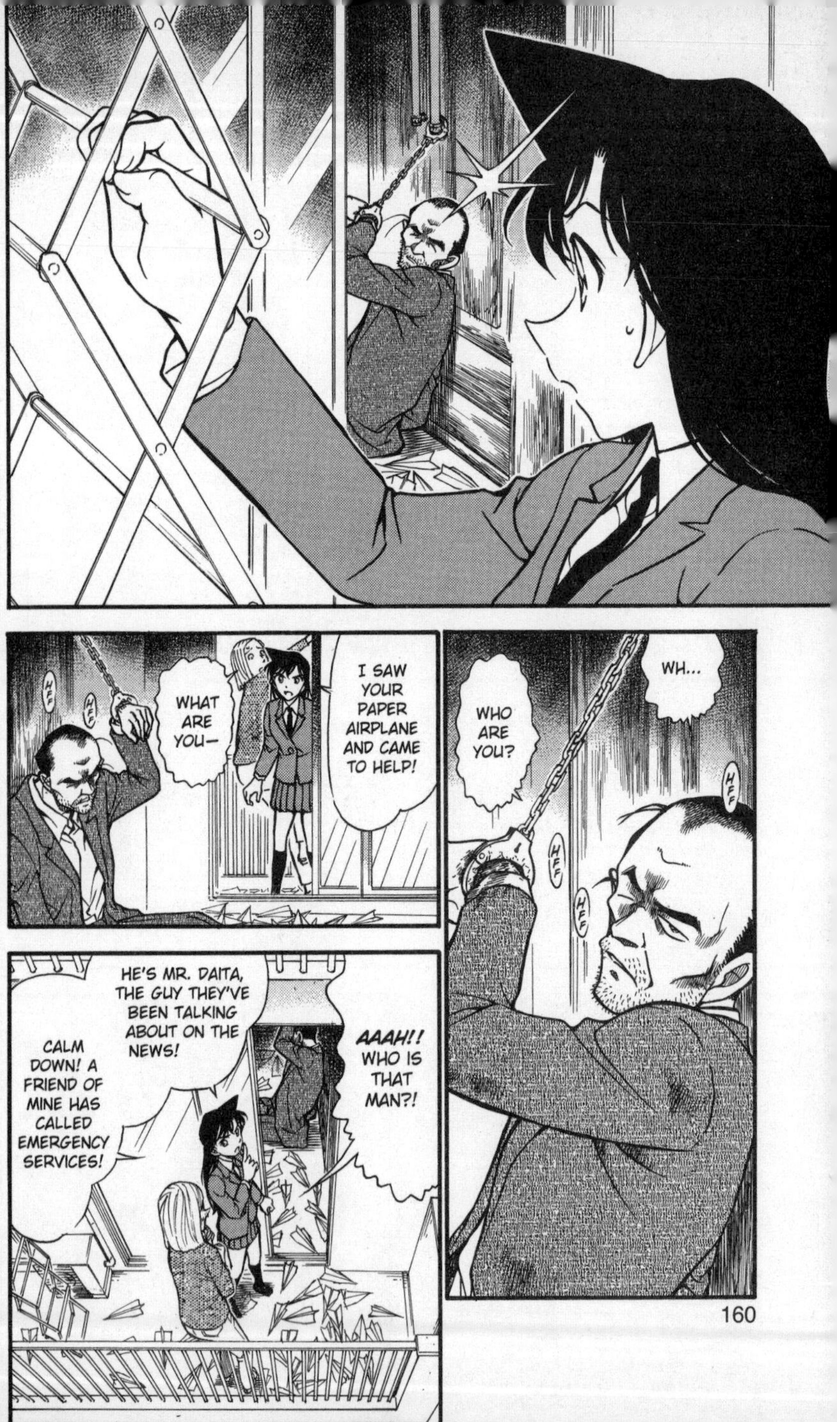

WH...
WHO ARE YOU?
HFF
HFF
HFF
I SAW YOUR PAPER AIRPLANE AND CAME TO HELP!
WHAT ARE YOU—
HFF
HFF
AAAH!! WHO IS THAT MAN?!
HE'S MR. DAITA, THE GUY THEY'VE BEEN TALKING ABOUT ON THE NEWS!
CALM DOWN! A FRIEND OF MINE HAS CALLED EMERGENCY SERVICES!

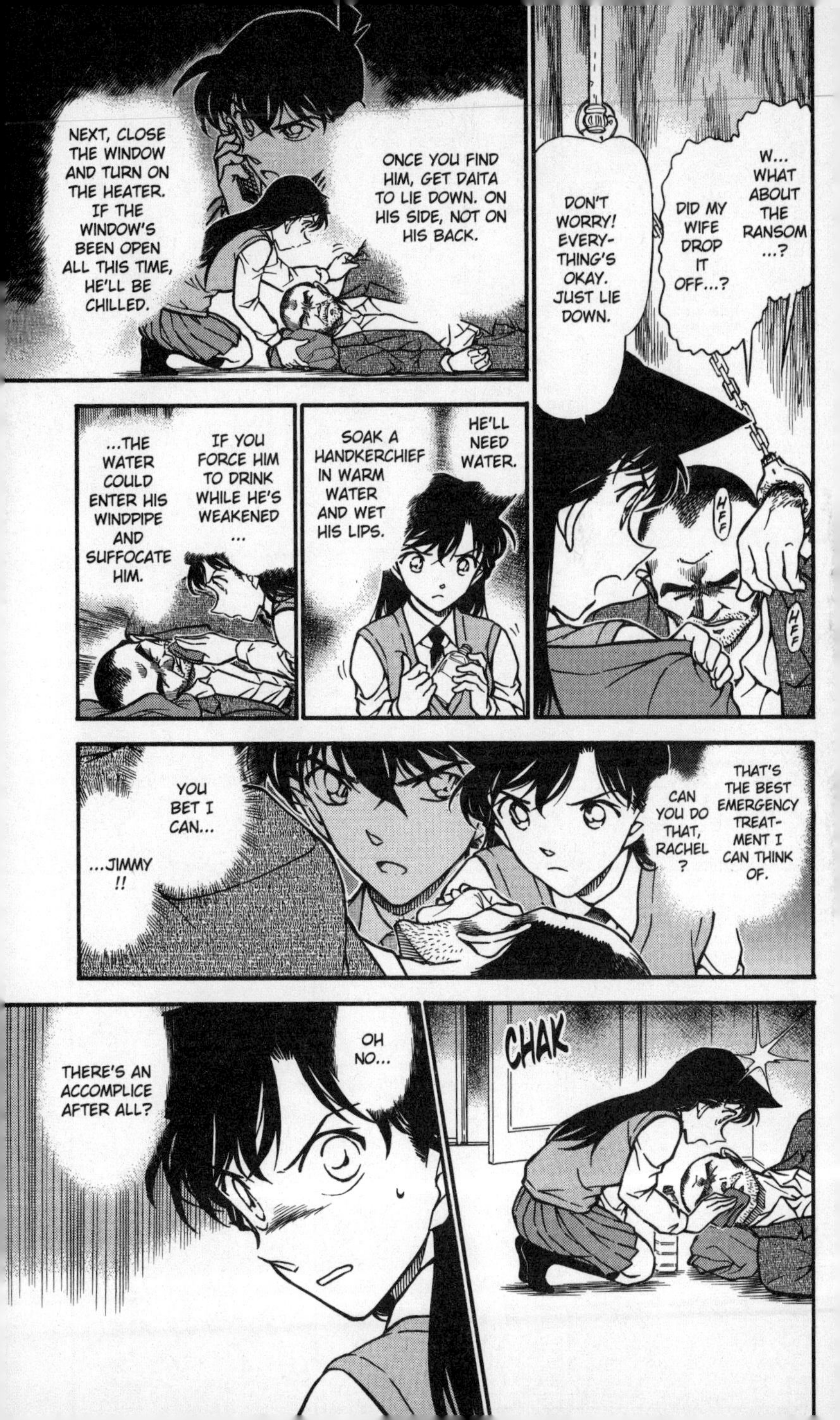
W... WHAT ABOUT THE RANSOM ...?
DID MY WIFE DROP IT OFF...?
DON'T WORRY! EVERYTHING'S OKAY. JUST LIE DOWN.
HFF
HFF
ONCE YOU FIND HIM, GET DAITA TO LIE DOWN. ON HIS SIDE, NOT ON HIS BACK.
NEXT, CLOSE THE WINDOW AND TURN ON THE HEATER. IF THE WINDOW'S BEEN OPEN ALL THIS TIME, HE'LL BE CHILLED.
HE'LL NEED WATER.
SOAK A HANDKERCHIEF IN WARM WATER AND WET HIS LIPS.
IF YOU FORCE HIM TO DRINK WHILE HE'S WEAKENED ...
...THE WATER COULD ENTER HIS WINDPIPE AND SUFFOCATE HIM.
THAT'S THE BEST EMERGENCY TREATMENT I CAN THINK OF.
CAN YOU DO THAT, RACHEL?
YOU BET I CAN...
...JIMMY !!
CHAK
OH NO...
THERE'S AN ACCOMPLICE AFTER ALL?

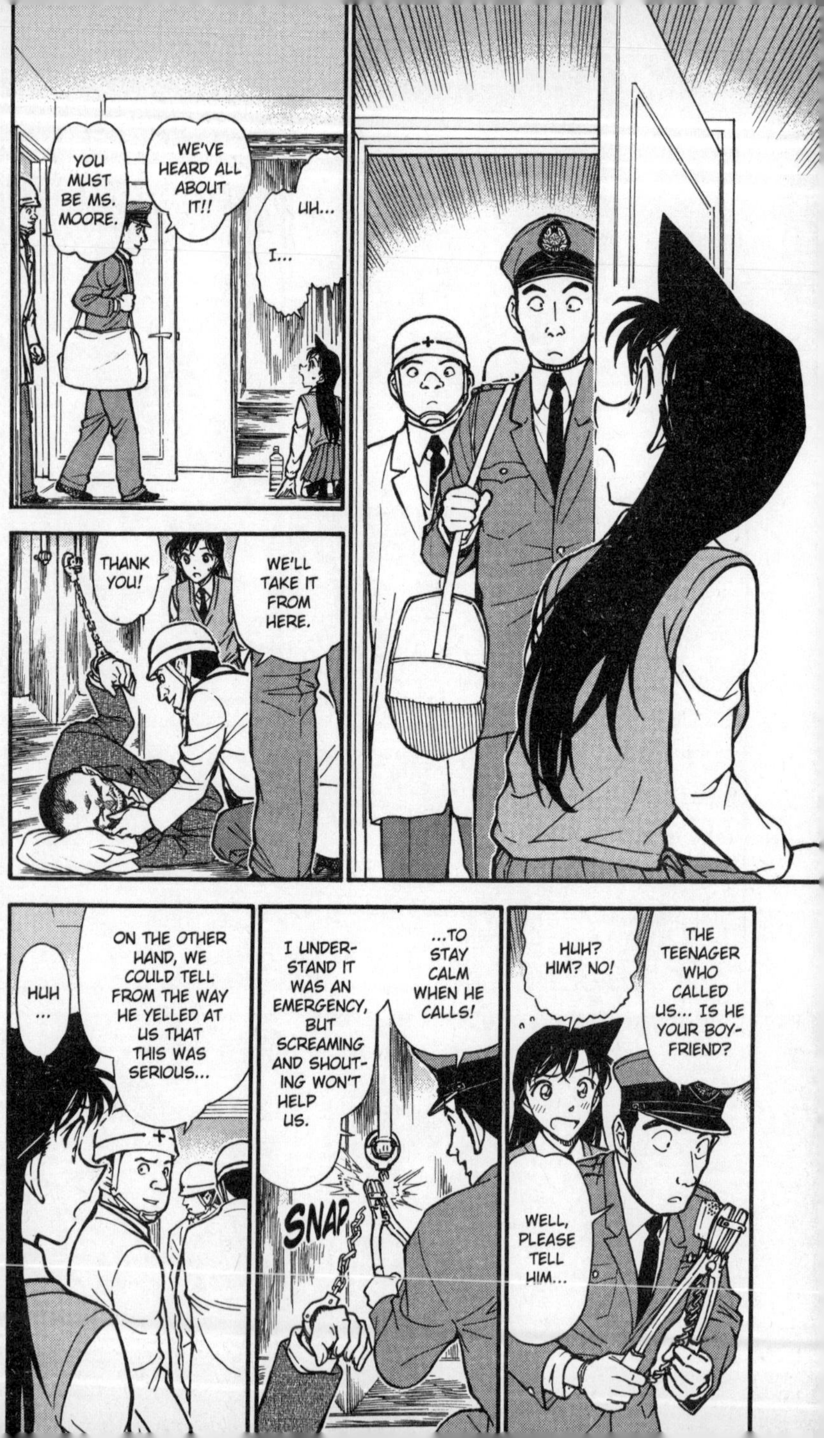
YOU MUST BE MS. MOORE.
WE'VE HEARD ALL ABOUT IT!!
UH... I...
WE'LL TAKE IT FROM HERE.
THANK YOU!
THE TEENAGER WHO CALLED US... IS HE YOUR BOY-FRIEND?
HUH? HIM? NO!
WELL, PLEASE TELL HIM...
I UNDER-STAND IT WAS AN EMERGENCY, BUT SCREAMING AND SHOUT-ING WON'T HELP US.
...TO STAY CALM WHEN HE CALLS!
SNAP
ON THE OTHER HAND, WE COULD TELL FROM THE WAY HE YELLED AT US THAT THIS WAS SERIOUS...
HUH ...

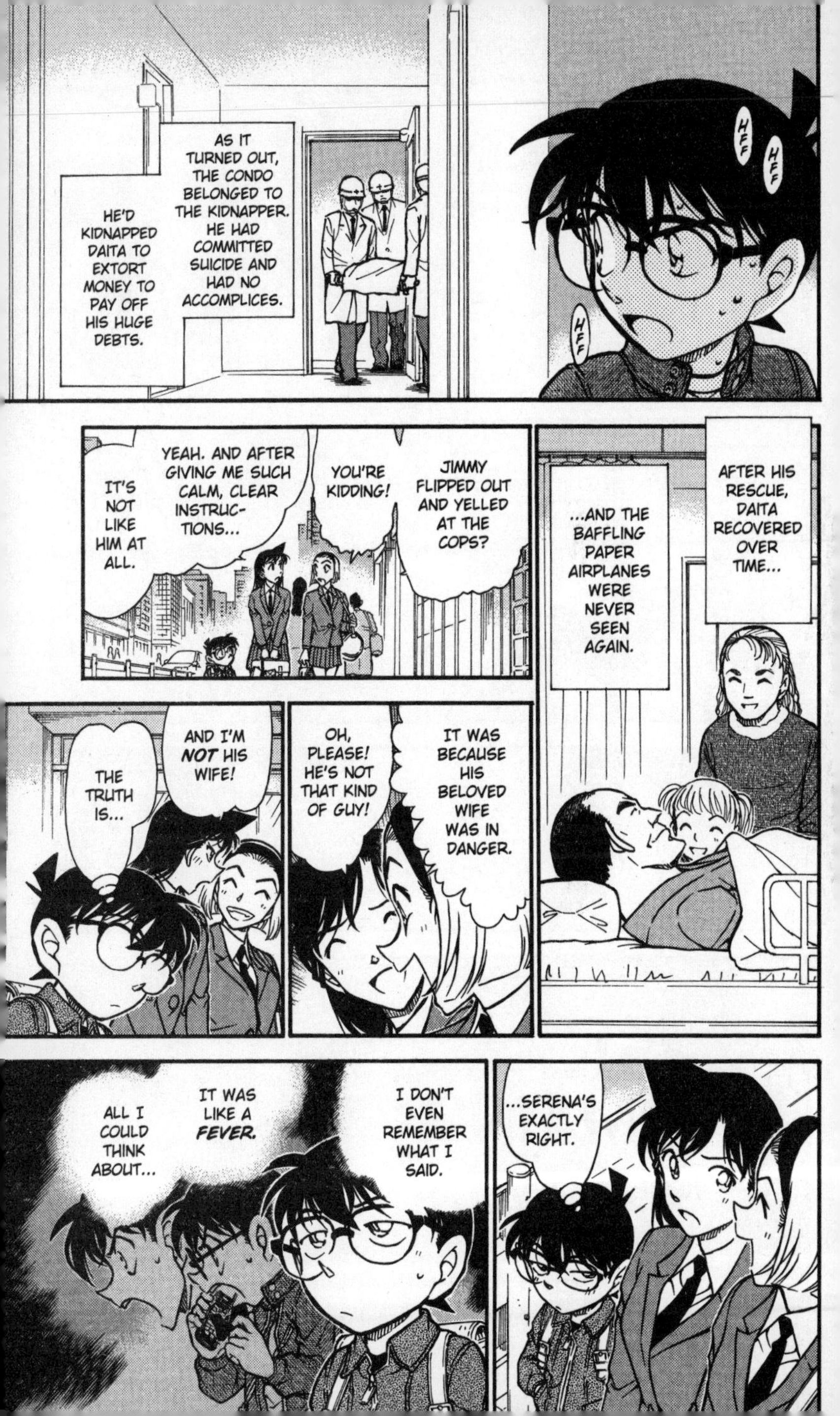
HFF
HFF
HFF
AS IT TURNED OUT, THE CONDO BELONGED TO THE KIDNAPPER. HE HAD COMMITTED SUICIDE AND HAD NO ACCOMPLICES.
HE'D KIDNAPPED DAITA TO EXTORT MONEY TO PAY OFF HIS HUGE DEBTS.
AFTER HIS RESCUE, DAITA RECOVERED OVER TIME...
...AND THE BAFFLING PAPER AIRPLANES WERE NEVER SEEN AGAIN.
JIMMY FLIPPED OUT AND YELLED AT THE COPS?
YOU'RE KIDDING!
YEAH. AND AFTER GIVING ME SUCH CALM, CLEAR INSTRUC-TIONS...
IT'S NOT LIKE HIM AT ALL.
IT WAS BECAUSE HIS BELOVED WIFE WAS IN DANGER.
OH, PLEASE! HE'S NOT THAT KIND OF GUY!
AND I'M NOT HIS WIFE!
THE TRUTH IS...
...SERENA'S EXACTLY RIGHT.
I DON'T EVEN REMEMBER WHAT I SAID.
IT WAS LIKE A FEVER.
ALL I COULD THINK ABOUT...

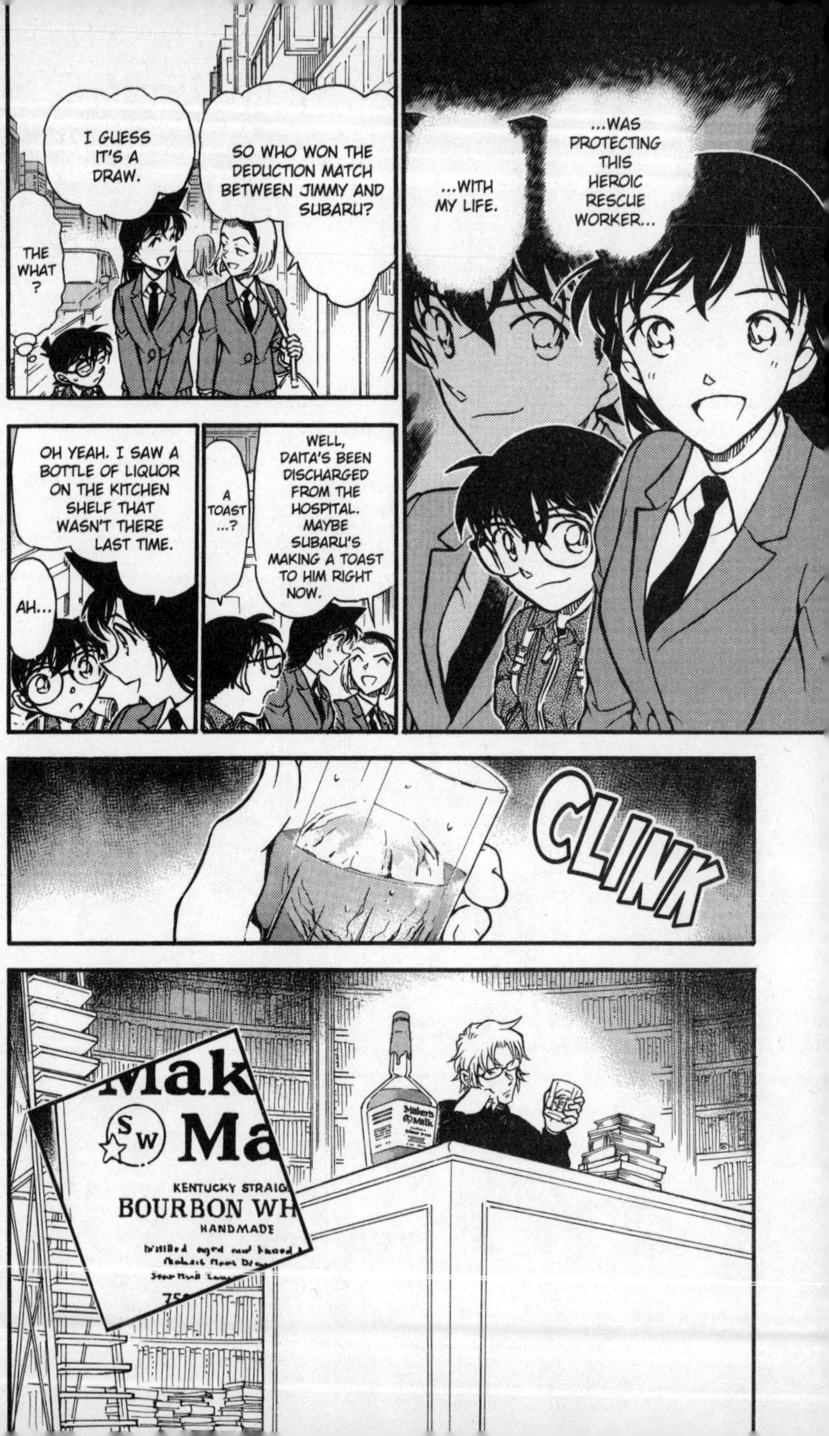
...WAS PROTECTING THIS HEROIC RESCUE WORKER...
...WITH MY LIFE.
SO WHO WON THE DEDUCTION MATCH BETWEEN JIMMY AND SUBARU?
I GUESS IT'S A DRAW.
THE WHAT?
WELL, DAITA'S BEEN DISCHARGED FROM THE HOSPITAL. MAYBE SUBARU'S MAKING A TOAST TO HIM RIGHT NOW.
A TOAST...?
OH YEAH. I SAW A BOTTLE OF LIQUOR ON THE KITCHEN SHELF THAT WASN'T THERE LAST TIME.
AH...
CLINK
Mak
Ma
KENTUCKY STRAIG
BOURBON WH
HANDMADE

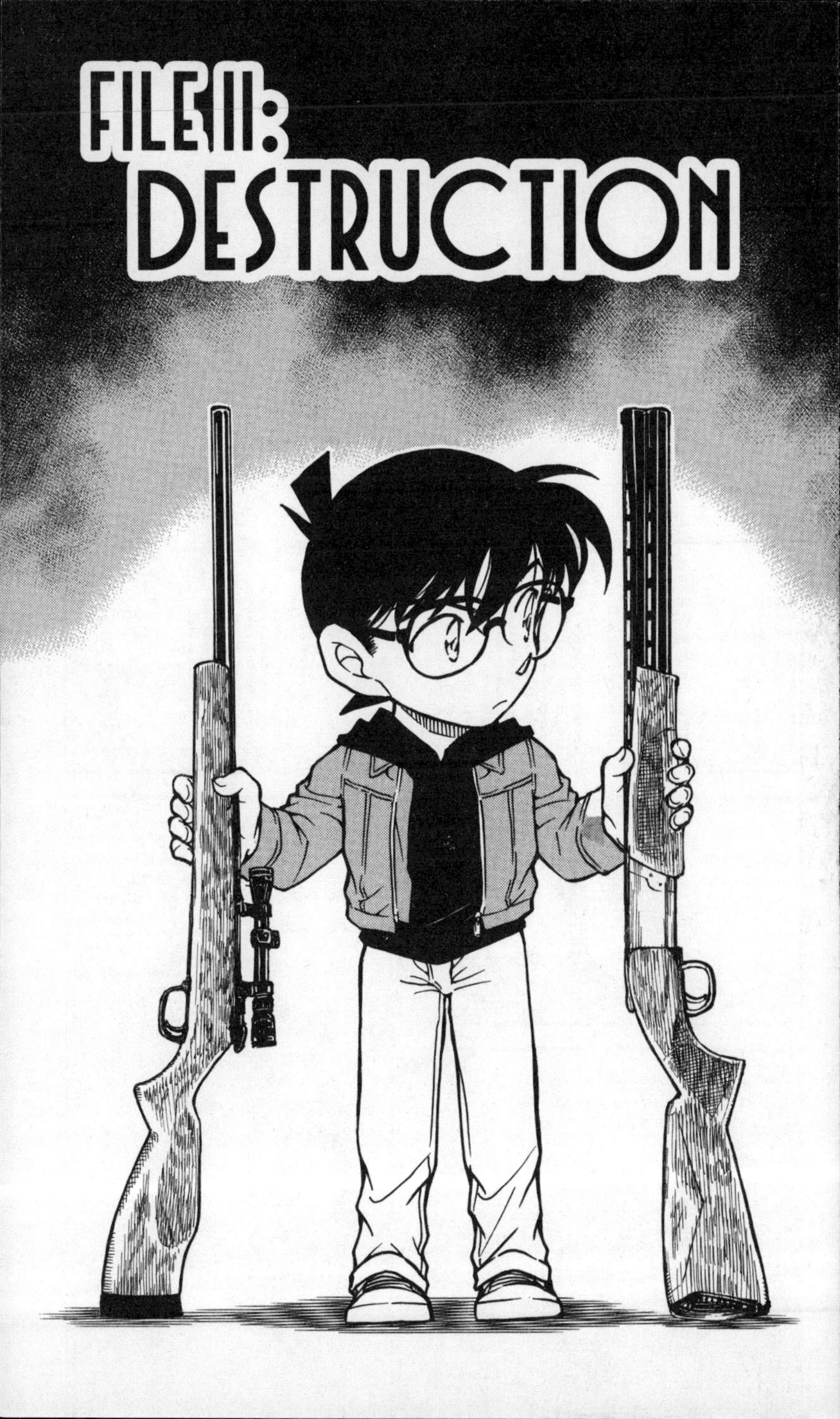
FILE 11:
DESTRUCTION

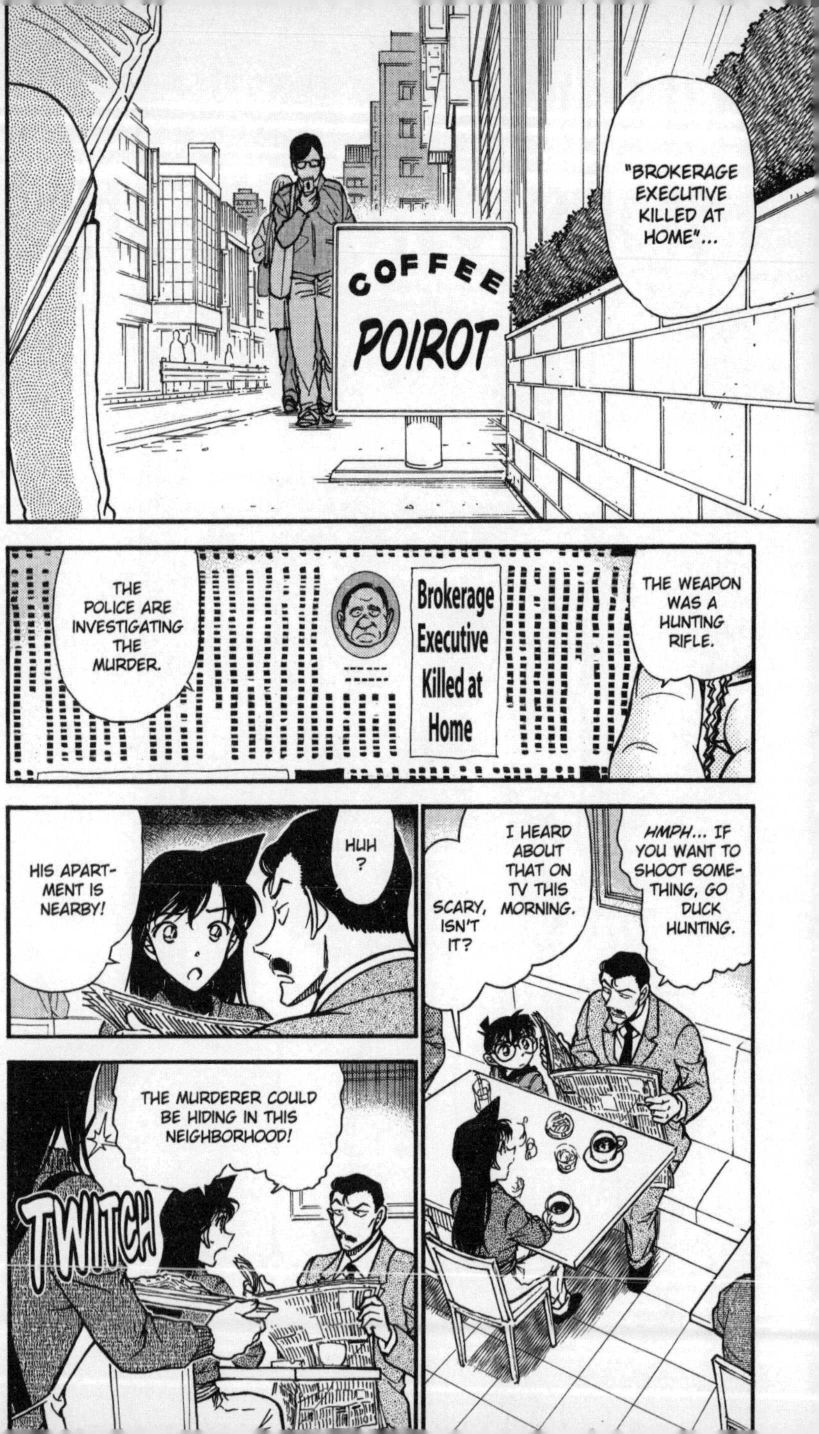
"BROKERAGE EXECUTIVE KILLED AT HOME"...
COFFEE POIROT
THE WEAPON WAS A HUNTING RIFLE.
Brokerage Executive Killed at Home
THE POLICE ARE INVESTIGATING THE MURDER.
*HMPH*... IF YOU WANT TO SHOOT SOMETHING, GO DUCK HUNTING.
I HEARD ABOUT THAT ON TV THIS MORNING.
SCARY, ISN'T IT?
HUH?
HIS APARTMENT IS NEARBY!
THE MURDERER COULD BE HIDING IN THIS NEIGHBORHOOD!
TWITCH

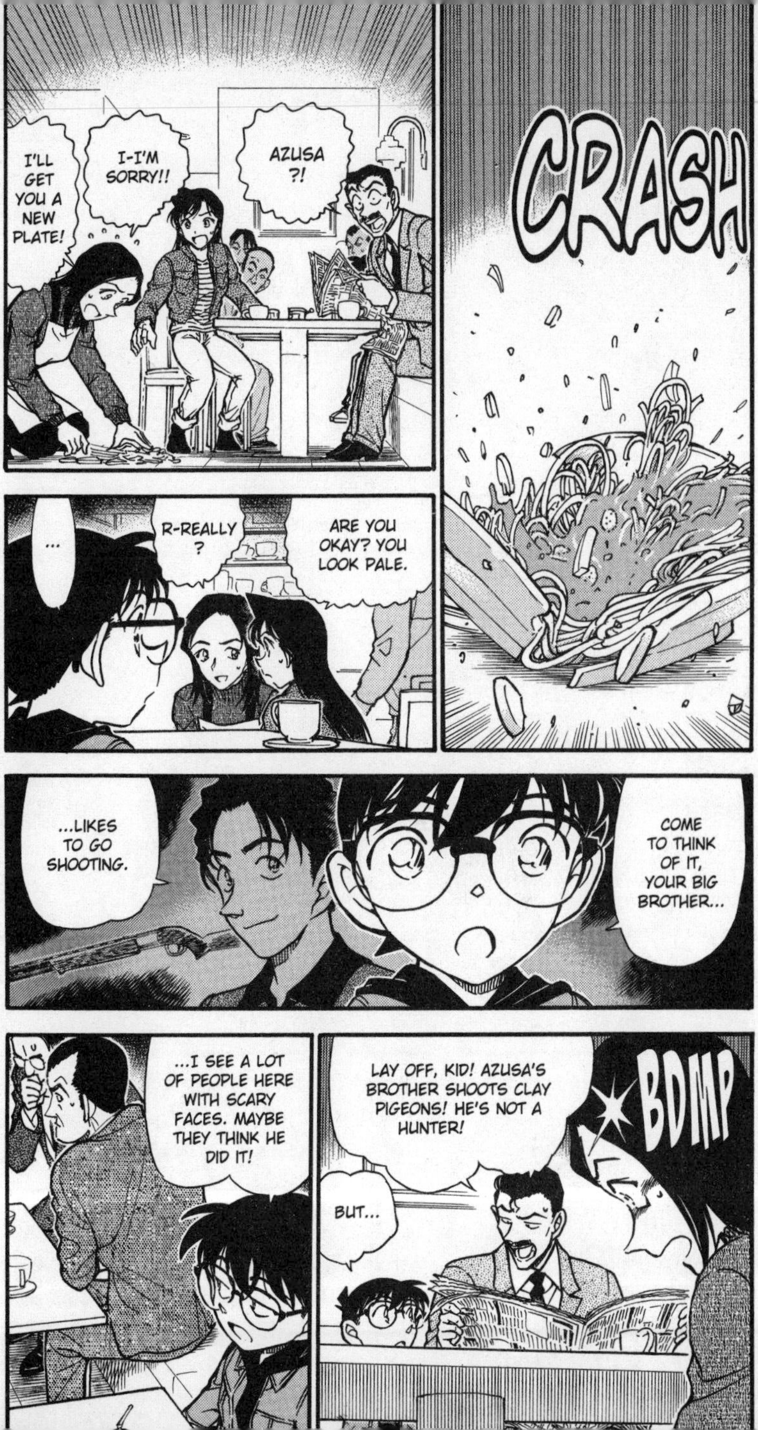
CRASH
AZUSA ?!
I-I'M SORRY!!
I'LL GET YOU A NEW PLATE!
ARE YOU OKAY? YOU LOOK PALE.
R-REALLY ?
...
COME TO THINK OF IT, YOUR BIG BROTHER...
...LIKES TO GO SHOOTING.
BDMP
LAY OFF, KID! AZUSA'S BROTHER SHOOTS CLAY PIGEONS! HE'S NOT A HUNTER!
BUT...
...I SEE A LOT OF PEOPLE HERE WITH SCARY FACES. MAYBE THEY THINK HE DID IT!

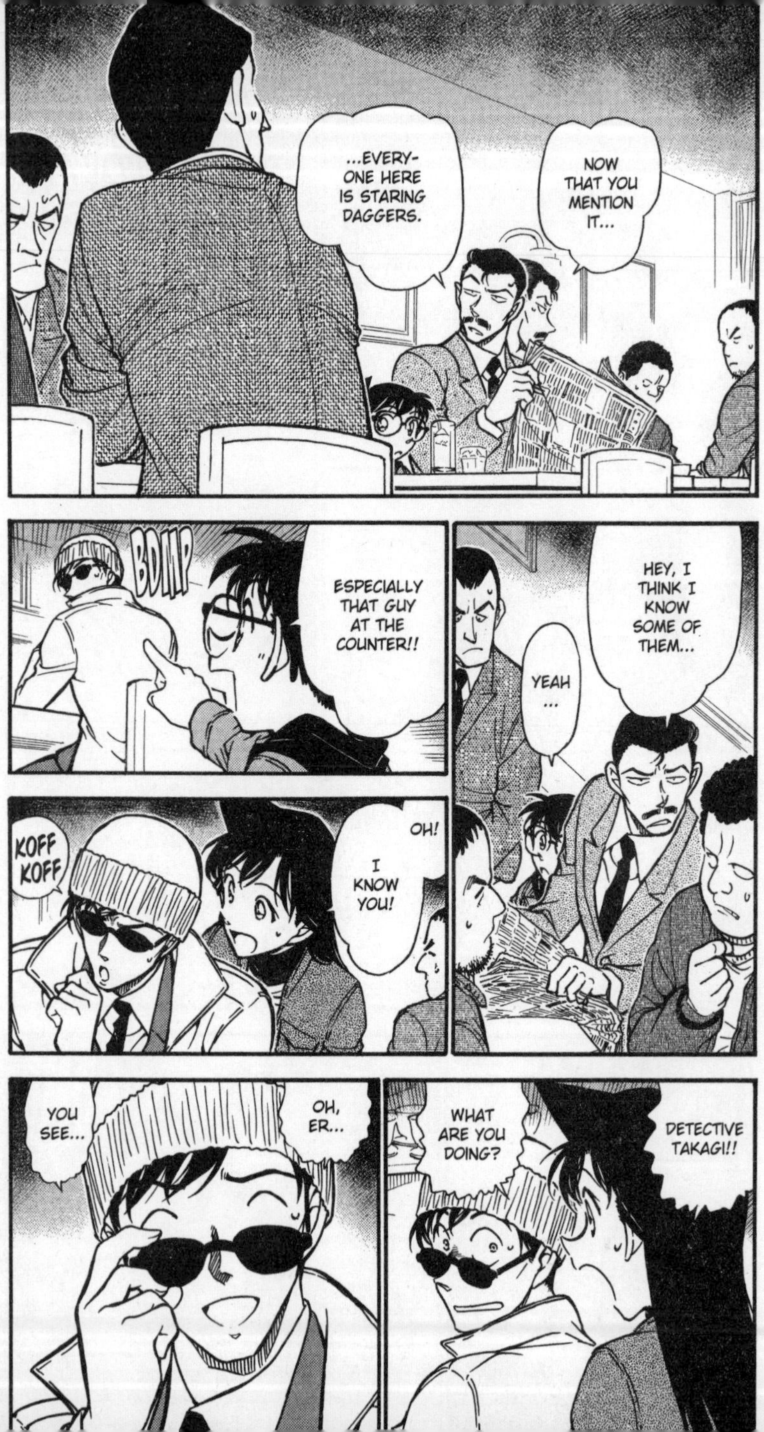
NOW THAT YOU MENTION IT...
...EVERY-ONE HERE IS STARING DAGGERS.
HEY, I THINK I KNOW SOME OF THEM...
YEAH...
ESPECIALLY THAT GUY AT THE COUNTER!!
BDMP
OH! I KNOW YOU!
KOFF KOFF
DETECTIVE TAKAGI!!
WHAT ARE YOU DOING?
OH, ER...
YOU SEE...

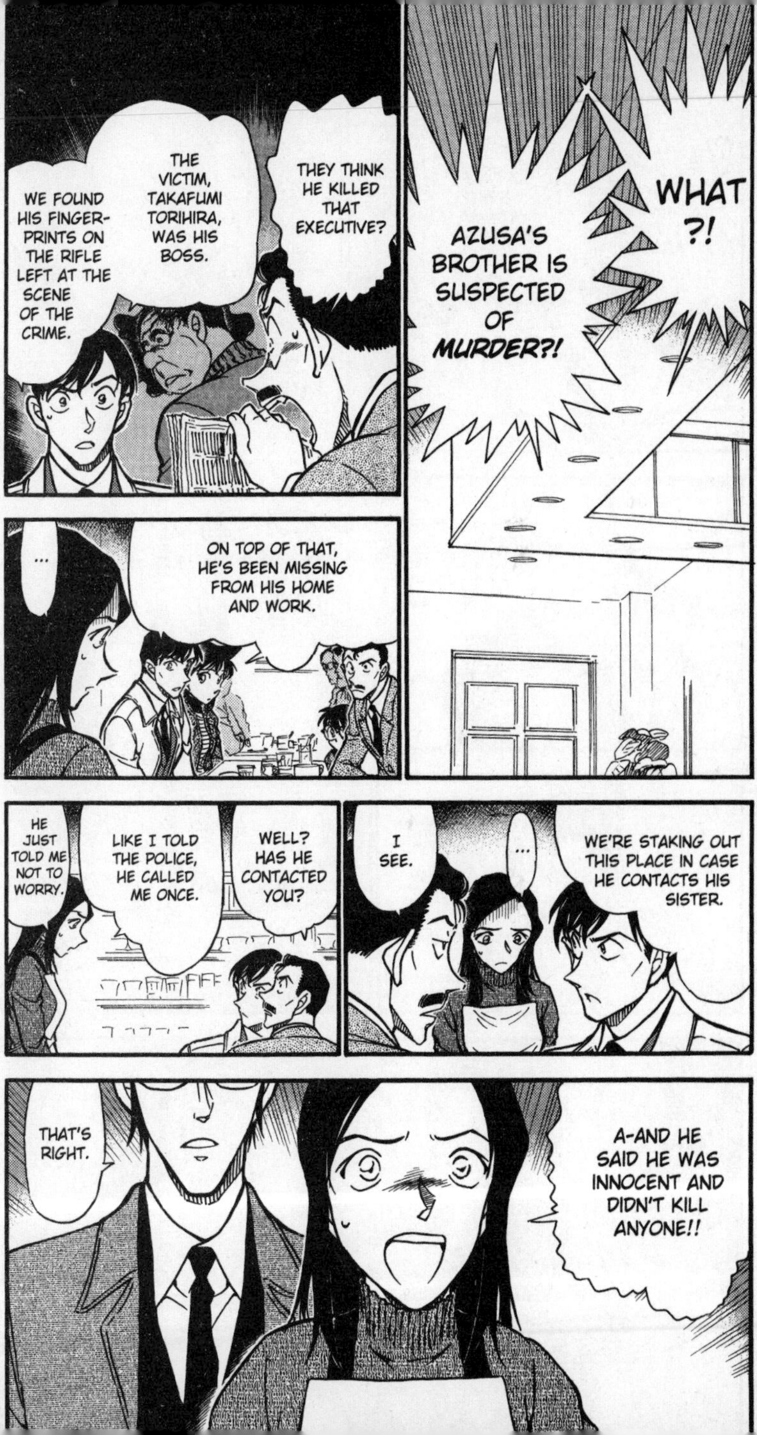
WHAT?!
AZUSA'S BROTHER IS SUSPECTED OF *MURDER?!*
THEY THINK HE KILLED THAT EXECUTIVE?
THE VICTIM, TAKAFUMI TORIHIRA, WAS HIS BOSS.
WE FOUND HIS FINGER-PRINTS ON THE RIFLE LEFT AT THE SCENE OF THE CRIME.
ON TOP OF THAT, HE'S BEEN MISSING FROM HIS HOME AND WORK.
...
WE'RE STAKING OUT THIS PLACE IN CASE HE CONTACTS HIS SISTER.
...
I SEE.
WELL? HAS HE CONTACTED YOU?
LIKE I TOLD THE POLICE, HE CALLED ME ONCE.
HE JUST TOLD ME NOT TO WORRY.
A-AND HE SAID HE WAS INNOCENT AND DIDN'T KILL ANYONE!!
THAT'S RIGHT.

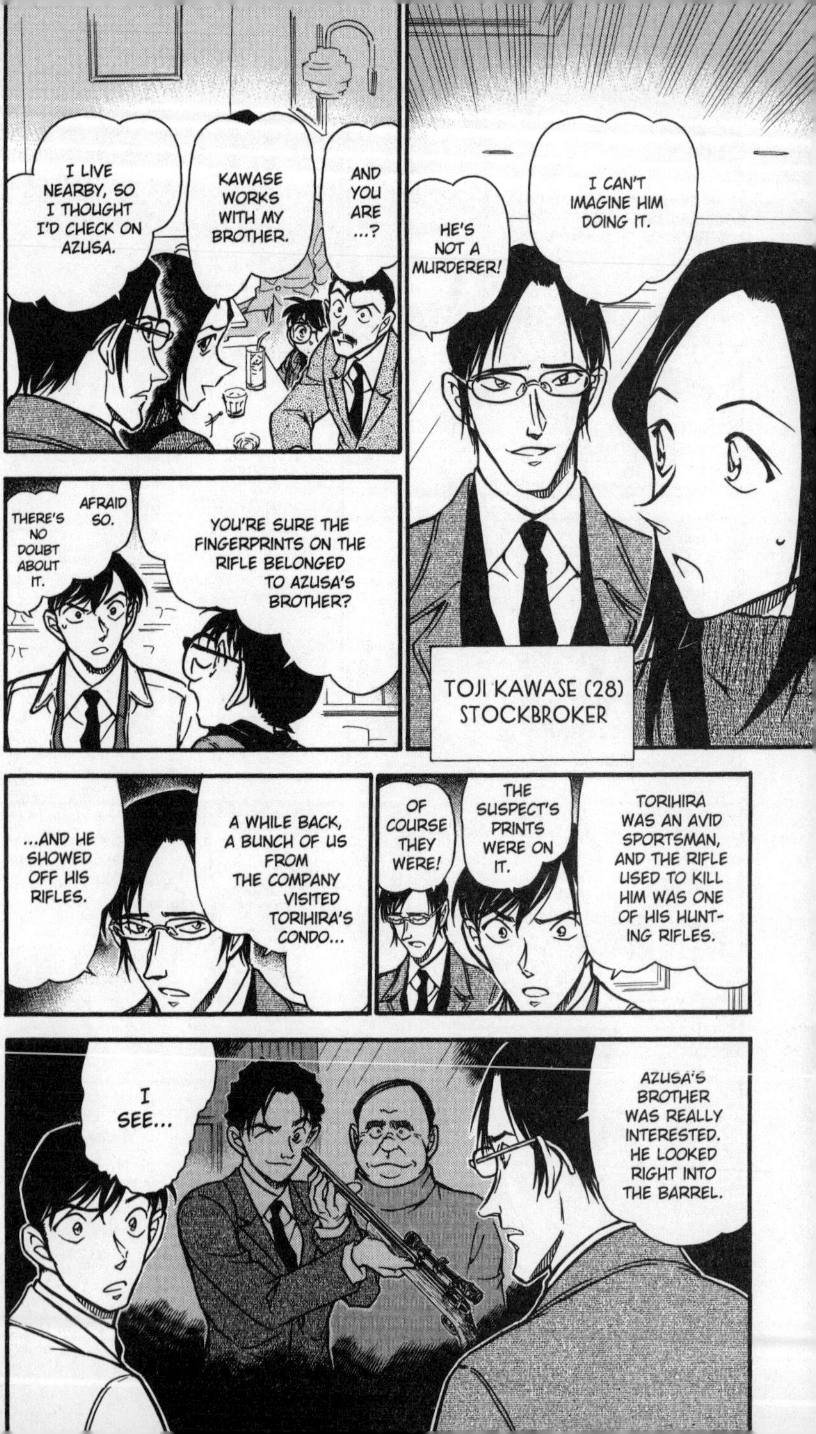
I CAN'T IMAGINE HIM DOING IT.
HE'S NOT A MURDERER!
TOJI KAWASE (28) STOCKBROKER
AND YOU ARE ...?
KAWASE WORKS WITH MY BROTHER.
I LIVE NEARBY, SO I THOUGHT I'D CHECK ON AZUSA.
YOU'RE SURE THE FINGERPRINTS ON THE RIFLE BELONGED TO AZUSA'S BROTHER?
AFRAID SO.
THERE'S NO DOUBT ABOUT IT.
TORIHIRA WAS AN AVID SPORTSMAN, AND THE RIFLE USED TO KILL HIM WAS ONE OF HIS HUNTING RIFLES.
THE SUSPECT'S PRINTS WERE ON IT.
OF COURSE THEY WERE!
A WHILE BACK, A BUNCH OF US FROM THE COMPANY VISITED TORIHIRA'S CONDO...
...AND HE SHOWED OFF HIS RIFLES.
AZUSA'S BROTHER WAS REALLY INTERESTED. HE LOOKED RIGHT INTO THE BARREL.
I SEE...

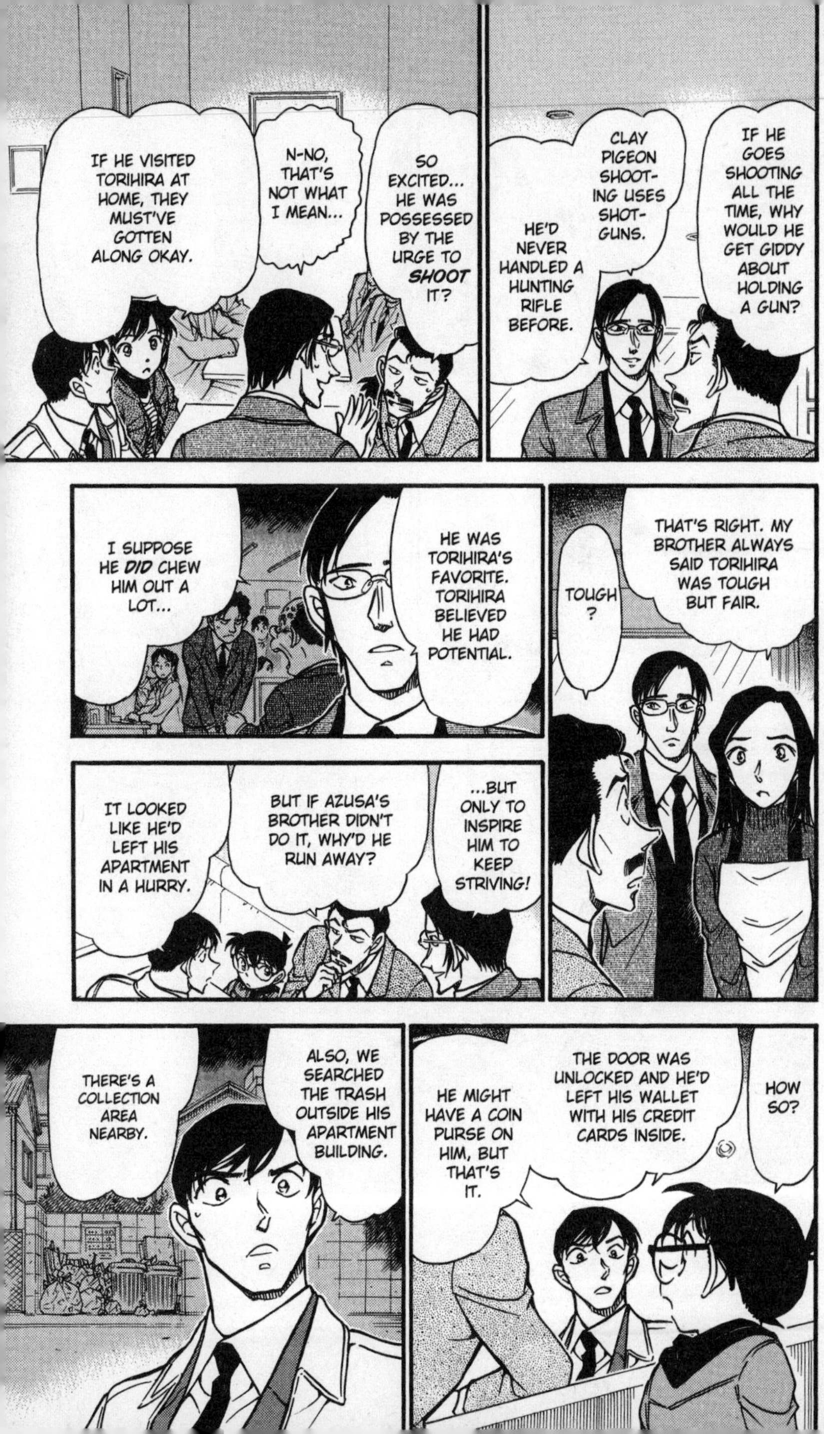
IF HE GOES SHOOTING ALL THE TIME, WHY WOULD HE GET GIDDY ABOUT HOLDING A GUN?
CLAY PIGEON SHOOTING USES SHOTGUNS.
HE'D NEVER HANDLED A HUNTING RIFLE BEFORE.
SO EXCITED... HE WAS POSSESSED BY THE URGE TO *SHOOT* IT?
N-NO, THAT'S NOT WHAT I MEAN...
IF HE VISITED TORIHIRA AT HOME, THEY MUST'VE GOTTEN ALONG OKAY.
THAT'S RIGHT. MY BROTHER ALWAYS SAID TORIHIRA WAS TOUGH BUT FAIR.
TOUGH?
HE WAS TORIHIRA'S FAVORITE. TORIHIRA BELIEVED HE HAD POTENTIAL.
I SUPPOSE HE *DID* CHEW HIM OUT A LOT...
...BUT ONLY TO INSPIRE HIM TO KEEP STRIVING!
BUT IF AZUSA'S BROTHER DIDN'T DO IT, WHY'D HE RUN AWAY?
IT LOOKED LIKE HE'D LEFT HIS APARTMENT IN A HURRY.
HOW SO?
THE DOOR WAS UNLOCKED AND HE'D LEFT HIS WALLET WITH HIS CREDIT CARDS INSIDE.
HE MIGHT HAVE A COIN PURSE ON HIM, BUT THAT'S IT.
ALSO, WE SEARCHED THE TRASH OUTSIDE HIS APARTMENT BUILDING.
THERE'S A COLLECTION AREA NEARBY.

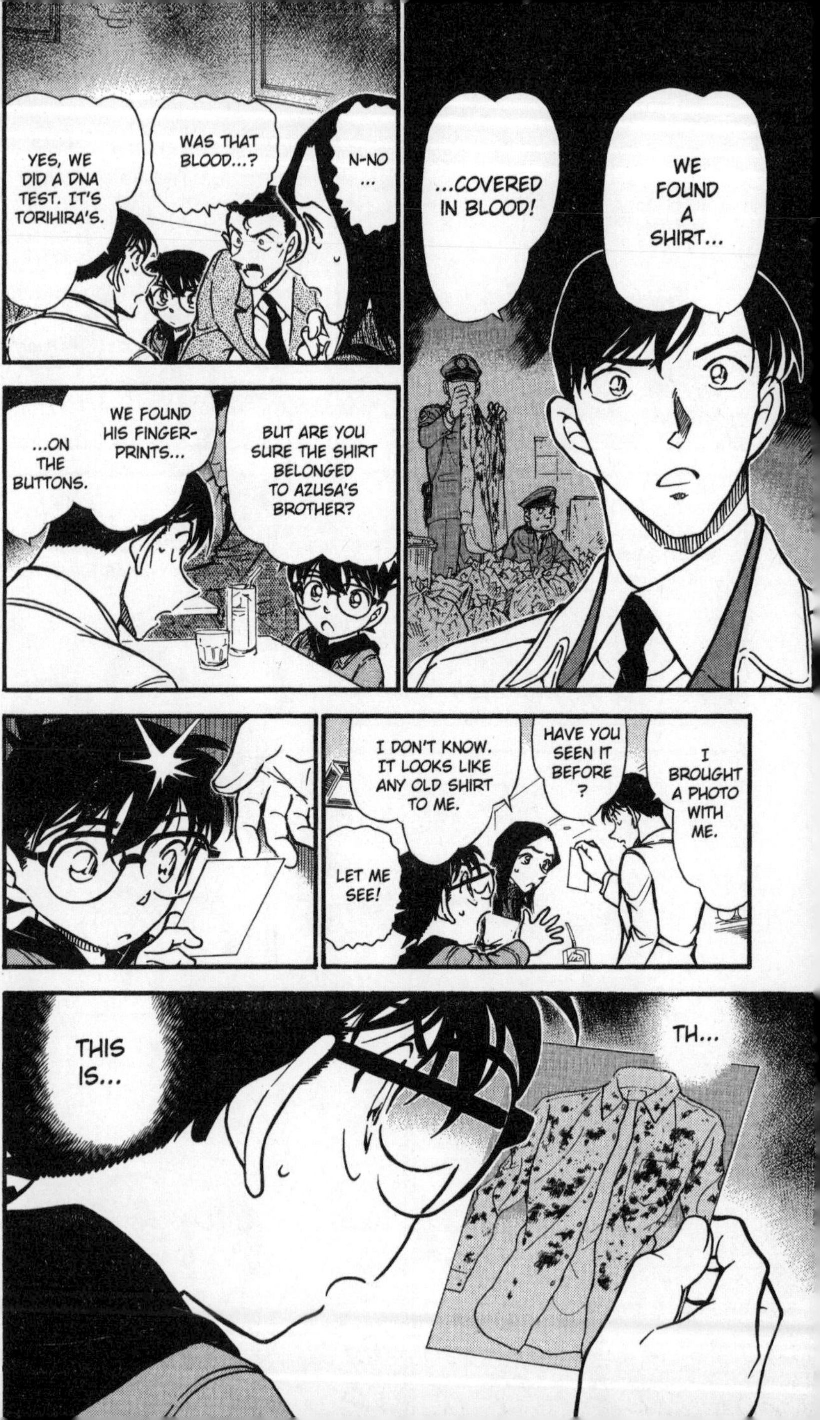
WE FOUND A SHIRT...
...COVERED IN BLOOD!
N-NO ...
WAS THAT BLOOD...?
YES, WE DID A DNA TEST. IT'S TORIHIRA'S.
BUT ARE YOU SURE THE SHIRT BELONGED TO AZUSA'S BROTHER?
WE FOUND HIS FINGER-PRINTS...
...ON THE BUTTONS.
I BROUGHT A PHOTO WITH ME.
HAVE YOU SEEN IT BEFORE ?
I DON'T KNOW. IT LOOKS LIKE ANY OLD SHIRT TO ME.
LET ME SEE!
TH...
THIS IS...

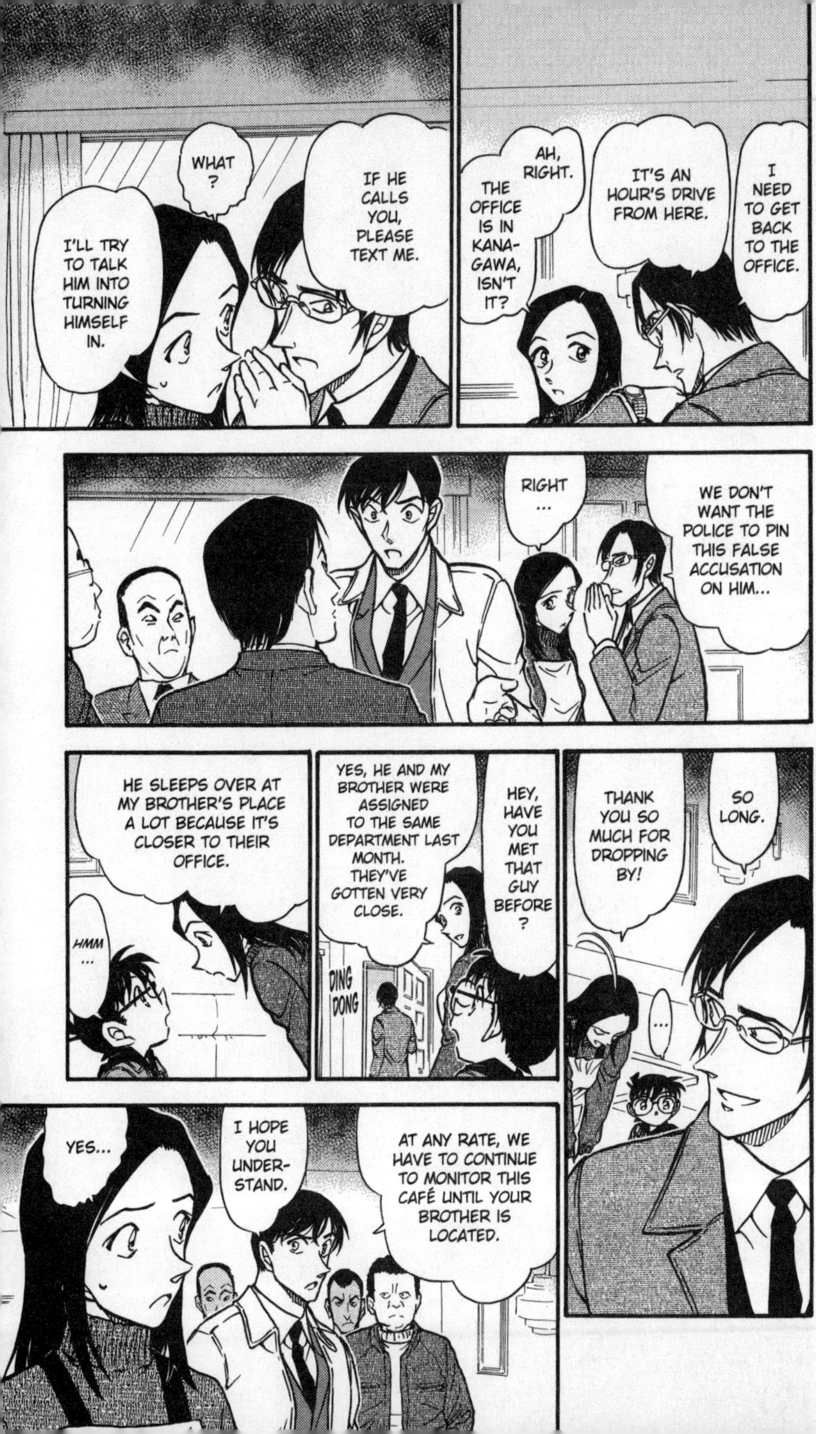
I NEED TO GET BACK TO THE OFFICE.
IT'S AN HOUR'S DRIVE FROM HERE.
AH, RIGHT.
THE OFFICE IS IN KANA-GAWA, ISN'T IT?
IF HE CALLS YOU, PLEASE TEXT ME.
WHAT?
I'LL TRY TO TALK HIM INTO TURNING HIMSELF IN.
WE DON'T WANT THE POLICE TO PIN THIS FALSE ACCUSATION ON HIM...
RIGHT...
SO LONG.
THANK YOU SO MUCH FOR DROPPING BY!
...
HEY, HAVE YOU MET THAT GUY BEFORE?
YES, HE AND MY BROTHER WERE ASSIGNED TO THE SAME DEPARTMENT LAST MONTH. THEY'VE GOTTEN VERY CLOSE.
DING DONG
HE SLEEPS OVER AT MY BROTHER'S PLACE A LOT BECAUSE IT'S CLOSER TO THEIR OFFICE.
HMM...
AT ANY RATE, WE HAVE TO CONTINUE TO MONITOR THIS CAFÉ UNTIL YOUR BROTHER IS LOCATED.
I HOPE YOU UNDER-STAND.
YES...

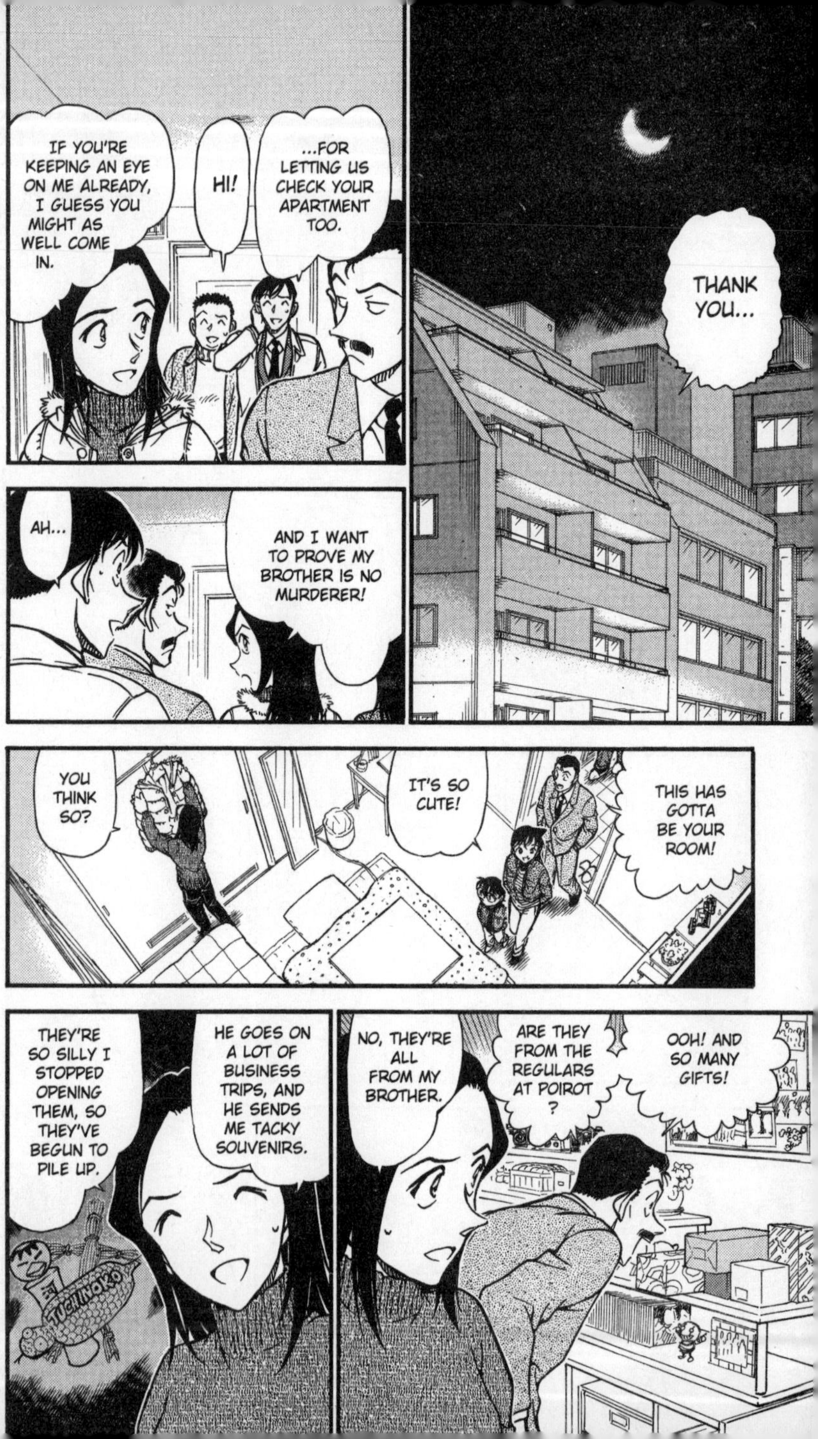
THANK YOU...
...FOR LETTING US CHECK YOUR APARTMENT TOO.
HI!
IF YOU'RE KEEPING AN EYE ON ME ALREADY, I GUESS YOU MIGHT AS WELL COME IN.
AND I WANT TO PROVE MY BROTHER IS NO MURDERER!
AH...
THIS HAS GOTTA BE YOUR ROOM!
IT'S SO CUTE!
YOU THINK SO?
OOH! AND SO MANY GIFTS!
ARE THEY FROM THE REGULARS AT POIROT?
NO, THEY'RE ALL FROM MY BROTHER.
HE GOES ON A LOT OF BUSINESS TRIPS, AND HE SENDS ME TACKY SOUVENIRS.
THEY'RE SO SILLY I STOPPED OPENING THEM, SO THEY'VE BEGUN TO PILE UP.

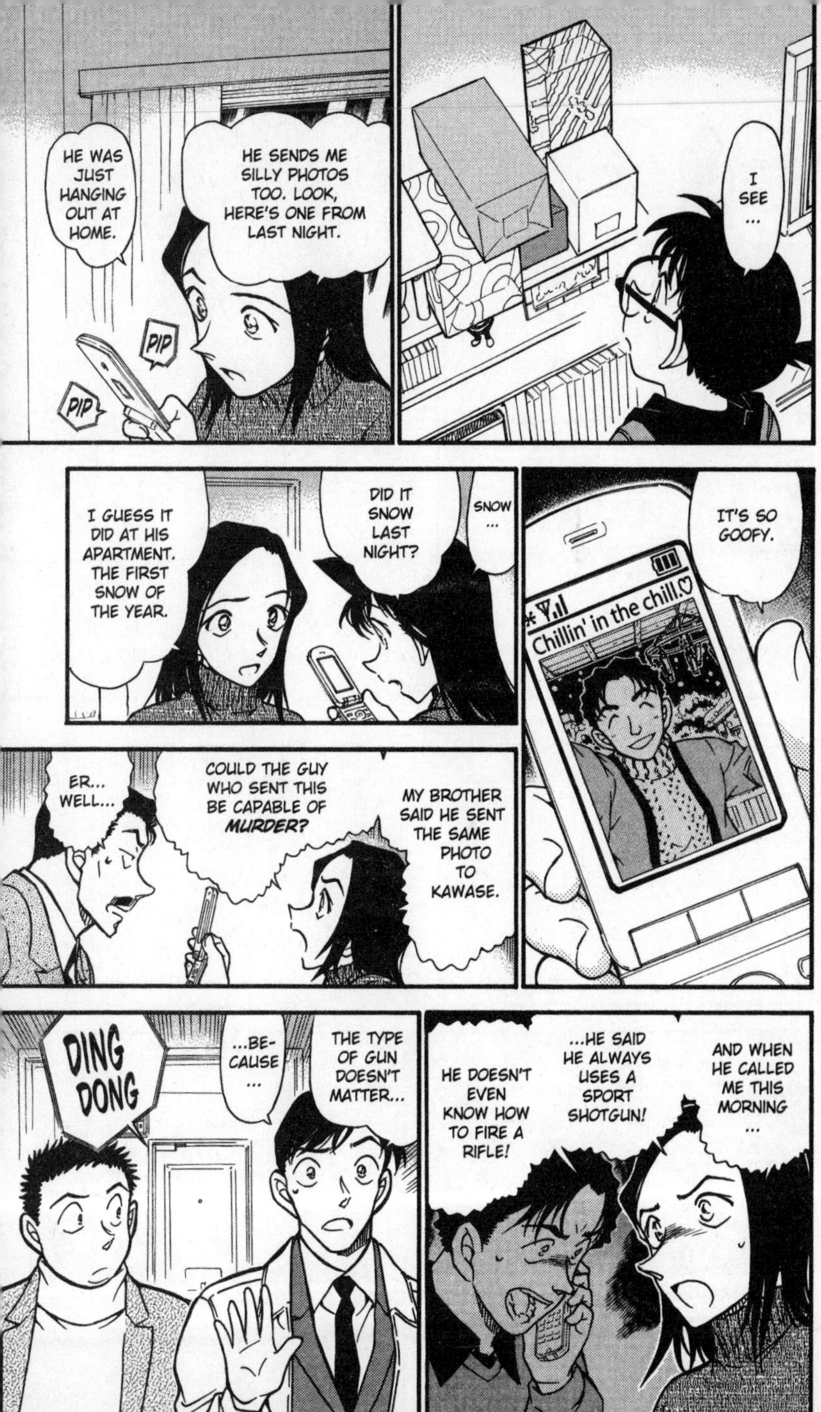
I SEE ...
HE SENDS ME SILLY PHOTOS TOO. LOOK, HERE'S ONE FROM LAST NIGHT.
HE WAS JUST HANGING OUT AT HOME.
PIP
PIP
IT'S SO GOOFY.
Chillin' in the chill.♡
SNOW ...
DID IT SNOW LAST NIGHT?
I GUESS IT DID AT HIS APARTMENT. THE FIRST SNOW OF THE YEAR.
MY BROTHER SAID HE SENT THE SAME PHOTO TO KAWASE.
COULD THE GUY WHO SENT THIS BE CAPABLE OF *MURDER?*
ER... WELL...
AND WHEN HE CALLED ME THIS MORNING ...
...HE SAID HE ALWAYS USES A SPORT SHOTGUN!
HE DOESN'T EVEN KNOW HOW TO FIRE A RIFLE!
THE TYPE OF GUN DOESN'T MATTER...
...BE-CAUSE ...
DING DONG

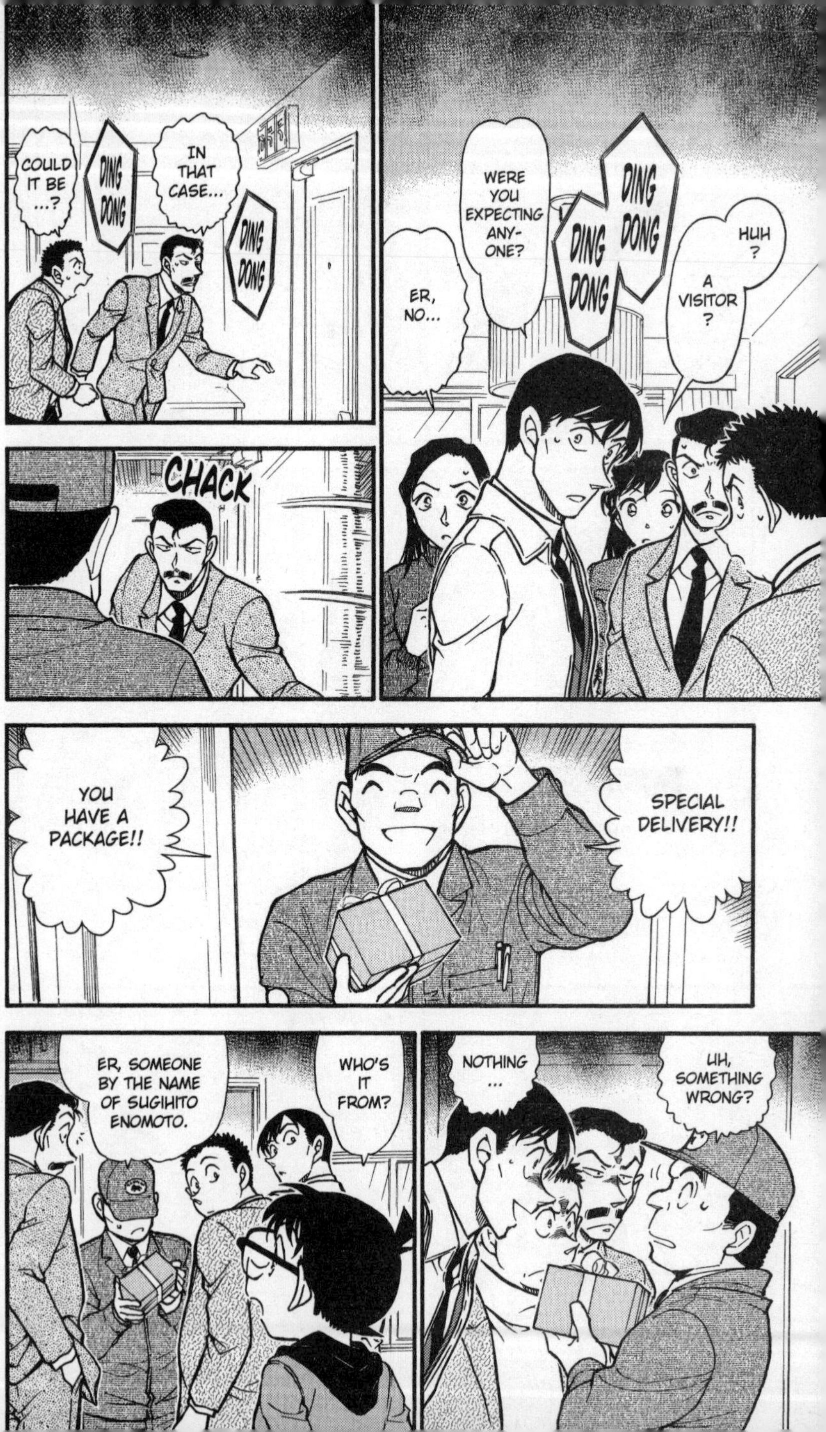

HUH ? A VISITOR ?
DING DONG
DING DONG
WERE YOU EXPECTING ANY-ONE?
ER, NO...
IN THAT CASE...
DING DONG
DING DONG
COULD IT BE ...?
CHACK
SPECIAL DELIVERY!!
YOU HAVE A PACKAGE!!
UH, SOMETHING WRONG?
NOTHING ...
WHO'S IT FROM?
ER, SOMEONE BY THE NAME OF SUGIHITO ENOMOTO.

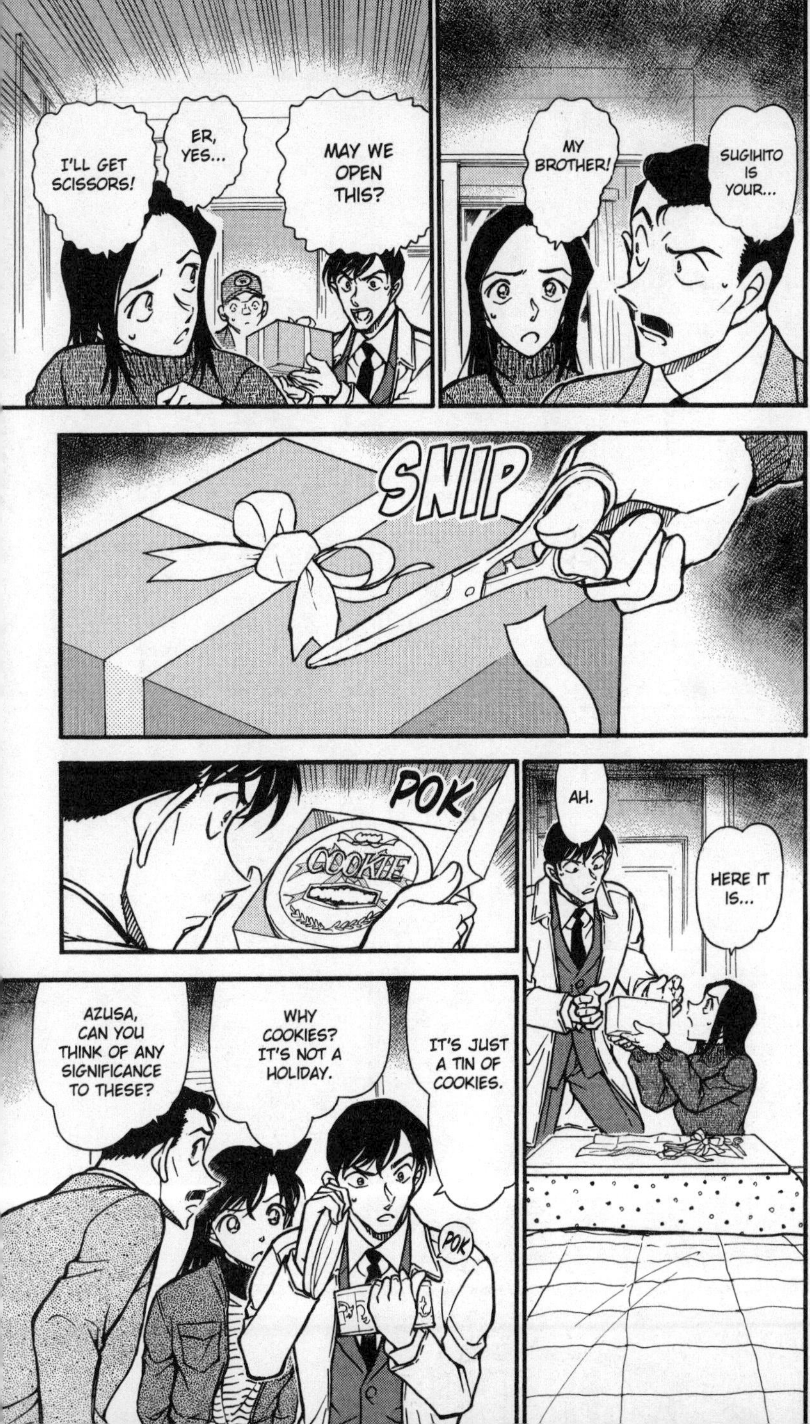
SUGIHITO IS YOUR...
MY BROTHER!
MAY WE OPEN THIS?
ER, YES...
I'LL GET SCISSORS!
SNIP
HERE IT IS...
AH.
POK
COOKIE
IT'S JUST A TIN OF COOKIES.
WHY COOKIES? IT'S NOT A HOLIDAY.
AZUSA, CAN YOU THINK OF ANY SIGNIFICANCE TO THESE?
POK

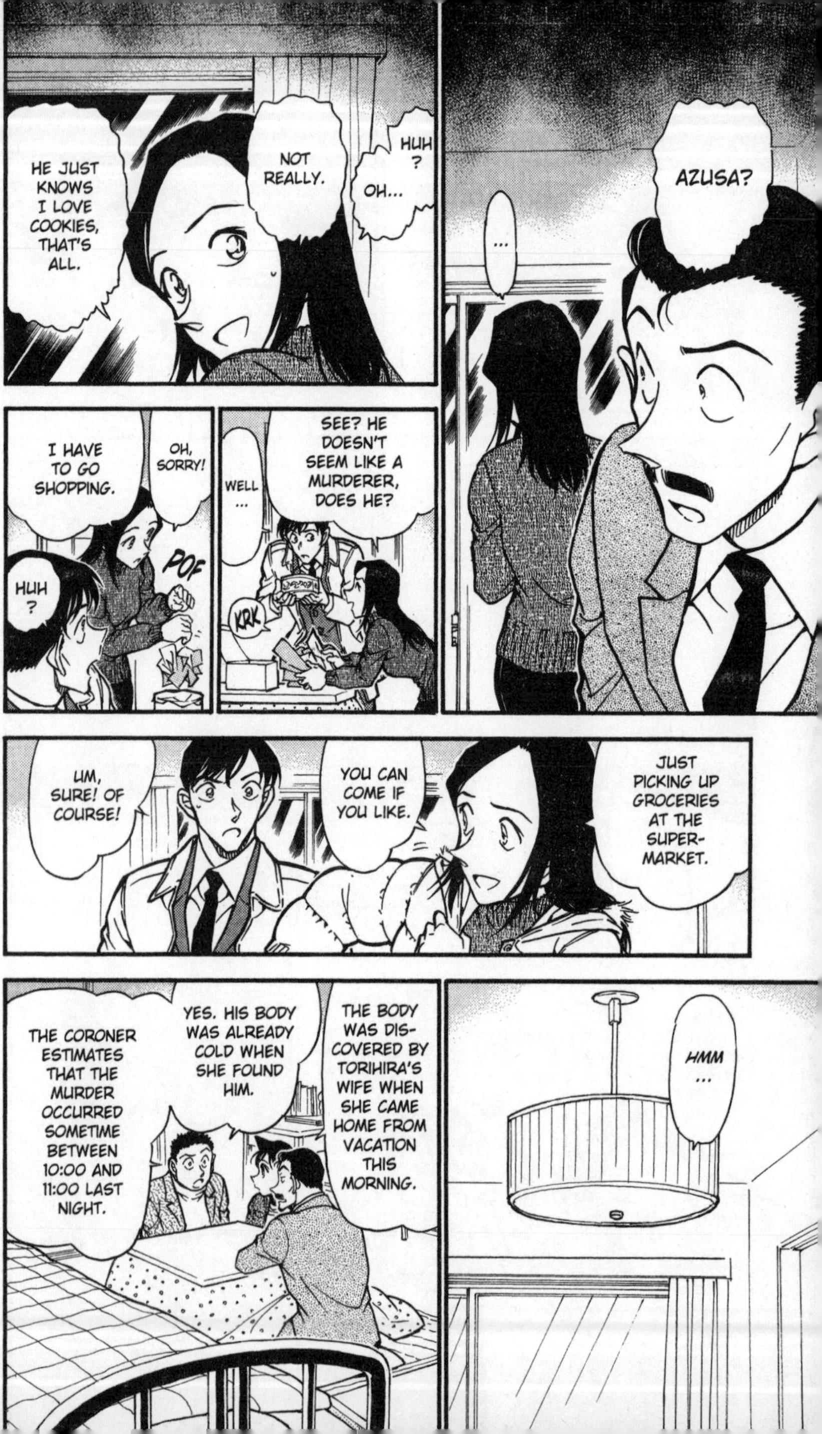
AZUSA?
...
HUH ?
OH...
NOT REALLY.
HE JUST KNOWS I LOVE COOKIES, THAT'S ALL.
SEE? HE DOESN'T SEEM LIKE A MURDERER, DOES HE?
KRK
WELL ...
OH, SORRY!
I HAVE TO GO SHOPPING.
POF
HUH ?
JUST PICKING UP GROCERIES AT THE SUPER-MARKET.
YOU CAN COME IF YOU LIKE.
UM, SURE! OF COURSE!
HMM ...
THE BODY WAS DIS-COVERED BY TORIHIRA'S WIFE WHEN SHE CAME HOME FROM VACATION THIS MORNING.
YES. HIS BODY WAS ALREADY COLD WHEN SHE FOUND HIM.
THE CORONER ESTIMATES THAT THE MURDER OCCURRED SOMETIME BETWEEN 10:00 AND 11:00 LAST NIGHT.

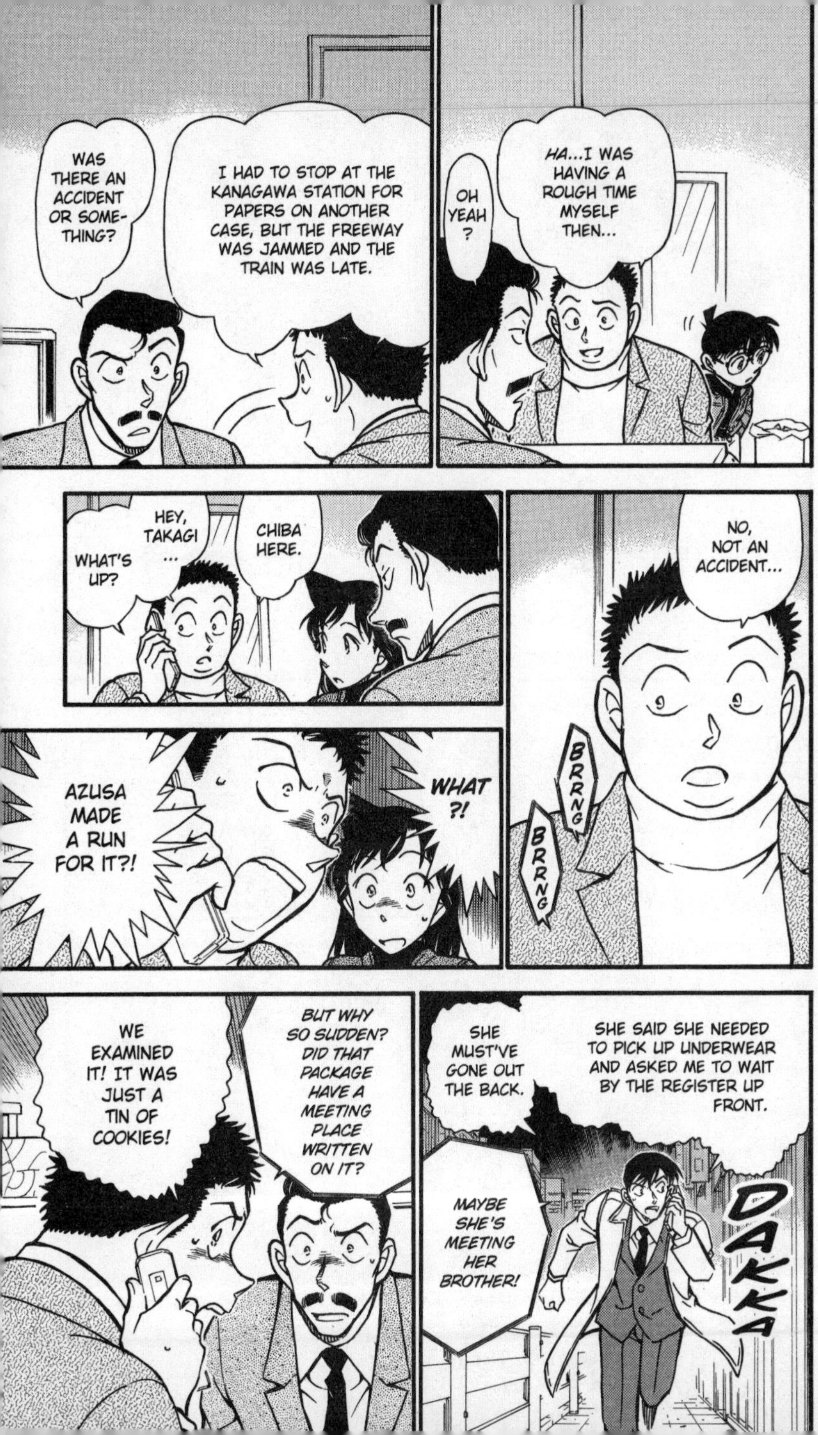
HA...I WAS HAVING A ROUGH TIME MYSELF THEN...
OH YEAH?
I HAD TO STOP AT THE KANAGAWA STATION FOR PAPERS ON ANOTHER CASE, BUT THE FREEWAY WAS JAMMED AND THE TRAIN WAS LATE.
WAS THERE AN ACCIDENT OR SOMETHING?
NO, NOT AN ACCIDENT...
BRRNG
BRRNG
CHIBA HERE.
HEY, TAKAGI...
WHAT'S UP?
WHAT?!
AZUSA MADE A RUN FOR IT?!
SHE SAID SHE NEEDED TO PICK UP UNDERWEAR AND ASKED ME TO WAIT BY THE REGISTER UP FRONT.
SHE MUST'VE GONE OUT THE BACK.
DAKA
MAYBE SHE'S MEETING HER BROTHER!
BUT WHY SO SUDDEN? DID THAT PACKAGE HAVE A MEETING PLACE WRITTEN ON IT?
WE EXAMINED IT! IT WAS JUST A TIN OF COOKIES!

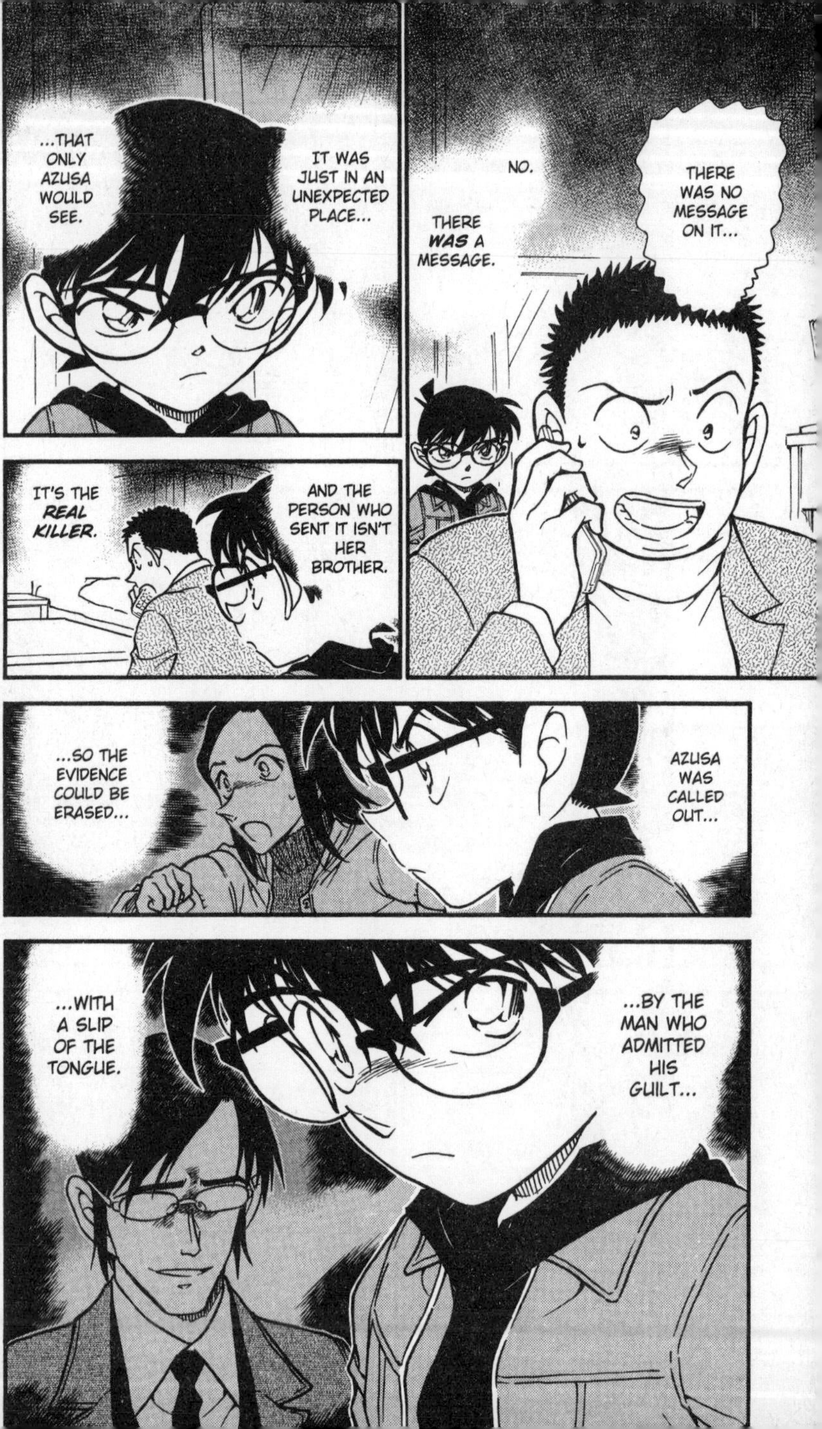
THERE WAS NO MESSAGE ON IT...
NO.
THERE *WAS* A MESSAGE.
IT WAS JUST IN AN UNEXPECTED PLACE...
...THAT ONLY AZUSA WOULD SEE.
AND THE PERSON WHO SENT IT ISN'T HER BROTHER.
IT'S THE *REAL KILLER*.
AZUSA WAS CALLED OUT...
...SO THE EVIDENCE COULD BE ERASED...
...BY THE MAN WHO ADMITTED HIS GUILT...
...WITH A SLIP OF THE TONGUE.

# Hello, Aoyama here.

I had the opportunity to take part in a panel discussion with writer Seimaru Amagi and artist Fumiya Sato, creators of the manga *Kindaichi Case Files*. I was alone but there were two of them...it felt like I was at an away game. I was worried they'd gang up on me, but they turned out to be very kind, funny people, and I really enjoyed talking with them. If you want all the details, read *Conan Kindaichi Magazine* issue 1*!! Heh...this sounds like an ad!

*Conan Kindaichi Magazine* issue 1 is only published in Japan.

# Gosho Aoyama's Mystery Library

## 61

## KOKO

Tortoiseshell Holmes is the most famous cat detective in Japan. But she was preceded by this volume's sleuth, the American cat Koko! Koko is a male Siamese cat with a handsome figure, silky fur and a taste for gourmet food; his full name is Kao K'o-Kung. In addition to his acute senses, he can jump extreme heights, he understands human language, he reads the newspaper and uses the typewriter... This multitalented feline truly has what it takes to be a detective. His owner—or, rather, the human at his beck and call—is Jim Qwilleran. A veteran reporter with a rather strange name, Qwilleran is the only person capable of analyzing Koko's whimsical behavior.

The author, Lilian Jackson Braun, has been working on her popular *The Cat Who...* series for over forty years. With this volume I'm entering the 14th year of *Case Closed*, so Conan is still nothing but a kitten compared to Koko... Heh.

I recommend *The Cat Who Could Read Backwards.*

[Editor's note: Braun has since passed away at the age of 97.]

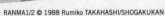

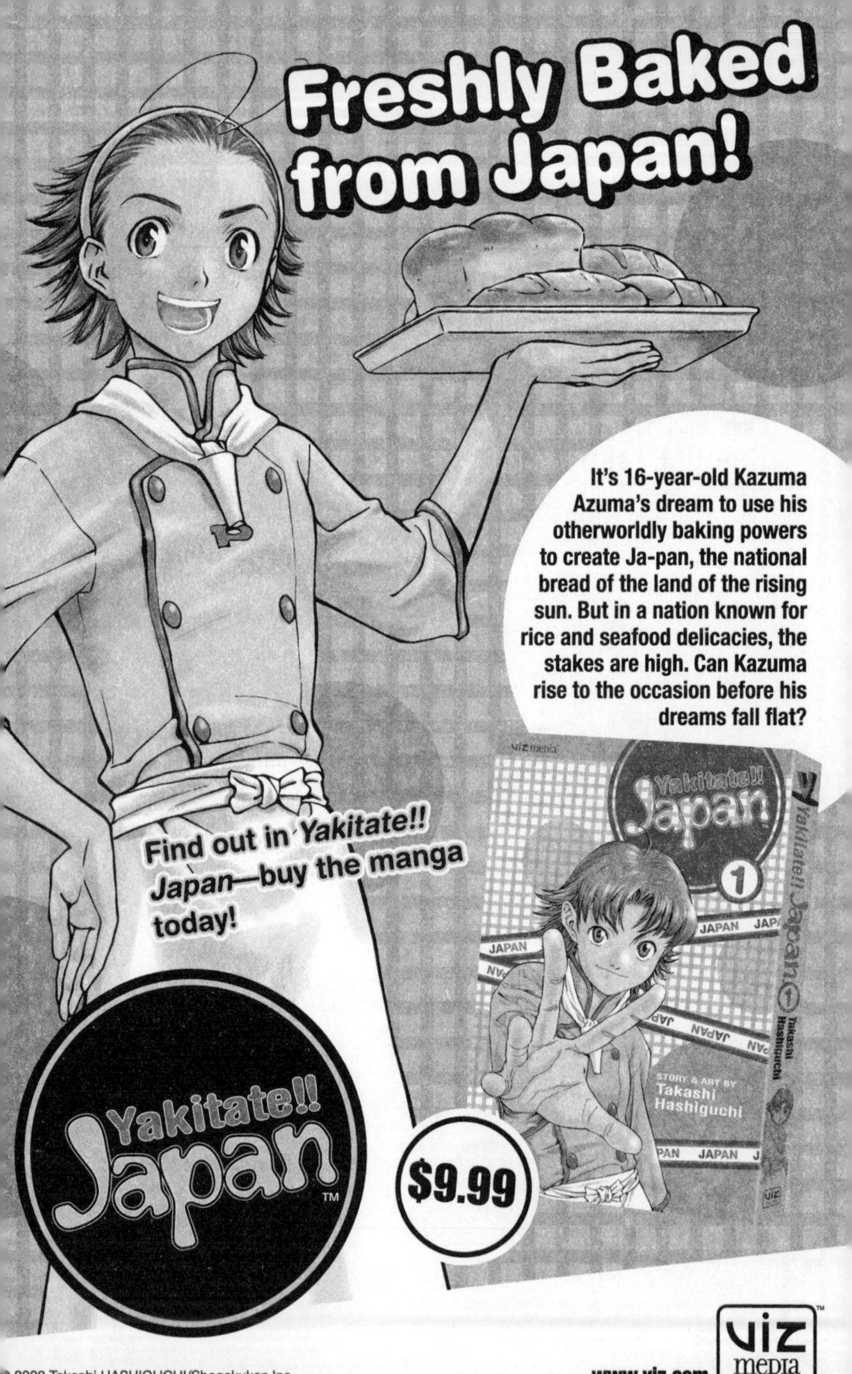
Freshly Baked from Japan!
It's 16-year-old Kazuma Azuma's dream to use his otherworldly baking powers to create Ja-pan, the national bread of the land of the rising sun. But in a nation known for rice and seafood delicacies, the stakes are high. Can Kazuma rise to the occasion before his dreams fall flat?
Find out in Yakitate!! Japan—buy the manga today!
Yakitate!! Japan TM
$9.99
viz media
Yakitate!! Japan 1
STORY & ART BY Takashi Hashiguchi
www.viz.com
viz media TM